THE PATH

Lonny E. Young

WESTBOW
PRESS®
A DIVISION OF THOMAS NELSON
& ZONDERVAN

WestBow Press books may be ordered through booksellers or by contacting:

WestBow Press
A Division of Thomas Nelson & Zondervan
1663 Liberty Drive
Bloomington, IN 47403
www.westbowpress.com
1 (866) 928-1240

ISBN: 978-1-9736-2468-4 (sc)
ISBN: 978-1-9736-2467-7 (e)

Print information available on the last page.

WestBow Press rev. date: 3/28/2018

The Bible talks a lot about walking with God, whether as individuals or the nation Israel. My prayer is that this devotional will help you have a more intimate walk with God.

When I was a child, my two brothers and I found this path along a creek bank. It was only wide enough for one person. Being the oldest I was in the lead, I kept looking back to see if my brothers were close behind. It was important that we stay together, so none of us got lost.

The same is true with our walk with God. Three things we need to keep in mind walking with God.

First, we must never get ahead of God. It's god who chooses the direction we take. If we are leading the choice becomes ours. We come to a fork in the road, a decision must be made. If we are leading we may take the wrong fork and leave God waiting at the fork. We must always allow God to lead!

Second, with God in the lead we must stay close. If we get too far behind we may not notice that He has taken a different path. We can then not follow because we've lost sight and contact. In order to follow we must always keep God in sight.

Third, we need to stay close and trust His leadership. God knows the perfect path to take. He knows His plan for our life. (Jeremiah 29:11-13). The path to prosper us and give us good success. In order to reach that goal, we need to follow His lead, stay close, for any course changes, and to avoid any pitfalls along the way.

I hope these daily devotions will help you stay close to God along this path we are taking. To be able to know when God says this fork or that fork, to slow down or to wait. That's the hard part. There may be times when God will stop for a bit. We want to forge ahead but God wants us to wait. There may be danger up ahead. We must learn to wait on God's direction.

This devotion is to encourage you to have a daily devotion. A time of reading and prayer in God's presence. It is also a road map for reading through the Bible in a year. A long journey, but it will go quickly, believe me. In this journey, we will get better acquainted with the God of the Bible. To learn to walk with him daily!

FOREWORD

We had visited church a couple of times. One evening the pastor came to visit. That night I accepted Jesus Christ as my Savior. That same night, after the pastor left, I went to my chair in the living room. I opened a Bible I had there and read Third John. I was so excited that I had read a whole book, I never stopped.

A short time later I found a schedule for reading through the Bible in one year. It wasn't long before I had marked in my Bible at the beginning of the chapters for that day. Genesis 1, I put 1/1, at Genesis 4, I put 1/2 and so on through the whole Bible. So, I just open my Bible at the bookmark and there was today's reading.

Our church had a Revival meeting. Our pastor asked the congregation to come up and write the names of those we knew to be lost. At the end of the Revival they passed out lists of about fifteen people on each list. I took my list and folded it and put it with my bookmark.

Every morning, after turning on the coffee pot, I read from a devotional by Sarah Young, then I open my Bible and read the list of names, I've added a few of my own, and then pray for those individuals. Next, I read my passages for that day. Following my reading I close my Bible and pray for my family, the sick, friends, and my church.

One year I decided to post on Facebook a verse each day. I went through the schedule and as I read the two or three chapters I circled a verse that spoke to my heart, or got my attention. That was the verse I posted. That was the birth of this devotional.

Now, after several readings, a verse will trigger so many thoughts of other verses that go along with what I'm reading. The more of the Bible we ingest the more God will and can bring to our minds. You begin to make the connections throughout the Scriptures.

Dedicated:
To my wonderful wife,
Mary,
our daughters; Tammy and Shannon

> Then God blessed the seventh day and sanctified it, because in it He rested from all His work which God had created and made. (Genesis 2:3)

Have you ever completed a long and hard task? Do you remember the feeling you had when it was completed? Wasn't that a glorious feeling?

Let's try to imagine the thoughts that went through God's mind when He had finished creating this wonderful world. God could very well have created everything in one second. With the power of His spoken word it could have all been brought into existence. But He chose to break it up into six days.

Someone once said, "how do you eat an elephant?" "One bite at a time." God even taught us a great lesson in His creation. Instead of being discouraged at what lies ahead, tackle it one step at a time.

As we approach this coming new year. There may be enormous tasks ahead. Remember this lesson "one bite at a time."

Jesus may have felt this same sense of "completeness" at the cross. In John 19:30 we read, "So when Jesus had received the sour wine, He said, "It is finished!" And bowing His head, He gave up His spirit."

Jesus had completed the task that God had sent Him to accomplish. To restore that relationship with the Father that was broken in the Garden of Eden. To make a way that sinful man can have a relationship with a holy God. To cover our sins in the shed blood of His Son.

Understand this was not Jesus' first choice. In the Garden of Gethsemane Jesus had asked that this "cup" pass from Him. Is there any other way I can accomplish Your will without going through the pain of the cross? God's answer was "no."

How many tasks have we encountered and refused to do them because they were too hard? Maybe we couldn't see how this could be done. If it's God will He will accomplish it. I saw a plaque once that said, "If God brings you to it, He will bring you through it." Remember that as you accomplish great things for God this year.

> This is the book of the genealogy of Adam. In the day that God created man, He made him in the likeness of God. He created them male and female and blessed them and called them Mankind in the day they were created. (Genesis 5:1-2)

I remember a few years ago being bit by the "genealogy" bug. I got on the internet and began writing to various relatives, etc. I compiled a booklet about our family tracing our "family tree" back to the Mayflower and then printing several copies and giving them to relatives. It was quite a blessing to me to see the hundreds of people that spring from two people that came to our great country on the Mayflower.

You may not be into doing the research and all that goes into finding out your Family Tree. Just take a minute and think back as far as you can. Where did you come from? Your grandparents maybe even your great-grandparents. Whether you realize it or not their traits were passed on to you through the generations.

In an eight-book series by Jack Cavanaugh entitled *An American Family Portrait* it tells of a boy in England who, through circumstances, migrated to American during the time of the Puritans and seeing the founding of our country. Through this series of eight books it travels from the time of the founding of our country through the generations to include the Vietnam era.

Through each generation there is a family Bible that is passed down from generation to generation to someone in the family that would continue their Christian heritage. A couple of times it would seem the line would end. But God found a way to continue the line.

I believe that when God created us He created us with a piece missing. Many people will spend their entire life trying different things to fill that void. Until they find a relationship with God they will search in vain.

Do you think about what you might pass on to the next generation? What kind of heritage are leaving behind? Think about it.

> And the LORD smelled a soothing aroma. Then the LORD said in His heart, "I will never again curse the ground for man's sake, although the imagination of man's heart is evil from his youth; nor will I again destroy every living thing as I have done. (Genesis 8:21)

How to please God? Look at Noah's response to God's judgment. He recognized the sovereignty of God. God is in control always. I wonder how many of the forty days that Noah spent on that ark did he question what he had done?

Yet we do the same thing. God has just brought us through a great storm, a calamity that takes our focus off God. We are on the trailing end of that calamity. What do we do? Do we say, "praise God for bringing us through it" or do we totally forget from whence came our salvation.

Here's something else Noah did. He didn't just say "thank you" to God and move on. Noah built an altar and offered up a sacrifice to God! He acknowledged that it was God who brought him through this trial by doing something physical.

God has brought us through a great storm. He has been by our side all along. He has comforted us and given us a peace through the whole ordeal. And our response is "thanks" and we move on. It's almost expected that God would bail us out. How arrogant! Where is the praise?

God watched over Noah from day one. He provided the materials, the labor and even caused the animals to gather on the ark. Noah felt he had to acknowledge God's presence and praise Him for being there when he needed Him.

As you read these three chapters try to put yourself in Noah's place. Where is your hope? When going through your own trials, where is your hope? And another thing is your offering of praise a "sweet smelling" offering in God's nostrils? Do your efforts at thanking God seem acceptable to you—how about God?

God made a promise to Noah. God has kept His promise! Who better to put our "trust" in than a God who will forever keep His promises! How many promises do you know in the Word of God? These are faithful promises from God!

I will make you a great nation, I will bless you, and make your name great; and you shall be a blessing. I will bless those who bless you, and will curse him who curses you; and in you all the families of the earth shall be blessed. (Genesis 12:2-3)

A very significant event occurred on May 14, 1948. The nation of Israel was recognized by the United Nations as a separate and distinct state. No longer part of Palestine but a Jewish state. A tiny country among some of the largest and most powerful countries in the region. A country that God promised, clear back in the days of Abraham, that He would bless.

Here is one of those promises that we talked about yesterday. A promise to the people of Israel. Egypt, after 1948, tried several times to attack Israel and to take the land back. God intervened and maintained Israel's place in the world. Still today many attack and try to undermine the sovereignty of a nation that God has promised to protect.

Someone once illustrated God's plan for His creation: First God began with a man, Adam. Next, He worked through a family, Abram. Third He put together a nation through Jacob, Israel. And forth He encompassed the world through His Son Jesus. And God wants to do a work through you as well. Take a minute and look at Jeremiah 29:11.

Some of the greatest minds and contributions to our world have come from the nation of Israel. God has truly blessed them! One reason you might want to consider, for God's blessing, is the fact of Abram's complete trust in God. God said pack up and leave and Abram obeyed. Didn't ask questions, didn't ask for an itinerary, a plan, but God gave him a direction and Abram left.

Do we trust God that much? One thing I have noticed in the New Testament is that God blesses "obedience". Jesus said, "if you love Me you will keep My commandments" (John 14:15). Did you catch that "if"? Abram was obedient to God's command "go". I think we see here, not only a promise to Abram, but a promise to us. If you trust God and obey His leadership—we will be blessed. What do you think?

Then Melchizedek king of Salem brought out bread and wine; he was the priest of the God Most High. And he blessed him and said: "Blessed be Abram of God Most High, Possessor of heaven and earth; and blessed be God Most High, who has delivered your enemies into your hand. (Genesis 14:18-20)

Melchizedek is an interesting guy. He first appears here in Genesis to Abram. A priest to bless Abram after his battle to rescue his family. Later he appears in the Psalms (110:4) and is talked about a lot in the book of Hebrews (Hebrews 5,6 and 7).

It was Abram that enlisted his servants and together they sought out their enemy and freed their family members who had been captured. Yet, notice who Melchizedek gives the credit, God Most High. Of course, we never take the credit for something God has done, do we?

I brought this contrast out to my Sunday school class a while back. This passage shows the side of God portrayed in the Old Testament. A Warrior, a mighty God, a powerful God! But in the New Testament we see a different side of the same God. A God that loves, and cares about His children. Sometimes it's hard to distinguish between the two. They are the same God.

We also see here the worship of God after a victory. We touched on this with Noah. Recognizing who we worship. Recognizing the One who brought the victory. Here the priest brings out wine and bread to celebrate the victory that God has brought.

Wine and bread, the same elements in the Lord's supper. That also is a celebration. A celebration of Christ's victory over sin and death. A celebration of remembrance of what Christ did for us on the cross of Calvary. Restoring a broken relationship with God.

If you have read the chapters leading up to this point you know we are early in Abram's walk with God. An important aspect in our walk is that God wants to show Himself faithful to His children. He wants us to trust Him every day. Abram had a challenge in his family and God was up to the challenge! We face many challenges every day, God is there if we call on Him. He is faithful to be by our side just as He was with Abram.

> And I will establish My covenant between Me and you and your descendants after you in their generations, for an everlasting covenant, to be God to you and your descendants after you. (Genesis 17:7)

The heading in my Bible says: *Abrahamic Covenant confirmed again and made everlasting.* Maybe Abram didn't understand, maybe he couldn't grasp the enormity of God's statement. The covenant that God made with His obedient servant would last forever! It would pass on down from generation to generation far beyond what Abram could possibly comprehend. God made a promise.

Try to grasp the importance of that Bible in your hands. It is called "the Word of God." Think about that a minute. These words have been handed down from generation to generation from Moses to Jacob to Joseph on and on to you this very moment. They haven't been edited, changed, or re-written. Oh, we have different translations and very minor changes but you know what I'm talking about. It's GOD's Word!

Do we give it the reverence it deserves? Do we really understand that almighty God sent, through His prophets, His mind, His thoughts, His will for us today, written down for our study?

Notice what He said, "to you and your descendants after you." It was meant to be passed on. From father to son, on and on.

I have read some very interesting stories about the efforts to try to destroy God's Word. It's interesting the efforts that Satan will employ to try to "change" or distort the very words of almighty God. Even in the very beginning, in the garden, the Serpent said, "did God say?"

I hope you are reading all the chapters that coincide with the chosen verses. The context is important to each of these verses. I think this is the third time God has reminded Abram of His covenant with him and by him, all of mankind.

One last thing. Notice that God uses the word "establish". It has been established from the beginning and when Jesus said on the cross, "it is finished" (John 19:30) the plan that God had envisioned from the beginning was completed. Restoring the relationship between a sinful mankind and a holy God.

"In your seed, all the nations of the earth shall be blessed, because
you have obeyed My voice." (Genesis 22:18)

I love this story! Read the context of this verse. It wasn't enough that Abraham was willing to leave his friends and the comfortable life he was experiencing in Ur and venture to land he didn't know existed. To follow the leading of a God he had just met. Who knows why God chose Abraham.

In this story, after God had FINALLY granted him the son God had promised, a miraculous birth at that. God had now asked Abraham to take his son up on a mountain and kill him. To build an altar and sacrifice him. Abraham waited a few days, hoping God might change His mind. NO! Look at verse 3 of chapter 22. It says, "So Abraham rose early in the morning and saddled his donkey." His response was immediate!

Have you ever tried to talk God out of something He has asked you to do? I have. It doesn't work. God has already set a plan in motion. You can't change it. Oh, you can refuse for sure but you will miss a great blessing and you will be OUT of God's will.

You don't suppose that God knew enough about the heart of Abraham that the reason He chose him in the first place was his willingness to be obedient. How do we respond when God leads us to try something new?

One more thing. Look at verse 1 in the same chapter. God said. "Now it came to pass after these things that God tested Abraham." He didn't tempt him He tested him. God is always putting little tests of faith in our lives. They not only reveal the extent of our faith but they can also strengthen our faith—when we pass the test.

One of my favorite verses is in Matthew. Matthew 9:29: Then He touched their eyes, saying, "According to your faith let it be to you." Jesus often used measuring terms related to faith. "Great faith" or "no faith" etc. Can faith be measured? How much God can use us for His purpose and His glory can be determined by the amount of faith we have in God. Do we have the faith to walk on water like Peter or are we like Thomas? (John 20:27-29)

And he said, "Blessed be the LORD God of my master Abraham, who has not forsaken His mercy and His truth toward my master. As for me, being on the way, the LORD led me to the house of my master's brethren." (Genesis 24:27)

This is a great story. Maybe something we might miss is that Abraham trusted God to bring into his life the right mate for his son. Abraham sent his servant back home to find a bride for Isaac. The servant arrived at the appointed place then asked God to reveal the right bride. God answered his prayer.

One lesson I have learned the hard way is to let God open the doors and not try to force them open myself. Of course, I know far better than God what is best for me, really? We have the ability to break through the doors. To travel down the road of OUR choosing and not Gods. But it never ends well!

Notice the testimony that Abraham had with his servant: "blessed be the Lord God of my master Abraham." Maybe the servant didn't know God personally but the testimony of Abraham was enough for his servant to trust Abraham's God. Maybe Abraham shared with him what God has done in his life. So much so that the servant prayed and asked, "Abraham's God" to show him the right wife for Isaac.

Have you ever prayed and asked God to show you the right path to take? To give you some wisdom in deciding. To choose the right road or the left road? How about in the choice of a mate to spend your life with? Do you trust God to make that decision?

One last thing. notice a little phrase toward the end of the verse: "being on the way." Just like when Abraham left Ur God didn't tell Abraham to go three miles to the big rock then left and go...etc. No God simply told him to go. It had to be a daily walk. A daily trust in God. Just as God provided the manna for Israel it was daily.

Remember Jesus prayer in the Gospels: "give us this day our daily bread." (Matthew 6:11). It was a daily thing. Our walk with God is a daily walk. Daily seeking direction and guidance. We must daily get into God's Word and seek His face in prayer for His will and plan and direction for our lives. It's a challenge that will bless your socks off!!

And the LORD appeared to him the same night and said, "I am the
God of your father Abraham; do not fear, for I am with you. I will bless
you and multiply your descendants for My servant Abraham's sake."
(Genesis 26:24)

Have you read these three chapters? Isaac follows in his father's footsteps.
When a famine strikes he runs to Egypt. Why? It's the "normal" thing to do.
It's the human response. It's the logical response. How many times have we been
confronted with a problem, or trial, and we seek the "logical" solution? When God
is hoping we will turn to Him.

In the verse above God appears to Isaac with a promise. The same promise
God made to Abraham. "I will be with you." The same promise Jesus made to His
disciples before ascending to heaven after the resurrection. A promise God has
made to His children from the very beginning.

I noticed something the other day in Genesis chapter 3. In this chapter
Adam and Eve rebelled against their heavenly Father. God expelled them from
the garden. But notice what Eve says in chapter 4 verse 1. "I have acquired a man
from the Lord." God continued to bless them both. Eve recognized that God's
hand was still on them. God never left them.

To me Isaac is just a link between Abraham and Jacob. I don't see that Isaac
did anything significant. Except that without Isaac there would not have been a
Jacob.

Many times, we think that our lives don't really mean anything. We've made
no impact on the world around us. We haven't made a difference, etc. We will
never know, this side of heaven, how we have impacted history. God just asks that
we trust Him and follow in His footsteps and do what He has asked us to do.

"Do not fear, for I am with you." How many times has God said those words
throughout the Scriptures. God in the Old Testament and Jesus in the New
Testament. That is probably the biggest challenge we face as His children. Trusting
God when things look bleak, hopeless, etc.

One more thing: Look at verse 28 in chapter 26. See the testimony that Isaac
has with his countrymen? "We certainly see that the Lord is with you." Maybe
that is the "legacy" we can leave behind. A testimony that God had His hand on
us. Isaac made a lot of mistakes, as we do, but God never left Him. God is as close
as the nearest prayer. Ask Him to comfort and encourage us as we seek His will
and purpose for our lives!

> Then Jacob awoke from his sleep and said, "Surely the LORD is in this place, and I did not know it." And he was afraid and said, "How awesome is this place! This is none other than the house of God, and this is the gate to heaven." (Genesis 28:16-17)

The house of God. Exactly where is that? In the Old Testament, it was considered to be the Tabernacle and later the Temple. In the New Testament, we are told that our bodies are the temple of the Holy Spirit (1 Corinthians 6:19). When Jacob awoke from his sleep he recognized the presence of God. It can be anywhere and at any time we can be in the presence of God.

I am a firm believer in the work and ministry of the local church. I also know that I don't have to go to a church to be in the presence of God. You will notice that Jacob didn't GO somewhere to be on holy ground. The place where he was at God made holy. The same is true for a church. When God's people gather together there is the presence of God.

Jacob is about to undertake an adventure that will greatly change his life. God will change his name and create a nation through Jacob. God began with a man, Adam. Then he used a family, Abraham. And now He will create a nation through Jacob.

Here we go again. Notice Jacob's state of mind in verse 17. "He was afraid." We are all afraid at some point in our lives. Most of the time it's the unknown that frightens us. We can usually handle things we can see or can defend. Many time's it is the "spiritual" things that frighten us. The most terrifying of course is an intimate relationship with Almighty God. When God intrudes in our lives we fear Him. We don't understand why the God of the universe would take note of us. It's scary!

Notice what Jacob said in verse 16. "Surely the Lord is in this place, and I did not know it." I wonder why Jacob didn't recognize God's presence. God is at work all around us and most of the time we fail to recognize it. I like what Henry Blackaby teaches in "Experiencing God". Find out where God is at work and join Him. Jacob was surprised to find God where he was at. Why are we surprised that God has an interest in what we are doing? Could we possibly be where God wants us, and thus wants to use us there?

One last thing. Notice that Jacob had an immediate response to God's presence. He took note of the event. In verse 18 he built an altar. Erected a monument to note God's presence. We need to take note of God's working in our lives. Keep a journal of God's working in our lives. Answered prayer, miracles, etc.

And she conceived again and bore a son, and said, "Now I will praise the LORD." Therefore, she called his name Judah. Then she stopped bearing. (Genesis 29:35)

Judah, the fifth son born to Jacob through Leah. Leah always interested me. She was the outcast. The older daughter that no one wanted. Jacob wanted Rachel, beautiful, young, etc. Jacob was tricked into marrying Leah. All in all, Leah bore Jacob 6 sons, Reuben (first born), Simeon, Levi (priests), Judah, Gad and Asher. Six of the twelve sons were born to the "least of these?"

I think it's also significant that Judah was the one son that continues the line from Adam, Abraham, Isaac, Jacob on through to the linage of Christ. See Matthew chapter one. Of course, they didn't know this at the time. Many of the things God does in our lives we have no idea the impact they will have in later generations.

The meaning of the name Judah is "praise." Notice Leah's response at the birth of Judah, "Now I will praise the Lord." Notice the scenario in these two chapters (29-30). Who has the power to provide children? Notice the women try everything possible to produce a child. Leah was the least favored and the most productive. God blessed Leah. It's in the power of God to grant children, or not, it's God's choice.

We try so hard to thwart the plan of God. Pills, invitro fertilization, abortion, etc. Children are the of blessing of God. The lack of children is the plan of God. He knows what's best. Many time's we refuse to accept the will of God.

I think Jacob's relationship with Rachel and his eventual four wives and twelve children are a study in relationships. Not only between Jacob and his wives but between Jacob and God. Jacob had his goals and priorities while God had His. Who do you think wins out?

Why did I choose this verse to emphasize in these two chapters? First, in the significance of Judah in the line of Christ. Second, that Leah is the least favored yet God used her to fulfill His master plan. Third, Leah recognized the source of God's blessings! Finally, Leah praised God for the precious gift. Many time's God blesses us daily with so many blessings and we want to take the credit, we think we did it all on our own. Yet, all God asks is that we acknowledge His hand in our daily blessings. Food, clothing, shelter, income the simple things we take for granted and yet God can take any one of these away at any time. Recognize the author of our life!

And He said, "Your name shall no longer be called Jacob, but Israel;
for you have struggled with God and with men, and have prevailed."
(Genesis 32:28)

Pause with me a minute. Go back to chapter 28 verse 20, 21. Did you notice the condition that Jacob put on God? IF God will do such and so THEN Jacob will call him God. Have you ever put "conditions" on God? IF God will do this THEN I will accept Him or obey Him.

Now notice that God did provide greatly for Jacob. Between 28 and 31 God did some miraculous things in Jacob's life. Was it because God wanted Jacob's obedience? Not Hardly. God led the way daily in Jacob's quest to know God. God showed Jacob what He was capable of.

God changed the names of just a few people in Scripture. Abraham and Sarah come to mind. God changed Jacob's name from "supplanter" to "God rules".

Notice in the verse above it is said, "for he struggled with God and with men." Until we have peace with God we will never have peace with men. And we see in Jacob's life that God was always seeking after Jacob until Jacob found God. That's the way it is with us today.

Did you know that when we are saved God changes our name? Maybe not our individual names but, in a sense, He changes our relationship with Him. In the gospel of John 1:12 it says, "But as many as received Him, to them He gave the right to become children of God, to those who believe in His name." In 1 John 3:1 it says, "Behold what manner of love the Father has bestowed on us, that we should be called children of God!"

I think maybe Jacob's relationship with God changed at this point. Jacob acknowledged God for who He is and God changed His relationship with Jacob from this moment on.

The same is true in our relationship with God. I wonder sometimes if we are really looking for God to "prove" Himself or is God at work all around us, leading us, teaching us, guiding us, to where we will open our eyes and acknowledge His presence all along.

Is God working on you? Are there events in your life today that point you to God? Has God already saved you and your looking for His will in your life? It took Jacob years to realize that God was working in his life. I pray it won't be years in your life!

"Then let us arise and go up to Bethel; and I will make an altar there
to God, who answered me in the day of my distress and has been with
me in the way which I have gone." (Genesis 35:3)

One of my favorite movies, entitled "The Lost Child" tells of this guy who
follows his wife to an Indian Reservation. There he gets into a conversation
with the chief of the tribe. He asks how they can live in this desert place. The chief
replies with a story, "A man once hired a servant to walk beside him every day to
remind him to praise his God. A place can be like that servant."

Do you ever venture back to the place where you met God? In your mind, at
least. Where God spoke to your heart. Do you have anything to remind you of that
experience? Maybe you made a note in your Bible. Maybe a bookmark? Something
to remind you of that experience.

Well, you say, I have the Holy Spirit to remind me. I have the peace of that
experience. I guess you haven't experienced how the world can gloss over those
precious moments. Moments when God was so real and His Spirit was "active"
in your life.

I think those reminders are important! The world has a way of drawing us
away from our close relationship with God the Father.

Jacob not only built an altar to praise God but he went back to that special
place where he met God. I've often wondered why Christians drift away from going
to church on a regular basis. For most of them that was where they me God. Why
would you not renew that relationship on a regular basis. "I don't need to go to
church to meet with God." I wonder why Jacob thought it was important to return
to the place he encountered God, to build an altar to praise God.

One last thought on this "altar" business. I believe we don't need to build
a physical altar to praise God. The testimony we leave behind to family and
friends is our altar. What better way to praise God than to have a testimony that
honors Him.

You might review the life of Jacob. It wasn't all that easy. He had many trials,
and times he questioned God. In the end, he returned to where he met God and
built an altar to his relationship with the Almighty.

Now Israel loved Joseph more than all his children, because he was
the son of his old age. Also, he made him a tunic of many colors.
(Genesis 37:3)

I hope your reading the chapters listed above. The context is important to understand what's going on. First, you remember that Israel is Jacob. God changed his name to Israel.

When Jacob left home to find a bride he went to his mother's family. It was love at first sight. When Jacob laid eyes on Rachel that was the girl for him. I can't go into detail here but in the end Jacob ended up with four wives, Leak, Bilhah, Zilpah and Rachel. Leah had six boys and a girl, Dinah, and Rachel only had two, Joseph and Benjamin. Joseph was the first born of his true love.

If you notice in verse two of this chapter Joseph was seventeen when this narrative begins. His family life was less than great. His brothers hated him. His father favored him above the rest. He, again, was the first born of the woman he loved.

Remember when you were seventeen? It is beginning to dawn on you that it was time to make decisions for your future. Your career, your marriage choices, etc. You knew the future was ahead of you and you had so many questions. What do you think was going through Joseph's mind as he went looking for his brothers that day?

I wonder how many stories Jacob told Joseph about what God had done in his life. The miracles God brought into his life. The wealth that God had blessed him with. The way he changed Ishmael's heart from hate to love, etc.

Jacob built a foundation in Joseph that would serve him well in the trials he would face later. Trials that we can't begin to fathom. Yet Joseph remained faithful to God. It wasn't a spur-of-the-moment thing. It was a foundation that Jacob had instill in Joseph early on that helped to keep Joseph trusting God.

Have you checked your foundation lately? Is it stable or is it rocky? Does it need some shoring up? I hope you will continue reading through your Bible with this devotional and let's see what God has in store for your life.

The LORD was with Joseph, and he was a successful man; and he was
in the house of his master the Egyptian. And his master saw that the
LORD was with him and that the LORD made all he did to prosper in
his hand. (Genesis 39:2-3)

Joseph should be dead! I hope you've read the chapters listed above. If you have
you know that thanks to Reuben, Joseph's brother, Joseph would have died in
a pit. Instead, Reuben suggested selling him to a passing caravan. So, Joseph went
from near death to being a slave.

Have you ever had a "near-death" experience? Something that when you look
back on it could have gone a different way and your life would have ended.

I have had three such experiences. It makes you want to rethink your life
choices. It makes you wonder just what God is up to. Wouldn't it be nice if God
would let us know when our time is up? Not me! That is the exciting thing about
a relationship with Jesus. God has the plan NOT you!

So, Joseph goes from a slave on a caravan to being a slave in Potiphar's home.
The conditions have vastly improved don't you think? Notice that it says Joseph
was successful. That can't be true. Joseph should be moaning and groaning about
his misfortune. "How could this happen to me?" "I don't deserve this!" Do you
think he would have been successful in Potiphar's house with that attitude?

So many time's we go through trials that test our faith. Is God really in charge?
Do you think Joseph asked that question? Remember we talked yesterday about
the foundation that Jacob had built in Joseph growing up.

It has always been my attitude when going through a storm at ask, O.k. God,
what are up to? What are you trying to teach me or trying to change in my life?
Joseph had the foundation to simply accept his circumstances. Learn from his
circumstances (Egyptian culture) and trust God that He is in charge and wait on
God to show him why he was going through this trial.

I think one thing that Joseph was sure of—God was with him in Potiphar's
house and would provide what he needed.

> And Pharaoh said to his servants, "Can we find such a one as this, a man in whom is the Spirit of God?" (Genesis 41:38)

So much has transpired to this point. Remember we noted that Joseph was seventeen when his father, Jacob (Israel), sent him to find his brothers. Here Joseph is thirty-years-old. Thirteen years that we can read about in thirty minutes. It's hard sometimes to comprehend that length of time. God has brought Joseph from being dropped in a pit, left to die, to Pharaoh's court.

I read somewhere once that there are only two men in the Bible, apart from Jesus of course, that there is nothing bad said about them. They are Joseph and Daniel.

Notice who Pharaoh has seen in Joseph. Wait a minute! I thought the Holy Spirit didn't come until Pentecost in the book of Acts. The Holy Spirit has been here since creation in Genesis. Read chapter one again. At Pentecost, the Holy Spirit became a PERMANENT resident in the believer. In the Old Testament, the Spirit came and left based on the need of God at the time.

It took thirteen years but Joseph is where God wanted him to be. Of course, if it was up to Joseph it would not have happened that way. So is the wisdom of God. You see Joseph had to learn the Egyptian culture to function properly. Joseph had to be moved from Canaan to Egypt. Time had to pass so his brothers would forget about what they had done. Pharaoh had to have his dreams. Joseph had to be available to interpret. A perfect plan to bring an unsuspecting Joseph to where he needed to be when he needed to be there.

Are you questioning God right now about some events in your life? I offer two suggestions: 1. Look back. See where God has brought you from. Have you learned anything from then till now? Have you seen God's hand in the past events? 2. Well, you can't look ahead because God has that all planned. Let me suggest you turn to Jeremiah 29:11-13. What an awesome promise from God's word. Notice he says, "to give you good success." God wants only the best for you.

May I offer another verse? Joshua 1:8. God lays some ground work for success in this verse. Check it out!

Now his heart yearned for his brother; so, Joseph made haste and
sought somewhere to weep. And he went into his chamber and weeps
there.

Пow let's see, what was God's plan for these last thirteen years? It was to bring
Joseph into Pharaoh's court to interpret Pharaoh's dreams. It was to save
Egypt from a famine. It was to save Jacob's family from the famine. It was to bring
Jacob's family to Egypt to spend the next 400+ years. I think it was to reunite
Jacob's family in love. To bring them together.

And who was Joseph's brother? Benjamin the last of Jacob's 12 sons. Rachel
died giving birth to Benjamin. The only two offspring of Rachel were Joseph and
Benjamin.

What does it take for you to weep? How happy or sad do you have to be to
weep? If I remember right the shortest verse in the Bible is, "Jesus wept." It's not a
sign of weakness to weep it's a sign of love and compassion. My children make fun
of me for weeping during a scene in a movie. Usually it's because someone in the
movie is weeping. It breaks my heart to see someone weep.

Joseph went into a private chamber to weep. To weep for joy to see his brothers
again. No hatred for what they did to him, no anger or revenge in his heart, only
joy to be reunited.

The Bible says that there will be no tears in heaven. Tears of sorrow maybe,
but there will be lots of tears of joy. Just imagine getting to see those loved ones
that have gone on before us, grandparents, spouses, children, you name it. The
reunion will be something to see—not a dry eye in the place.

Yes, Joseph was right where God intended for him to be, right when he
intended him to be there. Joseph waited patiently for God's leading in his life. I'm
sure there may have been times of questioning but he never lost his relationship
with his Heavenly Father. Trusting God to bring him to the time and place of
God's choosing.

Are you trusting God? I have no doubt He has a plan for your life! Are you
looking for His leadership and guidance to make the right choices?

And God sent me before you to preserve a posterity for you in the
earth, and to save your lives by a great deliverance. (Genesis 45:7)

REFLECTION: Do you see what Joseph is doing here? He is reflecting on what
God has done in his life. How God brought him to this point for a reason—to
preserve his family in this famine. How important is that? We must continually
reflect on what God is doing and has done in our lives. Why are we where we're at?
What lesson or purpose is God working at this point in our lives?

I know we are three weeks into the new year. I hope you have been keeping up
with the daily Bible reading. Don't forget to meditate on what you've read in the
scriptures and in this devotional.

During my working years I always tried to secure the week between Christmas
and New Years for a vacation week. I would try to finish up some loose ends and
start the year clean. Unfinished projects, etc. I wanted to go into the new year
with a clean slate.

At the same time, I wanted to reflect on what God had done in the past year,
a journal really helps at this point. I wanted to go back and see where God's hand
had been active during the past year. Then of course I wanted to think about and
look forward to what God might do in the coming year, which of course I had no
idea what He was going to do.

One other note about the verse above. I can see Jesus so clearly in that verse.
With His birth in Bethlehem you could almost see Him saying these words. He
came to bring a "great deliverance" did He not?

Joseph could see God's hand in the past thirteen years to bring him to this
point. Can you look back over the past year and see God's hand? That assumes that
you have a close relationship with the Father. Joseph's life reflected his relationship
with God. His patience to wait on God to work His plan in Joseph's life.

Sunday's would be a great time during the year to reflect on what God is
doing in your life. Take a few minutes on this day of rest to reflect on what God
is doing in your life!

"But as for you, you meant evil against me; but God meant it for
good, in order to bring it about as it is this day, to save many people
alive. (Genesis 50:20)

I would love to know what it is in Joseph's life that allowed him to have this kind
of relationship with God. We are talking thirteen years of nothing but trials,
hardships, etc.

At this point Jacob has passed away and now his brothers are worried that
Joseph will use this opportunity to seek revenge for the way he was treated. Joseph
assures them that God was in it all along. That's interesting. His brothers were
raised under the same roof, heard the same testimonies from Jacob. Why does
Joseph have better insight into God's plan and purpose?

Several years ago, I went through a month of three rather serious trials. At the
time, I was Sunday School Director, Deacon, Church Secretary. And of course,
I kept asking God WHY! Almost every time we talked I kept asking Him, why?
My drive time to work each day was forty-five minutes each way. I had ample
opportunities to discuss this with God. I still went to church each Sunday, did my
duties in the church. At one time, I offered to resign as a Deacon but the pastor
wouldn't hear of it. Anyway, about a year later I was driving to work, again asking
God why all this happened. Suddenly, clear as day, God said, "I wanted to find out
if you would be faithful." I had tears in my eyes all the way to work!

Whether God spoke to Joseph or not we don't know. There is no scripture
that tells of conversations between God and Joseph. Joseph did have a gift of
understanding dreams. It just doesn't say. He must have had a special relationship
with God. It never says he "questioned" God's planning. He just trusted God for
the outcome.

One verse I ran across in the New Testament sticks in my mind. It's in
Matthew 9:29 it says in part, "According to your faith be it unto you." Jesus
mentioned several times, "little faith," "great faith," etc. I would love to know the
measuring factor for faith. Another verse in Hebrews is great. Hebrews 11:6.
Joseph must have had AWESOME faith!

> And God said to Moses, "I AM WHO I AM." And He Said, "Thus you shall say to the children of Israel, 'I AM has sent me to you.'" (Exodus 3:14)

You know, I saw something in that verse I had never noticed before, such is the miracle of Scripture. Notice what God said to Moses: "I AM <u>has sent me to you.</u>" I never noticed what God did.

We have just finished up Genesis. Adam, Noah, Isaac, Jacob and Joseph, each one God used in a special way to continue His work on this earth. Do you think that God could NOT have accomplished this without the help of these men? Of course not. Almighty God can do whatever He pleases! So then, why do you suppose He enlisted these men?

I think it's in 1 Corinthians 1:27 where God says, "But God has chosen the foolish things of the world to put to shame the wise, and God has chosen the weak things of the world to put to shame the things which are mighty." Now why would God go to such lengths if all He had to do was speak it into existence?

Of all the Israelites that God could have chosen to free His people why did He choose Moses? Remember at the parting of the Red Sea? What happened? God could have done it before they even got there. No, He had Moses raise his arms THEN the sea parted. Was the power in Moses raising his arms or in God's power.

Ok, here's my take. I think God wanted to reward Moses' faithfulness. I don't think any Hebrews thought that the power was Moses. Remember what God told him to say, "Tell them I AM has sent you." The authority was God the vessel was Moses. Anytime we start thinking we have done anything apart from God we are headed for a fall. God uses each of us to accomplish His will and purpose but it is all God's doing.

There is a lot that has taken place in these early verses of Exodus. God's people were where God wanted them to accomplish what God wanted to accomplish, it was no accident. In 400+ years Israel had grown from seventy people to over 1 million. NOW they were ready to accomplish God's will and purpose!

And God spoke to Moses and said to him: "I am the LORD. I appeared to Abraham, to Isaac, and to Jacob, as God Almighty, but by My name LORD I was not known to the." (Exodus 6:2-3)

Elohim, Jehovah, Adonai, El-Shaddai all names for God in the Old Testament. Do the different names mean a different God, of course not, it's the same God? God is simply telling Moses that others have known one characteristic of God and Moses is about to see a different one.

Think about this: The God in the Old Testament who parted the Red Sea is the same God who calmed the sea for the disciples. The God in the Old Testament who rained Manna from heaven is the same God who fed five-thousand with two loaves and a fish. The God in the Old Testament who brought water from a rock is the same God who told a woman about Living Water. You get the picture?

God in Old Testament, had a different relationship with His people than in the New Testament. In the New Testament it's more personal, one-on-one. God never changes! God's approach to our relationship with him has.

If you notice before Moses and Joshua, God did all the fighting. When He freed the nation of Israel from Egyptian bondage God did all the work. As they eventually enter the Promised Land Israel must do the fighting. Granted God assisted greatly but Israel needed to learn to fight. One of the reason that He led them around to the Red Sea, to avoid conflict.

One other point. I remember hearing, as a young Christian, that we were to make two decisions when we got saved. One, we were to accept Christ as our Savior. Two, He was to become LORD in our lives. That should not have to be two separate decisions. When Jesus comes into our hearts HE becomes Lord. Our choice is whether to obey the leadership of the Holy Spirit or not. It doesn't change our relationship only our blessing.

Moses is about to enter the third and final chapter in his life. 40 years in Pharaoh's court, 40 years as a shepherd, and 40 years leading Israel.

So, Moses said to him, "As soon as I have gone out of the city, I will
spread out my hands to the LORD; the thunder will cease, and there
will be no more hail, that you may know that the earth is the LORD's"
(Exodus 9:29)

We are in the middle of the ten plaques God is bringing on Egypt. One
fascinating fact I learned a while back: Each plaque represents an Egyptian
god and God was demonstrating His power over these God's. One other thing.
I'm sure the Egyptian people were taking note of what God was doing. The people
of Israel were taking note as well, as God planned. God is always at work around
us if we but look!

As you read through these ten plaques I want you to notice something. Notice
that at times Pharaoh hardens his heart, we know that. How many times does
GOD harden Pharaoh's heart? You see it's not up to Pharaoh when this learning
process ends—it's up to God!

As we saw with Joseph and Jacob God has a specific plan and time frame He is
working with. In God's time the plaques will end and God will have accomplished
His purpose.

Going through a trial right now? I love what Dr. Charles Stanley says about
storms: God's omniscience (all-knowing) means He knows where we are at in the
storm. God's omnipresence (all-present) means He is with us in the storm. And
God's omnipotence (all-powerful) means He will bring us through the storm.

What might be going through the minds of God's people about now. Israel
wasn't exempt from all the plaques, just some. Remember they didn't believe Moses
when he first came and told them, God through him would deliver Israel.

Many times, as we read through the Old Testament we need to step back and
get the "big picture" of what God is trying to accomplish in Israel's life. Just as
many times we need to reflect over the past and see where God is leading us. In
some case's DRAGGING us! All to achieve His ultimate goal of bringing us to
where God wants us to be. We are the ones who make the process painful.

God is the Master Teacher and His lessons are hard sometimes. He is
teaching Israel to trust Him as they head to the Promised Land. They MUST
trust Him or perish!

Now the blood shall be a sign for you on the houses where you are.
And when I see the blood, I will pass over you; and the plague shall
not be on you to destroy you when I strike the land of Egypt. (Exodus
12:13)

When I accepted Jesus Christ as my Savior I accepted by faith that He died for my sins on the cross. It wasn't till a few years later that I asked myself, "WHY the cross. Why did Jesus have to die for me?" It wasn't until I made the connection in the Old Testament I realized why.

In Genesis, after Adam and Eve had disobeyed God and sinned and were cast out of the Garden of Eden we catch a glimpse of the foundation for the payment of sin. Genesis 3:21 says, "Also for Adam and his wife the Lord God made tunics of skin, and clothed them." That wasn't necessary, they had already clothed themselves in fig leaves. Insufficient! The principle is: "And according to the law almost all things are purified with blood, and without shedding of blood there is no remission." (Hebrews 9:22). Leviticus 17:11 says, "For the life of the flesh is in the blood, and I have given it to you upon the altar to make atonement for your souls, for it is the blood that makes atonement for the soul."

Do you remember the words of John the Baptist when he saw Jesus approaching for the first time? And looking at Jesus as He walked, he said, "Behold! the Lamb of God!" Why would John call Him that?

Look at the verse above. John was simply thinking of this verse in Exodus. The death angel passed by when he saw the blood.

I often, when I think of this principle, imagine God looking down on the earth and seeing millions of red dots all over the earth. Each person that has accepted Christ as Savior covered in the blood of Christ. This is one time that "seeing red" is a good thing.

Finally, one more passage 1 Samuel 16:7. God looks, not on the outward appearance, but at the heart. That's where God wants to see the blood applied. Unless God looks at the heart and sees the blood of His Son, God will turn His back on the sinner. That's why Jesus had to die on the cross!

> The LORD is my strength and song, and He has become my salvation;
> He is my God, and I will praise Him; my father's God, and I will exalt
> Him. The LORD is a man of war; the LORD is His name. (Exodus
> 15:2-3)

L et's back up a bit before looking at this verse. Look at chapter 14:31. Before
Moses goes into this song of praise look at the reaction of the people of Israel
after God's great deliverance: "Thus Israel saw the great work the Lord had done
in Egypt; so, the people feared the Lord, and believed the Lord and His servant
Moses."

Isn't that the way we are today? Even in Jesus' day they followed Him for the
miracles. When Jesus turned and told them what was expected of them, most
left Him.

Someone once told me that I could pray and ask God for an "amen" during the
day. A sign if you will, that God is taking care of me. I tried it a couple of times.
Praise the Lord it worked. The problem was I started asking Him every day. God
wants to make His presence known in our lives. Many time's we miss the miracles
all around us. Just getting to work and home safe can be a miracle. You want a real
miracle? Just be there when a child is born: THAT'S A MIRACLE!

In this passage Moses is offering a song to God to praise Him for delivering
them through the Red Sea and out of bondage to Egypt. I think Israel's memory
is about as short as ours. Not long after this great song of praise and thanksgiving,
Israel starts complaining about their troubles and wanting to go back to Egypt.

We are the same way. God's blessings in our lives last just a little less than our
memories of them. I told some teenagers once that I have lived what they have yet
to live, and they have lived what I have left. Read that over again. The older I get
the more "looking back" I do.

When we take the time reflect on our lives a question arises: "Can we see God
working in or lives?" That's my prayer for you. If you can't see anything, ask God
to remind you. Remember when God blessed Jacob and Jacob set a pile of stones
to remember what God had done. Just a hint, Joshua will do the same when they
enter the Promised Land. Remember God's blessings!

So, when they measured it by omers, he who gathered much had
nothing left over, and he who gathers little had no lack. Every man
had gathered according to each one's need. (Exodus 16:18)

"According to each one's need." Isn't that awesome. Do you remember the
story? Have you been keeping up with your daily reading? I hope we can
take this journey together.

Remember, we talked about how fickle the Israelites were. Every time Moses
turned around they were complaining about something. Now they are complaining
about the lack of food. Of course, you don't ever complain to God about something
you think you can't live without.

Well God decided to provide manna. The description is in the test. The thing
is, God also put some rules with this manna. They were to gather ONLY what
they needed each day, no more no less. Of course, some thought they would gather
"extra". They paid a price for that.

There is a very important principle here many overlook, when God establishes
some rules (scripture) it's important to pay close attention!

Does any of this sound familiar? Do you remember the Lord's Prayer in the
Gospels? "Give us this day our daily bread." Sound familiar? Why would God
want us to trust him daily? We are so fickle (just like Israel) we have plans for next
week, next year, the next ten years. But how much of that can change? All of it! It's
really in God's hands. Someone once asked me, "Do you know how to make God
laugh?" No? "Just tell Him your plans."

I'm sure Moses explained to the people just what God instructed him to
say. Just what you need, no more. It's a lot like the blessings God gives us, after
receiving this awesome blessing we wonder why it wasn't more, why it didn't come
sooner, why it was given in a certain way. So many questions instead of saying,
"thank you God!"

God provided water, manna, quail, safety, guidance, and still the people
complained. And what happens when they finally reach the Promised Land? They
refused to enter because they were afraid!

We are the same way. God provides so much for us on a daily basis but, we
anguish and fret if we lack just one thing.

> Now therefore, if you will indeed obey My voice and keep My covenant, then you shall be a special treasure to Me above all people; for all the earth is Mine. (Exodus 19:5)

Obedience! What a tough word. Jesus said, "If you love Me, keep My commandments!" (John 14:15) Again God is trying to get the point across to His people. Listen to Me and you'll prosper, disobey Me and you fail.

I guess, the first lesson we try to teach our children as soon as they are old enough to understand: obedience.

Let me get on a soapbox for a minute. Have you ever been with a family like this? They have a toddler, who just learned to walk, and of course they need to touch everything they come near. So, what is our response? We move the object instead of teaching them not to touch it (obedience). I never really understood the lesson being taught by removing the object.

It would be an interesting Bible study some time to search the Old Testament and see how many times God warned Israel not to disobey Him. Remember Moses? God gave a simple instruction but Moses, in his anger, disobeyed and Moses was refused entry to the Promised Land.

How many times has God, through His Holy Spirit, warned us not to do something, but we did it anyway? Remember the consequences? Not good I'm sure.

Keep that analogy of parents in mind. Why would the parents want to teach their children obedience? So, the parents can feel "in charge"? No, it is always for the child's safety and well-being. The same is true with God. God only wants the best for us. But, we must be obedient.

This goes all the way back to the Garden of Eden, doesn't it? A simply command, "don't eat from a certain tree." That act of disobedience opened the flood gates for sin in mankind. I'm sure Adam and Eve said to themselves, "what can it hurt?" I'm sure Israel said the same thing. It's not the act itself it's the trusting the one who issued the order enough to obey them. How important is obedience in the military? It could cost a life. In this case an eternity in hell for disobedience.

Then he took the Book of the Covenant and read in the hearing of the
people. And they said, "All that the LORD has said we will do, and be
obedient." (Exodus 24:7)

In the gospels, after Jesus' baptism He went into the wilderness to face the devil.
We are entering the wilderness. The rest of Exodus and the book of Leviticus
may seem like a wilderness but in every wilderness, there are oasis.

I wonder if, in your reading, you just kind of glossed over verse 11 of chapter
23. That is a very significant verse. God commanded His people to let the land rest
for one year in seven. Doesn't seem like much here. God allowed Israel to neglect
this principle for 490 years. Then the payment became due. To make things right
God removed Israel from Canaan for 70 years via the Babylonian Captivity. God's
laws will be obeyed!

Did you pick up on the three feasts mentioned? Why these feasts? Notice they
were regularly scheduled at least once a year. I believe there were seven feasts in all.

Remember we talked earlier about being "reminded" to worship and praise
God? These feasts are just that. Much like Christmas and Easter and you might go
so far to say Sunday worship can be a reminder of God, and our need to worship
and Praise Him.

I love that phrase "book of the Covenant" today that's the Scriptures. Much
of the purpose of this devotional is to encourage more time spent in God's word.
The more we read God's thoughts and His plan for us the closer we get to a deeper
relationship with the Almighty!

Here again Israel has promised to be obedient. Ever hear of a "foxhole"
confession? It's when things are going bad we look to God and make promises
of faithfulness IF God will get us out of the situation. Israel's faithfulness was so
fickle, well we talked about that.

How committed are you to a relationship with God? Does that relationship
only last as long as our trial? God is always there! God wants us to fellowship with
Him, talk with Him (prayer) seek His guidance and direction. . . And to trust His
leadership through His Spirit!

"And there I will meet with you, and I will speak with you from above the mercy seat, from between the cherubim which are on the ark of the Testimony, about everything which I will give you in commandment to the children of Israel." (Exodus 25:21)

God's priorities! It's amazing what is contained in these first twenty-five chapters.

First: the Passover story. Our salvation is the top priority for God. It was so important that God sent His Son Jesus to die on the cross for our sins and to have a relationship with us. Without that shedding of blood, as demonstrated with the applying the blood to the doorposts and lintel. The blood of Christ must be applied to our hearts to have that relationship with the Father.

Second: The Ten Commandments. The Law, instructions to live by. What God requires of us to live the kind of life that is pleasing to Him. Now notice that salvation came BEFORE the Law. The Law doesn't save us only the blood of Christ. The Law helps us to live the kind of life God meant for us to live. So how does the Law relate to today? The word of God, the Scriptures, the complete revelation of God is available when we read our Bible.

Third: The Tabernacle. It is God's desire that His people gather regularly to worship, fellowship, support and encourage one another. The main message of Jesus is love God, love one another. All through the New Testament with the establishment of the church by Jesus, the missionary journeys by Paul and the verse in Hebrews (10:25) exhorting us not to forsake the gathering together, etc. It is paramount that we gather together!

Salvation, Scriptures, worship and fellowship I see these three priorities in these twenty-five chapters of Exodus. If you're a child of God examine each of these and your relationship and obedience to God.

Read again the instructions for assembling the tabernacle. The Table of Shewbread, the Candlesticks, the Altar of Incense, etc. Each important, each representing an important part of our worship. One more thing. The trumpet, we will see later, the trumpet that is sounded to bring the people together for worship. I miss the sound of bells!

"And they shall know that I am the LORD their God, who brought them up out of the land of Egypt, that I may dwell among them I am the LORD their God." (Exodus 29:46)

I can almost hear the pleading in God's voice. God wants so much to have a relationship with us. He is reminding Israel of the power He demonstrated in bringing Israel out of bondage. The fantastic land that He has prepared for them.

I heard Dr. Stanley say once: "You are either headed into a storm, in a storm, or coming out of a storm." That was Israel. The problem is that most of the time Israel ignored the only source of strength and direction in those storms. It seems God is constantly reminding Israel of His power and Presence.

God had them build the Tabernacle here under Mt. Sinai and then carry it to the Promised Land. A constant reminder of His presence, He provided a pillar of fire by night and smoke by day, a constant reminder of His presence. He met with them (the priest or Moses) regularly in the Holy of Holies.

How about your travels to the Promised Land? You know we are only passing through this world. We are on a march to the Promised Land (heaven). What has God provided to remind you of His presence. The Scriptures, the Church and of course the presence of His Holy Spirit.

The tabernacle was to Israel much the same as the Holy Spirit is to us today. Constantly with us, guiding us, convicting us, etc. God's presence with us.

As we continue through Exodus and then through Leviticus try to picture the details that God lays our for our daily lives. Many of the laws will seem strange and certainly not applicable to us today. So why did God go to such pains to include them?

There is something there for us. You might want to look for those oasis, those verses that jump out and grab our hearts and draw us into His presence. He either speaks softly and comforts us or loudly and directs us. In either case take heed what the Spirit says be open and obedient to His voice. God has a message for you!

> "And I have filled him with the Spirit of God, in wisdom, in
> understanding, in knowledge, and in all manner or workmanship, to
> design artistic works, to work in gold, in silver, in bronze, in cutting
> jewels for setting, in carving wood, and to work in all manner of
> workmanship." (Exodus 31:3-5)

I've been in the ministry for over thirty years. Most of that time was in the Sunday School ministry, 2 1/2 years as a pastor. Anyone who has worked in ministry any length of time has seen this miracle. There is a need in your church. God always seem to raise the right person for the right job. That's assuming they are yielding to the prompting of the Holy Spirit.

Look at the verse above. God had given Moses the "plans" for the Tabernacle. Now the work begins. Now God stirs the Holy Spirit in certain people to accomplish that work.

Now you know, and I know that God could simply speak and the Tabernacle would appear. He spoke the worlds into existence. So why this calling certain men to accomplish this simple task? God has always desired to use His creation to accomplish His work.

I think of Phillip in the book of Acts. Just one of those God had chosen to be in the right place at the right time. How about Saul (Paul). The most unlikely person to carry the gospel to the gentiles, yet God chose him and used him.

Do you remember when God approached Moses to go to Egypt and free His people? What was his response. "I can't do it." Even after God showed him the power God would give him, he refused. Only after recruiting Aaron to speak did Moses consent.

Another interesting thing about workers in the church. Sometimes it may be something no one has ever thought of. A ministry that your church "could" be doing and God laid it on YOUR heart.

I think it's interesting that the verse above doesn't mention whether these men had this ability before God called them. The wisdom, knowledge, and understanding came from God. The effort and willingness to serve came from those men God tapped them on the shoulder. Has God laid some ministry on your heart? What's your response?

Now therefore, I pray, if I have found grace in Your sight, show me
now Your way, that I may know You and that I may find grace in Your
sight. And consider that this nation is Your people. (Exodus 33:13)

There is a lot going on in these three chapters. Here is one of those "oasis"
moments.

It's time for Israel to move on. God instructs Moses to make two more
tablets then God will write, again, His Ten Commandments on those tablets.
You remember Moses destroyed the first two when he saw Israel's sin, when he
returned from the mountain.

I think there is an interesting phrase in the verse above. "That I may know
you" what a desire to have today. I believe that is God's desire today as well. It was
a long rough time for God to reach Moses' heart. Remember the struggle Moses
had when God first recruited him. The issue, I think, was trust.

Now that God has proven Himself to Moses it's time to proceed to the
Promised Land. Notice also, in these chapters, that God promised to send an angel
ahead of them and to help them defeat the inhabitants of Canaan.

How important do you think it might be to find grace in God's sight? Is it
important to you? What does finding grace in God's sight mean to you? In the
Old Testament, the relationship between God and His people was different than
it is now.

Today God's grace indwells us through His Holy Spirit. God's covenant with
His people is confirmed through the presence of His Holy Spirit within us. The
New Testament calls it a "seal" unto the day of redemption. (Ephesians 4:30)

Israel is about to finish their journey to the Promised Land. Moses lifts a
prayer for God's guidance and, interestingly, a closer relationship with the same
God that has brought him this far. After all he has seen God do in his life he still
seeks a closer walk. How is your walk with God? Do you only meet and talk once
a week? How about a daily meditation? Do you seek Him only in times of distress
or is there an intimate relationship? Read Moses prayer again, look at verse 14.

> So, Moses gave a commandment, and they caused it to be proclaimed throughout the camp, saying, "Let neither man nor woman do any more work for the offering of the sanctuary." And the people were restrained from bringing. For the material, they had was sufficient for all the work to be done—indeed too much. (Exodus 36:6-7)

Just imagine going to church one Sunday morning and the pastor steps in the pulpit and announces that the church has all the money it needs and we won't be taking an offering this morning. Can you imagine the looks on the faces?

Moses, after requesting contributions to build the Tabernacle, in a short time has all the materials he needs and the Spirit led leadership and artists to complete the job. How many times have you been in a situation in a church where someone in leadership has asked for volunteers and no one raises their hand? All too often.

One other thing of note about this passage. Do you remember where the materials, gold, silver and precious stones, came from? Look at Exodus 12:36: "And the Lord had given the people favor in the sight of the Egyptians, so that they granted them what they requested, thus, they plundered the Egyptians." The materials for building the Tabernacle came from their captors.

God will provide for our needs! That is, to me, one of the most frustrating things about Israel's relationship with God. You can see it all through the Old Testament. Even the prophets were so mistreated when they dared to remind Israel of God's laws. Over and over God worked miracles and yet they refused to obey His simply commands.

After saying all that, I'm reminded that we are pretty much the same. God is at work all around us yet we wring our hands and fuss when a storm enters our lives.

I did a word search once on the phrase "remember me". I think it was maybe eight times or so. Why would we think that God would forget us? First, He sent His Son to die for us on a cross, second, we have the Holy Spirit living within us which gives us constant contact with the Father. If you understand the Trinity we have God living within us. And yet we think that God has forgotten us, that is sad.

> Then the cloud covered the tabernacle of meeting, and the glory of
> the Lord filled the tabernacle. And Moses was not able to enter the
> tabernacle of meeting, because the cloud rested above it, and the
> glory of the Lord filled the tabernacle. (Exodus 40:34-35)

Let's back away and get a "big picture" of the God that Moses is talking about here. We need to do this on a regular basis. Stop, back away and reflect on all that has occurred to this point. Expand our vision and get a review of what has happened.

The same God who walked with Adam and Eve in the Garden of Eden. The same God who closed the door of the Ark after it was loaded. The same God who, with His might, parted the Red Sea. The same God brought Israel out of bondage in Egypt. The same God who led the conquering of the Promised Land. The same God who was with Shadrach, Meshach and Abednego in the furnace of fire. The same God who was born a child in Bethlehem. The same God who fed 5,00 with two loaves and a fish. The same God who said, "suffer the little children to come unto me." The same God who paid for our sins on the cross of Calvary. The same God who told Thomas to touch his side and hands and believe. The same God who the disciples saw ascend into heaven. And, the same God who will return to claim a New Earth.

Oh, one more, the same God who dwells in us through the promise of the Holy Spirit. The same God that filled the tabernacle with His presence is the same God that dwells within us. Is that the most awesome thing you have ever heard?

I wonder what was going through Moses and Aaron's heads as they witnessed this awesome power and presence?

Did you finish out this chapter? Notice that when God was ready to move He led with a pillar. A question comes to mind. How much notice did God give the Israelites? A day, an hour? It doesn't say. I'm thinking when they rested they didn't fully unpack. I think they had to be ready to move at a moment's notice.

Are you ready to obey God at a moment's notice? Have you ever been sitting comfortably in your chair, during a commercial, and God says, you need to call (fill in the blank)? I'm busy right now I'll call them later. You have just missed a blessing!

> When his offering is a sacrifice of a peace offering, if he offers it of the herd, whether male or female, he shall offer it without blemish before the Lord. (Leviticus 3:1)

Have you read these four chapters? In my Bible, I went through and underlined a recurring phrase: "a sweet aroma to the Lord." What an awesome thought. Later God says He takes no pleasure in sacrifices. So, what do you suppose He is talking about here?

To me, I think God takes pleasure in anything that brings our focus on Him. Think about it. We are beginning our journey through the book of Leviticus. It's a tough book because we feel it doesn't pertain to us today. It's dry and boring. I would like you to think about something as we read through this book.

God has instituted the Feasts, the Offerings, etc. to bring our focus to Him. How distracted we are each day with our own problems, trials, even joys and we forget that God is with us (if you're a Christian). Through the presence of His Holy Spirit God walks with us, just as He did with Adam in the Garden.

I think it's interesting that several times in the prophets it says that the priest read the Law to the people. The Law is what we are about to read. I wonder if it was dry and boring to them then?

There are some worthy words in the above verse that are worth thinking about. "he shall offer it without blemish." How important is that requirement? If you look at the Passover passage in Exodus 12, again you will note that it was also a requirement then as well.

After Jesus had hung on the cross till he died the soldier went out to remove Him, and the two thieves with Him, to bury them. They had to break the legs of the two thieves to hasten their deaths. It wasn't necessary for Jesus, He was already dead. Because of the above verse and others like it the holy sacrifice could not be blemished. Our sacrifice on the cross of Calvary to pay for our sins, had to be "without blemish"!

As we travel through this book and look at the various laws and offerings, I want you think about two things. One, put yourself in Israel's place, what might it mean to them then. Second, how would this offering or law pertain to me as a child of God. What is God teaching me through this passage?

Then the Lord spoke to Moses, saying, "Speak to the children of Israel,
saying: 'He who offers the sacrifice of his peace offering to the Lord
shall bring his offering to the Lord from the sacrifice of his peace
offering." (Leviticus 7:28-29)

In my Bible, a reference to Ephesians 2:14: "For He Himself is our peace, who has
made both one, and has broken down the middle wall of separation."

Maybe if you read the verses above you might think that this offering was
to bring inner peace. Not so. Picture this Israeli bringing his offering to the
tabernacle and turning it over to the priest. What do you suppose his expectations
were? That he might walk away with inner peace? No. He wants to restore his
relationship with God.

When Adam and Eve were expelled from the Garden of Eden, God was
upset (to put it mildly) with them. They had disobeyed His express order and thus
brought sin into the world. Most of the time through the Old Testament, God is
not a "happy camper!" He is forever responding to the complaints of Israel.

This offering is a great picture of Jesus. In Isaiah Jesus is called the "Prince of
Peace." His death on the cross tore the veil between man and God. We now have
personal access to Almighty God through His Son. I guess that could be scary
when you think about it. But we must remember that Jesus is right there at the
right hand of God making intercessory for us,

This is such an important offering. How much does the world today strive for
inner peace? We spend millions of dollars on therapy, self-help books, etc. Peace
only comes from a personal relationship with God the Father.

Notice the instruction from God, "must bring his offering to the Lord." God
is not going to just, grant us peace. There must be an effort on our part, to show
God we earnestly seek this peace.

Here's another rich nugget from the New Testament: Colossians 3:15. "and
let the peace of God rule in your hearts, to which also you were called in one
body; and be thankful," What an awesome verse! You notice it doesn't say abide
in your heart. It says "rule" in your hearts. It must be preeminent! To have that
kind of relationship with God, that nothing in this world gets to you, must truly
be amazing!

And Moses and Aaron went into the tabernacle of meeting, and came
out and blessed the people. Then the glory of the Lord appeared to
all the people. (Leviticus 9:23)

The tabernacle of meeting. In the King James, it's called the tabernacle of the
congregation and, in the New Testament it's called the church. As soon as
God provided Israel with the Law, he gave instructions for the meeting place.
For the nation to gather together for two reasons. One, to worship the God
who had brought them out of bondage, and later gave them Canaan. Second, for
instruction. The instruction in the Feasts and the offerings and communicating
with God and His instructions for His people.

Nothing has changed! Either from the Old Testament tabernacle, the New
Testament church, or the church of today. It's basically the same purpose: worship
and instruction.

If you notice in this passage Moses and Aaron had completed the five
"offerings" and had entered the tabernacle to worship. Following that, they came
out and the glory of the Lord appeared to all the people. It's like God had put His
signature on the previous actions.

I think there is something to be said for the process here. They went in to
worship and God waited for them outside and appeared to all the people. The
presence of God was outside the tabernacle. The glory was outside the tabernacle.
God's work is done outside the tabernacle.

Too many of us think that our Sunday worship is sufficient for God. "I've
given to God now the rest of the week is mine." That is so not true. All through
scripture God desires a "daily" relationship. Far too many people today look at the
church as a "scheduled event" instead of time to worship God.

If a regular meeting place to gather and worship our heavenly Father were not
that big a deal, why do you suppose God went into such detail in the construction?
Oh, remember the words of Jesus, "Upon this rock I will build my CHURCH and
the gates of hell shall not prevail against it." (Matthew 16:18). The church was so
important to God that His Son made a very strong promise concerning it. The
devil has been working ever since to divide and destroy this all-important ministry.

> "For I am the Lord who brings you up out of the land of Egypt, to be
> your God. You shall therefore be holy, for I am holy." (Leviticus 11:45)

What an interesting verse. Here God is reminding Israel AGAIN who brought them out of bondage to Egypt. Who has provided for them and brought them to this point. The Law, the tabernacle, etc. Now He gives them a challenge: Be Holy!

An interesting companion verse can be seen in Galatians 5:1 it says, "Stand fast therefore in the liberty by which Christ has made us free, and do not be entangled with a yoke of bondage." Freedom in Christ, bondage to sin. Much the same principle as the Israelites.

Only through a relationship with God can we ever expect to be free. Now about this issue of being holy. I want to offer another thought. What is your definition of being holy? Is it being like God. Some say it is being like Jesus Christ. Jesus was the gold standard. If being like God means being holy wasn't that the same offer the devil made to Eve in the Garden? Genesis 3:5 says, "For God knows that in the day you eat of it your eyes will be opened, and you will be like God, knowing good and evil." Of course, what he said was a lie.

Let me offer another thought about being perfect: I think God is saying "be holy, for I am holy" means the closer our walk with God the closer we will be to being holy. Our relationship with God is His paramount desire. To walk daily, listening, obeying, serving God the best we can.

Of course, we will never achieve holiness! We can never expect to be as holy as God's Son. We understand that. Some have said that this is the goal to strive for. Granted, but I think it goes deeper than that. By acknowledging the impossibility, we tend to want to not try at all. That's not what God wants.

God reminds us of His love for us (brought out of bondage) and then encourages us to strive to walk as close to Him as possible. Of course, we will stumble, but God is right there to lift us up and strengthen our walk with him. Remember when Peter had the faith to step out of the boat? Then he looked around and saw the storm. Jesus was right there to lift him out of the peril. He is with us today, walking with us!

"As for the man whose hair has fallen from his head, he is bald, but he is clean. He whose hair has fallen from his forehead, he is bald on the forehead, but he is clean." (Leviticus 13:40-41)

Why in the world would you select this verse from these chapters? This verse touches on an interesting subject that is prevalent in Leviticus. Jesus also deals with it in the New Testament, "cleanness".

In Leviticus, anyone with leprosy, when they were out and about, if they encountered someone had to shout, "unclean, unclean" so the other person would know they had leprosy. Leprosy was very contagious and can be fatal.

In Jesus day, they still dealt with the disease. The interesting thing was that when Jesus encountered a person with leprosy, He touched that person to heal them. That was unheard of in the Old Testament and the people of Jesus' day as well. Now Jesus could have just said, "be healed" without touching them and they would have been healed. So why did He make it a point to touch them? That's who Jesus is!

I'm wondering if we have some around us who are afflicted with "leprosy" today. People that are beneath our touching. People that, maybe, we think God can't touch their hearts. It would be a waste of time for us to try to witness to them. Unspoken leprosy keeps us from reaching out to them.

Maybe that was the point Jesus was making. There is no one that God doesn't love. No one that God can't save. No one that God can't reach. It's we who have restricted the power of God. We have already judged them "unclean".

Just a note. I've noticed today that a lot of men are wearing hats (caps) into restaurants and buildings. When I grew up that was a definite a NO-NO! When you entered a building, you removed your hat. Then I got to thinking about it. The one's I know who don't remove their hats are ones who are going bald. They don't want to be seen with thinning hair. That's a shame.

Do you know someone who is "unclean"? You politely avoid them and especially don't share with them the grace of God through Jesus. Let me encourage you to remember Jesus and make an effort to touch them in some way. I kind word, a helping hand, etc.

"Then he shall kill the lamb of the trespass offering, and the priest shall take some of the blood of the trespass offering and put it on the tip of the right ear of him who is to be cleansed, on the thumb of the right hand, and on the big toe of his right foot." (Leviticus 14:25)

Have you lost it yet? You're not alone.

One thing I have noticed about the context of this verse, the verses before and after talk about using oil. This verse uses the blood of a lamb. According to a commentary I've read the trespass offering is an offering for unintentional sin against the Lord, holy things, or your neighbor. Making sure all the bases are covered!

In the New Testament book of Hebrews, the Lord Jesus is our priest. He has no need of all these ceremonies. Jesus simply appeals to the Father on our behalf and it's done. In fact, He paid for ALL our sins, past, present, AND unintentional with His death on the cross.

One other thing. The touching the ear, thumb and big toe I think it simply means we are covered! Everything is under the blood!

Have you noticed how much of a role the priest plays throughout these verses? Every Israeli had to go to the priest as a mediator to God. He brought the offering to the priest then the priest slayed the animal, extracted the blood and did what was prescribed for the application. Not just the blood, grain, drink, or whatever was needed.

The book of Hebrews refers to Jesus as our high priest. He has already taken care of whatever God requires to make atonement for our sin. I love what Jesus said on the cross, "It is finished!" (John 29:30).

God's plan from the Garden of Eden to today was completed on the cross. Jesus' death restored our relationship with the Father. Now because of the blood of Jesus we have access to the very throne room of God as His children.

Without the process of the sacrificial blood being applied, there is no power, no forgiveness, no reconciliation. Just like the old Baptist hymn: "There is power, power, power in the blood!" Amen.

"For the life of the flesh is in the blood, and I have given it to you upon the altar to make atonement for your souls; for it is the blood that makes atonement for the soul." (Leviticus 17:11)

There is a saying that goes around during the 4th of July celebration. "Freedom is not free". The cost of our freedom is the blood of so many soldiers, who fought to make and keep our country free. The same is true here. Adam's disobedience in the Garden came with a price. Man lost the freedom to be in God's presence. Therefore, Adam and Eve were expelled from the Garden. God provided animal skins to cloth them (Genesis 3:21). They were no longer eligible to be in God's presence because of their sin.

The same is true today. Because of our sin, God cannot allow us access to His presence. In Hebrews it says, "In burnt offerings and sacrifices for sin You had no pleasure." (Hebrews 10:6). And in Hebrews 10:4 it says, "For it is not possible that the blood of bulls and goats could take away sin." So why was God going through such lengths in Leviticus to stress these sacrifices?

God is laying the groundwork for His Son.

I often wondered just how long this sacrifice of a lamb on the altar in the tabernacle lasted. Till the next sabbath? Till the next sin offense. Till sundown the next day. Just how long was this sacrifice good for?

God needed a "permanent" solution. A way for mankind to restore their relationship with Him. ONLY the blood of the "only begotten Son of God" was sufficient to cover our sins past, present, and future. Jesus was the only answer to one having the authority to accomplish this for us.

Have you ever asked yourself, when Adam sinned in the Garden if God knew His Son would have to pay the price? Of course, He did. God is all-knowing. That was the price God had to pay for us to have self-will. God wanted that relationship with Him, and us, to voluntary. No strings! He paid a gigantic price to give us the option of receiving His Son as our Savior or to reject that option and choose eternity separated from God's presence.

He has done everything He could possibly do to make it possible for a relationship with Him. You must believe and accept this offering from God.

"You shall not take vengeance, nor bear any grudge against the children of your people, but you shall love your neighbor as yourself: I am the Lord." (Leviticus 19:18)

We don't pay much attention to the Old Testament today. It really doesn't pertain to us. We focus on the New Testament today. Take another look at this verse.

Next you might want to turn to Romans 12:19 in the New Testament. Paul writes to the church in Rome, "Beloved, do not avenge yourselves, but rather give place to wrath; for it is written, 'vengeance is mine, I will repay' says the Lord." And that referenced back to Deuteronomy 32:35.

How can this be? Well the same person authored all three references, the Holy Spirit. God takes full responsibility for justice being done. It's His call not yours. The thing I like about that, is that God can do a much better job than we can. The problem we have is that we want to retaliate now, we can't wait for God. That's sad. Another thing I've noticed is that a lot of times, by waiting on God, we discover whether that vengeance is warranted or necessary. It's best to leave it in God's hands. Besides think of the peace you get by turning it loose and trusting God's judgment.

Second, notice the second half of that verse. Sound familiar? Try Matthew 22:37-40 Jesus said to him, "You shall love the Lord your God with all your heart, with all your soul, and with all your mind. This is the first great commandment. And the second is like it: You shall love your neighbor as yourself. On these two commandments hang all the Law and the Prophets." Again, the same author, the Holy Spirit wrote both passages. The Old Testament Law and the New Testament summary by our Lord.

This is a clear-cut command, is it not? Why carry the burden of hatred and revenge around for years sometimes trying to determine how you're going "make things right" that's God's territory, is it not?

It seems this passage is dealing with our horizontal relationships also the same approach Jesus took. I like the analogy of the cross. The vertical relationship (God to man) and the horizontal relationships with our fellow man. Both, very important to God!

"And when you offer a sacrifice of thanksgiving to the Lord, offer it of your own free will." (Leviticus 22:29)

Simple words, but so profound! "A sacrifice of thanksgiving," you know that is all God wants from us? To recognize that God wants only the best for us AND that we worship Him freely.

Freely, that is SO important. That's what I want to talk about. Even from the Garden of Eden, God has always allowed us free will. Of course, God could have created us "dependent" on Him, but He didn't. He gave us everything we could possibly need and simply asked us to choose Him over the lies of Satan.

One of my favorite verses, of course, is Joshua 24:15 "As for me and my house, we will serve the Lord." A commitment Joshua made to God. I can just see the smile on God's face when Joshua made that statement.

Another great passage is 1 Kings 18. Elijah's confrontation with the priests of Baal. In verse twenty-one Elijah says, "How long will you falter between two opinions? If the Lord is God, follow Him; but if Baal, follow him." A clear option!

God has made that offer throughout our lives. Choose whom you will follow, obey, etc.

It's my theory that when God created us, He left a piece out. And mankind will spend their entire lives trying to fill that void, money, fame, things, sex, etc. Nothing will satisfy except a personal relationship with God. Besides paying for our sins on the cross, that is another reason why Christ came. We can relate much better with a God like Jesus than the one in the Old Testament. God couldn't seem to make the connection He wanted. How can I get across to man that I desire a closer relationship? I will go to earth and walk among them. Demonstrate my compassion and love and even to the point of dying for them on Calvary's cross.

"Free will" how important is that? We are not puppets with strings being manipulated by a powerful God. No, God's deepest desire is that we would choose Him over the things of this world. All that the world could offer cannot compare with what God offers!

"I am the Lord your God, who brought you out of the land of Egypt,
to give you the land of Canaan and to be your God." (Leviticus 25:38)

Why do you suppose God wants to keep reminding His people of what He had done? Surely, we can't understand why this is necessary. Just curious, what do you do when a trial approaches? Right away you turn to prayer, right? I don't think so.

"And to be your God." What an awesome thought. You see it's hard for us, because we know how the story ends. They refuse to trust God and God makes them wander in the desert for forty years, etc. The land is there's!

How many promises in the Bible do you know? How many have you claimed lately? Here God makes a promise to His people and when they reach the point of taking possession they cower in fear, refused to claim the promise.

I've heard this promise quoted so often when someone asks for a promise: "I'll never leave you or forsake you." Do you know this promise first appears in Deuteronomy? (31:8). You thought that was a promise Jesus made, didn't you?

Just what does that mean to you? It seems the Israelites forgot that promise as well. It is in the Law, the five books of Moses which they heard prior to entering the Promised Land. What did it mean to Israel? What does it mean to you?

That's why God must continually remind Israel of who He is. I just remembered a verse, I believe it appears twice in Judges (17:6, 21:25), "Everyone did what was right in his own eyes." You see that was the attitude of ten of the twelve spies sent to check out the Promised Land. They determined their chances by what they saw. So many time's we judge our circumstances and chances by our own ability, rather than trusting God to His ability.

We are almost through with Leviticus. I hope you have a new perspective on this book. There are so many rules and regulations, then in Jesus day they added another 600 more. And of course, if we kept every single rule we would be no closer to heaven than we are now. Always remember that God wants a relationship with Him and an honest effort to be obedient through love, not sacrifice.

"I will set My tabernacle among you, and My soul shall not abhor you. I will walk among you, and you shall be My people." (Leviticus 26:11-12)

This is an interesting chapter. In chapter 26 God lays out the consequences of disobedience. The pros and cons so to speak. Again, Israel knows the rules. We know the rules.

The word Tabernacle simply means "dwelling place" God has said that He would dwell with the nation Israel. Look at the middle of that verse: "I will walk among you" does that sound familiar? The last time God walked among man was with Adam and Eve in the Garden. Here again, He's telling them what it would be like to have a relationship with the Father.

In these five books of Moses I believe God does everything possible to win the hearts of His people. Remember, God started with a man (Adam), then a family (Abraham) and then a nation (Israel). It was Jesus who completed the plan and reached the whole world.

God went so far as to build a house where He offered to dwell within the nation. We saw in a previous verse that God dwelled in that Tabernacle, so much so, that Moses and Aaron couldn't enter.

This is just a foreshadow of today. Today when we accept Christ as our Savior we become children of God, a part of HIS family. That's the promise He makes to Israel in this verse "And you shall be My people." I have a mental picture of a loving father with open arms wanting so badly to hug his children. Much like Jesus talked about in His parable of the prodigal son.

O.k, so where did Israel go wrong? Before we leave Leviticus, let's think about Israel's relationship with God. God has made every effort and then some to connect with His people. Miracles galore, personal appearances, etc. And the first chance they get, they reject Him. Why is that? I can't imagine trust being an issue, can you?

After all, look what God did for them. Can you fill in the blank? Maybe think about your own life. What has God done in your life? Can you think of anything? Or maybe you believe that all you have and all you've accomplished you did it without any help. I wonder if that might be Israel's attitude. Until we can acknowledge God's presence and power we will never be able to trust Him!

> But the Levites shall camp around the tabernacle of the Testimony, that there may be no wrath on the congregation of the children of Israel; and the Levites shall keep charge of the tabernacle of the Testimony. (Numbers 1:53)

Just a minute! Look at the next verse, verse 54, it reads: "Thus the children of Israel did; according to all that the Lord commanded Moses, so they did". In chapter one they took a census of each tribe, all twelve of them. In the above verse, assigned duties, etc. Did you notice? When God is specific, do this, do that, Israel complies. But you ask them to trust God and go into the Promised Land where there are giants, now that's another story.

I have often believed that if God put a price tag on salvation, He did, but that's for another time, say you brought 10,000 dollars to a church near you and the pastor, and even the word of God said that guaranteed you access to heaven there would lines out the door and around the block. We would beg, borrow or steal the ten thousand dollars, to make it happen, why? Because it's something tangible something we can do. Just like Israel. When God gave them specific instructions they obeyed. When God brought them to the Red Sea they were lost as to what to do next.

Whenever I buy a new Bible I first go to the New Testament and physically underline every time the word "faith" appears. Did you know the word only appears twice in the Old Testament (KJV)? Why is this word important? It's exactly the point I'm trying to make.

Exercising faith requires trusting God. No instructions, no game plan, just trust God for the outcome or direction. Can you imagine the amount of faith it would take to go into the mission field? Just total trust in God. Another good example is a farmer. He spends hundreds of dollars buying seed only to throw it into the ground and trust that God will provide a harvest. It is totally in God's hands. Oh, we can spread some fertilizer, irrigate, etc. But it's God that provides the harvest.

That's our salvation! Nothing we can do, it's all on God and faith that God will keep His word. That's the key in John 3:16, "whosoever believes in Him." It's faith in Jesus that brings salvation. Not ten thousand or a million dollars, it's free, it only cost the life of God's Son.

According to the commandment of the Lord they were numbered by
the hand of Moses, each according to his service and according to
his task; thus, were they numbered by him, as the Lord commanded
Moses. (Numbers 4:49)

Did you catch that one little word in this verse? "Service", each according to his
service. God had specific tasks for each tribe, mainly the Levites regarding
the tabernacle. In chapter ten God even gives specific details in the order that the
tribes were to march from one place to another.

Three tribes were to leave first, then the tabernacle, then the rest. For the
protection of the tabernacle.

Here Moses is told by God to number the people. Later Moses and later
David would take it on themselves to number the people, much to their regret.

Why do you suppose God wanted them numbered here? Soon they would be
entering the Promised Land, well that was the plan. I think God wanted to boost
their faith. Help them realize the size of their army. Even though God would do
the fighting.

It's like what God might do for us. He grants a special blessing in our lives
to encourage our faith for a bigger task ahead. Something else I've noticed about
God. The more you trust Him the greater He works in your life. If we are obedient
in the small things God is willing to trust us in greater things. I believe there is a
verse that says that.

Notice in the verse above, not only according to his service but also according
to the task. God never puts more on us than we can handle. Just like entering the
Promised Land. If measured my Israel's standards they didn't have a chance. But
if looked at through God's eyes they were more than equipped! The power was
God's the faith needed was Israel's.

I wonder if Moses questioned the census. Why was this necessary? Many
times, God will ask us to do something that seems weird, or strange. Just do it!
God always has a plan and purpose for what He asks us to do. Like I said before
it may be just to see if we will obey His leading.

Has God laid on your heart to do something? What is your response?

The Lord bless you and keep you; the Lord make His face to shine upon you, and be gracious to you; The Lord lift up His countenance upon you, and give you peace. (Numbers 6:24-26)

Have you ever felt God's hand on your life? The heart of this verse says pretty much the same. His face to shine on you, His countenance on you, etc. It's an awesome feeling.

I was pastor of a small church for 2 1/2 years. No college, no seminary I just told the Pulpit Committee that "I love the Lord." Purely God's hand that allowed me to be their pastor. Two and a half years of watching God to amazing things through me and with me.

I've heard this verse quoted several times by a Rabbi on TV. I'm wondering if this might be the Hebrew version of The Lord's Prayer. If it is I'm sorry. By that I mean it would come to mean as much as the Lord's Prayer means to us.

Have you ever noticed that the more familiar we become with passages in the Bible the less we think of them? Take John 3:16. We know that by heart, most of us, we know the words by heart but do they have any real meaning?

The above verse seems to be that kind of verse. A Hebrew child is taught that verse early on. His parents teach it to him. He grows up knowing the verse but not the God it's talking about. The same with John 3:16. It tells us what God gave up for our relationship with Him, and that we must believe in Him.

Being a Christian is SO much more than that simple verse. Yet, somehow, we think that if we memorize that verse we're in. God wants so much more from us.

I think it's interesting that this verse follows God's instructions for being a Nazarite. Certain restrictions for a closer walk with God. Follow the rules and your "set apart" for God's use. Israel is good at following instructions but lacks the heart connection.

This is a beautiful verse, just as John 3:16 or the Lord's prayer. When we can get past the "words" and know the God of the Word and have that relationship that the center of this verse talks about, God's presence, then we have what God intended for us. A daily walk with God's hand on our life.

> Now the leaders offered the dedication offering for the altar when it
> was anointed; so, the leaders offered their offering before the altar.
> For the Lord said to Moses, "They shall offer their offering, one leader
> each day, for the dedication of the altar." (Numbers 7:10-11)

I believe this is the longest chapter in the Bible apart from the 119th Psalm. The funny thing is that once you have read the offering for the tribe of Reuben then it is repeated for each tribe thereafter.

A long list of animals and utensils as an offering to God. God has brought them from Egypt where they were slaves with little or nothing to the point of making this great offering. God has blessed each person, family, tribe and the nation far beyond their dreams.

It was stretched out over 12 days. One day for each tribe. Each day they were reminded of what God had done for them. It was brought as a dedication to the altar. As we have seen previously, the altar where God made Himself known.

I can see the soldiers now going through each camp compelling all the members to come up with the items for the offering. Threatening them with bodily harm forcing them to give.

I'm sorry, I couldn't resist. I'm just kidding of course. They offered willingly, excitedly, expectantly, praising God in the process. It's what we had talked about before. Any acknowledgment of God must be freely given. God has never forced anyone to do or give anything against their will. Even Jesus in the Garden of Gethsemane asked if there were any other way, and then freely offered Himself, as God required.

God wants the same from you. There is nothing compelling your relationship! God would not hear of it. He desires our relationship to be completely voluntary. His heart longs for it. His Holy Spirit dwells within us, as proof of His desire for a closer relationship. Of course, the Spirit doesn't live in someone who has rejected Him.

It's tempting to skip over the other tribes once we have read the list of offerings. Don't do that. Each tribal leader, representing his tribe brings with open arms that which was required. Looking forward to their day, their opportunity to give. To be a part of what God was doing in their midst. What an awesome feeling!

> And it shall be, if you go with us—indeed it shall be—that whatever
> good the Lord will do to us, the same we will do to you." (Numbers
> 10:32)

I pondered this verse for some time. Then I remembered the principle used here is also told by Bro. Henry Blackaby in his book, *Experiencing God*. The principle he teaches is this: Find out where God is at work, then join Him there.

That's what Moses was telling his father-in-law. You see, God was using Moses in a great way. So, he advised his father-in-law to join him and not only see what God was doing, but be a part of the miracles.

Are you a part of what God is doing around you? Of course, the local church is a great place to start. Is God moving in your church? Is God moving in your life? Why not?

We must always keep this episode is prospective. Where Israel was when God called Moses. Where Moses was when God called him. Where God had brought them from, to where God was taking them. One day, one step at a time. Each day God had some new task for them or some new destination, some new purpose God was directing.

Is God "active" in your life? Where is God leading you today, this week, this year? Are you trusting Him or do you argue or disagree with what you perceive as His plan? Ask Him!

Now He's not going to tell you what is coming up. He will give you a peace about a certain direction or task. It doesn't take faith when God spells out the future. It's all about trust. Trusting God that He knows the path, and the right time to move forward.

Have you noticed in these chapters how God used a pillar of smoke by day, and a pillar of fire by night, to tell Israel when to move and when to rest. It also gives direction, but more important when! That is key. We tend to be in a hurry and want to get ahead of God which will never work.

Are you a part of what God is doing in your community, in your church? You're missing a blessing. One of the greatest blessing a child of God can have is to be a part of something God is doing. We can be a part of miracles! If you haven't noticed yet in these chapters that God uses people to accomplish His will. Is God using you?

Then Moses said to him, "Are you zealous for my sake? Oh, that all the Lord's people were prophets and that the Lord would put His Spirit upon them!" And Moses returned to the camp, he and the elders of Israel. (Numbers 11:29-30)

What a prayer. With all the static Moses has been getting from his people, even his sister and brother, he must feel like he's pushing a boulder up a steep hill. I'm sure he has wanted to give up several times.

He asks an interesting question here. "Are you zealous for my sake?" He is questioning their motives about someone else's service. Jesus had the same problem. I think it was Peter that said, "shall we rebuke someone serving that isn't part of our group.

Another funny thing about that verse. "that the Lord would put His Spirit upon them." Guess what? That's exactly what Jesus did when He ascended to heaven. He sent the Holy Spirit to indwell ALL His children. Everyone that confesses Christ as their Savior receives this very same Spirit.

Maybe we can ask ourselves the very same question. How about two questions. One, Are you zealous for anything? If so what are you zealous for? Is it sports related? Is it possessions related? Is it someone you care about? What motivates you to go the extra mile, to get excited about? I hope it's something to do with the Lord.

I remember when I first started teaching a Sunday school class. I was scared to death. Then when I saw a light go on in the faces of my students I became so excited I couldn't wait to get to church and teach and study for a lesson. When you see God at work you can't help but get excited!

Moses is questioning the motive of the one asking the question. Why are worried about him, how about your own zealousness. What gets you out of bed in the morning? What motivates you? Is it personal gain or doing for others?

Let me recommend Bro. Blackaby's book: *Experiencing God.* It is an awesome book. There I go using that word again. I'm sorry but it's the best word I can use to express my excitement. It's a great study! The parallel between this passage and the one in the New Testament is interesting.

Then the Lord said to Moses: "How long will these people reject me? And how long will they not believe Me, with all the signs which I have performed among them? I will strike them with the pestilence and disinherit them, and I will make of you a nation greater and mightier than they." (Numbers 14:11-12)

The twelve have returned from surveying the Promised land. I hope you are reading these chapters. First, they are amazed at what the Promised Land contains, bounty wise. They are also afraid of what the land contains, giants. The vote is 10 to 2 NOT to trust God and claim the land.

Can you read the frustration and disappointment in God's words? One note, turn to verse 22. Look what God says, "Because all these men who have seen My glory and the signs which I did in Egypt and in the wilderness, and have put Me to the test now *these ten times*, and have not heeded My voice." (emphasis added). God has had it. No Promised Land for this generation.

If my memory serves, God wanted to destroy them at Mt. Sinai as well. Both times Moses intercedes. God wanted to start all over, just destroy the bunch of them and start all over. Did you notice Moses' argument? What would be God's testimony to the Egyptians? What would the Egyptians say?

These verses are so interesting. Notice that once Israel was confronted with God's response to their lack of faith, now Israel wants to obey. Nope! You have made your decision now you must pay for your decision. This reminds me of heaven. Heaven? Yes, when so many unbelievers reach the judgment and say, "Oh, it is true. O.k, I repent and accept Jesus." Then, as Jesus said, "I never knew you, depart from Me." (Matthew 7:23)

Two key words in the verse above. Reject and believe. That is the key. That is the same scenario today. Those who reject the story of the cross and God's sacrifice to pay for our sins and, as John 3:16 says, "whosoever believes in Me" that is the key that opens the gates of heaven. Read Romans 10:9-10.

Is there a limit to God's patience? In Romans it also says, "And gave them up to a reprobate mind." (Romans 1). God will only wait so long.

Then the Lord said to Aaron: "You shall have no inheritance in their land, nor shall you have any portion among them; I am your portion and your inheritance among the children of Israel." (Numbers 18:20)

I wonder if that would satisfy us. Notice God says, "I am your portion." Is that enough?

When God said that, did He mean that Aaron and the priests would not enter the Promised Land? No, of course not. It meant that they would be set apart. God would provide special land and property for them. God would make special provision for them.

If you notice, both in Numbers and in Leviticus God went into great detail about the priest and the priesthood. Specific detail both in their dress and their procedures. Besides giving them details on the offerings and sacrifices. Much is said of the priests.

Of course, in the New Testament, especially in Hebrews it describes Jesus as our High Priest. He has made the sacrifice. He stands before the Father on our behalf. He makes petition to God on our behalf. So, in the Old Testament, we get the picture and in the New Testament, we get the real thing.

Much is the case in the Old Testament. Whether it's the life of David, Abraham, Samson, Elijah, and so on. Each gives us a glimpse into the mind of God. What God wants, how He responds to sin and disobedience.

You can't have one without the other.

What portion of our lives does God have. God told Aaron that God would be their portion. How can we measure that? I've often wondered if we might measure it in time. Such a valuable commodity today. Some people treasure that commodity so much that they are not even willing to give God three hours on Sunday. There is just too much else to do. We work all day during the week. We have chores that need to be done on Saturday. We just need a day of rest. Granted! God even set aside one day in seven to rest in Exodus 20.

To rest, that means God's not included in that rest. I did a sermon once on a verse in Hebrews about entering God's rest. Can you truly rest on the Lord's day without including Him? I want to encourage a little effort to meet with God in the God's house, on the Lord's day!

Then the Lord spoke to Moses and Aaron, "Because you did not
believe Me, to hallow Me in the eyes of the children of Israel, therefore
you shall not bring this assembly into the land which I have given
them." (Numbers 20:12)

Did you read these chapters? I think it so funny. Funny, seriously! Yes. Do you
remember not long ago that Moses had to talk God out of destroying Israel?
He wanted to wipe them out, and start all over. Why? Because He had had enough
of their disobedience.

Now God told Moses specifically what to do. "speak" to the rock and water
will come out. Now Moses had had enough of Israel's complaining so in a rage he
struck the rock twice. As a result, Moses was denied entry to the Promised Land.

How many times have we said or done something in anger that we wish we
had never said or done? It's so frustrating, isn't it? We can see this all through the
Bible. Anger can destroy relationships! It didn't do much for God and Moses'
relationship at this point. God did allow Moses to see the Promised Land, from
Mt. Pisgah (Numbers 23:14) he was not allowed to enter.

The Bible says not to let the sun go down on our anger. Why? It eats us alive.
Have you noticed how much being angry can affect your whole life? From sleep, to
eating, to our disposition, etc. Sometimes the person or thing we are angry about
isn't around to receive our wrath.

Notice here also that it wasn't Aaron who struck the rock but he will pay for
Moses anger. That also happens as well. Others can pay for our anger. Sometimes
we destroy things that are precious to us out of anger. Things that can never be
replaced.

So, what might be a good solution? Jesus said, "pray for those who despitefully
use you." (Matthew 5:44). The minute we bring this anger to God He begins
working on our heart, the source of our anger. The more we pray for, and about
what we are angry about then God works on the solution. Remember a verse we
saw earlier? "Vengeance is Mine, and recompense" (Deuteronomy 32:35) The
moment we fully turn our anger over to God He begins to work. The key is that it
MUST be turned over to Him. God will not meddle as long as we have our hands
on it. Not until we release it to Him can God begin to settle the situation.

Just think of the peace you will receive by giving it to God.

Then Balaam answered and said to the servants of Balak, "Though Balak were to give me his house full of silver and gold, I could not go beyond the word of the Lord my God, to do less or more." (Numbers 22:18)

What an awesome attitude. Can you imagine knowing the will of God so clear that you can say to someone who offers you the moon to do something and you say no. That takes faith!

I'm not really a fan of this portion of scripture. Why? I have a hard time distinguishing between Balak and Balaam. I get confused easy! Many times, I had to stop and think which is which.

Balak is the guy who wants to curse Israel. Balaam is the prophet that Balak is hiring to curse Israel. The funny part of the story is that three times Balak calls on Balaam to curse Israel Balaam ends up blessing them.

At first Balaam refuses. Balak keeps asking, pleading, you see in the verse above he offers Balaam a house full of gold and silver. What is that to Balaam, to be on the wrong side of God.

What is the world offering you to deny God? To turn your back on His provision. To refuse to follow Jesus by faith. Is it worth it? What price would you put on an eternity in heaven or hell? Think about it.

"I could not go beyond the word of the Lord," What a fantastic (I'll try another word) statement. As a long-time Sunday School teacher, it has always been my contention that it is impossible to know the will of God apart from the word of God. It is scary how little God's children know about His word. Therein lies the boundaries that God has placed AND the blessings that He has promised. But because we are so ignorant of His word we suffer not knowing.

I hope you have been keeping up with the daily reading. It takes less than a half hour. In my devotions, I read a devotion from Sara Young, I pray for a list of lost people I keep in my Bible, then I read my two or three chapters, then I pray for family, friends, sick, etc. It all fits together in a quiet time with God and His word. I could not imagine beginning a day without this time.

First you must set a time to meet with God. Then prepare a routine. Follow it each day. The beginning of a relationship with God!

Therefore say, "Behold, I give to him My covenant of peace; and
it shall be to him and his descendants after him a covenant of an
everlasting priesthood, because he was zealous for his God, and made
atonement for the children of Israel." (Numbers 25:12-13)

This brings up an interesting point. Does this seem cruel that God would kill
all these people? And this is also a method that Satan uses to derail the work
of God. Just like in the Garden of Eden. Contaminate the work. Draw away God's
people from their purpose.

I've often wondered if this might be Satan's tactic in our country. Some
surveys say we are 80 to 90 percent a Christian nation. Yet we lead the world in
pornography, drugs, divorce and abortions. How can this be? I've often wondered
how we can rationally excuse this.

It works in families, in churches and in nations. Paul warned of it in some
of his epistles. Infiltrators in the church that teach another doctrine. Divide and
conquer that's the devil's tactic.

In this passage Baal and other cults had crept into the Israeli camp. Drawing
God's people to idol worship. We struggle individually as well. I don't have to read
my Bible, I don't have to go to church, I don't have to pray. I'm saved and going to
heaven why should I need to do these things? Then ask yourself a question. How
close is my relationship with the Father? Do I feel His presence when I get up in
the morning to face a new day?

Why did God heap such blessing on Phinehas? He was willing to do
something. That's the hard part. Most would rather ignore the problem, maybe it
will go away. A huge problem in churches. Confrontation is not easy, but necessary!

"Because he was zealous for his God." We talked earlier about being zealous.
Change is brought by God's people who are willing to take a stand. One question.
Where was God's people when prayer was taken from our schools?

Is God way off base seeking "purity"? Let's see, I think we looked at a verse
that said, "Be ye holy, as I am holy." (Leviticus 19:2) did we not? This is part of that.
I believe it is said in Peter's epistles that we are a "royal priesthood" (1 Peter 2:9)
does it not? Now what would that entail? What is contaminating your relationship
with God?

"Let the Lord, the God of the spirits of all flesh, set a man over the congregation, who may go out before them, who may lead them out and bring them in, that the congregation of the Lord may not be like sheep which have no shepherd." (Numbers 27:16-17)

The choosing of Joshua. Joshua was an understudy of Moses. Joshua walk with Moses and saw how God used Moses, worked through Moses and blessed Moses. Preparing Joshua to take the reins of leadership. Notice how Moses words this:

"Let the Lord God, the God of the spirits of all flesh, set a man over the congregation." It wasn't Moses who chose Joshua, it was God. God's man for God's people.

This can be the most important choice a church will ever have to make. It must be God's man. A lot of prayer must take place. Notice also that Joshua is likened to a shepherd. This is very interesting. Let me ask you a couple of questions. Where was Moses for forty years before going to Egypt to set God's people free? Where was David when God chose him to be Israel's king? They were both shepherds. An interesting quality for leadership.

I know you remember one of Jesus' titles. "The Good Shepherd" (John 10:11). Isn't it interesting that He is called The Good Shepherd AND, The Lamb of God?

In the gospel of John, the writer spends a great deal of time describing how the Good Shepherd takes care of His sheep. How the sheep hear His voice and respond. (John 10) Great passages.

How important is it to have a shepherd? Both in the Old Testament, and in the New Testament, and today. There must be a leader. The picture that Moses gives "sheep which have no shepherd" is very important. Forgive me, but it also shows the importance of a good pastor. And the importance of attending church. You are sheep whether you like it or not. You attend church, hopefully, for direction from the word of God. The pastor not only teaches from it but lives it before the congregation. Leadership, direction, guidance, all from the word of God.

I think it is important to remember that it was God, and not Moses, who chose Joshua. Who is your shepherd? God or the world?

> And they said to Moses, "Your servants have taken a count of the men of war who are under our command, and not a man of us is missing."
> (Numbers 31:49)

Again, I hope you are reading along. Have you noticed that Israel has had some battles prior to entering the Promised Land? God is always in the training or teaching mode. God wants His people prepared to face the trials ahead. Sometimes the little trials in our lives are to prepare us for things ahead.

Did you notice the priest name? Eleazar is now the High Priest. Aaron has left to be with the Lord. Moses will leave soon. The baton is being passed on.

Following their battle with the Midianites the servants take another count. They left with twelve thousand troops. God said one thousand from each of the twelve tribes. He also said that all of Israel would share in the bounty.

We are coming close to the time of entering the Promised Land. We have one more book of the Law to read, the book of Deuteronomy. Deuteronomy is said to be a recap of the first four, we will see.

In the New Testament "the Law" is referred to several times. These five books are what is referred to. Notice the words of Jesus, "I came not to destroy the Law, but to fulfill it" (Matthew 5:17). Why would God want to destroy something He had put so much effort into?

How is the Law important to us? There are a lot of "principles" given in the law that help us understand who Jesus is, and why God chose to visit us through His son.

One of the important reasons Israel had these battles before even entering the Promised Land was to build their faith that God was with them. Notice in this verse, "not a man of us is missing." God protected them. God is constantly working in our lives to strengthen our faith. The victories we experience in life are because of God's watch care.

Don't miss verse 50. Notice that Israel recognized where the blessings came from. Each man brought an offering from the spoils of the victory. It doesn't say ten percent but each brought as God prospered them. Have you thanked God lately for His provision? Has God blessed you recently? Thank Him!

> For the Egyptians were burying all their firstborn, whom the Lord had killed among them. Also on their gods the Lord executed judgments (Numbers 33:4)

This is such a statement to be revisited! Notice the last part: "Also on their gods the Lord executed judgment." That was the reason for TEN plaques. You notice in Exodus that Pharaoh was ready to release them after the third or fourth plaque. "But God hardened his heart." (Exodus 9:12) You see God wasn't ready to leave until ALL the Egyptian gods were dealt with.

It seems cruel to read that God killed all their first born. Other passages in the Old Testament where God requires the life of the women and children. That's hard to accept today in our society. But God knew that these women and children could potentially draw Israel into idolatry. We are the same way today. That's why God cautions in New Testament not to be "unequally yoked" (2 Corinthians 6:14) that is united with an unbeliever. Not just in marriage but in business and other areas of life.

Is God is dealing with some god's in your life? The question is, what does God have to do to defeat these gods? What will He have to do in your life to remove these gods?

Toward the end of this chapter God gives them some commands after entering Canaan. Destroy the inhabitants, the idols, engraved stones, etc. Cleanse the land basically. Clean house before settling in. It is so important that Israel obey this command.

Do you remember in Genesis 31, when Jacob and his four wives left Laban and headed home? Remember what Rachel did? She hid, in her luggage, idols that were her parents. She was bringing them along. Laban went looking for them and his daughters. We want to cling to things that have absolutely no power but are precious to us.

God defeated the idols of Egypt and He can defeat the idols in your life. The question is what will God have to do to remove them from your grasp?

I think it is interesting that in these five books God has done everything in His power to demonstrate His love and provision for Israel, when it comes time to trust God to defeat their enemies they run. Why is that I wonder?

"Therefore, do not defile the land which you inhabit, in the midst
of which I dwell; for I the Lord dwell among the children of Israel."
(Numbers 35:34)

What do you suppose God meant by "not defiling the land?" I would guess
that it is the one thing that God hates the most. I've read the Old Testament
several times. The one thing that sticks out to me—idols. God hates anything that
comes between Him and His children.

Remember when Moses came down from Mt. Sinai? (Exodus 32) What
did he find the Israelites had done? A golden calf. We already talked about what
Rachel took from her parents and Jacob destroyed them as soon as he found them.

That's fine for the Old Testament but that doesn't apply to me today. Oh,
be sure that it does. Remember the definition of an idol: Anything that comes
between you and God. That can fall into many categories! Even time can be an
idol. What you do with it as opposed to what God wants to do with it.

God warned Israel as they were about to claim a rich land for themselves.
Think about something, about this blessing they were about to receive. There were
cities already built they didn't have to build. There were vineyards already planted
and producing that the children of Israel didn't have to lift a finger. On and on,
everything they could possibly want just handed to them.

God would do the fighting. God provided, and yet.

Before we end this book let's take another overall look at what God has done
to this point. God has brought them out of a 400+ years of bondage where they
were enslaved. Parted the Red Sea before their very eyes. Gave victory after victory
over their enemies, Fed them from heaven with Manna. Continuously provided
water even with all their complaining. Gave them the Ten Commandments, the
Feasts and instructions for sacrifices, etc.

What did God ask? I believe it was the first commandment: "Thou shalt have
no other god's, before Me." (Exodus 20:3) God is a jealous God. Israel will find
this out in so many ways.

How about you? Is there anything between you and God? What takes priority
in your life? Pray and ask God to open your eyes.

The Lord your God, who goes before you, He will fight for you, according to all He did for you in Egypt before your eyes, and in the wilderness where you saw how the Lord your God carried you, as a man carries his son, in all the way you went until you came to this place. (Deuteronomy 1:30-31)

This is Moses' last opportunity to convince Israel to trust God.

Have you read the poem "Footprints?" I hope so. An interesting point made in that poem is that the person had to "look back" to see there were only one set of footprints. You could use that poem with this verse. You see what Moses said? "As a man carries his son." The heart of this verse is the Footprints poem.

He reflects back to Egypt. The miracles that God performed to free the nation. If you've done any study of our nation's founding you can almost see God's hand in the same process. Oh, sure God didn't part the Red Sea but our "farmers" defeated the most powerful army at the time.

The great thing about scripture is how relevant it is to every day. Here's the challenge that Moses presents to the people: Remember!

Israel is going to need that faith built on remembrance to help them when they enter the Promised Land. Canaan was promised to them all the way back to Abraham. Hundreds of years have passed and it's time to fulfill that promise.

The forty years of wandering is over. The generation that refused to obey God's offer has passed away, except for Joshua and Caleb. The judgment has been fulfilled.

Do you remember a line in Exodus? Exodus 1:8 "There arose a new king in Egypt who knew not Joseph." That is where Israel is at now. This is a new generation that hasn't seen the miracles that God has done in Egypt. They obey God out of faith and the stories that were passed down.

There is a verse in Matthew that fits here. Matthew 9:29 it reads in part, "according to your faith be it unto you." Israel will finally receive the promised land by faith. Be sure to read these chapters as we finish up these five books of Moses. These are Moses last words.

> Oh, that they had such a heart in them that they would fear Me and
> always keep all My commandments, that it might be well with them
> and their children forever! (Deuteronomy 5:29)

What an awesome prayer! You know for all the "preaching" that Moses did to the people. The heart is what needed to change. How many people attend church Sunday after Sunday and hear sermon after sermon and the words never penetrate their hearts? It's like Pharaoh's hardened heart.

We also see a great promise. "that it might be well with them and their children." It's like having the secret formula for happiness and success but refusing to open the envelope. It's sad. That's where faith comes in. Just like the previous paragraph. The answer is right there but it doesn't sink in.

Do you remember Jesus example of the "broad way", and the "narrow way" (Matthew 7:13-14) remember what He said? "Few there be that find it." It makes me think of a missionary in a small church in a foreign land. Year after year, preaching and teaching and seeing no fruit. It is so easy to give up.

Let's use another New Testament example. The sower and the seed (Matthew 13). That missionary is planting seed that will someday produce fruit. Moses wants to see the same thing. We kind of skip over the battles that were fought in their forty years of wandering but each one a lesson in God's power. Adding to their faith!

I did a word search one day for the word "heart" it's fascinating! Try it. There are so many variations of the kinds of heart. The saddest reference would be, to me, a stony heart. It is so hardened that the truth cannot penetrate.

In Deuteronomy Moses will set the scene to begin to enter the Promised Land. He will, of course, recap God's leadership from Egypt to their present location. Here is where Moses leaves them, (Deuteronomy 34) walks up the mountain and God takes him. I don't think it's a coincidence that Moses is one of the two who arrive on the Mount of Transfiguration (Matthew 17) with Jesus; Elijah being the other. Neither one, are described as dying in the Old Testament. Take your time and meditate on this book!

> Therefore, know that the Lord your God, He is God, the faithful God who keeps covenant and mercy for a thousand generations with those who love Him and keep His commandments. (Deuteronomy 7:9)

There's that phrase again. It keeps popping out at me. "Keep My commandments" even Jesus said, "If you love Me you will keep my commandments." (John 14:15) You're going to see this a lot more.

As a parent of two children this obedience thing is important. One of the hardest tasks as a parent is teaching your children to obey you, isn't it? We would wish it was simple, just do as I say. It's not that simple. Punishment must follow disobedience. There is no getting around that. If there isn't, there is rebellion!

It has always fascinated me about the Garden of Eden. Here God created this perfect environment. He then puts in it everything that Adam and Eve could ever want. Then He puts this tree in there and says, "don't touch." Why? Why did He put it in there if they were not to touch it? I wonder if "obedience" had anything to do with it. Of course, we know that disobedience to God is sin.

There are so many examples throughout scripture that show the pros and cons of obedience and disobedience. When God called Abraham out of paganism Abraham didn't hesitate, didn't ask questions he just obeyed God.

God told the children of Israel that He would take them to a land filled with milk and honey. When they got there, they rebelled. Again, the idea of consequences for disobedience. As in the Garden as well.

So why is obedience so important. I think it's because of what it demonstrates. Trust, love, a desire to please. Those are the attributes God was wanting from Adam and Eve. Instead they fell for Satan's lies, that they would be equal to God.

"Mercy for a thousand generations." All the way to the cross and beyond. God's mercy! Even after Adam and Eve had sinned by disobeying God, God provided the sacrifice for their sin. (Genesis 3:21)

I like what Eve said later after their first born, son, Chapter 4:1, Now Adam knew Eve his wife, and she conceived and bore Cain, and said, "I have acquired a man from the Lord." God had not forsaken them. God's mercy is boundless even in our disobedience.

"And now, Israel, what does the Lord your God require of you, but to fear the Lord your God, to walk in all His ways and to love Him, to serve the Lord your God with all your heart, and with all your soul, and to keep the commandments of the Lord and His statutes which I command you today for your good?" (Deuteronomy 10:12-13)

About six-hundred years later the prophet Micah wrote a similar verse: "He has shown you, O man, what is good; And what does the Lord require of you but to do justly, to love mercy; and to walk humbly with your God?" (Micah 6:8) I much prefer the verse in Deuteronomy.

Maybe Micah is easier to memorize. Moses has some additional requirements that I like. "Walk in His ways, and to love Him, to serve the Lord" just a couple. And at the end of Moses' verse is says, "with all your heart and soul."

Now I will give Micah some credit his verse is addressed to "O man" and Moses is addressed to Israel. But we know that "All scripture is profitable for doctrine, reproof and instruction in righteousness." (2 Timothy 3:16). There is that phrase again in Moses' verse, "Keep His commandments." You might as well get used to it, God wants obedience. It's the next closest thing to His heart. The closet thing? A relationship! He wants us to be obedient out of love, out of a desire, like the Moses' verse "to walk humbly with your God." God's desire is that we walk with Him through life, side by side.

Think about that picture for a minute. Your walking along this path with God. You talk with Him on a daily basis. Suddenly you want to go down this path. God refuses. Why? You've chosen the wrong path. The neat thing is that God knows what is ahead, you don't. Now which path do you want to take?

Isn't it interesting the word God uses at the beginning of this verse. "What does the Lord *require* of you?" It's not a suggestion, it's a requirement. To walk with God, you must be obedient to God. That's why Adam and Eve were expelled from the Garden, was it not? The biggest battle God had with Israel is its disobedience. So, frustrated, as we've seen that He wanted to destroy them and start all over. I'd like to encourage you to think about "walking with God" and what that entails in your life. Think about it.

"Observe and obey all these words which I command you, that it may go well with you and your children after you forever, when you do what is good and right in the sight of the Lord your God." (Deuteronomy 12:28)

Have you given up yet? You've made it through Leviticus and it's going to get exciting in Joshua. Slow down, like Moses says here, "observe." Pay attention to, one, what God has done, two, what He is telling us. This recap is very important. Both for us and for Israel.

Notice Moses references the next generations. That is so important. It's the concept of building a firm foundation. One of my favorite passages in 1 Corinthians 3. It stresses the need for Jesus Christ to be our foundation. A working relationship with God is part of that foundation. In the gospel of John, the author says, "In the beginning was the Word, the Word was God and the Word is God." Later in verse 14 of chapter one John says, "And the Word became flesh and dwelt among us." The Word meaning Jesus. Why did Jesus choose to walk among us? That personal relationship. Walking with His disciples daily. That's what God wants with us.

"When you do what is good and right." Do you realize that you are being watched! Not only your family, friends, co-workers but the people you meet every day. Especially if they know you are a Christian. They are watching you. But most importantly God is watching. That's the reference Moses is making here. "in the sight of the Lord." Everything we do is in plain sight of God. Not only that, but as Christians we have the Holy Spirit of God living within us.

What happens, as a Christian, when we slip up and do something not pleasing to God? God lets you know it! His Holy Spirit speaks directly to your heart. There is one problem. We have learned to turn off that Holy Spirit or to ignore it. Another problem? We can't turn off God's eyes. He sees us every minute of every day. Nothing escapes Him. We might turn off, or ignore the Holy Spirit but not God.

It always comes down to choices, doesn't it? Like Moses said, "good or bad" did you notice there are no gray areas? You can't just go half way. Either you do as God says or you don't. I like what Dr. Stanley says, "Partial obedience is dis-obedience." It's that simple. Wait a minute. Are you getting the idea that the Bible is a book of rules? Heavens no! It's a book about a relationship with God Almighty.

"And it shall be with him, and he shall read it all the days of his life,
that he may learn to fear the Lord his God and be careful to observe
all the words of this law and these statutes." (Deuteronomy 17:19)

Who is the "him" in this verse? Read this chapter again. It's about a king, a ruler, a president if you will. Anyone put in charge over others. Moses, writing long before David tells Israel they will have a king. Catch this, "Whom the Lord your God chooses." (17:15). God must do the choosing.

For many years I have watched the choices our country makes in its leadership. One thing I watch is the "condition" of our country. Granted, this verse says God sets up those who rule over us. Can God use an ungodly nation to set up a godly king? Of course, look at the books of First and Second Kings. God can do anything He chooses! But, I watch to see who our country chooses. It gives me insight as to the spiritual condition of our country.

Now what do you suppose Moses is talking about "and he shall read it all the days of his life."? The word of God of course. It is so cool to look back in history at what our Founding Fathers thought about the Bible. You don't hear much about that today, do you? Today we can't even get them to follow the Constitution let alone scripture.

One other thing before we leave this chapter and today's study. I want you to note three things that God forbids a ruler to have: (1) "not multiply horses." (v. 16) (2) "multiply wives" (v. 17) (3) "greatly multiply silver and gold." (v. 17). Here's a trivia question: Who broke all three of these rules? Solomon. Yep, the wisest man in history. Disobeyed God's rules. Sad!

O.k, that's great for kings and rulers what about me? Of course, it applies to you as well. The key in this verse that applies to us today is being obedient to the word of God. What a concept. We've never heard that. I'm sorry, I'm being sarcastic. But it's true.

You wonder why we keep pounding this principle? Because God wants only the best for us but we keep trying to do it our way and expect God to bless it. It doesn't work that way.

The more we can incorporate God's principles into our lives the more God will walk with us and guide us daily!

For the Lord, your God is He who goes with you, to fight for you
against your enemies, to save you." (Deuteronomy 20:4)

There is this scene in "You've Got Mail" where Meg Ryan is frustrated because
she can't come up with a one-liner to put her antagonist in his place. She thinks
of one later but not now she needs one. Tom Hanks offers to give her some zingers
to use. Then Hanks warns her; If you use them and it works there will inevitably
be a period of remorse and regret for saying it.

So, what does this verse have to do with Tom Hanks and Meg Ryan?
Remember, we talked earlier about "walking with God"? That God wants to walk
with us through life and guide us on the right road to take. In this verse God not
only walks with us but fights our battles. How many times have you thought of
just the right thing to say, later, after the opportunity had passed? Too many times!

Wait a minute! How many times have you said something in the heat of the
moment and wished you could take it back? Again, what does this have to do it
this verse. God fights our battles.

That is such a vital purpose of the Holy Spirit. He will give us the words to
speak at just the right time and in the right circumstance. That's if we haven't
locked Him away someplace. If He is allowed to have control. If God is walking
with us!

I'm sure you have heard this so many times to let God do the fighting. There is
a time to fight and a time to wait. God knows the right time and the right weapon.
You see, we want to deliver that zinger right now, "in your face". God does a much
better job of making your point in HIS time.

I love this concept. God Almighty walking beside us through life. Is that
sacrilegious? I think not. It wasn't for Adam and Eve. Think about those in the
Old Testament that it is said, "they walked with God." It's not that unusual. I think
it's something God wants more than anything. In fact, remember, He indwells us
through the Holy Spirit.

That's an interesting thought. How many of your "close" friends know that
much about you? How close do you let those around you into your life? My guess
is not much these days. God wants much more that casual He wants intimate!

Look down from Your holy habitation, from heaven, and bless Your people Israel and the land which You have given us, just as You swore to our fathers, a land flowing with milk and honey. (Deuteronomy 26:15)

First, a thought about heaven. In this verse Moses is liking heaven to the Promised Land. That's interesting because they went into the Promised Land the same way we will enter heaven, by faith. Israel denied the power of God the first time. By trusting God to provide for them they were able to enter the second time.

The same is true for us today. God provides the means to enter heaven, His son Jesus Christ. By trusting in that power, we can have access to heaven. Deny that power and we are doomed. I'm sorry but it is that simple. So much of what God shows us in the Old Testament is simply a word picture what the New Testament fulfills.

And you thought when we left Leviticus we were through with the laws and instructions. God is trying to teach us all through scripture. Consider Galatians 6. The principle of sowing and reaping. God may have taught the same lesson in the Old Testament by illustration but the principle is the same.

Again, Moses emphasizes that God has "given you the land." It's a done deal. They simply must claim it. That's interesting because it's the same with heaven. Jesus in John 14 tells us that Jesus, the Son of God, has gone to prepare the Promised Land (heaven) for us. We need to accept that gift by faith.

Just like, as we look back at this story we can't understand why Israel would not just walk right in and claim the land. Today we don't understand how someone could deny the gift God gave us through His Son, access to heaven.

Whenever I think of heaven I get this mental image of the closing scene from "The Robe". The throne room and Richard Burton and Jean Simmons walking from the throne into the clouds. The throne being the place where God is seated. It has also been a fantasy of mine of being able to sit with Jesus for, maybe, fifteen minutes and talking. Of course, I probably won't do much talking for being choked with tears, tears of joy of course!

"The Lord will establish you as a holy people to Himself, just as He has sworn to you, if you keep the commandments of the Lord your God and walk in His ways." (Deuteronomy 28:9)

Did you catch that huge word in the middle of this blanket promise? The word "if". You see God's blessings don't come without strings. I think sometimes we think that because we are His children (Christians) that we should automatically receive God's blessing. It doesn't work that way.

God has nursed Israel along from the time of the nations' creation from Abraham. I know of two incidents where God wanted to destroy Israel but was talked out of it. If you think you can talk God out of anything. I think this was more a test for Moses than for Israel.

Remember in 1 Peter 2:9, But you are a chosen generation, a royal priesthood, a holy nation, His own special people, that you may proclaim the praises of Him who called you out of darkness into His marvelous light. Now who do you think Peter was talking about? Christians!

Many think, that because of Israel's disobedience and idolatry God had put Israel aside. Some say Jesus' curse of the olive tree signified that transfer. He simply set Israel aside for now. Israel will always be God's people. Just as a Christian will always be children of God.

If your children disobey you and curse you and leave home are they no longer your children? Surely not. God has much more patience with us that we have with our children. I believe the word is grace.

We talked about this before. The hardest lesson to teach our children is obedience. Sometimes they have to get out into the world and be confronted by authorities before they learn.

The same is true with both Israel and God's children. For Israel, they learned one lesson by spending forty years in the wilderness, but it is short-lived.

How about you? What lesson is God trying to teach you right now? The trick is to recognize God's hand in the teaching and to learn the lesson. Some lessons are harder to learn than others. Some lessons we refuse to learn until it's almost too late.

A good way to find out is pray. Ask God to show you!

"And the Lord, He is the One who goes before you, He will be with you,
He will not leave you nor forsake you, do not fear nor be dismayed."
(Deuteronomy 31:8)

Is this a fantastic promise? We will never be alone. Many time's we refuse to acknowledge His presence. As a child of God, we have God's presence within us in the person of the Holy Spirit.

There is a key point in the first few words. "He is the One who goes before you." If you've read any American history you know that these were the scouts that explored the wilderness and created trails for settlers to follow and make their homes. Without these brave explorers, the settling of our great country would have been impossible.

Now, as the verse says, imagine that God is out in front of us. He travels the future seeing what obstacles and pitfalls are ahead in our path. Then He guides us through them. Notice I didn't say around them. I said through them. There are lessons to be learned when we travel through these trials.

Sometimes when I'm driving through the country I try to imagine what it might be like for settlers to travel over the hills and creeks and valleys. Of course, they didn't have paved roads or gas stations along the way. It was said the ruts in the Oregon Trail were almost two feet deep, from so much travel by wagons.

That's why one of my favorite verses is Jeremiah 29:11-13. God has already mapped out our life. Only to prosper us. So then why do we have so much trouble? We get out of His will. We take a road not of His making. We want to do our own thing. When just around the corner God has a great blessing in store. But instead we take a detour.

I want to mention that these verses in these three chapters catalog God's blessing and curses. Obedience brings blessings, disobedience bring curses. It's just that simple. Now contrast these chapters with Jeremiah 29:11-13. God doesn't mince words in declaring where He stands. Just as in the Garden of Eden the choice is yours. You choose the path. I pray it's the one that you and God are walking together, and one of your choosing.

Don't miss the promise that He will not leave you. He's there, you simply have to lean on Him and not your own devices!

> Yes, He loves the people; All His saints are in Your hand; They sit down
> at Your feet; Everyone receives Your words. (Deuteronomy 33:3)

Moses begins these chapters by singing a song. Interesting. Worship in our churches begins the same way. O.k, I've got to clarify something. I said earlier that Moses was taken up like Elijah. Look at verse 6 of chapter 34. it says, And He buried him in a valley in the land of Moab, opposite Beth Peor, but no one knows his grave to this day. Many believe that the reason Moses appears with Elijah is that God took him. You decide.

With these chapters, we have finished the Law. The reference to the Law in the New Testament pertains to these five books. Before the New Testament was written this was God's word. The Law and the Prophets. Studied and read in the synagogues.

You will also note in chapter 34 that God takes Moses up on Mt. Nebo to view the Promised Land. God also gave Abraham a tour of the Promised Land when He called Abraham's family to follow Him.

Look at verse 10 of chapter 34. "But since then there has not arisen in Israel a prophet like Moses, whom the Lord knew face to face." You can make what you want of that verse.

The point I want to make about Moses is that I don't think anyone demonstrates the "walking with God" that we have been talking about better than Moses. Granted they had their disputes. But Moses, except for that one incident, was totally obedient to God.

Those words in the above verse remind me of a passage in the Psalms. Psalm 31:15a "My times are in Your hand." Is that an amazing thought? I'm trying to keep away from using awesome too much. Just think about those words for a minute. "Our time is in God's hand." He is in control. Get a grip on that.

From Moses being put in a basket and sent down the Nile to standing here on Mt. Nebo and viewing the Promised Land, Moses was under God's direction.

Notice in verse 7 of Chapter 34. "Moses was one hundred and twenty years old when he died." What an interesting life. 40 years in Egypt, 40 as a shepherd and 40 leading God's people.

> "This book of the Law shall not depart from your mouth, but you shall meditate in it day and night, that you may observe to do according to all that is written in it. For then you will make your way prosperous, and then you will have good success." (Joshua 1:8)

This is one of my top five favorite verses. Here, as I mentioned, the reference to the book of the Law. Today that means the Bible. So many verse in the Bible to encourage reading and heeding the word of God.

So much is made of the stock market today. It's risen over 5,000 points in the last year. So many people have their life savings there. Many pension plans are grounded in the stock market. But this verse says our prosperity comes from God. Have you heard anything about Bitcoin. It's the new currency. Don't forget the age-old argument about gold. There are so many different directions to go, how do you know what is the right one?

Take another look at the verse above. There are two simply rules to be prosperous. Read and meditate on the Word of God daily! And "observe to do according to all that is written therein". Simple, right? How are you doing this year with this Bible reading plan? Did you make it through Leviticus?

How about daily? Or do you skip a day or two and then try to catch up. It doesn't work. When you get up in the morning do you plan out your day? You have a schedule or a plan of what you want to accomplish, right? It's all a matter of priorities, isn't it? It's what you deem important, right? If this verse doesn't convince you to schedule 30 minutes with God I don't know what will.

This verse also says, "day and night" I look at this as meaning ALL DAY. All day our mind and thoughts should be on God. Remember we said, as Christians, we have God within us as the Holy Spirit. Talk to Him. Ask Him directions. Thank Him for just missing that car in traffic. Thank Him for that extra money you found, etc.

This is a good verse to memorize. I'm not big on memorizing verses. I do try to memorize the address: Joshua 1:8. Also think about the context. Joshua is about to enter the Promised Land. No Moses this time, he is on his own, him and God that is. And God gives him two rules to encourage him!

So, He said, "No, but as the commander of the army of the Lord I have now come." And Joshua fell on his face to the earth and worshipped, and said to Him, "what does my Lord say to His servant?" (Joshua 5:14)

There are two key events here. In chapters 4 and 5 there are two great lessons to take note of. In chapter 4 is the story of the stones. God instructed Joshua to make a pile of twelve stones in the middle of the Jordan. Interesting that no one will see the stones or know that they are there. So why would God have Joshua do it. Notice that God made a point that this is where the feet of the priests and the Ark traveled. It's holy ground. An act of praise.

The second set of twelve stones, again representing the twelve tribes would be stacked on the other side of the Jordan as a memorial to what God brought about in this place. The miracle that was done. Every time someone looked at the pile of stones it would remind them of God's power.

How do these stones apply to us? One, God is at work in our lives whether we see it or not. And second, we should have some reminders of God's power in our lives. I love the concept of a Christmas ornament symbolizing an event that year. Thank you, Hallmark. But what do we have to remind us of God's working in our lives? How about a journal? I've been keeping a journal since 1999. It's is amazing to look back through those books and see where God has led me. It's such a blessing to be reminded of God's hand on my life.

Chapter five is so good! Notice that, after crossing the Jordan and being in enemy country that God orders all His people to be circumcised. So, what you say? Look in Genesis chapter 34. Two sons of Abraham used this ritual to destroy their enemies. Dinah's brothers told the people, pagans, that if they circumcised themselves that then she could marry the prince. They did and the two brothers killed them all. They were helpless.

So, God told Israel to render themselves helpless in enemy territory. Why? They could have done that on the safe side of the river. God is always at work trying to encourage us to trust Him. If this story doesn't help you trust God I don't know what will. Fantastic story!

> Then the men of Israel took some of their provisions; but they did not ask counsel of the Lord. So, Joshua made peace with them, and made a covenant with them to let them live; and the rulers of the congregation swore to them. (Joshua 9:14-15)

The church I once attended had this Christmas festival every year. It was the beginning of December and we needed to set up the three festival buildings. They were simple buildings, just a few sheets of plywood. I'll never forget this story.

It was a Saturday, we all had other things to do. We didn't even take time for donuts. Anyway, we took all the pieces out and began assembling them. NOTHING FIT. It just wouldn't go together. We worked at it for two hours. Finally, someone suggested that we had not begun with prayer and that we should stop and pray. We did. Everything fit and we finished in an hour.

This was a simple situation. These travelers came from a far land. Simple enough, we will just make a treaty with them.

One of the points that God stressed to Joshua when they entered the Promised Land, was that they were to destroy ALL the inhabitants. That seems cruel but God knew if they survived that would lead Israel away from God. His instructions were very clear!

These people tricked Israel into signing a treaty. Totally contrary to God's wishes. Notice the end of verse 14. "but they did not ask counsel of the Lord." Just like the illustration above.

Most of the time we think that some decisions are not important enough to bother God with. A simple 10 second prayer many times could save hours of grief. Just counsel with the Holy Spirit living within you. What should I do? What should I say? What should I NOT say?

Look at verse 16. I hope you are reading these chapters along with this devotional. Verse 16 says," and it happened, at the end of three days, after they made a covenant with them, that they heard they were neighbors who dwelt with them." Contrary to God's command.

These people would be a thorn in Israel's side for generations. Because they didn't take a minute to ask God's guidance. Oh, that reminds me. You might reread the story of Ai.

> So, Joshua took the whole land, according to all that the Lord had said to Moses; and Joshua gave it as an inheritance to Israel according to their divisions by their tribes. Then the land rested from war. (Joshua 11:23)

To obey God, to walk in His will, is an amazing thing. The rewards, notice the end of this verse, "Then the land rested from war." Ah, peace and tranquility. But think of the cost of finally doing it God's way. Over forty years of wandering in the wilderness, a whole generation passed away to finally achieve what God had promised them in the beginning. Was it worth it? To this generation I'm sure.

I'd like to point out a verse in Deuteronomy, if I may. Deuteronomy 1:39, "Moreover your little ones and your children, who you say will be victims, who today have no knowledge of good and evil, they shall go in there, to them I will give it, and they shall possess it."

They, the children, were the excuse that Israel used for not trusting God and entering the Promised Land. Those "victims" now become the victors.

Each of the twelve tribes received an inheritance in the Promised Land. Two and a half tribes had their inheritance on the other side of the Jordan but they all received a portion of land from God. Land that was conquered by Israel. Land that God gave them.

"According to all that the Lord had said." I can't stress this enough. They could have been there forty years sooner. Nothing had changed in the land. The giants were still there. But God gave them the victory when they finally trusted Him and did what He told them to do.

Something I'd like to remind you of. Remember when Israel finally crossed the Jordan? What happened? The priests picked up the Ark, stepped into the water and the water parted. Remember the Red Sea? Moses simply raised his arms and the Sea parted. How much faith do you suppose was needed at the Jordan to do what God asked? Ok, how much faith did take to march around Jericho seven times, not knowing what was going to happen.

God asks us, sometimes, to do things that are not logical, as Dr. Spock would say, but God has a plan. For one thing when it works out who gets the glory? You or God? Trust God, Israel finally did!

Hebron therefore became the inheritance of Caleb the son of
Jephunneh the Kenizzite to this day, because he wholly followed the
Lord God of Israel. (Joshua 14:14)

Caleb reminds me of Barnabas in the New Testament. Caleb stood with Joshua
when they were out-voted. Caleb stood with Joshua all through the wilderness
wanderings. I think I heard this quote attributed to Ronald Reagan: "It's amazing
what can be accomplished when it doesn't matter who gets the credit."

It was Barnabas who introduced Saul to the disciples when they were so
afraid of Saul. After Saul's conversion, it was Barnabas who accompanied Saul on
his first missionary journey. You don't hear much about Barnabas. That's the way
these special people like it.

They remind me of the pianist and organist in a worship service. They seldom
get any recognition but the worship service would be so flat without them. I'm glad
on occasion our church applauds our pianist and organist.

Sunday school teachers, office personnel, deacons, etc. Many time's these little
noticed servants are the backbone of a growing church.

Caleb received Hebron as an inheritance. Look back a couple of verses. Notice
that Joshua gave Hebron to Caleb but he had to conquer it. Caleb must be in his
sixties or older and yet he has the desire to take what God had given him. Hebron
is still there today. You can see it if you visit Israel.

The division of the land makes little sense to us today. You might want to
look at it differently though. This was the fulfillment of God's promise. The actual
dividing up of the conquered land. Each tribe according to its population received
God's inheritance.

Don't miss the end of this verse. "Because he wholly followed the Lord God
of Israel." Can you say that? Are you walking in God's will? I can tell you there is
no better place to be. When you know you are in the center of God's will it is a
fantastic place to be.

A major part of knowing God's will is getting in His word. Reading,
meditating, praying, attending church, etc. All these activities help us to discern
God's path for us and helps keep us on that path. Caleb had that relationship and
God blessed him!

> Now the whole congregation of the children of Israel assembled at Shiloh, and set up the tabernacle of meeting there. And the land was subdued before them. (Joshua 18:1)

As soon as Israel claimed the land they set up their church. That's what it is. A place to gather and worship and praise God. Think about it.

A couple of verses I'd like you to take note of in today's reading. First, chapter 16 verse 10. "And they did not drive out the Canaanites who dwell in Gezer; but the Canaanites dwell among the Ephraimites to this day and have become forced laborers." Just what we talked about earlier. Totally against God's command when they entered the land. Second, chapter 17 verse 13, "And it happened, when the children of Israel grew strong, that they put the Canaanites to forced labor, but did not drive them out." Isn't this what happened in Egypt when Israel came to visit in Exodus?

This has such a parallel in our own lives. What "little" sins are you allowing in your life? It doesn't hurt anybody. It's just a little one. When you start thinking this way, you are thinking just like Israel did in Joshua. "It can't hurt" right? Don't fall for that. What harm can just a bite from some fruit cause, right?

Let's get back to this tabernacle (the church). As a young Christian, I so looked forward to Wednesday night prayer meeting. Because it was like a "re-charging" time. I needed to be reminded, especially of the power of prayer. It still amazes me when I go to prayer meeting. This special time demonstrates the power of prayer and faith. For busy people in the middle of their busy work week to think that it is important to gather together for prayer, to me, shows their faith in prayer and in God.

We have seen a couple of verses that talk about, that there was peace, that land was subdued. We still have 6 more chapters and yet a lot of land to be conquered. Maybe we are content where we are. We're settled. There is still work, to do. Our walk with God needs constant updating, checking, examining, re-evaluating. Oh, it needs maintenance too! We can never be satisfied with our relationship with God. God is always stretching us, testing and trying and growing our faith in Him. He wants to use us to our greatest potential. God knows our capabilities and wants the best for us. To glorify Him!

> Not a word failed of any good thing which the Lord had spoken to the
> house of Israel. All came to pass. (Joshua 21:45)

I was privileged once to get to hear Dr. W.A. Criswell at First Baptist Church in Dallas, Texas preach on the Word of God. We went to Dallas to attend the Southern Baptist Convention. Ever since the night of my conversion I have had a hunger for God's word. To study, read, and teach. A Sunday School Director for over thirty years. I truly believe that the more of the Word of God we have in our hearts the more God can use us.

You can underline this verse. That is a promise from God. If you doubt me, look at the promise in Revelation 1:3 and 22:7 basically the same promise. They that read and heed the Word of God are blessed!

Did Israel do all that God asked and said? Not a chance. The Old Testament is full of Israel's disobedience. Israel's disobedience and God's patience and grace to continue to lead and bless them.

I hope you will read each of these chapters as we travel through God's word. My favorite term is to "chew" on God's word. The picture of a cow chewing on some grass, over and over, getting every morsel of vitamin and flavor from every mouth full. That's Bible study.

And another challenge for the year. Find a Bible teaching, preaching church. So many times, I have been as blessed by the people I meet and talk to as by the sermon preached. Many people equate church with preaching, that's just part of it. Get into a class. Fellowship. The early church in the book of Acts felt that fellowship was important in their worship experience.

If you get anything from these daily studies watch Israel. How God deals with them, how He loves and directs them can rightly be demonstrated in our own lives. God loves Israel just as much as He loves us. The life lessons that God tries to teach Israel are life lessons for us daily! That's why I emphasize the Tabernacle so much.

When I was pastor at Freeman we had a bell in the tower. I loved to ring it on Sunday morning. It was rung on and off, but I rang it. Especially on New Year's Eve. That bell reminds me of the trumpets mentioned in Old Testament: A call to worship!

"And if it seems evil to you to serve the Lord, choose for yourselves this day whom you will serve, whether the gods which your fathers served that were on the other side of the River, or the gods on the Amorites, in whose land you dwell. But as for me and my house, we will serve the Lord." (Joshua 24:15)

What a summary for the book of Joshua, and Israel to this point. Question: Do you know the first commandment? It's key! I think it's one of the biggest desires of God. It's, again, number one to God. Exodus 20:3, "You shall have no other gods before Me." Now look at the first part of the verse above. What was Joshua's challenge to Israel?

Idols, idols, idols. Israel wrestled with this more than anything else. From the golden calf at the foot of Mt. Sinai to the pagan worship brought to Solomon through his many wives. Anything that comes between us and God is an idol!

So, what is an idol? There are great passages in both Psalm 115: 3-8 and the same description in Psalm 135:15-18. I don't want to take room here. I encourage you to read these verses! I do want to point out the end of each passage: "Those who make them are like them; so is everyone who trusts in them."

Israel could never seem to leave them behind. Just like Rachel in the book of Genesis (31:34). And neither can we. Why do we give such power to inanimate objects? When we have the power of God living within us!

The last part of this verse is quoted and plaques and posters are made from these words. But look in our churches today. Where are the spiritual leaders today? Look at any congregation and it is a majority of women. Understand I don't object, God will use anyone and anything to reach a family. His goal of course is to reach the husband and father! The spiritual leader should always be the man of the house. It was God's plan from the beginning!

In the Garden of Eden when God came looking, who did He ask for? Who was accountable? Adam! Think about all that Joshua had witnessed from God. Joshua was with Moses when God freed Israel from Bondage. Joshua was in captivity in Egypt when Moses arrived on the scene. Joshua saw God deliver Israel and conquer the Promised Land. "You shall have no other gods before Me!"

> When all the generations had been gathered to their fathers, another generation arose after them who did not know the Lord nor the work which He had done for Israel. (Judges 2:10)

We are entering one of the hardest books to read. Not in terms of reading but in terms of frustration. I have used this book many times to illustrate the patience and grace of God. At what point are you ready to give up? God never gave up on Israel.

The beginning of this verse is so important. Generations arose that did not know the Lord. That's just scary. After what Joshua said, and to find so many generations fell away from following God. It's so important to teach our children and grand-children about God and having a personal relationship with Him.

Someone once said that, "we are one generation away from paganism." It's happening in our country now. We are slowly and methodically ridding ourselves of the presence of God. Not the presence of His Spirit, don't misunderstand me. I'm talking about, prayer in school, carrying a Bible, etc.

When I returned from Vietnam I was told that I should not wear my uniform off the base. It tended to upset people, to cause contention. That is where we are with religious symbols today. We shy away from public displays for fear of offending anyone. Maybe that's how Israel got in this condition.

Take your time through this book. Digest each chapter. My pastor pointed out that as you work through Judges the nation draws further and further away from God. From the verse above that wasn't that hard.

Look at the cycle through the whole book. God sends a pagan nation to get Israel's attention. Eventually they turn to God and ask for help. God sends a deliverer. They are taken out of bondage. The nation enjoys peace. Then they drift back away from God. God sends a nation to get their attention, and on and on.

Is God using something in your life to draw Him back to you? A sin, a circumstance, a lost friend? What will it take for you to ask God to save you? How long will it take to realize your need of God? God's grace is so awesome! Find it in this book!

> And the Angel of the Lord appeared to him, and said to him, "The Lord is with you, you mighty man of war!" (Judges 6:12)

Did you notice verse 11? Where was this mighty man of valor? Hiding in a winepress from the Midianites. You will notice all through Judges how God uses the neighboring nations to judge Israel. God can use anyone or anything to get our attention. His soul purpose was? To bring us back to a relationship with Him.

I don't know if you noticed or not, but every time I've seen the reference to "the Angel of the Lord" the word angel is capitalized. Many believe that this reference is the pre-incarnate Christ. Interesting.

One more thing. I love the phrase," the Lord is with you." I don't remember Gideon praying and asking God's help. He didn't seek God's intervention. God was watching Israel. In verse one of chapter six, it says Israel had been in bondage for seven years. Take note of how long Israel is in bondage with each judge. How long it takes them to cry out to God.

One of my favorite passages in the New Testament relates to this incident. 1 Corinthians 1:27, "But God has chosen the foolish things of the world to put to shame the wise, and God has chosen the weak things of the world to put to shame the things which are mighty." You see how God works? God can even use you!

Notice the servants that God uses in Judges to accomplish His will. The last one anyone would choose. Why would God use such unworthy vessels? When they succeed who gets the glory?

Look at the challenge for Gideon. Later he reduces his army from 22,000 to 300. That's crazy! Is it? Who gets the glory? One other thing to note in this chapter six. God helps Gideon, even after his fleece thing, by giving him a small victory before he takes on Midian. God is in the "teaching" trade. He will not lead us where we are not equipped to go. By equipped, I'm referring to our faith. He will grow our faith to the point where He can use us for greater and greater battles.

There is some discussion about putting out fleeces to determine God's will. I've used them. The point is finding God's will in making decisions. Whatever works for you. Frequent prayer, fleeces, toss of a coin. It all boils down to trusting God!

Thus, the children of Israel did not remember the Lord their God, who had delivered them from the hands of all their enemies on every side. (Judges 8:34)

News flash! Israel did not remember God. Like that is unusual. Of course, we don't have that problem. I wonder how long after God parted the Red Sea and Israel walked across on dry land did Israel start complaining again? You see this is the same scenario throughout the book of Judges. Notice the length of time they are in bondage until they cry out to God.

I think this is a key reason why we need weekly worship in God's house. If for no other reason than to keep reminding us of God's presence. Reminding us of answered prayer, the ability to pray, and the need to pray. Just the sharing in a Sunday school class of God's blessing in testimony can really encourage us.

Don't forget verse 35. They not only forgot God's deliverance but the role Gideon played in it. Ungrateful? Isn't it nice we don't have to deal with that today. I'm sorry I couldn't resist a little sarcasm. It seems each generation gets farther and farther from God and neglects the real reason for our blessings.

God chooses whom He will, to accomplish what He will, all to His glory. Do you want God to use you? Are you walking with Him? In the back of my Bible I've written some lyrics from a gospel song by Phil McHugh. "One day Jesus will call my name. As days go by I hope I don't stay the same. I want to get so close to Him there's no big change, on that day that Jesus calls my name." That's how you are ready when God needs a helping hand.

That's another thing. We all know that God doesn't need anybody or anything. He spoke the world into existence. He can accomplish whatever He wishes just by speaking it. So, why would God need any of us? Who gets the glory when God does something fantastic through one of His servants? What does that say to other Christians who wonder if God is at work in their lives?

Just think of a dad who sees his child accomplish something on his own, how proud he is that his child accomplished it. That's how God feels when His child trust Him to take that extra step.

"Yet you have forsaken Me and served other gods. Therefore, I will deliver you no more. Go and cry out to the gods which you have chosen; let them deliver you in your time of distress." And the children of Israel said to the Lord, "We have sinned! Do to us whatever seems best to you; only deliver us this day, we pray." (Judges 10:13-15)

There is an interesting story in the Bible about idols. The major sin that God hates the most and Israel failed in so miserably.

It begins in Numbers chapter 21. Israel had rebelled and God sent a plague of serpents. When they bit someone, they died. Of course, Moses was sought to plead to God for it to be removed. God told Moses to construct a cross with the bronze serpent on it. He did, and God told Israel that when they were bitten they were to look on this cross and they would be spared. So, the plague passed. So, what became of the cross?

In 2 Kings 18 the cross appears again. This time they have given it a name, Nehushtan. In chapter 18 a man named Hoshea became king. One of his first acts was to remove all the idols from the land. Now look at verse 4, "He removed the high places and broke the sacred pillars, cut down the wooden image and broke in pieces the bronze serpent that Moses had made; for until those days the children of Israel burned incense to it, and called it Nehushtan."

Something that Moses had constructed from God, the people had turned into an idol. You know, if God wanted to, He could have preserved the original writings of Moses and the prophets. This might help to understand why He didn't. The writings would have become idols.

There's another lesson. We can make anything an idol. That's what frustrated God about Israel. They would so quickly turn to lifeless idols made of clay or gold than to trust the living God who delivered them from Egypt.

I think this is the third time God has threatened to disown Israel. Yet God is faithful. His patience is everlasting. Unless you want to think about this verse in Romans: "Therefore God gave them up to uncleanness, in the lusts of their hearts, to dishonor their bodies among themselves." (Romans 1:24). There is a point when God will just back away and take His hand from us. He will still hear our plea "God save me"

> Then Manoah said to the Angel of the Lord, "What is Your name,
> that when Your words come to pass we may honor You?" And the
> Angel of the Lord said to him, "Why do you ask My name, seeing it is
> wonderful?" (Judges 13:17-18)

I have seen this twice in my lifetime. Years ago, I went with a group to Rev. Jack Hyles church outside of Evansville, Indiana. It was an annual Pastor's Conference. One night this young black preacher came to the pulpit. I had never heard this before. This fella began just saying the names of Jesus. Bread of life, Savior, the Door, Jesus, Emmanuel, etc. The longer he talked, just saying the names of Jesus, the louder the group of pastors got. By the time he finished the crowd was standing and shouting! The most amazing sight, I'll never forget it. No three points and a poem. No quoting scripture, unless you say the names of Jesus as scripture. Just the names of Jesus.

One Sunday morning, I was watching Dr. Charles Stanley. There was a quartet and they began singing the names of Jesus. The song was great, but again, just the names of Jesus. When they finished the congregation was standing, applauding and cheering. The power of Jesus name.

This verse always reminds me of Isaiah 9:6. "For unto us a Child is born, unto us a Son is given; And the government will be upon His shoulder. And His name will be called Wonderful, Counselor, Mighty God, Everlasting Father, Prince of Peace. Of the increase of His government and peace there will be no end."

Isaiah was written hundreds of years after Judges. The same messenger? Who can say. What angel would call himself wonderful?

In verse 19 the couple referred to the visitor as Lord. Of course, this episode refers to the birth of Samson. One of the more prolific characters in the book of Judges. Samson is a great study. Many thoughts as to the deeds and misdeeds of Samson.

This story is like the one where Samuel is born. Hannah has a similar plea for a child. Both barren. Both prayed for a child. Both answers from God. I firmly believe that children are a "gift" from God. We can try to destroy them and we can try to plan for them but it is God's will that will prevail. When the child is conceived it is by the will of God and God has a plan for that child!

> Then Samson called to the Lord, saying, "O Lord God, remember me, I pray! Strengthen me, I pray, just this once, O God, that I may with one blow take vengeance on the Philistines for my two eyes."
> (Judges 16:28)

Have you ever prayed, "remember me, God"? I did a word search on that phrase once. It was interesting. I think it only appeared about five or six times. Why would you ask God to remember you? Is there some reason that He might forget you? Not likely. That would be like us forgetting one of our children.

We may feel, at times, like God has forgotten us but more likely it's the other way around. We are just voicing our own desire. We have finally remembered that God is there. Much like we see Israel in this book.

Of course, God answers his prayer and Samson dies in the process. But Samson is forever in scripture. There are so many in the Bible that we can relate to. We can see our lives, our hopes, our struggle with God in different characters in the Bible. Samson's problem was that he thought his strength was in his hair. That God used material things to accomplish His perfect will. It was Samson's life that God used. They may have seemed at odds, but Samson always seemed to accomplish what God wanted him to accomplish, despite his faults.

God is working in your life right now. You may not know it yet. He is just waiting for you to say, "remember me Lord." If your lost, He is waiting for you to seek His forgiveness and ask His Son to save you. To come into your heart and change your life. If you're already a child of God He is waiting for you to ask, "what would you have me to do?"

Samson is a great study. He always seemed to be doing the right thing for the wrong reasons. He accomplished what God wanted concerning the Philistines but seemed to do it the hard way. God wants to use you as well, but He wants your total surrender, to trust Him, to follow the leadership of His Holy Spirit that dwells within you (if you're a Christian).

It's still early in the New Year. Think back to the beginning of this year. Has God been showing Himself in your life? Is He trying to get your attention about something? Listen and trust His guidance!

"When you go, you will come to a secure people and a large land. For
God has given it into your hands, a place where there is no lack of
anything that is on the earth." (Judges 18:10)

The Danites have not received their portion of the inheritance in the Promised
Land. We are nearing the end of the book of Judges and it does not have a
happy ending as you will soon see.

In this verse, they have stopped at a Levite's house to seek direction. God tells
the Levite priest about some land they may claim as their inheritance.

Notice in verse 30 of chapter 18. From what tribe did the Danites get their
priest. The tribe of Manasseh is not God's choice for priests. The priest must come
from the tribe of Levi. Secondly, they have stolen the idols that Micah had made
for himself. Idol worship. You get the feeling as you read these verses that God is
nowhere, to be found.

God is not. Israel has created their own gods, their own worship, their own
religion. They have no memory of a true relationship with the God of their fathers.

Chapter 19 really shows how far Israel has come. The book of Judges is a tough
book to read. And yet, we can see the same thing happening in our world today.
The farther away from God we get the worse it's going to get.

I read a book recently, Richard Beeman's *Plain, Honest Men*. It's an in depth
look at the process of writing our Constitution. Our nation is at a crossroads.
The Revolutionary War is over and now we must set up a new nation. Two or
three from each of the thirteen colonies. Each with their own interests, their own
priorities, their own agenda. They came together and created one of the most
astounding documents in world history, apart from the Bible of course. Of course,
God wrote the Bible.

The men of those days had limited education, limited resources, but one thing
they had in common. They were all learned, Christian men, in the scriptures. That
influence flowed into this amazing document.

In the book of Judges Israel has lost its way. There is no more divine guidance,
no divine intervention. Maybe God wanted to see just how far they would go. Not
like He didn't know already. God's timing is perfect to accomplish His perfect will.

In those days, there was no king in Israel; everyone did what was right in his own eyes. (Judges 21:25)

This is such a sad verse. We saw in chapters 19-21 the total absence of God. The people had quit seeking God's intervention. Quit seeking God's input. The sad part about this verse is, it could be written today.

Many of us noticed the other day, that when Dr. Billy Graham passes there is no spiritual leadership in the wings. When you think of the President's that Dr. Graham knew and visited with and counseled it's just amazing. Where is the next spiritual leader coming from?

I remind you again of yesterday's devotion. Israel had come to the point where spiritual decisions were based on what was convenient. "What was right in their own eyes." Today, with so many denominations and contrary interpretations, etc. How can we know the truth? How can we know God's will for us and our nation? That's why God gave us His word.

One of the biggest reasons for this devotional is to encourage this journey through God's word. 30 minutes maybe 45. Reading a portion every day. Myself, I've had to read it several times just to absorb the meaning. Rarely, I will seek a commentary. There are so many translations available today. What is important is YOU understanding for yourself what God is saying to you!

Just a thought. If every man did what was right in his own eyes does that make him equal with God? It almost sounds like the Garden of Eden all over again. Remember the comment Satan told Eve? "You will be like God, knowing good and evil." (3:5) Really?

I would like you to chew on that verse above for a while. That verse is written twice in Judges, here and in 17:6. When God says something once it's important! When God says something twice it's very important to take note. A very vivid picture of the spiritual condition of Israel now.

One thing I've noticed about reading God's word this way instead of chronological is that after a book like this we need something like the book of Ruth to cheer us up. After Leviticus and Deuteronomy, we have the book of Joshua. God always has a way of bringing us back to Him. Just like He will with Israel.

"The Lord repay your work, and a full reward be given you by the
Lord God of Israel, under whose wings you have come for refuge."
(Ruth 2:12)

Does the Lord keep account? Of course, He does. In the book of Revelation, we are given crowns for our various deeds, five I believe. These crowns are not to wear, they are to present to our Lord as tokens of praise.

One interesting thing that's not really talked about is Naomi's influence on Ruth. There had to be quite a testimony to make Ruth want to leave her homeland and stay with Naomi. In verses 16 and 17 of chapter one. To have that much dedication to Naomi and her God.

Some people call it "providence." God's providence is clear all through Ruth. A case of being in the right place at the right time. Being where God wants you when He wants you there.

The last part of that verse reminds me of the verse in the Psalms that says, "How precious is Your lovingkindness, O God! Therefore, the children of men put their trust under the shadow of Your wings." (Psalm 36:7). God's protection was truly with Ruth.

All kinds of New Testament verses are flooding my thoughts. Here's one: "Therefore, my beloved brethren, be steadfast, immovable, always abounding in the work of the Lord, knowing that your labor is not in vain in the Lord." (1 Corinthians 15:58). Mark that one down!

You would think the author of Ruth was thinking about this verse when he spoke of Ruth. Of course, the author of Ruth also wrote First Corinthians, the Holy Spirit.

Ruth reads like a fairy tale, doesn't it? It's not. God meant it to show that being faithful has many rewards. Most of the time we may not see God's hand in our circumstances but He's there to be sure. Why would Almighty God be interested in Me? If you're His child He is very much interested in you. He wants you to succeed. Not as the world measures success but as God measures success. Success to God is a closer walk with Him. A relationship of trust and faith and service that God can use to further His kingdom.

Oh, notice verses 17-22 of chapter 4. Ruth is in the line to Christ! (Matthew 1:5)

"No one is holy like the Lord, for there is none besides You, nor is there any rock like our God." (1 Samuel 2:2)

Hannah is a mother without a child. Hannah prayed and bargained with God. "I will give him to the Lord all the days of his life." (2:11) God answered that prayer. The birth of Samuel the prophet. Samuel will transition us from the book of Judges to king David by way of king Saul. There are some great lessons to learn in the books of Samuel, Kings and Chronicles. The early years of the reign of kings.

Isn't Hannah's reference to God kind of strange? Why would she call Him a rock? Have you ever been to New York City? The site of those buildings so high is unreal. Do you know why they can build those buildings so high? There is a solid foundation of rock under those buildings. Nothing better!

What better foundation to build on than solid rock! One of my very favorite chapters in all of scripture is found in the third chapter of First Corinthians. "For no other foundation can anyone lay than that is laid, which is Jesus Christ." (3:11).

Isn't that what Hannah said? Oh, in the same chapter of 1 Corinthians is this verse: "Do you not know that you are the temple of God and that the Spirit of God dwells in you." O.k, if you're the temple of God's Spirit how is your foundation?

Let's look at it as a former Sunday school teacher: How much of the word of God is in your foundation? That would make it as solid as possible.

I must tell this story. When I taught high school kids I would bring a bunch of Legos every week. I explained that this Lego (they got one a week) represented a "truth" they would receive in this class today. As these truths mounted they would begin to form a foundation. Just as these Legos could be joined together to form one solid piece. A few weeks later I asked where these Legos were at? All but one said they were at home in a drawer. One young lady reached in her purse and pulled out a block bigger than a cell phone. She got the message.

These daily readings are meant to add to and solidify your foundation, your relationship with God is built on your knowledge of the word of God. Add to it faithfully!

> Then Samuel spoke to all the house of Israel, saying, "If you return to the Lord with all your hearts, then put away the foreign gods and the Ashtoreths from among you, and prepare your hearts for the Lord, and serve Him only; and He will deliver you from the hand of the Philistines." (1 Samuel 7:3)

I hope you have read these chapters. The ark is a central theme of these chapters. You see the ark was Israel's "good luck charm" much like Samson thought his hair was where his strength was. Very often we attribute blessings to inanimate objects when God is the real source. When Israel lost the ark in battle they gave up. The Philistines captured them. Only by the power of God was the ark returned.

Now notice what Samuel said, "Return to the Lord with all your heart." Is that not key or what? Our actions, our logic, our futile efforts are useless if our hearts are not in it. Believe me God knows!

So many times, when we celebrate Communion or the Lord's Supper we neglect a very important part of that passage that explains the Supper. 1 Corinthians 11:28 says, "But let a man examine himself, and so let him eat of the bread and drink of the cup." Now we are to examine our hearts if we are right with God and our fellow man.

Idols again! From Genesis to here God wrestles with Israel about idols. Until our focus is on Him, and not a piece of clay or gold image we can never please God. Again, Samuel says, "put away the foreign gods!" Prepare your hearts for the Lord!

Now what do you think He means by "prepare your hearts for the Lord?" Examine. Yes!

I want to offer a little current example. When do you prepare your heart for worship on Sunday? Sunday morning on the way to church? Please! I think Saturday should be designated a "preparation day!" Begin thinking about meeting God the day before. Plan your wardrobe, etc. Prepare your heart. Anticipate what God might do on the Lord's day.

"Prepare your hearts for the Lord" another thought concerning these words. Ask God to speak to you on the Lord's day. Through someone you meet, through His Holy Spirit, through the message, Ask God!

> And the Lord said to Samuel, "Heed the voice of the people in all that
> they say to you; for they have not rejected you, but have rejected Me,
> that I should not reign over them." (1 Samuel 8:7)

This is a key verse to remember when you are sharing your faith. When someone rejects your message and your efforts, remember that they are rejecting God, not you.

Did you notice the motivation behind Israel wanting a king? Look at verse 5, and said to him, "Look, you are old, and your sons do not walk in your ways. Now make us a king to judge us *like all the nations*." (emphasis added) We want to be like every other nation. What an excuse.

As a young preacher, I often wished that I could preach like Chuck Swindoll or Charles Stanley. Then God made me realize that He created me just as I am! If I was like them one of us would not be necessary. God created us unique, one of a kind, rejoice in that fact!

As for Israel wanting a king. I am one of the very few that believe that it was God's plan from the beginning. Humor me! Check out these verses and draw your own conclusions: Genesis 49:10, (Saul was from the tribe of Benjamin). Deuteronomy 17:14-20. Genesis 38. Deuteronomy 23:2 and finally Ruth 4:18-22 now count the generations from Perez to Jesse.

God never wanted to forfeit His reign. He wanted to appoint a "Godly" ruler to lead, through His leadership. That is the challenge for us today. Seeking God's man to be our president, our governor, our mayor, even our pastor. God should always be in leadership. Several times in the New Testament we are admonished to obey those appointed over us.

Samuel is interesting. He is the transition from the Judges to a king. Notice that it was Samuel's testimony that prompted the people to ask for a king. His son's failings disheartened the people and caused them to seek a king.

Another thing about appointing Saul as their first king. It was God's choice but it was what Israel wanted. God gave Israel what THEY asked for not what God wanted. They didn't seek His will. They basically got ahead of God. That is never good!

Do you have a desire? What is it motivated by? Do you want God's best or your desire? God's will and timing or yours?

"Only fear the Lord, and serve Him in truth with all your heart; for consider what great things He has done for you." (1 Samuel 12:24)

I just heard a great message from Dr. Stanley about fearing the Lord. That word appears all through the Old Testament but it doesn't mean "afraid" it simply means to reference God. I have an "r" word for you: Relationship.

Notice what else this verse says: "and serve Him in truth with all your heart." We are forever confronted with what is truth. With the internet and social media and so many ideas bombarding us daily it is hard sometimes to know what is true. Renew your commitment to finish reading the whole Bible. There is so much truth here that you will want to read and reread it over and over.

Just the book of Proverbs alone is a lifetime study of God's truth!

I mentioned this before. I was listening to my grandson the other day talking about an event he had participated in and thinking, write it down. He was so vivid in his description. That's what we need to do when God does something in our lives, write it down. Then, later, we can reflect on it, and it strengthens our faith and walk with God. If you're not doing that I want to encourage you to begin now.

Oh, today is the Atheist holiday. Did you know that? Yes, Psalm 14:1 says, "The fool has said in his heart, 'There is no God.'"

Look back to verse 20. "Do not fear" again. Even though they rejected God's leadership He has not turned His back on them. He, Samuel, reminds them to continue following God.

Saul is a great study. He reminds me of Samson. There was so much potential there. Both Saul and Samson just wanted to do things their own way. God had His hand on them in the beginning but they drifted further and further away from God's leadership. The power of pride is a deadly foe.

How earnestly are you seeking God's guidance? God's path, God's will in your life. Remember the lesson here of Israel. I think it was God's plan to make David king. But Israel couldn't wait for God's plan they wanted a king, and they wanted him now. We will see in the following chapters the price Israel would pay. Pray daily for God's wisdom and guidance in our lives!

But the Lord said to Samuel, "Do not look at his appearance or at his physical stature, because I have refused him. For the Lord does not see as man sees; for man looks at the outward appearance, but the Lord looks at the heart." (1 Samuel 16:7)

" "You don't get a second chance at a first impression." Have you heard that expression? How quickly we judge. Have you had anyone tell you, "you're not going to like this person"? They have decided who you're going to like or not like. Have you formed an opinion based on your friend's comment? I hope not.

Ok, so how do you form an opinion. Their looks? Their words? Their mannerisms? Why do you judge at the first meeting? Take a clue from what God told Samuel. Judge by their heart. How can you know their heart? Listen to their speech. In Matthew 15:11 Jesus says, "Not what goes into the mouth defiles a man; but what comes out of the mouth, this defiles a man." and verse 18, "But those things which proceed out of the mouth come from the heart, and they defile a man."

David, as we will see, through all the threats from Saul never bad-mouths Saul. Never speaks evil of him, though he tried to kill him several times. David had a unique relationship with God that was evident in his actions. Except when he rebelled. Rebellion is never in God's best interest.

I will remind you of the context. It didn't take God long to see what was in Saul's heart. Saul showed his heart on several occasions. So, God went looking for His choice from the very beginning. God sent Samuel to Jesse's house. Jesus has several sons. Notice that right away Samuel decides who God's choice is. Of course, we don't do that. We are willing to wait on God's choice, right? Come on! We would have done the same thing. The one WE thought would be the perfect king. If you think about it, that's how God chose Saul, "the people's choice".

This is another great verse to remember the address. There is a key principle here that we need to remember! God judges, not on the outward appearance, but on the heart. This can also apply to our works for God. What is our motivation? Do we serve God to please Him or to please our peers? God knows. We're not fooling anyone, especially God.

"Then all the assembly shall know that the Lord does not save with sword and spear; for the battle is the Lord's, and He will give you your hands." (1 Samuel 17:47)

This is David's reply to Goliath's rantings. There is a great story within this story. We all know the story of David and Goliath don't we. The part that's interesting, and what this verse applies to, is this. When David volunteered to fight Goliath, Saul offered him his sword and shield and the trappings of a warrior. Look at verse 39, chapter 17. David fastened his sword to his armor and tried to walk, for he had not tested them. And David said to Saul, "I cannot walk with these, for I have not tested them." So, David took them off.

Do you see? David wouldn't use weapons he had not tested. He used a sling and some stones. He had defeated lions and bears with those. The same is true with us. Have you "tested" God? Have you really tried the weapons of God? The weapon of prayer? The weapon of the truth of God's Word? How about the weapon of salvation by trusting in Christ as your Savior? Take a minute and read Ephesians 6. The 'armor of God' chapter. That is the armor God wants us to use!

There is another great lesson here. You know, of course, God could have killed Goliath on the spot, right? So, why didn't He? God was, even now, working first on David's faith also on that of Israel. Of course, evidently David's faith didn't need much work. Israel's faith was in Saul and where did that get them? God's plan was to work through David to encourage David and, remember what David said, "for the battle is the Lord's" when we give God the glory it's amazing what He can accomplish through us!

David is talking here to a nine-foot giant but his words are for Israel and Saul as well. God uses anyone and anything to accomplish His will and purpose. David had no idea when he left his father's house to bring lunch to his brothers that he would face a nine-foot giant. David was ready when he left for whatever God would put in his path that day. Those years in the pasture, tending his father's sheep, writing Psalms brought a special relationship between him and his God. I'm sure David spent many an hour praying to God. And he saw what God could do with his sling. Training for a day when he needed it!

"And you shall not only show me the kindness of the Lord while I still live, that I may not die; but you shall not cut off your kindness from my house forever; no, not when the Lord has cut off every one of the enemies of David from the face of the earth." (1 Samuel 20:14-15)

This relationship between Jonathan and David is a great example of the principle that Henry Blackaby used in his book *Experiencing God.* "Find where God is at work and join Him there." You see both Saul and Jonathan knew that David would be the next king. Saul chose to try to kill David at every opportunity. Jonathan joined with David even though it was against his father's wishes.

These chapters are a great study. It's a shame that some have tried to make more out this relationship, David and Jonathan, than it was. The culture of the day was that when a new king took over the throne he would kill or destroy all that remained of the previous king. That's what Jonathan is afraid David might do. Jonathan is asking for grace when Saul is no longer king and David reigns.

It's sad how hard Saul's heart was toward David. Not only David but it seemed he had turned his back on God. There is some debate as to whether Saul made it to heaven or not. That's for you to decide from these passages. What was Saul's motives, please God, or himself? It does say earlier that he prophesied, was filled with the Holy Spirit. But in the Old Testament that was not a permanent condition.

This relationship between Jonathan and David is worth a study. Again, a contrast of walking with God or against Him. Jonathan saw God working in David's life. Saul saw God use David to defeat Goliath and instead of rejoicing in God's presence he was threatened. Envy was also a big factor. Maybe Saul thought that since he was king God should bless him. You didn't see Saul running out to defend God's honor against Goliath.

Look around you. Do you see God's hand on anyone in your circle? Are you helping and encouraging them or are you jealous? Find out where God is at work and join Him there. The point Mr. Blackaby was making was that instead of trying to create a ministry or looking for some way to serve God, find out where God is working. A church is a great place to start. Find a church where God is working, and join Him.

> Then he said to David: "You are more righteous than I; for you have rewarded me with good, whereas I have rewarded you with evil." (1 Samuel 24:17)

Guess who is speaking here? If you've read the chapters you know. Saul. The sad part is that this isn't the first time that David has confronted Saul. From the beginning, when David defeated Goliath and the people praised David more than Saul, Saul has been out to kill David.

If you know anything of the New Testament does this verse sound familiar? Jesus says in Luke 6:35, "But love your enemies, do good, and lend, hoping for nothing in return; and your reward will be great, and you will be sons of the Most High. For He is kind to the unthankful and evil." This is a principle Jesus spoke often of. "Love your enemies."

Another interesting thing about David. David knew that God had chosen Saul as king. More than once David had opportunity to kill Saul but, as David put it, "I will not lift my hand against God's anointed". (1 Samuel 24). David was not the judge of Saul's relationship with God. David simply did the godly thing and let God take care of the judgment.

So many times, we think we need to take a hand in something we perceive as wrong. Pray first. You may be getting in God's way of dealing with the situation. Of course, He may be using you to accomplish that. That's why it's so important to pray FIRST!

Notice in verse 21 that Saul made the request that Jonathan made in the previous chapters. Again, this was the custom in those days. A new king destroyed the house of the old king. Maybe here Saul knew the inevitable.

Saul could very well be the story of many Christians today. That initial great feeling of being saved and going to heaven then slowly the world seeps in and gradually pulls them away from God. At some point God removes His hand from their life and they continually drift farther and farther from God.

The key is to recognize that God has taken His hand from you. Pray, repent seek that same relationship you once enjoyed. Just like the Prodigal son, God will welcome you with open arms!

"Please forgive the trespass of your maidservant. For the Lord will certainly make for my lord an enduring house, because my lord fights the battles of the Lord, and evil is not found in you throughout your days." (1 Samuel 25:28)

Abigail is one of my favorite characters of the Old Testament. She also is a great lesson, along with Jonathan. The lesson being, that God can use us no matter our circumstances!

I hope you have read these three chapters. The servants of David have an unpleasant meeting with Mr. Nabal. Attitude is everything and Mr. Nabal needs an attitude adjustment. God will do that later.

Notice Abigail's response to her husband. She gathers the food they had requested and goes out to meet David. Notice in this verse that she, just like Jonathan, recognized God's hand on David. Do you think God takes note of our response to God's servants? Of course, He does. These are people God has chosen to accomplish His will and how we respond to them is important to God.

Notice in the middle of the verse above, "because my lord fights the battles of the Lord." Here's a good place to remind you that God's anointed can very well be the pastors God has called to ministry. How we treat or respond to these servants reaches God's attention.

There are so many servants in the church, serving God willingly. This is a good example to think about how we treat them.

Abigail does the right thing despite her circumstances. The same with Jonathan. Too many times we let our circumstances dictate our response to situations and to God. Don't do that! Like Abigail she did what was right. I have always been curious at Nabal's response when Abigail returned. Maybe God began dealing with him right away.

Notice also both in Abigail and Jonathan that God took care of the situation. Too many times we want to deal with it in our own strength. God will not fight a battle that we have our hands in. Only when we have taken our hands off and allowed God to do His thing will He respond.

Do you think God knows your situation? If you're not a child of God you have no allies. God wants to show Himself strong in your situation but you must trust in Him first!

> Now David was greatly distressed, for the people spoke of stoning
> him, because the soul of all the people was grieved, every man for his
> sons and his daughters. But David strengthened himself in the Lord
> his God. (1 Samuel 30:6)

While David was away from his home base in Ziklag, raiders came in and kidnap his family and people. When he returned the people blamed David for the invasion. The Amalekites had taken his women and children. The rest wanted to stone him.

I love the last part of this verse. "But David strengthened himself in the Lord his God." This is only possible because of one thing. We've talked about it before and no doubt will talk about it many more times. It is a staple in our relationship with God. That's the key word "relationship". I think a lot of people think that a once-a-week visit to your neighborhood church is enough for a relationship with God. No way!

I've noticed in several movies that when two characters wish to have a conversation one will say, "walk with me". They talk while they are walking together. That's the picture I want you to get into your mind. Walking with God. That assumes, of course, you are both going in the same direction. Someone once said that when nothing is happening in your life you need to check who you are walking with. No trials, no testing, just everything is smooth. Make sure it's God who is beside you.

Never make decisions when you are grieved about something. I think it was Charles Stanley that gave me these warning signs. He said to think of the word H.A.L.T. he said to never make decisions in these four circumstances: Hungry, Angry, Lonely, Tired. Great advice. The people are angry about what has happened and wanted to take out their anger on David. Remember the word HALT.

Where does your wisdom and strength come from? That is an important question to ask. David's strength came from God. Samson's strength came from God, not his hair. Where does your strength come from? One other thing, check your walk. How close are you walking to your source of strength? Here's a better way to put it. Where is your faith? What are you trusting in?

"Now then, do it! For the Lord has spoken of David, saying 'By the hand of My servant David, I will save My people Israel from the hand of the Philistines and the hand of all their enemies." (2 Samuel 3:18)

Time to back away again, and get that big picture. We have moved from Judges to the final judge, Samuel. Samuel, by the will of the people, not God, has chosen Saul from the tribe of Benjamin to be their king. Saul has proven to be just what God told Israel they would get. Because they got ahead of God's Plan. Through 1 Samuel we saw the reign of Saul, the anointing of David by Samuel (1 Samuel 16:11-13). The kinship of David and Jonathan and finally the death of Saul and Jonathan.

In 2 Samuel, we will see the rise of king David. The Philistines have conquered Israel with the death of Saul. David's first task is to free Israel. David was anointed king of Hebron (remember, Caleb's inheritance) then finally he is anointed the king of Israel.

Now, notice in this verse how God is choosing to free Israel. "By the hand of My servant David." I've talked about this before. God has no "need" of using His children to accomplish His will. He can simply send a bolt of lightning, etc. God "chooses" to use His children for two reasons: One, that God would get the glory. We can do nothing apart from God. Two, He wants us to trust Him, obey Him, and serve Him. In so doing who reaps the blessing? We do. We get to see just what God can do. I think it was D.L. Moody who said, "There is no limit to what God can do with a life fully committed to Him." I heard that quote early on in my walk as a Christian and was determined to see just what God can do. He still amazes me at just what He can do!

I think that many times as we read the Bible we miss two aspects in our reading. The first is time. The events we read about may only take less than thirty minutes but takes several years to accomplish. We need to stop and realize the time frame. Second, we need to look for God's providence in the events that occur. They may not be spelled out. The book of Esther is a great example. The word God is not used in Esther but that doesn't mean He is not totally in control of all the events.

Is God using you in some powerful way today? Watch for His hand in the events that transpire through this week.

APRIL 9   2 SAMUEL 4-7

"Therefore, You, are great, O Lord God. For there is none like You, nor is there any God besides You, according to all that we have heard with our ears." (2 Samuel 7:22)

There are two interesting parts in these four chapters. The first part of these chapters deals with Uzzah. You might know this story. David wanted to move the ark of the Covenant from Abinadab's home to Jerusalem. So, he got this brand-new cart and had Uzzah and Ahio put it in the cart to bring to Jerusalem. The problem was in Exodus 21:14, that's where God instructed the ark to be built it included a pole on each side of the ark and instructions that the tribe of Levi oversaw transporting it. Well, this little mistake cost Uzzah his life. It is important to take note of David's reaction. How do you respond when things don't go the way you think they should? David was angry with God.

Maybe later, David consulted his scrolls of the books of Moses. Because later David did it right and accomplished his wish. When God puts roadblocks in front of our desires there is a reason. Usually it must do with timing, but sometimes it's about method. God may have a better plan. Prayer is always good at this point.

Chapter seven is one of my favorite chapters in 2 Samuel. In my Bible, beginning in verse 19 through to verse 29 I have underlined the word "servant". That word appears no less than eleven times in these verses. Why is that so significant? Realize who is talking. The king of Israel, God's chosen people. The one that God used to slay Goliath, to lead Israel, in battles victorious, etc. If anyone should have some pride or be puffed up just a little it would be David.

Do you remember what Jesus said in Matthew 25:23, "His Lord said to him, 'Well done, good and faithful servant; you have been faithful over a few things, I will make you ruler over many things. Enter into the joy of your Lord." Is that not awesome? David hit it right out of the park.

David's attitude toward God has always been one of servant. Of course, David made mistakes, as do we, but David always came back to God to make amends. Always sought that close relationship with his master. I like the part in that verse in Matthew, "you have been faithful in a few things." God doesn't ask for great things just faithfulness!

99

"Be of good courage, and let us be strong for our people and for the cities of our God. And may the Lord do what is Good in His sight." (2 Samuel 10:12)

If you will check out the first chapter of Joshua you will find these words four times, "Be strong and of good courage." Do you know what it means to step out of your comfort zone?

David sure did! Remember his upbringing was as a shepherd. Of course, Moses had the same training. What would it take for God to get you to try something you have never tried before? That's getting out of your comfort zone.

I wasn't saved till I was thirty-five. Within six months I was teaching a Sunday School class. When I was in high school and had to give a book report I would stay home! I was VERY shy!

I became a deacon, then associate pastor. Then a church called me to preach in view of a call to be their pastor. I was scared to death. They recognized this and let me preach two Sunday's before voting on me. When the Pulpit Committee questioned me on my credentials, no college, no seminary, I said, "I just love the Lord." They called me.

I served as their pastor for two and a half years. The church doubled in attendance. All God's doing, for sure! I did my first baptism, many weddings and funerals. I led our community Easter service one year. My first hospital visit was to minister to a couple who had lost their baby to S.I.D.S. Every day I would see God work miracles with a former truck driver who dropped out of school in the tenth grade. All because I was willing to trust God. To venture out of my comfort zone. To wake up every morning and say, "What are you going to do today, God?"

God was working daily in David's life. The victories on the battle fields, the leadership of God's people. All from a shepherd boy who was willing to trust God and get out of his comfort zone.

You cannot begin to understand the joy of watching God work miracles, using you to accomplish His will. I have so many great memories of those two and a half years I will never forget. The greatest memory was what God accomplished with a willing heart and the leadership of His Holy Spirit.

"But now he is dead; why should I fast? Can I bring him back again?
I shall go to him, but he shall not return to me." (2 Samuel 12:23)

I will talk about this verse in a minute, but first. There is another verse in this chapter that pertains to the verse above. Verse 7 says, "Then Nathan said to David, 'you are the man'! Thus, says the Lord God of Israel". David had committed a grievous sin. Adultery and murder and thought he could get away with it. Noting escapes God's eyes. God used Nathan to confront David.

I hope you will read these chapters. The above verse pertains to God's judgment on David and Bathsheba for their sin. The child that Bathsheba birthed would die. David had grieved and beg God to spare the child. The child died. Sin has consequences!

There is a wonderful truth in this verse. First, it tells us that children go to be with the Lord if they die in infancy. David accepted God's judgment. Too many times when God deals with us in our lives we want to "blame" God instead of ourselves.

David recognized that, one day, they would be reunited in heaven. That gave him peace. To me, one of the greatest demonstrations of God's grace was that Bathsheba conceived again and gave David another child, Solomon.

God was not through with David. God's judgment included strife throughout David's family for the rest of his life. Not only his family but his kingdom as well. So much so that God would not allow David to build His Temple but passed that on to his son, Solomon.

Besides the great lesson of the verse above we cannot forget that the biggest lesson David was to learn and we should as well; there are consequences to sin! We may have received God's forgiveness. As far as God is concerned that slate is wiped clean. But the consequences can last a lifetime.

David made so many mistakes. But over and over, he confessed and repented and God used David in so many miraculous ways. It says in scripture that David was a man "after God's own heart." (Acts 13:22, 1 Samuel 13:14) How can that be? With all the mistake's he made. I like the way that is worded. Think of it this way. David was a man who "sought" God's heart. Oh, he made mistakes, we all do, but David always made it right with God!

Then the king said to Zadok, "Carry the ark of God back into the city. If I find favor in the eyes of the Lord, He will bring me back and show me both it and His dwelling place." (2 Samuel 15:25)

I need to remind you to read the chapters above, each day. You might want to read the scripture then this devotion. It will make more sense. The rebellion of Absalom is part of that "consequences" that we talked about yesterday. Absalom had won the heart of the people. So much so that David had to flee his home.

Notice in this verse that David said, "If I find favor in the eyes of the Lord." David, though he had his faults eventually sought God's favor. Lapse of judgment, mistakes yes, but always returned to God and his will. When God told David, he couldn't build the Temple, well we will talk about that later.

Zadok had brought the ark with them when they fled the city. David instructed Zadok to return the ark to Jerusalem. This is a good place to notice something about this ark and the nation Israel. At some point the ark became a "good luck charm" to Israel. They felt that all they had to do was lead, in battle, with the ark and they would be victorious. That is not what God intended. Do you use some spiritual things as "good luck charms?" Your Bible for instance. Do you read your Bible hoping to gain good luck? I hope not. Remember Nehushtan?

Look at the following verse: "But if He says thus: 'I have no delight in you,' here I am, let Him do to me as seems good to Him." David throws himself into God's hands. Can you do that?

Think about David's situation. He is at the mercy of his son. He has been run out of Jerusalem and fleeing for his life. Remember the code of the kings. Remove anyone who threatens your throne. I don't believe Absalom would have been above killing David.

David always seemed to have a special relationship with God. Even with all his mistakes, why is that? Take your time through these chapters and learn about David. To me David and Peter (New Testament) are so much alike. They seem to make mistakes regularly yet God used them in mighty ways, again why?

God knew their hearts. God knew they simply wanted a closer walk with God, they stumbled, but always came back to God!

"For I, your servant, know that I have sinned. Therefore, here I am,
the first to come today of all the house of Joseph to go down to meet
my lord the king." (2 Samuel 19:20)

Now that we have survived Leviticus do you remember one of the offerings in
the book? I believe it was the "sin offering" (Leviticus 4) that pertained to
unrecognized sin. Sin that we unknowingly commit. We have done something
wrong but didn't know we did it. Is that weird or what? God has even provided
for sin we don't know we committed. I wonder how many Israelites made that
offering just to be safe?

Do we have such an offering? Of course, it's called grace. The blood of
Jesus Christ is so powerful it will even cover those sins we don't realize we have
committed. The neat thing is we have the Holy Spirit to bring those sins to our
attention.

Ok, the Spirit brings that sin to your mind, now what. Well, let's debate it
with God. Let's first try to deny it. When that doesn't work we say, "it's not that
bad" like one sin is worse that another. Next, we make excuses and say, "the devil
made me do it" well of course he did but that doesn't excuse it.

So how do we deal with sin? Look at the verse above. We confess it.
Acknowledge we sinned, ask forgiveness and move on.

Have you ever heard the phrase "forgive and forget" well that's not possible?
Oh, we can forgive but our minds are wired as such that forgetting isn't possible.
Of course, the Bible says that God forgets, which is great for us. So why don't we
forget? Those little reminders are to keep us focused on God. When our mind
brings up those sins that we thought we have taken care of with God, we have, they
are to remind us of God's grace. Remind us what our relationship with God cost
Him. We need to be reminded every day that God can, and does forgive us. That's
why it's important to absorb these chapters about David. God put these chapters
in here to show us what grace means. The constant struggle David had with his
relationship with God is the same things we struggle with.

Even the apostle Paul struggled with his relationship with God but in the end
Paul obeyed God. Can we say the same thing?

As for God, His way is perfect. The Word of the Lord is proven; He is a shield to all who trust in Him. "The Lord lives! Blessed be my Rock! Let God be exalted, the Rock of my salvation! (2 Samuel 22:31,47)

This verse recalls a verse in Hebrews 13:15, "Therefore by Him let us continually offer the sacrifice of praise to God, that is, the fruit of our lips, giving thanks to His name." Any believer knows you can't praise God enough. With our realization of what God has done for us, we can't praise Him enough.

That's where David is at. Remember we looked at what Absalom had done or attempted to do to David. David sought God, trusted God, and God brought him back to Jerusalem in triumph. In these verses in chapter 22 David is making a sacrifice of praise!

When was the last time you brought an offering of praise to God? You know you can do that every day, but especially on the Lord's Day. Our worship service begins with songs of praise. Our time of offering is a time of praise. Our Bible study is a time of praise. And, our Sunday school hour is a time of praise!

Look at the fantastic words in the beginning of verse 31. "As for God, His way is perfect; The word of the Lord is proven; He is a shield to all who trust in Him." Talk about praise. The thing is that these are words of "experience." God has been with David from the shepherd's field to the throne of Israel. It's when David acted on his own he got in trouble!

Again, in verse 47 God is likened to a Rock. Like Jesus said, "Upon this Rock I will build my church." Peter the rock? Not hardly, the Rock of our Savior Jesus Christ. The solid foundation in 1 Corinthians 3.

Here is a song that is not in the Psalms. The Psalms being the hymn book of the day. Here one of David's songs is used. I wonder what David's voice sounded like? You know it doesn't matter. God is praised when the music is from the heart, not the mouth.

I love what Ephesians 5:19 says, "Speaking to one another in psalms and hymns and spiritual songs, singing and making melody in your heart to the Lord." Is that not awesome?

Do you catch yourself during the days repeating the words to a hymn? I love it, God is pleased!

Then the king said to Araunah, "No, but I will surely buy it from you for a price; nor will I offer burnt offerings to the Lord my God with that which costs me nothing." So, David bought the threshing floor and the oxen for fifty shekels of silver. (2 Samuel 24:24)

I think it is interesting that this verse comes up on "tax-day." There is an awesome story here. David, again, wanted to praise God. God had stayed a plague He had brought on David. If you've read the chapters you know the details. The point is that David desired to praise God for His mercy. A plague brought on by David. A sin, repentance, then praise.

The property and the animal for sacrifice, the owner offered to give them to David for his offering for free. Cool, we're taught to accept all gifts with grace and thankfulness, right? No when David wanted to praise God David wanted it to mean something to him. He insisted that he pay for the land and the sacrifice. An offering that costs nothing is just that.

I learned the hard way about giving. A tough lesson. But a lesson none the less. Too many people associate their giving with the church. They measure it as supporting the church or ministry. I don't recall any reference to that in scripture. The giving is to God, plain and simple. So, whatever your excuse is, take it up with God not the pastor or deacons.

I remember one of the purposes of Paul's travels and missionary journeys in the book of Acts was to collect offerings in the various churches. Those offerings were not for Paul's ministry or any church, those offerings were for the poor in Jerusalem.

When we give an offering, it is taking it out of our hands and putting it in God's hands period. What God chooses to do with it is His business. God simply asks us to give.

When David sought to make this offering his one thought was to praise God. Remember we talked yesterday about a "sacrifice of praise." David is simply saying, "it's not a sacrifice if it doesn't cost me something."

I've thought about this in reference to Wednesday night prayer meeting. For someone to take time out of their day, dress up, drive to church, just to pray is a sacrifice of praise!

> "And keep the charge of the Lord your God: to walk in His ways,
> to keep His statutes, His commandments, His Judgments, and His
> testimonies, as it is written in the Law of Moses, that you may prosper
> in all that you do and wherever you turn." (1 Kings 2:3)

The passing of king David. I hope you are reading these chapters because there is a lot of skullduggery going on. This verse is David's challenge to his son Solomon. Right off the bat there were some who tried to deprive Solomon of his throne.

If you had the opportunity to pass on some wisdom to the next generation what might that be? This verse is a good example. The problem is that Solomon paid as much attention to his father's wisdom as the next generation pays to our wisdom.

Why is it that when we can pass on our vast "experience" the next generation feels they need to make the same mistakes. Remember the definition of insanity: "Doing the same thing over and over and expecting different results." That's what David was faced with. What amazes me is that Solomon is touted as the smartest man in history. The point of this scripture, I hope, as it is with all of scripture is that we might learn from the mistakes of others.

I want you to note from this point on how many references God makes to David. Some of the following judges are said to have either followed in David's footsteps or not.

Solomon is a pivotal point in the history of Israel. A lot of changes take place following his reign. I'm always fascinated by the reference to "walking" in the ways, etc. To walk is an act of going somewhere, not standing still. Traveling to a destination. When we walk with God both us are traveling together to the same destination. Picture that for a minute. How is your walk with God?

Notice these words: His ways, commandments, judgments, testimonies, and Law. If you want some homework read the 119th Psalm and underline each of these words. The 119th Psalm is all about the word of God.

David leaves some parting words, warnings really. Obey the Law. The Law that was handed down from God to Moses. That would be wise advice to our "next generation!"

"Therefore, give to Your servant an understanding heart to judge Your people, that I may discern between good and evil. For who is able to judge this great people of Yours?" (1 Kings 3:9)

It's so frustrating to me. Solomon gets off to such a great start. We like to make jokes about how he lost his way with all the wives he married but the real reason is that he was drawn away from God by the lure of idols. Why that is, I wish I knew. But then we fall for the same diversions today. How easily we are drawn away from, praying, Bible study or church. Just the same as Solomon, the wisest man who ever lived.

This verse is Solomon's answer to God who asked what shall I give you? Solomon simply asked, notice, "an understanding heart" not wisdom, not riches but an understanding heart. How hard is that to come by today? Compassion, forgiveness, encouragement, etc. Solomon just wanted to lead his people faithfully.

There is an important element in Solomon's downfall that we might want to take note of. Notice how Satan attacks Solomon. Not with armies or even lies. Satan attacks his family. That method is still valid today. Disrupt the family life and bring disharmony and confusion to so many people. The sad part is that it can go on for generations.

Notice in verses 6-9 in this chapter that Solomon uses the term "Your servant." Much like his father, David, did earlier. It would be worth taking note how these two men looked at their relationship with God. They were servants!

"Discern good and evil" does that sound familiar? Remember Genesis 3:5, "For God knows that in the day you eat of it your eyes will be opened, and you will be like God, knowing good and evil." Solomon asked for the same knowledge that Satan offered Eve. Does God want us to discern between good and evil? Yes, but not from experience. Solomon already knew God's wishes. God gave them in the Ten Commandments. Yet we still question and search and try and try to find out on our own. The instructions and limits are right there, but who takes the time to really try to please God?

Also keep in mind that these commandments weren't meant to get us to heaven. They were meant to point out our sin!

"Concerning this temple which you are building, if you walk in My statutes, execute My judgments, keep all My commandments, and walk in them, then I will perform My word with you, which I spoke to your father David." (1 Kings 6:12)

I mentioned before to be on the lookout for references to David. King David seems to be the standard with which God measures a relationship with Him. Notice in this verse, Solomon is building the temple that David was not allowed to build.

I want you to think back to David's response to God telling him he could not build the temple. That was David's desire, that was David's dream, then God says no. What was David's response? Instead of going ahead anyway, or cursing God's decision, or turning his back on God, David purposed to gather the materials for his son to build the temple. That is the man who was after God's own heart.

Here again, in this verse God stresses the importance of being obedient to His Law. The five books of Moses, God's Law. Did David keep the Law religiously? No. Did David repent of his disobedience and beg God's forgiveness? Yes. I think it's important to understand David's relationship with God.

Again, in this verse is the reference to "walking" with God. I can't stress this enough. It is a daily thing, a moment by moment seeking God's direction, advice, counsel, etc. Most don't even bother with Sunday worship. If Sunday worship was not important to God why would He go to such lengths to give instructions on the temple?

It would be interesting to contrast David's walk with God, to Solomon's. Their obedience, etc. Look at this verse again. Do the conditions sound familiar? Of course, they do. They were given to Moses, passed on to David and now God is passing them on to Solomon. Jesus passed them on to us with two commandments that reflected the same ten commandments. Look at Matthew 22:37-40.

"Then I will perform My word with you." Do you think it's wrong for God to put conditions on His blessings? Of course not. How can you "walk with God" if you're in rebellion? You're not walking the same path. God will not walk with someone who is in sin. I stress again God's purpose for us—A relationship built of obedience!

> And he said: "Lord God of Israel, there is no God in heaven above or
> on earth below like You, who keep Your covenant and mercy with Your
> servants who walk before You with all their hearts." (1 Kings 8:23)

This theme is tough to keep reminding you about. Over and over we have seen through our journey from the Garden of Eden to this point in the history of God's people. Let me remind you of something in the Garden. God put a forbidden tree in the Garden THEN told Adam and Eve not to eat of it, why? Obedience. What was their response?

God took His people to Mt. Sinai and gave them the Ten Commandments. While Moses was on the mountain God's people constructed an idol. God judged them, almost destroyed them if not for Moses intervention. (Exodus 32) Now we see David and then Solomon. God's message is still the same, obedience.

I don't remember the word mercy being used till now. Of course, if it weren't for God's mercy Israel would have been destroyed long ago. It is the same for us today. Here's a little note about the apostle Paul's writings. Check out Paul's salutations in his letters. In all of Paul's letters he begins with, "grace and peace" in the salutation. Now look at Timothy and Titus. These books are known as "pastoral epistles" notice his salutation in these books.

It might be important here to point out the measure of obedience at the end of this verse. "with all your hearts" it has been said that many people will miss heaven by eighteen inches. They have the head knowledge of who Jesus is but they haven't invited Him into their hearts. That is sad. It could be said of Solomon. With all his knowledge, he missed the point. Solomon's heart was drawn away by the women he chose to be with. All being pagan worshippers.

Who has influence in your life? Are they children of God? Who sways or impacts the decisions you make? Notice in the verse above, "who keep Your covenant." that is an imperative in seeking advice. Dr. Stanley once said, "if the advice you receive is contrary to the word of God, STOP." God gave us His word for a reason. All through these books and verses we see stressed over and over, obey my commandments. Stressed over and over!

"Blessed be the Lord your God, who delighted in you, setting you on the throne of Israel! Because the Lord has loved Israel forever, therefore He made you king, to do justice and righteousness." (1 Kings 10:9)

As an unbeliever, I used to think that there were two valleys to every mountaintop. Later, when I came to know the Lord I realized that there are two mountaintops for every valley. It all depends on perspective.

I hope you have read these chapters. The verse above is a quote from the Queen of Sheba who has come to see Solomon because the word had reached her of all that God has done for him. The queen is amazed, look at verses 4-7. She said, "the half was, not told me." after viewing it for herself she was amazed.

Notice how she words the verse above, "Blessed be the Lord YOUR God." That is a hint of the valley were going to look at next.

Look at verse 3 of chapter 11. And he had seven hundred wives, princesses, and three hundred concubines: his wives turned away his heart. I don't think it was the number as much as their influence over his life. Isn't it interesting how easily we can be led astray from our walk with God?

Remember back in Deuteronomy 17. God warned the future king of Israel to be warned of collecting, horses, wives, and gold. Solomon had an abundance of all three. A warning from God. Has God warned you of something? Has He made it clear that you were to avoid certain things. Heed the warning!

One last comment. Look at verse 34 of chapter 11. "However, I will not take the whole kingdom out of his hand, because I have made him ruler all the days of his life for the sake of My servant David, whom I chose because he kept My commandments and My statutes." Sound familiar?

David wasn't perfect by any means but God had a special relationship with him. Notice that God gives the reason why He and David were so close. "because he kept My commandments and My statutes". God seeks obedience from His children. The more we walk after Him the closer we are to His will.

> "And all Israel shall mourn for him and bury him, for he is the only
> one of Jeroboam who shall come to the grave, because in him there
> is found something good toward the Lord God of Israel in the house
> of Jeroboam." (1 Kings 14:13)

Here is a pivotal point in the history of Israel. The decision that Rehoboam makes will forever divide Israel into two kingdoms. The Northern ten tribes and the Southern two tribes, Judah and Benjamin. Again, I encourage you to read these chapters.

I don't know about you but I keep getting Rehoboam and Jeroboam confused. Someone once told me to remember that Jeroboam "jumped". It was Jeroboam who led the rebellion against Solomon's son Rehoboam.

Look at verse 16 of chapter 14. "And He will give Israel up because of the sins of Jeroboam, who sinned and who made Israel to sin." As you continue through Kings you need to keep this in mind as well. From here on Israel (Samaria) will be the name of the Northern ten tribes, while Judah is the name of the southern tribes. It can get confusing, just look at the context.

There will be many, many kings in the next chapters. For the most part Judah had godly kings, with exceptions of course. The northern kingdom never had a godly king. God would eventually use Assyria to remove the northern tribes. Babylon would remove the southern tribes, but they will return. I don't want to get too far ahead. Just a little heads up.

One interesting thing we can see even with Rehoboam. A lot of times there is little influence of the father on the son. A godly king can be from the worst father, and the other way around. It all boils down to God's influence on the individual. That's key! A king could bring a great revival and turn Judah back to God and the next king, his son, would do the opposite.

What influences you? Television, a school teacher, parent, grand-parent, friend? Where are they leading you, on what path are they leading you? We've already talked about the need to be walking on the same path as God. Keep in mind the reference yesterday about how much God loved David and why!

> Asa did what was right in the eyes of the Lord, as did his father David.
> (1 Kings 15:11)

There are two phrases that you will want to keep an eye for. The one above, "did right in the eyes of the Lord." The second is in verse 14, "high places." You notice that Asa didn't remove the "high places." This is where Israel or Judah kept their idols. This is where they went to worship instead of the temple. The kings would bring a great revival but refuse to remove the high places which would eventually infect the revival.

The time periods can be hard to understand. "In the 18th year of Jeroboam the son of Nebat, Abijam became king over Judah. Jeroboam was king of the Northern tribes and Abijam was king of Southern tribes. It can be confusing. It's not important, it was how they recorded events. The important thing we want to take note of, is, how they responded to their relationship with the Lord.

You see Asa was one of the good kings. Look at verse 14 again, But the high places were not removed. Nevertheless, Asa's heart was loyal to the Lord all his days. Notice it's the heart that is the measure. We can fool people with our speech and our actions, but God knows the heart!

This has an interesting application. We have all the outward appearances of a faithful Christian. Do we have any "high places" in our heart where we are trying to hide things from God? Secret sins of, unforgiveness, envy, prejudice, greed, etc. These can be our high places. Where we hide our secret idols.

Take note as we go through these various kings, how many refuse to destroy the high places.

Another thing you might make a note of. I hope you have read these chapters. Notice how many times the kings resort to help from neighboring nations. There always seemed to be war between the north and south as well. God's people and those who have turned their backs on God.

Oh, David is mentioned again. How about that, the measuring stick of a relationship with God. You would do well to study the life of David on your own.

"Hear me, O Lord, hear me, that this people may know that You are the Lord God, and that You have turned their hearts back to You again." (1 Kings 18:37)

Oh, this is one of my favorite stories in the Old Testament. The thing that amazes me is the brevity of his, Elijah's, prayer. Just the few words shown above to call down fire from heaven to prove the power of God.

I know you have read these chapters. 950 prophets. 450 prophets of Baal and 400 prophets of Asherah. I can hear Elijah now quoting Joshua, "choose you this day who you will serve." (v.21) Basically the same challenge. Shame on Elijah for mocking these prophets look at verse 27. Maybe their god is asleep, and must be awakened.

Now I want you to note the confidence of Elijah. He not only mocked them. When it was his turn he did everything he could to demonstrate God's power. To the point of pouring buckets of water on the altar first. Elijah had a walk with God that was so close he trusted God every step of the way.

This verse always makes me think of Jesus and Lazarus. Look if you will at John 11:41b,42. Jesus addresses the tomb of Lazarus and says, "Father, I thank You that You have heard Me. And I know that You always hear Me, but because of the people who are standing by I said this, that they may believe that You sent Me." Is that not amazing!

What was the point of these two prayers? Not to call the power of God. Both had already known God's power. The point was to be a testimony to those around them. In a sense pointing and saying, "to God be the glory. Look at God's power!" Granted it also spoke of the faith of Elijah and Jesus for sure. What a measure of faith on Elijah's part!

I heard a story of two farmers. There was a terrible drought. Both farmers had prayed and prayed for rain. One farmer was on his knees in the barn. The other farmer was out plowing his field in preparation for rain. Which had the greater faith?

Elijah's faith was such that he did everything he could to make it harder on God to burn the sacrifice. Yet God not only consumed the sacrifice but the altar as well.

> Then a man of God came and spoke to the king of Israel, and said,
> "Thus says the Lord: 'Because the Syrians have said, "The Lord is God
> of the hills, but He is not God of the valleys," therefore I will deliver
> all this great multitude into your hand, and you shall know that I am
> the Lord." (1 Kings 20:28)

O.k, here's a pop quiz: Who is the king of Israel, northern or southern kingdom. Israel is the northern kingdom. I guess this shows the relationship the northern king had with God. There are many theories about Ahab. He did some good things and bad things. Elijah drove him nuts. So, was Ahab saved or lost? It's simple, we don't know his heart.

That is the same dilemma we face today. How many times have we tried to determine whether a person was lost or saved by their actions? We can't help it. That still doesn't make it right. In Matthew. Jesus says, "Beware of the false prophets, who come to you in sheep's clothing, but inwardly they are ravenous wolves. You will know them by their fruits. Do men gather grapes from thorn bushes or figs from thistles?"

Thus, can be a dangerous practice. I've heard some say, "we are just fruit inspecting." You are also judging a person's heart. Remember what God told Samuel, "only God knows the heart." (1 Samuel 16:7).

This also brings up a pet peeve of mine. Too many of God's children want to put God in a box. That's what the Syrians have done. They can't conceive of God doing anything more than they are able to comprehend. We do the same thing. We put God in box by thinking that God can't do certain things. A box of our making, not God's.

If only the end of this verse were true. "And you shall know that I am the Lord." Ask Israel. How many times has God shown His power and then Israel turns right around and says, "woe is me, where is God?"

This is one of the greatest challenges as a Christian to trust God to take care of anything God puts His mind to. Don't put Him in a box. God is more than capable to accomplish anything He wishes. We just must believe. Remember Elijah?

How many battles has God won? You can't count them. How about in your life? How many times has something happened in your life, a blessing, and you can't explain it? What do you say, "I was sure lucky" lucky is not in the Christian vocabulary!

So, the king said to him, "How many times shall I make you swear that you tell nothing but the truth in the name of the Lord?" (1 Kings 22:16)

This is a funny story. So, relevant to today. The king wants the truth BUT, it must coincide with what he wants to hear. He wants a certain answer BUT, it must be the answer he wants. Have you ever read your Bible that way? There's a verse that tells you something you don't want to hear. Instead of remembering that these are the words of God you want to discount them. Oh, the prophet was talking to Israel, or a certain person, not me. This doesn't apply to me.

Even when the prophet said what the king wanted to hear he knew the prophet was making fun of him. The king didn't want the truth. I think the New Testament talks about this, "For the time will come when they will not endure sound doctrine, but according to their own desires, because they have itching ears, they will heap, up for themselves teachers; and they will turn their ears away from the truth, and be turned aside to fables." (2 Timothy 4:3-4).

Would you know the truth if you read it? The first question you have to ask is, "what is the source of the truth?" Can you trust the source? If it is the Bible you can trust it. Throughout history millions have put their faith in the word of God and it has never failed.

If a friend of yours lies to you. Do you trust them afterward? Of course not. They must earn that trust back. O.k, answer this. How much faith does it take to believe the word of God. Let me quote one of my favorite verses: Matthew 9:29 Then He touched their eyes and said, "according to your faith let it be to you." How many times does Jesus marvel at those who demonstrate great faith? 99% of the time it's from a Gentile. He gets so frustrated with His own disciples.

This king is frustrated with the prophet. He threatens him to tell the truth but then doesn't believe him. Just a note. That also applies to the work of the Holy Spirit. How many times has God's Spirit warned us not to do or say something and we ignore Him and do it anyway? And what has been the results? It never works out.

God only wants the best for His children, BUT they must be willing to listen and obey!

> Then it happened as they continued on and talked that suddenly a
> chariot of fire appeared with horses of fire, and separated the two of
> them; and Elijah went up by a whirlwind into heaven. (2 Kings 2:11)

I've talked about this before. Many have said that this is the reason that Elijah appears with Moses on the mount of configuration with Jesus. Elijah did not die.

This also fulfills a promise that Elijah made to Elisha. Because of Elisha commitment to Elijah, Elisha carried on the ministry of Elijah. Sounds confusing, I know but there is a great lesson in this chapter. God is looking for that kind of commitment from us. How many Christians miss out on God's working in their life by a lack of commitment.

It saddens me, as one who has seen both sides, how much a Christian, misses out on God's blessing because they simply put God on the back burner. They are so excited when Jesus comes into their life, but it is short lived. They soon get wrapped up in the world and events around them and that excitement "cools."

Elisha saw what God was doing in Elijah's life. Elisha wanted the same relationship with God. Elijah told him that if he saw God take him up that he would pass on the mantle to Elisha. In this chapter, you see the transfer of power. A commentator once said that Elisha perform exactly twice as many miracles as Elijah. Elisha received a "double" portion of God's blessing. Why? He was faithful to follow Elijah and by that, God.

I don't know why but this reminds me of the two men in the gospel of Luke walking on the road to Emmaus (Luke 24). When Jesus joined them, and spoke to them. There's that word walk again. Companionship, fellowship, a relationship built on a connection that is constant and regular.

Do you think it was an accident that Elijah's mantle was left behind? I don't. We leave many things behind when we depart this earth. As Christians, we have a responsibility to leave a testimony that honor's God. A testimony that the next generation can build upon, can rely on and use as inspiration to continue the work. What an awesome challenge. I know many older men who have that testimony with their family. What a blessing. It also makes leaving this earth much easier. I pray this devotional will inspire a closer walk with the Lord!

So, he answered, "do not fear, for those who are with us are more than
those who are with them." And Elisha prayed, and said, "Lord, I pray,
open his eyes that he may see." Then the Lord opened the eyes of the
young man, and he saw. And behold, the mountain was full of horses
and chariots of fire all around Elisha. (2 Kings 6:16-17)

"**O**pen their eyes." How many times have we prayed that? We talk and talk,
and witness till we want to give up, but God says, "keep on, keeping on."
In a sense, this is a physical picture of a New Testament principle. You see all the
words in the world will not bring someone to salvation in the Lord, EXCEPT the
Holy Spirit convicts them first. (John 16:8)

You might say that it is the work of the Spirit that "opens their eyes." Until
God's Spirit works on their heart and opens the eyes of their heart to their need
for a relationship with God they are like this servant who is scared to death of
what might happen.

Notice how Elisha accomplishes this. He prayed. I know of so many stories
of relatives who have prayed and prayed for a loved one to be saved. Years pass and
finally God opens their eyes and realize their need for God. It not only takes prayer
it takes faithful, consistent prayer.

Here's another concept that if the child of God ever got a hold of would change
their whole walk. God's presence is ever with us, and His power! The servant never
realized the army that surrounded them, God's army. He saw the army in front of
him, not God's army around them. Remember what Jesus said to Peter? Look at
Matthew 26:23, "Or do you think that I cannot pray to My Father, and He will
provide more than twelve legions of angels?" Jesus was being arrested. He said to
His disciples, "put away your sword." God has it all under control.

Too many times we want to take matters in our own hands. We want to do
what God, we think, should do. God has other plans. They could not understand
why Jesus had to die.

Look at the lesson. God is ready and able to assist us. We must ask for that
help. In this case it is simply to "open our eyes" and know that God is present.
Remember not only our physical eyes but the eyes of our heart. To recognize our
need of God and to accept that help and salvation from the Lord.

Yet the Lord would not destroy Judah, for the sake of his servant
David, as He promised him to give a lamp to him and his sons forever.
(2 Kings 8:19)

Remember we noted earlier that Judah is the Southern Kingdom comprised
of the tribes of Judah and Benjamin. These tribes will be spared and allowed
to eventually remain in the nation of Israel. God was reminding Jehoram of that
promise.

I mentioned this before. Let me ask you this question. When you think of
king David, what comes to your mind? Let me guess, one of two events. David
and Goliath or David and Bathsheba. Right? That's a shame. It would do you well
to study the life of David. Just as in the verse above, God's relationship with king
David is something to seek.

We all make mistakes. Have you ever tried to rationalize or explain away
those mistakes? Of course, we have. How does God look at those mistakes? It
depends on our response to God's response. If God has chastised you about that
mistake, as He did with David, what was your response? Was it like Adam and Eve
and blame someone else or was it like David, I repent and beg Your forgiveness. "I
have sinned!" That is the response God is looking for.

Here again God was ready to destroy Judah. Yet because of a promise He
made to David, God repented. Jesus makes the same promise to us! Because of
what Jesus did on the cross of Calvary, God will never leave us if we claim the
blood of Christ. When we become children of God, God will never give up on us!

Notice in verse 18 of this chapter. "He walked in the way of the kings of
Israel." Remember I said that none of the kings of Israel followed God. Most of the
kings of Judah did, but not Israel. This was God's way of saying here is a southern
king who didn't follow God.

Think about something here. God continued to watch over Judah because
of king David. Our relationship with God is not based on what our father or
grandfather or any other relation did. Our relationship with God the Father is
based on our relationship with God the Son, nothing more or less!

O.k, take a moment and examine your relationship with God!

> Then Jehoiada made a covenant between the Lord, the king, and the
> people, that they should be the Lord's people, and also between the
> king and the people. (2 Kings 11:17)

Here is one of those contrast I was talking about. I hope you have read these chapters. Athaliah had become the leader of Judah. Jehoiada claimed the throne. It's important to note what his first duty was. Look at verse 18. He destroyed the temple of Baal. One other thing of note. Look at verse 21 of chapter 11. "Jehoash was seven years old when he became king." Read the account of this king. Interesting!

What does the word covenant mean to you? We make covenants all the time. Today they are called contracts. We put our signature to them, sometimes they may be just a handshake. Of course, a handshake today is meaningless. A lawyer can't argue a handshake.

What do those "covenants" mean to you? Evidently not much on man's side or Israel's side in the Old Testament. How many times did Israel make a covenant with God to obey His commandments and before the week was out, they broke it. Take note of the ups and downs of the kings of Judah in this book.

What about God's covenant with us? Has it ever been broken? God is faithful in every promise He has made to us. Two problems! One, we don't know half the promises God has made to us. Second, we don't claim those promises because we don't know them. Understand some of the promises, especially in the Old Testament, are for Israel alone, but many, many are for us today. Wait till we get to the Psalms and Proverbs!

One last point. Have you noticed a phrase used for each king? "His mother's name was Zibiah of Beersheba." (12:1). Why would God deem it important to note the mother's name instead of the father? That's worth thinking about.

Look at verse 2 of chapter 12. "which Jehoiada the priest instructed him." Remember he began his reign at seven years old. He needed instruction. What better input for a young king than from the five books of Moses (that was all they had then). Remember what Proverbs says, "Train up a child in the way he should go, and when he is old he will not depart from it." (Proverbs 22:6)

> But the Lord was gracious to them, had compassion on them, and regarded them, because of His covenant with Abraham, Isaac, and Jacob, and would not yet destroy them or cast them from His presence.
> (2 Kings 13:23)

Is there any way to measure God's patience? Both in the book of Judges and here in Kings. I would have given up a long time ago. Notice, God reminds them of what? Not His covenant with David. David was in Jerusalem, David represented the southern kingdom. No God used Abraham, Isaac, and Jacob, essentially His covenant with the nation of Israel before it became two kingdoms. Because of His covenant He would extend such grace to the north that only God could extend!

Eventually God would remove His hand and Assyria would come in and remove the southern kingdom, all ten tribes for good. God will wait only so long, He will extend every opportunity, make every effort to get your attention, but sooner or later, without repentance God will remove His hand. Does that mean there is no hope? Of course not! God's ear is always attentive to our pleas. Unfortunately, the northern kingdom never sought God's forgiveness!

There are lessons to be learned from each of these kings, both northern and southern. The thing that fascinates me is that one king could be a godly king and do all the right things and his son could totally reject God and do all the wrong things. Why is that? I wish I knew that answer. Of course, the opposite is true. A horrible king, rejecting God, could have a son who wholly follows God!

We were talking in our Sunday school class about why certain things were not in the Bible. I mentioned that if God told us everything that happened we would not be able to carry the book. God has put in His word what is sufficient for a relationship with Him. Once we become a child of God His Holy Spirit will reveal much more than is covered in His word. Not that it adds to His word, don't misunderstand me. God's Spirit will unlock deeper meanings and truths we had never noticed before. I don't know how many times I have read a passage for six times and on the seventh time I get it! Of course, a lost person has no clue of the truths of God's word without His Holy Spirit!

They feared the Lord, yet served their own gods—according to the rituals of the nations from among whom they were carried away. (2 Kings 17:33)

I forgot to mention Samaria. That is the capitol of the northern kingdom and the northern kingdom is sometimes referred to as Samaria. Notice the mention of "high places" and the idols that were there. This is the reason God chose to remove the northern ten tribes. God uses Assyria to punish, and remove His people from their inheritance. Assyria brings in a lot of their people into the region. We will see the effects in the New Testament gospels.

Do you notice the wording of this verse? "They feared the Lord, yet served their own gods." Is that not a commentary on today. How many "professing" Christians do you know that live like the devil? That's sad, and God will not wink at it. Satan loves to copy the things of God. That's where Samaria comes in. Samaria is a "copy" of Jerusalem. A Jerusalem want-to-be. With temples to false gods etc.

O.k, let's look at the last part of that verse. Remember when Israel came into the Promised Land? What was God's instructions? Destroy the inhabitants. Did they? No. One verse in Joshua said, "And it happened, when the children of Israel grew strong, that they put the Canaanites to forced, but did not utterly drive them out." (Joshua 17:13).

It's just a little oversight, right? When God gives instructions, it is meant for our good. By allowing this "little" sin it caused ten tribes to lose their inheritance. The Canaanites corrupted God's people into following false gods. It was like a cancer that continued to grow until it killed the body.

This is so true of us today. We don't need prayer in school. Everyone should have the "freedom" to choose. It's a woman's body to do with as she pleases, right? It seems we have taken the word "freedom" to mean a lot more than God intended. We are free to choose. But our choices must be in line with God's standards. Statutes, judgments, ordinances, commandments, etc. These are not optional! We even have the "freedom" to choose to obey God or not. But be careful, are you willing to accept the consequences? Remember the northern kingdom.

"Now therefore, O Lord our God, I pray, save us from his hand, that
all the kingdoms of the earth may know that You are the Lord God,
You alone." (2 Kings 19:19)

Isn't it interesting how often we turn to God when things are going bad? We can
be going our merry way for years then suddenly something happens and NOW
we want God to take a hand. Maybe you need to be introduced first. That's like
totally ignoring a neighbor for years then suddenly you need his help, wow.

This is the beginning of the end. God has sent Assyria to remove Israel from
their land. Because of the prayer of Hezekiah that judgment has been postponed.
Through the prophet Isaiah God speaks to Hezekiah. It is amazing just how deep
the grace of God is. Over and over the ten tribes refuse to listen to God yet God
continues to give them opportunity after opportunity to repent. Finally, God has
had enough. Aren't you glad, He gives us chance after chance to have a meaningful
relationship with Him.

Hezekiah was a king of the southern two tribes. Here Assyria attempted to
take them. God delivered them. I have been talking like Hezekiah was a northern
king. God delivered the south but not the north. Look at the end of chapter 19.
This attack on God's people cost Sennacherib his life.

I just want you to keep this picture in mind. The two divisions of Israel,
northern ten tribes and southern two tribes. All the same people. The same people
that God gave an inheritance to. Yet ten refused to follow the very God that gave
them the victory. The south struggled on and off with obeying God but God never
gave up on them.

Hezekiah always seemed to be seeking God's help. Either in battle or in
sickness. The thing, I think, that kept God near was Hezekiah's faith. He turned
to God in times of trouble. Where the northern tribes turned to their idols. God
wants us seeking Him all the time. Sure, it seems that it is only when we need help.
There should also be times of praise. But because of our faith we turn to the one
true God who hears us. That's why it is so important to maintain that relationship
with God. Is there anything between you and God that hinders!

"And I will not make the feet of Israel wander anymore from the land which I gave their fathers—only if they are careful to do according to all that I have commanded them, and according to all the law that My servant Moses commanded them." (2 Kings 21:8)

Good old Manasseh. Here was one of those evil kings who ruled the southern kingdom. Notice verse two of this chapter, "And he did evil in the sight of the Lord, according to the abominations of the nations whom the Lord had cast out before the children of Israel." One more note, look at the beginning of verse 3, "For he rebuilt the high places."

Manasseh was king for fifty-five years. One of the longest reigning kings. Notice, Hezekiah was his father. Here is the example I was writing about earlier. From one of the best kings to one of the worst, father, son. I guess we could go all the way back to Cain and Able.

I want to remind you about reading the listed chapters for each day. When you get a "big picture" of the events we are looking at you can better understand what God is doing. To really grasp the context of the Old Testament you need to read all of it!

Again, look at the next verse, "But they paid no attention, and Manasseh seduced them to do more evil. "

How closely do you follow the leaders of our country? How informed are you about what is going on in your government? You would be surprised how much the actions of those in leadership affect our lives. The great thing about America is that we have a voice in who our leaders are. Israel didn't!

We also can affect our own lives. We make decisions every day that can affect the rest of our lives! I decided, as a teenager, to not finish school. I got my G.E.D. in the United States Air Force, but that decision has haunted me for the rest of my life.

Of course, the greatest decision I ever made was to ask Jesus into my heart. But that wasn't until I was thirty-five. I had so much to catch up on!

One last thought. Look at verse 12 of this chapter. "Therefore, thus says the Lord God of Israel: 'Behold, I am bringing such calamity upon Jerusalem and Judah, that whoever hears of it, both his ears will tingle." There are consequences to ignoring God and the prompting of His Holy Spirit.!

> Then the king stood by a pillar and made a covenant before the Lord, to follow the Lord and to keep His commandments and His testimonies and His statutes, with all his heart and all his soul, to perform the words of this covenant that were written in this book. And all the people took a stand for the covenant." (2 Kings 23:3)

In the first two verses of chapter 23 I underlined the word ALL. Look how many times God used that term (five). Everyone gathered together, why? To read the word of God. Oh, and where was that book of the covenant found? In the temple, the house of the Lord. If you are attending a church and there is no Bible to be found or read, if your Sunday school class doesn't teach the word of God—Run!

Josiah, in the verse above, makes a commitment, not only of himself but the nation to heed the words of the Law. I'm not going to quote it but in verse five Josiah removes the high places!

One more reference. Look at 23:21,22, "Then the king commanded all the people, saying, 'keep the Passover to the Lord your God, as it is written in this Book of the Covenant. Such a Passover surely had never been held since the days of the judges who judged Israel."

Here is a nation that was almost defeated by Assyria and this new king, Josiah, found the Book of the Covenant, the Bible in those days. And began to read and follow the instructions that God had given in the Book. Remember the Passover was described in Exodus, instituted in Leviticus. It is a constant reminder of what God has done for us.

I don't think there is a better picture of what Christ has done for us than the Passover picture in Exodus 12. When the death angel sees the blood on the door he will "Passover" those inside who had the faith in God's command to apply the blood to the doorposts.

Notice the commitment, in this verse, by Josiah. "with all his heart and soul." It didn't mention his mind, interesting. How many decisions do we make relying on our mind, head knowledge? How many decisions are made by the heart? Micah 6:8 and Deuteronomy 10:12-13 say, heart, mind and soul. All must be a part of our, decision making process. I wonder how many people have missed heaven because the requirements were so simple that it didn't seem possible? They analyze with their mind but miss heaven with their heart.

Shem, Arphaxad, Shelah, Eber, Peleg, Reu, Serug, Nahor, Terah,
and Abram, who is Abraham. The sons of Abraham were Isaac and
Ishmael. (1 Chronicles 1:24-28)

These are some tough chapters to read. Let me challenge you to look over these
names. The reason I chose these verses above are the names. These names link
Noah to Abraham. These are the same names listed in the eleventh chapter of
Genesis. Then in Genesis we go from Abraham, Isaac, Jacob and Joseph. Except
Joseph doesn't figure in the "scarlet thread" we are looking at. In the 39th chapter
of Genesis we find the connection to the last chapter of Ruth. Perez is mention in
Genesis, in Ruth we take the genealogy to David. David, Solomon, Rehoboam,
etc. When you read these verses look for names that you recognize from your
reading this year.

Since we are talking about names I want to give you two more names that are
not that significant in the genealogy but may be interesting. They may be familiar
names, but maybe not in the Bible.

The first is Ichabod. He appears in 1 Samuel chapter four. Israel had just
lost a battle and the Ark of the Covenant was captured by the Philistines. When
the news reached this mother, she gave birth to a son. She said this, Then, she
named the child Ichabod, saying "The glory of the Lord has departed from Israel!"
because the ark of God has been captured and because of her father-in-law and her
husband. (4:21). I think there is a telling picture here. I think Israel's faith was in
the ark and not in the God who reigns over it! That's not good. Israel had placed
their faith in the ark and not the God of the ark.

The second name I want to look at is Ebenezer. He appears in 1 Samuel
chapter 7. In verse 12 we read, Then Samuel took a stone and set it up between
Mizpah and Shen, and called its name Ebenezer, saying, "Thus far the Lord has
helped us." One of my favorite Baptist hymns is, "Come Thou Fount of Every
Blessing" and in verse 2 that word "Ebenezer" is used. Always reminds me of the
Bible verse.

So, what is the point? Here are two contrasting events. Ichabod meaning the
glory of God has departed. And Ebenezer meaning God has helped us. I think
of those two perspectives in our relationship with God. Which describes your
relationship?

And Jabez called on the God of Israel saying, "Oh, that you would bless me indeed, and enlarge my territory, that Your hand would be with me, and that You would keep me from evil, that I may not cause pain!" So, God granted him what he requested. (1 Chronicles 4:10)

Have you read the book about this verse? I haven't. It's interesting how God can put little islands of hope and encouragement in the middle of dull passages. Here we are reading along about these names that mean little or nothing to us then up pops Jabez. He does the same thing in Genesis. Look at chapter five. Your reading along, again another list of genealogies, life span and when they died then in verse 24 this verse pops out, "And Enoch walked with God; and he was not, for God took him." Isn't that interesting? Does that mean he didn't die or God decided to take him home? It's just dropped in there and if you're not looking carefully you miss it. It says, "he walked with God." We have been talking about our walk with God, haven't we?

That's the point of this verse about Jabez isn't it? That God would be with Jabez and that God would bless him. Don't we all desire that relationship? Another thing, Jabez asked, that God would bless him. Is this a "name it and claim it" type relationship? I think not. The New Testament is quite clear that God is not a Viza or Mastercard.

I mentioned yesterday about a hymn called, "Come Thou Fount of Every Blessing." I first noticed that hymn in a movie called, "Love Comes Softly." In the movie, a farmer had lost his barn and tries to explain to his wife that God was still with him. He explained that just because he was walking next to his daughter doesn't mean she will always be safe. The same is true with God. God desires that intimate relationship, but that doesn't mean no harm will come.

Now that my children have grown and left home I still worry about them. Do I want the best for them? Yes! I can't be with them twenty-four seven. Even if I was that doesn't mean something won't happen. The peace that comes with walking with God comes from just knowing He's there! Knowing that He wants the best for us. But then when trials happen He is also right there with us to encourage us, pick us up, and put us back on track. To me that is what walking with God is all about!

> But Aaron and his sons offered sacrifices on the altar of burnt offerings
> and on the altar of incense, for all the work of the Most Holy Place and
> to make atonement for Israel, according to all that Moses the servant
> of God had commanded. (1 Chronicles 6:49)

No, you haven't missed anything. First and Second Chronicles are a recap, or review of previous events. Now that we've finished the genealogies we are going back. Think of it like the gospels. Another "angle" of the same story. Someone once said that First and Second Samuel were from man's viewpoint and Chronicles was from God's viewpoint. Whatever the case there are some things covered here that were not covered in Samuel. Just as in the gospel accounts.

We are about through with lists. Be patient, continue to read. God is simply reminding us of the past events to prepare us for Ezra and Nehemiah.

There is an interesting passage here that supports what I have long suspected. God loves music. Look at verses 31,32. Talking about the choir members who sing before the Lord. I don't think it is an accident that every "worship" service begins with music. For me those old gospel hymns prepare me for worship!

Lately when I get to church early, before the service begins I pick up a hymnal and begin with page one and go through and see how many I know the tune to. Of course, then I sing it to myself. I'm surprised at how many I know. Of course, I have been attending for over thirty years. Just that little time blesses me so much.

How would you like to be known as "the servant of God?" Here they are talking of Moses of course. Remember, I quoted this before. The most awesome words we could possibly hear when we get to heaven would be the words of Jesus saying, "Well done thou good and faithful servant" (Matthew 25:21).

It's going to seem endless, these lists of names and places. Don't give up. It's like looking at your family tree. See if there are names you recognize, things you hadn't known before. Remember that this is the word of God. Did you notice the nugget (verse) above? There are gems like this all through God's word. Little islands that you would miss by skipping over them.

These were the heads of the fathers' houses by their generations, chief
men. These dwelt in Jerusalem. (1 Chronicles 8:28)

Here is a good place to give an observation I made a few years ago. It's about the
word Jerusalem. Do you notice anything interesting about that word? Take a
close look. Look at the heart of the word. JER-USA-LEM. Yes, the letters U.S.A.
I don't begin to know the mind of God. I just think that it's very interesting.

More names, more genealogy. I got hooked on genealogy a few years back. I
managed to trace both my ancestry and my wife's back to the Mayflower. Speaking
of the Mayflower if you ever have opportunity to read the Mayflower Compact.
This was the first "constitution", if you will, of the settlers when they began
colonizing our country.

Why was it so important for Israel to track their genealogy? You remember
a few days ago I made the point of following the lineage from Abraham to Judah
to David and then Solomon. Judah was one of twelve sons. He was the fourth in
line. That was the line God chose to provide the vehicle for His Son to be born on
this earth. In Matthew, if you notice, Matthew begins with Abraham. Matthew's
gospel was written, primarily, to the Jews. Luke's gospel goes all the way back to
Adam. Luke was written to Gentiles. This is a fascinating study to follow.

Ok, let's get personal. How about your Christian genealogy? Both my wife and
myself are not sure about our parents. Again, we weren't saved till our thirties. Our
daughters are saved. Each generation must pass on their Christian heritage. I think
Israel is a good example with the northern kingdom, turning to idols once they
separated from the southern kingdom. Once they moved away from Jerusalem
they thought they could establish their own place of worship in Samaria. It didn't
work.

Remember Uzza? Only the Levites could handle the ark. Genealogy was
important there. Remember Saul, he was from the tribe of Benjamin. Abraham
said the scepter would not pass from Judah (Genesis 49:10). The rulers were to be
from the tribe of Judah. Israel got ahead of God's plan.

How far back can you trace your "Christian" heritage? Is it something to be
proud of or are you the first in your family? Cherish it!

> So all Israel was recorded by genealogies, and indeed, they were inscribed in the book of the kings of Israel. But Judah was carried away captive to Babylon because of their unfaithfulness. (1 Chronicles 9:1)

When was the first time you heard the word "captivity" referring to Israel? Until I had begun reading the Old Testament regularly and thoroughly I had no idea what it meant and why God would allow the southern kingdom to be captured. We talked about this earlier.

God told Israel in Leviticus to allow the land to rest one out of every seven years. (Leviticus 25:3) They didn't! So, this went on for 490 years. God's punishment? Remove the people for 70 years. God will have His will done one way or the other. The challenge is to recognize it. Of course, Israel had it written in the Law.

Notice the verse says, "Judah" was taken. That is the name for the southern kingdom consisting of the tribes of Judah and Benjamin. These two tribes, despite a few bad kings, remained faithful to God. For the most part, they did not destroy the "high places" but there were several revivals and recommitments. The same cannot be said for the northern ten tribes. They never had a godly king. Therefore, God sent the Assyrians to remove them from the land forever.

I am not forgetting the promise that God made to Israel that there would always be a remnant. I guess in a sense "Jerusalem" was that remnant.

Why this endless list of names? Remember this was Israel's document of record. So why do we call it God's word? Is all of it God's word? Let me ask you this, what would you remove? Do you have any authority to believe some and ignore other parts? Let me give you a verse in Revelation: For I testify to everyone who hears the words of the prophecy of this book: if anyone adds to these words, God will add to him the plagues that are written in this book; and if anyone takes away from the words of the book of this prophesy, God will take away his part from the Book of Life, from the holy city, and from the things which are written in this book. (Revelation 22:18-19)

I call this my copyright for the book of the Bible. Some say it only applies to Revelation. The whole Bible is God's word!

> Therefore, all the elders of Israel came to the king of Hebron, and David made a covenant with them at Hebron before the Lord. And they anointed David king over Israel, according to the word of the Lord by Samuel. (1 Chronicles 11:3)

I mentioned before that David was anointed three times. Once by Samuel at his father Jesse's house. Next as king of Hebron, and then as king of Israel here. I think it's interesting that Hebron is the territory that God gave to Caleb after claiming the Promised Land.

You notice that Jerusalem is referred to as "the city of David" (11:5) in the gospels Bethlehem is called the city of David. Bethlehem is only six to eight miles outside of Jerusalem, a suburb you might say.

Only chapter ten is given to the brief events of Saul. Then in chapter eleven it begins with David's anointing. Why would God write another book recording the events in David's life? Like I said, it's the same principle as the reason for four gospels. If you had a party and invited five guests to the party. Then in a week you asked each of the five guests what happened at the party there would be five different answers. All attended the same party. All participated in the same events but each had a different perspective of the same event.

Myself, I think God wants us to know David intimately. God wants the same fire, the same dedication, the relationship with us that He had with David. But David wasn't perfect! That's the point. God doesn't expect us to be "perfect" He expects us to WALK with Him. As we go through the Old Testament I'd like you to notice the number of times God uses the word "walk" referring to a relationship with Him.

We not only have the picture of a "relationship" but we also see that we are both headed somewhere, a destination. In Jeremiah 29 it says that God has a plan for us. King James uses the word "thoughts" but it's the same idea. God is walking with us to a destination of God's choosing. He wants to walk with us to guide us, protect us, and to teach us along the way!

David is as a pioneer was in the forming of our country. David led the way, blazed the trail, if you will, now we need to follow that trail. David noted the pitfalls that we are to avoid and marked the oasis for our refreshment. Study and watch David as we read through Chronicles!

"For because you did not do it the first time, the Lord our God broke out against us, because we did not consult Him about the proper order." (1 Chronicles 15:13)

O h, there is so much here! First, this chapter clears up a lot about Uzza in 2 Samuel. Why God chose to strike Uzza. I guess David missed this lesson in Sunday school.

When God gives specific instructions, He expects them to be carried out. God, in Exodus, in the creation and transport of the Ark of the Covenant gave instructions that there would be rings on each side where poles would be inserted and the "priest" would carry the ark. (Exodus 25:14)

You will notice in the verses surrounding this one that David made it a point to consult with the Levites. Just out of curiosity, where do you get your spiritual advice? Tv, radio, or the Word of God? How about, maybe, praying and asking God for direction?

There have been so many mistakes, you can read some in scripture, that have been made by not consulting God in prayer. Remember the Gibeonites in the book of Joshua chapter 9? They came to Joshua claiming to be from a far country. Their whole purpose was to deceive Joshua and get a treaty with Israel. Notice what Joshua did when Israel was defeated at Ai? God helped him solve that.

You have a decision coming up shortly. How are you going to know what path to take? As a believer, I think it is so important that we listen to God's Spirit within us. I don't know how many times I've started down a certain path and God's Spirit never gave me a "peace" about that path. Sometimes it just takes a simple prayer at the moment of decision. We will see that when we get to Ezra.

One other note. If you're wondering, we will get to the gospels in the first week of October. Be patient. Meanwhile chew on as much of the Old Testament teachings as you can. It doesn't change just because Jesus arrived. Jesus said, "I didn't come to destroy the Law but to fulfill it!" (Matthew 5:17)

I've been bragging on David a lot. But in the case of Uzza David learned a lesson the hard way. How do we learn our lessons? How much of God's "principles" do we know and apply to our daily lives. Just a thought. You know Jesus practiced prayer regularly, do you?

"So, let it be established, that Your name may be magnified forever, saying, 'The Lord of Hosts, the God of Israel, is Israel's God.' And let the house of Your servant David be established before You." (1 Chronicles 17:24)

Just a note about yesterday's reading. Look at verse 18 of chapter 15. Remember I said you never know what you might find in genealogies? I have this underlined in my Bible. Do you see it? One of these guys is named "Ben." Really? With all these names so long and hard for us to pronounce we find Ben.

Here's another passage, probably the same event but I can't help but note it. Beginning in verse 16 of this chapter make note of how many times David refers to himself as "servant." (10). You might think that someone who walked as close to God as David did, that he might use a different word to describe his relationship with God. This was David's heart. Therefore, God blessed him so much. Therefore, David is the standard used to measure all future kings.

First and second Chronicles aren't that long. Kind of a brief overview of how Israel arrived at being removed from their land by Babylon and Assyria. It's almost an introduction to Ezra and Nehemiah. Take the time to review these events. Is there a lesson here for me?

These ten references to "servant" are in a prayer that David is offering to God. That is his heart. David asked that his house be established before God. Remember Saul's approach? He thought that by killing David his house would be established. That's not God's plan. God's ways are always best!

Here in this chapter (17) we see also where David wanted to build the temple for the ark. At first Nathan said, "go ahead." But God later, in a dream Nathan had, told him no. So, David threw a fit and refused to listen to God any further. NO! David accepted God's judgment and proceeded to gather all the materials for Solomon. It's in this same chapter that David prays his "servant" prayer.

What is our response when God closes a door? We know for sure that it is the right thing, right? God must be wrong, He can't know the circumstances, really? The same God that wants only the best for His children will deny you something good, I don't think so!

Then King David said to Ornan, "No, but I will surely buy it for the full price, for I will not take what is yours for the Lord, nor offer burnt offerings with that which costs me nothing." (1 Chronicles 21:24)

Now why would God think it necessary to repeat this episode again? (2 Samuel 24:24). Remember all scripture was written through the leadership of the Holy Spirit. Remember what 2 Timothy 3:16-17 says, "All Scripture is given by inspiration of God, and is profitable for doctrine, for reproof, for instruction in righteousness, that the man of God may be complete, thoroughly equipped for every good work." That is such an important concept that we must grasp.

David sinned by taking a census God did not approve. God gave David a choice of punishments. I hope you've read these chapters. David chose three days of plague. David was looking to restore his relationship with God. He was told to build an altar. David went to Ornan to purchase the materials and the offering. Ornan offered them to David for free. As a favor to David. How easy it would have been to take the offer and make peace with God. But David didn't

Even Adam and Eve saw the price for their sin. When God expelled them from the garden He could have just let them leave with their fig leaves. No, there was a blood price that needed to be paid (Genesis 3:21). God is forever trying to restore our relationship with Him. Even to the point of sending His Son to the cross to restore that relationship. The point is that we paid <u>nothing</u> for the restoration. It was all God's doing. We didn't have to lift a finger—just believe!

For many, that is too high a price to pay, can you believe it?

It's not like that amount of money was going to hurt David. He was rich, he could afford it. That isn't the point. You know it! The point is the principle of the act. David had to show God that he wanted to restore that relationship. Have you reached out to God? How is your relationship with the Almighty?

That is the great thing I like about the Old Testament. The principles are taught by illustration, by story, by example! For me the book of Proverbs is hard to grasp, even some of the teachings of Jesus or Paul, but to have them demonstrated in the life of David brings them home like no other! What have you offered God lately?

For David said, "The Lord God of Israel has given rest to His people, that they may dwell in Jerusalem forever." (1 Chronicles 23:25)

Did you catch that? Where does peace and rest come from? Only God can make the world around us peaceful! The kingdom may have peace. But David's family is another story.

Remember, God said David could not build the temple because there was strife. A lot of the "strife" was in David's family. How much was of David's own making is hard to say. Remember in Exodus that sometimes God hardened Pharaoh's heart. The strife in David's life was in direct response from God for his affair with Bathsheba.

God had forgiven David, David had made amends with God but there are still consequences! Mark this down. God's forgiveness does not negate the consequences for some sins.

I want to remind you of David's response to God denying David the desire to build the temple. This is very important. As a Christian for over thirty years I talk to people all the time that think they will get even with God for something they think God did to them by turning their back on God. It doesn't work that way. Your turning your back on the one person who can remedy the situation. Your blaming the wrong person. You should be looking at yourself and thanking God that He is always there reaching out to restore that relationship.

I think I have read through the Bible several times using this schedule. I still have so much to learn. I will never get tired of opening His word in the morning and seeing what God has to say.

Each verse, each chapter, even though I've read it dozens of times, this morning will speak to a need I have that day. It still amazes me!

Just the study of David's relationship with God challenges me to seek that kind of relationship. Fellowship with the God of the universe is not sacrilegious It's what God desires more than anything. To have a close, intimate relationship with His children. Not only through His word but also through listening and obeying the promptings of His Holy Spirit that lives within us.

Be patient with these readings. So, we look at a verse again, maybe it's something that needs to be reinforced! Myself, I'm so dense I need to read something several times before I get it!

But David did not take the number of those twenty years old and
under, because the Lord had said He would multiply Israel like the
stars of the heavens. (1 Chronicles 27:23)

It doesn't seem like a big deal, does it? But it is a great example of David's obedience
to God's direction. Do you remember this promise? It was given to Abraham in
Genesis 22:17. God keeps His promises.

We have talked about the relationship David had with God and how David
made so many mistakes yet he walked with God. Let's refresh our memories!

Do you remember God's relationship with Abraham? For now, we will begin
with Abraham. Adam is pretty much the same story. Abraham's faith in God was
such that he left a very prestigious environment, packed up his family and led only
by God's Spirit went to Canaan. Great, except when it came to God's promise of
offspring what did Abraham do? He tried it his way, or more accurately Sarah's
way. Anyway, it didn't work. Did God give up on Abraham? Of course not. How
about Jacob? Jacob wrestled with God for a long time about His leadership. After
God blessed him with Laban, four wives thirteen children and flocks and herds,
Jacob acknowledged God and built an altar to God at Bethel.

Let's look at Saul. God called Saul to be their first king. It went to Saul's
head. So much so that God removed His hand from Saul. Saul was so desperate
to find God that he sought a fortune teller. Saul refused to trust God and walk
in His ways.

Then theirs David. Again, David made some grievous mistakes for sure. But
he always came back to God, asked forgiveness and repented.

You know the point I'm trying to make. First, God is always ready to make
amends and restore the relationship with Him. It's we who refuse or are reluctant
to approach God. That's sad. Second, we all make mistakes, sometimes we drift
away from God sometimes it's deliberate rebellion. Either way, again, God wants
to restore that relationship. But do you?

It's so much easier to live without God and all His rules and convictions.
Really? Think about that for a minute. A heavenly Father who wants only the
best, and you reject Him.

"O Lord God of Abraham, Isaac, and Israel, our fathers, keep this forever in the intent of the thoughts of the heart of Your people, and fix their heart toward You." (1 Chronicles 29:18)

What a cool prayer! I have stressed many times how David, when told he could not build the temple gathered all the materials, look at verses 16 and 17. Who does David give the glory to for the abundance of materials to build the temple? God of course! Hey, that was my idea, God only helped. Seriously! That's part of David's walk with God. Knowing where every blessing comes from. Just getting out of bed in the morning is a blessing from God.

David is just overwhelmed by God's daily blessing. To see his son, Solomon, doing what David wanted to do. David offers up this prayer. Thanking God just for the privilege of seeing it.

Twice in this verse David mentions the heart of the people. That is a key point. You see, what is the step we take when we become a child of God? We ask Jesus to come where? We want Jesus in our heart! Not in our mind, or thoughts, but solely in our heart. Because that's where love is. What better place for the Son of God to dwell. We know that Jesus dwells there in the person of the Holy Spirit!

The God of Abraham (imperfect Abraham), the God Isaac and Israel (Jacob). Can you say that? The God of my father—. I hope so! It is important that we can pass on our spiritual heritage as well as our family heritage. Understand you are not saved because your father or mother was. This is a decision you must make for yourself.

What an awesome request: "and fix their heart toward you." That should be the prayer of every parent. That their children would fix their heart toward God. Fix is the picture of a permanent direction. Like a sailor getting a fix on the stars for guidance. Determined by a fixed object to determine their direction. That's what God wants us to do. Get a fix on God's direction and head that way.

As we finish First Chronicles ponder what we have read. Half of the book, it seems, was taken up with genealogies. A chapter on Saul and the rest with David's life. Leading up to Solomon taking the throne. Try to ponder why God would want to review these facts. What is that He is trying to get across in our walk?

But who is able to build Him a temple, since heaven and the heaven
of heavens cannot contain Him? Who am I then, that I should build
Him a temple, except to burn sacrifice before Him? (2 Chronicles 2:6)

I have noticed something about Israel. It seems they tend to put their faith in the things of God instead of God. Whether it's the Ark of the Covenant or the Temple. We saw that with Nehushtan in 2 Kings. They take the things of God and turn them into idols. Which God hates. Constructing the temple didn't keep God from sending them into exile. It was disobedience!

This is an interesting picture. Solomon is talking about the enormity of God and yet, as Christians, we have God living within us in the person of the Holy Spirit. Wow!

Solomon, as king, is preparing to construct one of the seven wonders of the ancient world. We can only surmise the grandeur of this magnificent structure. God goes into great detail about this temple. In Ezra, they remnant that returns tries to build a replacement temple. The older people cry because it didn't match the original. Again, they missed the point. It's not the building it's the relationship.

Have you seen pictures of the cathedrals on the east coast? Magnificent. Yet how many are packed with believers? How many of our grand churches are full of believers? Are they going there to meet with God or to enjoy the grand edifice?

And yet in the lowest Christian their dwells the Holy Spirit. In 1 Corinthians 6 we read, "Do you not know that your body is the temple of the Holy Spirit who is in you, whom you have from God, and you are not your own? For you are bought at a price; therefore, glorify God in your body and in your spirit, which are God's." (6:19-20)

I'm not making light of the Temple. It was God's will and God's direction but I think Israel missed the point. At one time, it is said that God filled the temple with His presence. Chapter five of second Chronicles describes God's filling the temple with His "Shekinah" glory! But to them temple became a demonstration of God's presence instead of their obedience to His commands. God wants an intimate relationship not an object between us and Him.

Take a minute and examine your relationship with the Almighty!

If My people who are called by My name will humble themselves, and pray and seek My face, and turn from their wicked ways, then I will hear from heaven, and forgive their sin and heal their land. (2 Chronicles 7:14)

What an awesome verse! How many revivals have been built on this verse alone? It's a challenge and a promise from God. Here is that theme again, obedience to God's commands. I was reminded again this morning about what Jesus said in John 14, verse 15, "If you love Me, keep My commandments." It is just that simple.

If My people (Christians or Israel?) who are called by My name will humble themselves and seek my face. I think that gives the idea of an up close and personal relationship with God. I know I keep stressing that point but we can see throughout the Old Testament how Israel missed the point, except David! I think David had the right idea. David knew where he stood with God. Right from the beginning in his battle with Goliath David knew where his strength lay.

I want to challenge you to remember this verse. I'm not big on memorizing. At least you can remember the address. 2 Chronicles 7:14.

Don't skip over that little word "pray" in this verse. God said that we communicate with Him through prayer. For something we neglect so freely, it was paramount in Jesus' life. Read the gospels, how many times does it say that Jesus got alone and prayed. He prayed in the garden three times to try to change God's mind, but in the end obeyed His Father!

Notice, of course, that God has some requirements to His blessing. Humble yourself, pray, seek His face, etc. THEN I will heal their land. Don't miss that. God wants, so much, to have that intimate relationship with us. We want so much for God to bless us. You can't have one without the other!

Most of the time this verse is used prior to revivals to essentially "prepare" the congregation for revival. Most people think the purpose of revival is to win people to Christ. We measure a revival by the number of professions made. A revival is just what this verse says, getting God's people back on track. Focused on God, prayer, cleaning up some things in their life—then revival happens!

> "Blessed be the Lord your God, who delighted in you, setting you on
> His throne to be king for the Lord your God! Because your God has
> loved Israel, to establish them forever, therefore, He made you king
> over them to do justice and righteousness." (2 Chronicles 9:8)

This verse sounds like something maybe Solomon might have said. It's not. These are the words of the Queen of Sheba. It's hard to look at this verse, when we know what happens. Solomon had such a blessing from God. Solomon simply asked God to be a good king. God blessed him beyond his expectations. And what did Solomon do with that special relationship with God? He squandered it! He was led astray. If Solomon can fall prey to the wiles of the devil what chance do we have?

The Queen of Sheba was so impressed with what GOD had done for Israel. She recognized that God was working through Solomon. It wasn't Solomon's doing.

This can so easily happen to us. We marvel at what God does and sometimes we begin to think that it's all us. That is why God uses the simple things to confound the wise. The Queen said that God had established Israel forever. He has. Just think of the miracle in 1948. Years had passed. It seemed Israel was no more. Then in 1948 Israel was recognized by the United States and other countries as a sovereign nation. Never count out the providence of God. His promises are as sure as the sunrise each morning!

I think it is interesting that in both passages, both in 1 Kings and here she refers to God as Solomon's God. I wonder if Solomon ever shared his faith with her? Interesting thought. She clearly recognized where his greatness came from.

In these same chapters, we see the end of Solomon's reign. The reign is passed on to Rehoboam, his son. It's a shame Rehoboam didn't seek God's leadership in the decisions he made. Isn't it interesting that Rehoboam consulted the old men, then his peers, but it never says he consulted God.

Solomon can be a great example of our approach to God's wisdom. The book of Proverbs talks a lot about wisdom. We see clearly that Solomon's wisdom came from God. So why did he get drawn away by his wives? It is so easy to be drawn away from God's influence. The problem is we "let" it happen, instead of staying focused on God's will for our lives we begin thinking we know more than God!

"For the eyes of the Lord run to and fro throughout the whole earth,
to show Himself strong on behalf of those whose heart is loyal to Him.
(2 Chronicles 16:9)

Don't miss the truth of this verse. Do you know anyone who tried to run from God? Jonah, thought he could run away from God's call. It cost him some nights in the belly of a big fish! Do we think we can hide from God? Of course, we do. Otherwise this "Christian" nation wouldn't have the degree of sin that is so prevalent! We don't think God is watching, or maybe we think He just winks at our transgressions. Judgment is sure, though maybe not swift!

I heard a youth minister once tell his students that according to the Bible God is with us everywhere we go. Even in the back seat of your car. That got their attention.

I love the last part of that verse. Again, the reference to the "heart," a heart that is loyal. That is so critical. I begin to sound like a broken record talking about that relationship with God, but it's true. Until you make that commitment to "walk" with God daily and talk to God in prayer, and worship Him on the Lord's day in His church there is no loyalty there.

There are so many blended families today. Some parents only get to see their kids occasionally depending on which parent has custody. It is so hard to maintain a close relationship in that situation. Can that be the case with God? How much time do you spend with God verses time spent in the world?

School is a great example. Our children spend many hours a day in their classroom listening to a teacher fill their heads with who knows what. They spend maybe one hour a week in a Sunday school class. Maybe two if they get to hear a sermon. The difference is overwhelming! The influence is scary!

I remember the quote I heard once from, I believe it was D.L. Moody, "The world is yet to see what God can do with a life fully committed to Him." That really impacted me as a young Christian. In a since I think that is what this verse is saying. God is always looking for someone willing to take that daily walk with Him, and follow where He leads!

"Nevertheless, good things are found in you, in that you have removed
the wooden images from the land, and have prepared your heart to
seek God." (2 Chronicles 19:3)

This is one of those verses you can meditate on for some time. The "nevertheless" about Jehoshaphat is that he doesn't choose his friends very well. Jehu has rebuked him for his alliance with Ahab. But notice what Jehu says, "good things are found in you." That is so much how God looks at us. When we don't think there is any hope, God sees a spark in us that no one else sees. We need to pray and ask God to reveal that special gift He has given us.

Notice what Jehoshaphat has already accomplished. He removed the idols from the land. We talked earlier about the "high places" here Jehoshaphat has removed what puts a wedge between God and Judah. He has done a good thing, Jehu commends him for that, it's a start. For us the start is accepting Christ as our Savior. That begins our relationship with the Father.

After becoming a Christian God gives us a gift. A special gift comes with the indwelling Holy Spirit. A gift that God uses to serve Him. Notice the important step that Jehoshaphat has done on his own. "prepared your heart to seek God." That is so important! Look at Jeremiah 29:13, "And you will seek Me and find Me, when you search for Me with all your heart." There is a requirement to seeking God! "With all your heart."

How do you prepare your heart to seek God? Of course, as we have discussed many times, you need to begin with a relationship. Next you need to ask God what His plan is for your life. God's not going to tell you the schedule for the next three weeks, He wants you to trust Him. He will guide you, moment by moment, if you listen! It must be a commitment on your part.

God did some great things through Jehoshaphat. He also made some bad judgments. Just like David, God blessed Jehoshaphat for his seeking God's guidance. That is our daily challenge. The Holy Spirit inhabits us for a reason. To many times we just ignore Gods prompting and leadership and try doing things our own way. It won't work. That's all part of that relationship thing.

> Then the Spirit of God came upon Zechariah the son of Jehoiada the priest, who stood above the people, and said to them, "Thus says God: 'Why do you trespass the commandments of the Lord, so that you cannot prosper? Because you have forsaken the Lord, He also has forsaken you." (2 Chronicles 24:20)

It's interesting how many times God's word talks about "prosper". We all want to prosper. I don't mean getting rich. I mean making ends meet, getting along comfortably. Here is one of my favorite verses pertaining to prospering, "This Book of the Law shall not depart from your mouth, but you shall meditate in it day and night, that you may observe to do according to all that is written in it. For then you will make your way *prosperous* and then you shall have good success." (Joshua 1:8) (emphasis added)

Let me urge you to note these two verses in the front of your Bible and check them out regularly. Joshua 1:8 and Jeremiah 29:11-13. Talk about gems! Both promise a blessing if we seek God's guidance and meditate on His word. There are others that we will add as we go along. We already covered Joshua 1:8 when we were in Joshua. God also tells Joshua to "be of good courage."

That last verse is so sad. The problem is that if we continue to ignore God's prompting God will forsake us as He did Israel and Judah. Now if we are a child of God He simply puts us on a shelf and doesn't use us. If we are lost that is so dangerous! God's ear is always attuned to use when we seek salvation. But His convicting, Spirit may just move on.

Notice the measurement that God used here, "transgress the commandments of the Lord." That's obvious. When you ignore God's Law there are consequences. It's just like an unruly child. You can ignore him just so long before he does something you can't ignore any longer. Then you must act. God is the same way. He looked the other way when Israel refused to let the land rest one in seven years (Leviticus 25:3). Then the bill finally came due.

It's the same with our rebellion as a child of God. God may seem to ignore it for a while but one day that bill will come due. Then God will make things right, one way or another.

He sought God in the days of Zechariah, who had understanding in
the visions of God; and as long as he sought the Lord, God made him
prosper." (2 Chronicles 26:5)

What a fantastic principle. There's that word prosper again. Here we get the
formula to prosper. Understand this isn't a sure thing. We have seen with
the prophet Samuel that God looks on the heart (1 Samuel 16:7). The motive is
simple, glorify God. We will see later with one of the minor prophets that when
God began to bless them, they ruined it to their own desires. They fell away from
God. There are many entrepreneurs that will tell you that it was God who blessed
them. They recognize the source of their blessing.

Look at the verse before this one. There's that familiar phrase, "And he did
what was right in the sight of the Lord." Wouldn't that make a great notation on
a headstone? Here's another king who took the throne at a very young age (16).
Looking for wisdom and guidance, both from his peers and the Spirit of God. His
counselors also had to know what God was up to.

There is a time limit here. Did you catch that? "As long as he sought the Lord."
Here is a picture of that walk, and relationship I have been talking about. Picture
two people, you and the Lord, walking on this path. God is leading and you are
being blessed beyond imagination. Then suddenly you say, "I think I'll go this way."
God doesn't follow. What do you do? Go your own way of course! And you have
left the power that has brought you these great blessings. How long do you travel
that road before you realize your mistake?

This principle is so critical. I know because I did just that. And it has taken
me years to get back on that road. It's not worth the struggle, believe me!

I think there's a Baptist hymn that goes, "where He leads me I will follow."
What a great message. It's a challenge really. So how do I know where God is
going? That's the work of God's Holy Spirit living within the believer. When you
take off down that separate path He will tell you. But then we say, "I know what
I'm doing, trust me." Really? You know more than God?

Underline that word "prosper" here and look at the context!

Moreover, King Hezekiah and the leaders commanded the Levites to sing praise to the Lord with the words of David and of Asaph the seer. So, they sang praises with gladness, and they bowed their heads and worshipped. (2 Chronicles 29:30)

If you want to have some fun tell someone to look at verse 3 in chapter 4 of Hezekiah. See if they search their Bible. Hezekiah just sounds like it should be in the minor prophets.

Maybe we get the picture that the northern and southern kingdoms had no influence on each other. If you have read these chapters you see that most of the time they fought with each other. Look at verse 19 in chapter 28. "For the Lord brought Judah (southern kingdom) low because of Ahaz king of Israel (northern kingdom), for he had encouraged moral decline in Judah and had been continually unfaithful to the Lord." It reminds me of the birth of Jacob and Esau how they fought in Rebekah's womb. Two nations of God's people fighting among themselves.

Hezekiah was one of the great kings of the south. He made great reforms, attempting to bring the people back to God. (29:2). You can see the contrast between the northern kingdom and the southern by the two rulers, Ahaz and Hezekiah. Why God removed the northern ten tribes and allowed the Judah to return after their captivity with Babylon.

Here, again, the singing praises. What a great way to praise God. The theological messages in the hymns of old are precious! You can almost feel God's presence in the hymns. One thing that amazes me the most are the hymns of Fanny Crosby. Just look at the lyrics of her hymns. They are so vivid and up-lifting and yet Fanny Crosby was blind. Maybe she didn't have her eyesight but her relationship with God was amazing!

"They sang praise with gladness, and they bowed their heads and worshipped." Isn't that awesome? That is a picture of worship and praising God. A picture, I might add, you get nowhere else but in the house of God. I believe that is why Jesus was so adamant about establishing His church. (Matthew 16:18). We must come together regularly, if for no other reason, that to encourage one another, sure we can study our Bible and pray by ourselves. It's the fellowship that encourages us!

"With him is an arm of flesh; but with us is the Lord our God, to help
us and to fight our battles." And the people were strengthened by the
words of Hezekiah king of Judah. (2 Chronicles 32:8)

Here is Assyria again, trying to conquer the southern kingdom. God will use
this nation to punish Israel (northern kingdom) but He will use Babylon for
the south. Hezekiah recognized where the power is. It's interesting that he uses
the term "flesh" to describe the power of Assyria. If your familiar with the New
Testament, especially Paul's writings the flesh is how Paul describe the battle a
Christian faces each day.

We fight this battle every day. Do we trust in our own strength or do we
trust God? There is that element of faith that measures just how much we trust
God and then ourselves. Where does our faith lie? In fact, your eternal destiny is
based on your faith. Do you believe what God said through His preacher Paul?
"For by grace you have been saved through faith, and that of yourselves; it is a gift
of God." (Ephesians 2:8).

And of course, one of my favorite is in Matthew 9:29, "Then He touched their
eyes, saying, according to your faith be it unto you." The words of Jesus. That is
where Hezekiah's strength lay. Where is yours?

We are nearing the end of second Chronicles. We have traveled a long way.
Tomorrow I want to back out and take another overall view of where we have
traveled. It's always important to do that in our own lives. Where were we? Where
are we now? How did we get here? Where do we want to go from here? The
important question is, where is God in this journey?

One last note here. Look at verse 20 in chapter 32. "Now because of this
King Hezekiah and the prophet Isaiah, the son of Amoz, prayed and cried out to
heaven." There is where Hezekiah got the victory. Our relationship with God in
prayer is so important.

I heard a story about Dr. Jack Hyles, a pastor of a large church in Indiana. He
told us that every Sunday there were a group of believers in a small room in his
church praying for him through the whole service. Praying for God to move in a
fantastic way. Believe in prayer?

"Go, inquire of the Lord for me, and for those who are left in Israel and Judah, concerning the words of the book that is found; for great is the wrath of the Lord that is poured out on us, because our fathers have not kept the word of the Lord, to do according to all that is written in this book." (2 Chronicles 34:21)

What a profound way to end these six books (Samuel, Kings, Chronicles). Think back to our journey. We left the book of Judges in sad shape. Israel had fallen about as far as they could. Samuel, the last of the Judges, was told by the people, "we want to be like the other nations, we want a king." God gave them the desires of their heart, not God's heart. That didn't turn out to well. Then God raised up David.

We go from king David through his son Solomon to the book of Kings. An assortment of rulers, the nation Israel is split in two. Assyria takes the northern kingdom out of their homeland forever and Babylon removes the southern two tribes to Babylon, the Captivity period. We went from the low of the book of Judges to the high of the completion of Solomon's Temple to the low of being removed from their homeland.

Up and down, why? It all comes back to walking with God. When Israel listened to God and obeyed God, God took care of them. Even the good kings, like David, had their problems, but God was with them. David is a great example!

Notice in the verse above. The king, Josiah, discovers the Bible (Law). The five books of Moses. Look at his reaction. I remember when I was saved and this overwhelming hunger for God's word. To read it, study it, meditate on it. Sunday school, preaching, Bible study, I couldn't get enough. That is as it should be! How much time do you spend in God's word? I don't care if you stay in one book for a year or you follow this "through the Bible" schedule. Get into God's word!

Meditate on these last six books. Think about the journey the nation of Israel took. The further they strayed from God the worse it got. The closer they walked with God the more God blessed their efforts. It's true today, maybe not as profound as in the Old Testament, but just as sure. God is working today to change hearts and lives!

> Who is among you of all His people? May his God be with him, and
> let him go up to Jerusalem which is in Judah, and build the house of
> the Lord God of Israel (He is God), which is in Jerusalem. (Ezra 1:3)

Cyrus? Persia? What happened to Nebuchadnezzar and Babylon? Remember this is seventy years after Israel or Judah was taken captive. The sentence is up and God has ordained that the southern kingdom should return to the Promised Land. There is something I hadn't noticed here.

I noted that Israel's history, began with the Passover in Egypt. It is God's priority that interests me. From the Passover (salvation) to Mt. Sinai (Law) to the construction of the Tabernacle (church or worship) I think we can see what God's priority is. First, A relationship with Him through accepting Christ as our Savior. Second, His word, the Scriptures, the Word of God. Read the Gospel of John chapter one. And, third, worship, His church as Jesus put it in the New Testament. (Matthew 16:18)

What is interesting still is the priority of His restoration in Jerusalem. Logically you would first build a protective wall THEN reconstruct the Temple. No, God says, priority one is the temple. You see God doesn't deal in our logic but His priority. May I refresh your memory again?

Remember in Joshua when Israel was finally going to enter the Promised Land. What did God tell Joshua to do? First, cross over the Jordan then have his whole army circumcised. That is, proceed into enemy territory and then render your army helpless for three days. Why not do that "before" you cross the Jordan? Again, God's priority not our logic.

So why does God do things that way? If it was logic who gets the glory, we do. If it's God's way, God gets the glory! Enough said!

Here again we see another principle of God. God could have restored the temple just by speaking it into existence. But He chooses a man to fulfill the task. A man who takes on a hopeless, enormous task, just by faith, and the leadership of God—and works a miracle. Digest the events of this little book of Ezra and watch how God works through a man who is willing to take a step of faith and believe God to work a miracle!

> For Ezra had prepared his heart to seek the Law of the Lord, and to do
> it, and to teach statutes and ordinances in Israel. (Ezra 7:10)

I said once that I had done a word search in my Bible program for the phrase "remember me." I would love to do another search on the phrase "prepared his heart." Just what do you think that means? It might mean checking with God for a peace and direction for the next challenge in his life. It could mean drawing strength from God's presence in his life to accomplish what might seem an impossible task. You meditate on that thought, "prepare your heart."

There's that Sunday school teacher again. Ezra's assignment was to rebuild the temple. Why would he be concerned with teaching and obeying the Law? The Law is the foundation of purpose for our lives. God's desire is our obedience and thereby a strong relationship with Him. I've mentioned this before, John 14. This is cool. John 14 is one of my favorite chapters and then to find this sentence spoken by Jesus is so cool! "If you love Me, keep My commandments." John 14:15.

The very best way to have that special relationship with God is to obey His word. What happened to Adam and Eve? God just said, "don't eat of that tree" but what did they do? All through the Old Testament we see kings who followed God's commands and those who didn't. It's just that simple!

This was an important time for the remnant who returned to Israel. Ezra had all kinds of problems trying to accomplish his task. Opposition from Satan, etc. When you finish this book, notice something toward the end. What did the people of Israel do? The same thing that cost them their land in the first place. They allowed pagans to mingle with God's people.

When the New Testament says not to be unequally yoked (2 Corinthians 6:14). God had a reason for including that in His word. Most think this is primarily for marriage. It's not just that, it's in business, in relationships, etc. Any opportunity the devil must draw us away from God he will use it. We talked about walking that path with God. It is so easy to be drawn off the pathway, a side trip, or road, to take us away from the voice of God. Don't be tempted! Stay on the right path, don't be distracted from the relationship!

"Arise, for this matter is your responsibility. We also are with you. Be of good courage, and do it." (Ezra 10:4)

I have noticed something with these two books, Ezra and Nehemiah. God chooses a man, starting out alone many times, to accomplish His will in a certain area. Those who recognize God's working, maybe walking with God at the time, join that person and accomplish God's task. To me that has always been the purpose of a pastor. First, determine God's will. Second, enlist God's people. Third, follow God's plan. No man can do it alone.

Too many pastors feel that they need to do it alone. That was never God's plan. Remember Moses? God sent Moses up on a mountain. But it was God's people, once they got right with God, who contributed to, and built the tabernacle.

One of the amazing things that happened to me as a pastor. I was visiting a member in the hospital. A nurse asked if they wanted a hospital minister to stop by. They said, "No, our pastor is here." You can't imagine what that meant to me. I have often wondered why it meant so much to have "your" pastor visit in a hospital. I believe that pastor "represents" the presence of God. What better place to have the presence of God than in a hospital.

Here, Ezra has the unenviable task of carrying out God's word. From the beginning God made it clear to Israel to remain without pagan influence! By inter-marrying with the surrounding nations they were bringing their idols into their home. Strictly forbidden by God.

What influences have invaded your home? Of course, the TV is always a threat. Now we have the internet as close as our phones. They devil is working overtime to distract us from listening to God, by whatever means possible. The best counter is what Paul wrote in Ephesians 6, "Put on the whole armor of God, that you may be able to stand against the wiles of the devil." Then he goes on to describe each element necessary to combat the devils lies. My favorite is, of course, the sword of the word of God. The only offensive weapon. The more of God's word we have committed to our minds, the better equipped to do battle. You might say the sharper the sword. Speaking of sharp, don't forget Hebrews 4:12. Check it out!

"O Lord, I pray, please let Your ear be attentive to the prayer of Your servant, and to the prayer of Your servants who desire to fear Your name; and let Your servant prosper this day, I pray, and grant him mercy in the sight of this man." For I was the king's cupbearer. (Nehemiah 1:11)

In my Bible, next to this verse I have Matthew 6:33, "But seek first the kingdom of God and His righteousness, and all these things shall be added to you." but I also like the next verse. "Therefore, do not worry about tomorrow, for tomorrow will worry about its own things. Sufficient for the day is its own trouble."

Here is that lone individual, whom God has commission to go to Israel and restore the wall. They have been in captivity in Babylon for seventy years. I think it's interesting that he is still tuned to the things of God. Babylon has not invaded his faith!

This is a great chapter. Nehemiah acknowledges Israel's sin before God. It almost sounds like he is taking responsibility. We represent our nation. What we do reflects on our family, our nation and our God, as children of God.

Notice Nehemiah's station. The cupbearer was the one who not only served the king his wine, but also sampled it first to see if it was poisoned.

Now here, Nehemiah refers to himself as servant, as he was. I think this adds to the prayer David prayed. David was the king of Israel, yet saw himself as servant before God. (2 Samuel 7) That is OUR station in life. Be we, President of the United States or a waiter in a restaurant, we are all servants of God.

Nehemiah was about to face a king who could bless him or have him killed. What better place to pray first. I can't tell you how many times I have prayed and asked God to give the right words to say. That all comes from our relationship to the Holy Spirit. Is He in control, or are we? Who is doing the talking? Who has control of our thoughts? Have you ever said just the right thing at just the right moment? That was God working. Trust Him!

Ezra, Nehemiah and Esther are the last of the "historical books" in the Old Testament. Stories that demonstrate God's truth!

And it happened, when all our enemies heard of it, and all the nations around us saw these things, that they were very disheartened in their own eyes; for they perceived that this work was done by our God. (Nehemiah 6:16)

Just out of curiosity, do you remember what Rahab said to the two spies in Jericho? She hid them from the king of Jericho and when it was safe she sent out. Her comment to them was, "For we have heard how the Lord dried up the water of the Red Sea for you when you came out of Egypt, and what you did to the two kings of the Amorites who were on the other side of the Jordan, Sihon and Og, whom you utterly destroyed." (Joshua 2:10)

Now think for a minute, why did so many people follow Jesus? Was it His teaching? Not really! When He told them what God expected of them many left Him. So much so that He asked His disciples if they would leave. No, the others followed for the miracles.

The point I want to make is all through the Old Testament God gives us story after story of His miracles. One more, remember what Joseph told his brothers, after the death of their father? Joseph knew who brought him to Pharaoh's court. Look at verse 20 in chapter 50 of Genesis. "But as for you, you meant evil against me; but God meant it for good, in order to bring it about as it is this day, to save many people alive."

God is very active all around us. Trying to get our attention, and maybe even the lost world. They question why certain things happen and don't realize that God is at work. It's up to you to tell them the good news! Just as in this passage. God is using Nehemiah in a great way. His enemies don't understand what has happened.

Notice that they knew who had accomplished this. They recognized God's hand. Just like with Jesus. Check it out. So many times, Jesus marveled at the faith of the Gentiles and the lack of faith in His own disciples. Look at the story of the centurion who told Jesus He didn't have to come to his house, just speak the words. This was a Roman centurion.

How about your faith? Is it enough to believe that God can and will use you to work miracles? He can, as long He gets the glory!

And Ezra blessed the Lord, the great God. Then all the people
answered, "Amen, Amen!" while lifting up their hands. And they
bowed their heads and worshiped the Lord with their faces to the
ground. (Nehemiah 8:6)

Do you wonder where we get some of the "traditions" in our churches? Look
at the verse preceding this one. "And Ezra opened the book in the sight of all
the people, for he was standing above all the people; and when he opened it, all
the people stood up."

Have you ever had an evangelist who asked everyone to stand for the reading
of God's word? I have. I understand the principle. But just like Israel, does it mean
anything? We can "honor" God all the time, in public. What God wants is that
honor in our hearts!

That would be an interesting word search. I wonder how you would search it?
Here the people, after Ezra blessed the Lord, the people said, "Amen, Amen!" You
know their history. What about us. How quickly, on Monday morning at work,
do we quickly forget the commitments we made to God Sunday?

I don't pay much attention to the physical actions, especially of Israel. What
matters most to God is the heart. Now, don't misunderstand me! I am all for a
habit of weekly worship in God's house. But put away the "I'm a Christian" face
and come to church seeking God's presence in your heart.

I will say, there is one habit that bugs me. It's not a physical thing but it's what
people say, or don't say. It really bugs me when people refuse to end their prayer in
Jesus' name. They say, "in His name" or "in Your name." I only capitalize so you
know who I'm talking about. Is it so hard to say Jesus' name? O.k, off my soapbox!

I hope you've read these chapters. Notice in chapter 9 that Israel's people sign
a covenant. The verses acknowledge who God is, but look where they have come
from. I'm sorry, I need proof. Words are cheap. That's the way it is with most
Christians today. They can say just the right things at just the right time. We have
memorized the "Christian" lingo but our hearts are far from God.

That's my biggest challenge in these pages. To encourage you to not only talk
the talk, but walk the walk. Remember that walk?

Also, that day they offered great sacrifices, and rejoiced for God had made them rejoice with great joy; the women and the children also rejoiced, so that the joy of Jerusalem was heard afar off. (Nehemiah 12:43)

The wall is complete. Nehemiah had accomplished his goal, his calling. Great rejoicing, and praising God. Have you ever felt that feeling? The feeling that God had accomplished something through you. You notice I didn't use the word great? It doesn't have to be great you just must know that God did it through you!

Notice that the party was heard afar off? It is so important that when God does something in our life that God gets the glory, both for our own peace and for a testimony to those around us.

God tapped Nehemiah on the shoulder to do a great deed. Nehemiah prayed that God would give him the right words to convince the king of God's calling. God did. Nehemiah trusted God to provide the men and resources to accomplish that deed. God did.

Did you notice chapter thirteen? I think I need to remind you that we are not talking about the Bible we hold in our hands. Nor the 39 books of the Old Testament. We are talking about the five books of Moses. Including the end Exodus and the book of Leviticus. Those boring books that are so hard to read.

After what Israel has been through I can see the people eagerly taking in every word. Absorbing the very word of God. The Law, handed down to Moses on Mt. Sinai and found among the ruins in Jerusalem and read again for the first time in over seventy years. Imagine.

How are you doing in your quest to read through the Bible in one year? Struggling? I hope God has blessed you in so many ways. I hope I have challenged and encouraged a closer relationship with God by spending this time in His word.

Our last chapters in the book of Nehemiah. Ponder the awesome task that God called Nehemiah and Ezra to accomplish. Israel was empty of God's people. The northern kingdom was taken away by Assyria and Babylon had removed Judah and Benjamin, the southern kingdom. And God has brought them back. Amen!

"For if you remain completely silent at this time, relief and deliverance will arise for the Jews from another place, but you and your father's house will perish. Yet who knows whether you have come to the kingdom for such a time as this?" (Esther 4:14)

Mordecai was so wise. Notice in the verse above that he told Esther that God was going to accomplish His will no matter what Esther did. I wonder sometimes if we think we could thwart God's will or derail His plans by not participating. Not going to happen. What happens is that we miss the blessing.

It's just like that time that God laid on your heart to try something out of your "comfort zone" and you refused because of what people might say or do. You're the one who missed the blessing of seeing what God could do in your life. I know, that happened to me.

We had a "Watchnight Service" in our church. I was watching a movie about a martyr named Hess. I left the chapel and went to get a drink. God was so real in my life He was speaking to me so clearly. God wanted to use me, but would I trust Him? I hadn't been saved that long. I had just started teaching a Sunday school class. What did God want with me? Not long after that night I had surrendered to the call of God to the gospel ministry. For a very shy person this was a big step. I don't mean to carry on about my testimony. Just to say I know what I'm talking about.

I can't tell you how many people have told me the best way to learn the Bible is to start teaching. I love it. It is so true! So many focus on Esther, the book was named for her. The true hero of this book, apart from God of course, is Mordecai. If you watch him, he had that relationship with God I've been talking about. A walk with God, that caused him to enlist Esther to approach the king.

Do you think it was an accident that the king "just happened" to be reading, that night, what Mordecai had done to save the kings life? The neat thing about Esther is that the word God is not mentioned yet He is all through the book. That's how God works in our lives. We must be looking, and aware of His hand working in our daily walk.

Think about these two servants of the king. Neither looking for the ministry but God used both to accomplish a great work!

"For how can I endure to see the evil that will come to my people?
Or how can I endure to see the destruction of my countrymen?
(Esther 8:6)

When I think about a couple of events prior to Haman's departure I wonder about the king's relationship with Esther. When she first approaches the king in the throne room. She didn't know what to expect. Yet, the king, offered to give to her up to half of the kingdom (5:3). Then at that faithful dinner when the king thought he had attacked Esther, his rage was interesting. I'm a romantic. I think there was more there than king / queen relationship. That's just me.

Here, in this verse, Esther realizes what Mordecai had told her. That her people were about to be eliminated and she has the opportunity to stop it. The point is, we can't stand by and see our friends and relatives make a terrible mistake and miss heaven. So, what are we to do?

I'm sure, if you've attended church for any length of time, you have heard a message that implores you, for your friends and loved ones sake, to witness to them. I don't know how many I've heard. One of the more popular sermons of the past was "Sinners in the Hands of an Angry God" by Jonathan Edwards.

So how do we reach those we care about? The same sentiment that Esther expressed above. First you pray. Do you have a list, if you need one, of family and relatives? You need to pray every day, "If there is anyone who doesn't know Your Son as Savior, please put someone in their path to share with them the gospel of salvation through Jesus." Co-workers, classmates (Sunday school or school). Neighbors, etc. By praying you recruit the power of the Holy Spirit to begin working on their hearts to convict them, and bring to Christ. (John 16:8)

You may be the one God chooses to enter their path to share with them the gospel. Who knows. By praying you enlist the help of the Holy Spirit. He must act first, by convicting the lost, of their need of a Savior. Then God will put someone in their path to share the good news.

Esther was reluctant at first, but when Mordecai told her of the need of her people she was willing to risk death to talk to the king. Are we willing to risk, rejection, a little embarrassment to win someone?

Why is light given to a man whose way is hidden, and whom God has hedged in? (Job 3:23)

Before we look at this verse I want you to put yourself in Job's shoes with the first three chapters. I have used these chapters many times when counseling about bad things that come into our lives. In my Bible, I have underlined this phrase, "While he was yet speaking." You see Job didn't receive the bad news about his family, his servants, his wealth over several days. No, he received the worst news, over and over, one right after the other in maybe a ten minute, span. Boom. Boom. Boom!

The word hedge suggests a prayer principle that I heard years ago. The minister said, "when you pray for your children, ask God to put a hedge around them, to protect them from Satan." Remember the first three chapters? God "allowed" these things to Job. When we ask God to put a hedge we are recruiting His protection. We can't be everywhere always with our children. God can!

Job is not one of my favorite books. I still have a problem understanding what's going on. Bear with me and we'll see what we can glean.

Job is depressed! Really? Remember how he received this news. So, how would you respond. Blame God? Most do. It's all God's fault. God should have stopped this. Especially taking my children. That's not fair! Really? Where is the verse that says we are automatically granted grace? Remember Job is a "godly" man. He's a deacon, Sunday school teacher, a pillar of the community. This shouldn't happen, really? So, what do we deserve? As children of God we should seek a relationship that says, "not my will but Thine be done." Can you do that? Jesus did (Luke 22:42) in the garden just before going to the cross. Can you pray that?

The light. It's interesting that Job is depressed, hurt, discouraged, his wife told him to curse God and die (2:9). That was what Satan expected and wanted. But Job was walking too close to God to fall for that trick. Myself, when things like that happen, trials, etc. I pray, "Ok, God what is it you are trying to teach me?" God never does anything without a purpose in mind! We need to seek that purpose!

"Behold, happy is the man whom God corrects; Therefore, do not despise the chastening of the Almighty." (Job 5:17)

As much as I have problems with Job there are some great verses in this book. This is one of them. I like what Dr. Charles Stanley said about storms, "We are either entering a storm, in a storm, or just coming out of a storm." Storms are a fact of life. This verse really picks up on what I ended yesterday's devotion with.

Ever get a "spanking" from your parents? Today that's not heard of. Whether we want to admit it or not, when our parents correct us it's because they love us. Something else to consider. Our parents have been through much of what we attempt before we know better. They are simply trying to protect us!

I remember telling my dad once, (much to my regret) "I'm going to do what I want, but I would like your advice." I would love to know what he thought at the time. You say, "why that's terrible." Is it? Don't we tell God that all the time?

It's clear in the Bible, one, that God loves us (John 3:16). Second, that God has a perfect plan for our lives (Jeremiah 29:11-13). So why do we fight Him? Of course, we know better than God what is best for us. We have certain goals and plans and God isn't going to deter me! Really?

Why would a man be happy, if God corrects him? Like we said above, God loves us to much to keep us from falling into bad habits. How many have said, later in life, why didn't someone warn me about this? If they did would you have listened? That's the beauty of God's Holy Spirit living within us. He convicts us when we make those wrong turns. The problem is He is so easy to ignore. God will not PUSH us to where He wants us to go. We must go voluntarily. The nice thing about God also is, He will not say "I told you so." Our own conscience will take care of that.

I want to reiterate what I said yesterday. It is so important! If God is correcting you about something, listen. If you are going through that storm, ask God, "what is the lesson you want me to get from this?" Sometimes it may be just to get us to change directions. Much like God did with Jonah. Think about it.

> God is wise in heart and mighty in strength. Who has hardened himself against Him and prospered? (Job 9:4)

This is all true. The question is, "how long will it take?" Some people take a lifetime before they realize how much God cares and He has a better plan. The first time I saw Jeremiah 29:11-13 was on a scented packet in someone's bathroom. I looked at that verse and thought, "I'm glad someone has a plan, because I don't." I can't stress how much these verses have meant to me. The address has been etched in my memory. Of course, God has conditions to His plan. "Seek Me."

Remember the Bible content that we have read so far? What has God done with Israel? From parting the Red Sea to bringing His people back into the land He promised them. Mighty deeds and working through His servants. God will accomplish His will. Just ask Esther. God has the power to do whatever He wishes, BUT, He desires to use His children to accomplish these mighty deeds.

Oh, there's that word prosper again. I really feel sorry for those, especially His children, who have turned their back on God. What they are missing out on is amazing. Excuse the metaphor, but it's like having a very rich father and turning your back on him because you disagree with him. That is a sorry example but multiply it a thousand-fold then you might get it.

Did you notice that word hardened? Where do you remember that from? Pharaoh and Moses. Sometimes it says Pharaoh hardened his heart, sometimes it says God hardened Pharaoh's heart. What would it mean to you to have a "hardened" heart? No amount of evidence, or arguing can convince you otherwise. It sounded right. You have charted a course and that's where you're going, right? That's sad.

That's also a picture of God's Spirit speaking repeatedly, and you ignoring it. It's like someone talking to you, but at the same time getting farther and farther away. Remember we've used the picture of God walking with us daily? Suppose you come to a fork in the road. You want to go left, He wants to go right. As you part, God keeps warning you you're going the wrong way. The father apart you get the fainter the voice. That's what happens when we choose our way.

Though He slay me, yet will I trust Him. Even so, I will defend my own
ways before Him. He also shall be my salvation, for a hypocrite could
not come before Him. (Job 13:15-16)

There is so much in this verse. "Yet will I trust Him." That's really what it's
all about isn't it? I marvel sometimes at how many people take the time to
come to a mid-week prayer service. To take the time in the middle of their busy
week, dress up, drive to church for a one-hour prayer and Bible study. To me, that
shows the depth of their faith, even to some extend their walk with God. It sure
demonstrates their priorities.

To be honest I don't get the next part. "I will defend my own ways before
Him." You have no defense. Of course, how many of us want to argue God's plans
for us with the Almighty? One of my pet peeves are people who think they know
better than God. Believe me there are many. Again, I refer to Jesus in the garden.
"Nevertheless, not My will but Thine be done." (Matthew 26). Maybe this is what
Job was talking about. Jesus asked God if there were any other way. But in the end
Jesus knew the plan.

Then there is the next part. "He also shall be my salvation." I have a question
for you. Did God see Jesus on the cross when He saw Adam in the garden of
Eden? I think so. Of course, He had hoped that Adam and Eve wouldn't sin. It
has always been our choice. God would have wanted it another way. But that's the
risk He took when He gave us free will. It has always been our choice. But that
doesn't mean that God didn't know what choice we would make. So, God had to
provide a means for us to restore that relationship with Him. He chose His Son
to make that sacrifice.

That's why, I believe, that God spent so much time on the Old Testament.
He had to paint a very clear picture of what Jesus would accomplish on the cross.
Remember John the Baptist remark when he first saw Jesus? "Behold! The Lamb
of God that takes away the sin of the world." (John 1:29).

One last question. How many hypocrites do you suppose will stand before
God? There may be many but none will enter heaven. Of course, that is the big
reason most people give for not going to church. Really? Do you seriously think
that excuse will work for God? The church that His Son established for our
worship of Him. And that's the excuse you have?

"Are you the first man who was born? Or were you made before the hills? Have you heard the counsel of God? Do you limit wisdom to yourself? (Job 15:7-8)

This is a great verse. God is essentially saying, "who do you think you are?" Is He not?

I'm curious about Job's four friends. Remember Job's current condition. God has allowed Satan to do his best to turn Job away from God. It hasn't worked. Of course, Job has questions but never doubts God's sovereignty. His friends, here it is Eliphaz, seem to me to try an intellectual approach. Try to reason with him. Job's not buying it.

I think his friends don't understand the relationship Job has with God. They try to put Job in their box. They try to make Job relate to God the way they do. Have you ever known someone who had a special relationship with God?

As a baby Christian, I had the opportunity to spend many hours with preachers and men of God. I absorbed it like a sponge. Our youth group would go on a week-long bus trip to Kentucky from Missouri. Many hours, just talking and learning. As baby Christian's we learn from observing those Christians around us. Later, as we grow. We begin to feed ourselves. Those early years can be critical.

A New Testament writer talks about starting out with milk then progressing to solid food. (Hebrews 5) Most of us never get passed the milk. We get saved and think that's all there is, that's all I need and stop. God has so much more for us than milk.

If you want to know about wisdom wait till we get to the book of Proverbs. Solomon talks a lot about wisdom and knowledge in the Proverbs. There is a difference you know.

You know Job has no shortage of counseling from his friends. Chapter after chapter. But if you notice, on this journey, the real answers come from His discussions with God. If you're looking for answers to what God is doing in your life, ask Him. Let me give you an experiment. Turn off the TV. Turn off your phone. Nothing going on around you. Now, sit still for ten minutes. I think it's called meditation. Anyway, my guess is you can't do it. Why?

"Oh, that my words were written! Oh, that they were inscribed in a book! That they were engraved on a rock with an iron pen and lead, forever! For I know that my Redeemer lives, and He shall stand at last on the earth." (Job 19:23-25)

In December of 1998 I saw this TV movie with Neal Patrick Harris and Debbie Reynolds called "A Christmas Wish." A nephew was going through the journals of his departed uncle and discovered a mystery. I won't elaborate but it's well worth watching.

Because of this movie it triggered something and motivated me to begin keeping a daily journal. Just one page, a day. I began in 1999. For over twenty years I kept that journal. It is amazing to look back over those years. I think these will mean more to my grandchildren than to me.

I can fully understand what Job is talking about. The idea I want to get across is that it's too late to reflect when you could have started today. It's so important to begin writing your events today than twenty years later trying to remember them. Woulda, coulda, shoulda, don't fall into that category!

I was sitting with a group of people the other day. A fellow was telling this story about when he went fishing. I was thinking, "you need to write that down." So many people have stories to tell but don't take the time to write them down. Not for you, but for those who come after you. So much of our country's history has been researched through diaries left behind by our ancestors.

Now, do you get the point that Job is making? Let me tell you my take. Job wants to tell all those who come after him about the grace of God. The miracles that God has brought to him. Notice in verse 25, "For I know that my Redeemer lives." That is worth writing down. I have always believed, and others will back this up, that the greatest witnessing tool is your personal testimony. How God has changed your life. You can quote all kinds of scripture, but until you tell them what God has done in your life, it's just words on a page.

One of the neat things about keeping a journal is that you can write down those unexplained events and then see later how God used that to work a miracle in your life!

"Now acquaint yourself with Him, and be at peace; thereby good will come to you. Receive, please, instruction from His mouth, and lay up His words in your mouth." (Job 22:21-22)

How acquainted are you with Him? The surest way is to spend time in His word. Get to know the power and purpose of God in the Old Testament and then in the New Testament get to know God personally through His Son Jesus. That's why I love to use the picture of walking with God. There is just something intimate about strolling with someone beside you and sharing your thoughts.

In these verses Eliphaz is exhorting Job to have a closer relationship with God. Really? Here is a guy who by the world's standards has every right to curse God. Yet, even with his wife's urging, refuses to blame God. He has lost everything, yet Job clings to his relationship with God.

That's great advice. I'm wondering about his motive. Look at the second part, "thereby good will come to you." I can hear Job now, really?" How many people think that if they go to church every week and pray every day that no bad thing will happen to them? That's sad. God never promises that.

Again, I love the analogy used in "Love Comes Softly." It's not that bad things won't happen but that when they do God is right there, walking beside you, lifting and encouraging, and bringing peace through that storm. But, He must be there walking with you. Not someone you only meet on Sundays. Someone you have a close relationship with.

"Lay up His words in your mouth." That is the whole point of this devotion. Get into the word of God. Not to tell someone next year that you read through the whole Bible, but to input His words into your mind to be accessed later when you need them. The story of Joseph, the faith of Joshua in chapter 24. The special relationship David had with God. The miracles done through Moses. The Passover picture in Exodus 12. The Ten Commandments in Exodus 20 and Deuteronomy, etc. All these pictures are engraved in your mind. God will bring them up when you need them. They also give insight into who God is and, oh, don't forget Jeremiah 29! What an awesome picture of the relationship and love that God has for His children. And the promise of a plan!

And to man He said, "Behold, the fear of the Lord, that is wisdom,
and to depart from evil is understanding." (Job 28:28)

The book of Job is said to be one of the oldest books in the Old Testament. Long before David or Solomon, Abraham or Judah. It's interesting because of his reference to wisdom. Solomon has so much to say about wisdom in Proverbs. I mentioned earlier the two words wisdom and knowledge. Many people think they are the same. They are not.

It was explained to me that, briefly, wisdom is simply the "application" of knowledge. We can have a head full of knowledge but absolutely no common sense, which is another word for wisdom. I've known a few like that. They have a whole list of degrees but can't change a light bulb.

One fact you can take to the bank. If your knowledge does not include the word of God it is all useless. The word of God, some have called it, absolute truth, is essential to understanding knowledge. That's why I commend the Old Testament so much. Many times, we learn from "experience." Not reading a textbook. The Old Testament is full of examples guided by experience. How God works in and through various people in the Bible.

The New Testament is more of the textbook, except for the gospels. Even the gospels are illustrations of God's desire for a more personal relationship. So much so that God decided to come to earth to fellowship and teach man what was important to Him. And to demonstrate His love for us. Not just in word, but in deed.

I'm sure we will talk about this word again. I think I've talked about it before. "The fear of the Lord." The word fear is not what normally comes to our minds. To God the word fear is "respect" "reverence" etc.

God's enemies should fear Him, not His children. It's such an interesting contrast. God wants us to "reverence" Him and at the same time to have a personal intimate relationship with Him. Can you do both? Only with God. To reverence God, He expects us to obey Him, to keep His commandments. Even Jesus said, "If you love me, keep My commandments." (John 14:15). Think about it. Is that not the same kind of relationship we want with our own children, intimacy and respect? "Depart from evil" is that keeping His commands?

> But there is a spirit in a man, and the breath of the Almighty gives
> him understanding. (Job 32:8)

I may have mentioned this before. I believe that when God created us, He left out a piece from our spirit. As we grow older we search for that missing piece. We try all kinds of things, food, relationships, things, wealth, recognition, etc. Trying to find that missing piece. It's only when someone introduces us to Jesus, and we invite Him into our hearts do we discover that missing piece. The missing piece brings peace!

I think the first time I had a Bible of my own was when I was inducted into the United States Air Force. I was given one of those pocket New Testaments. While I was on a train headed to Lackland, Air Force Base in San Antonio, Texas, I opened it and tried to read it. I was scared to death. The first time I had left home, literally on my own. I opened to the gospel of Matthew and began reading. WRONG! I never got out of the first chapter. The genealogy did nothing for me. No one told me to start with gospel of John.

The point is, it made no sense. Later, I shared this earlier, that once I had asked Jesus into my heart, I couldn't get enough of God's word. It was like I was starving and I found a banquet before me. That's what Elihu is talking about here. "The Almighty gives him understanding." Job has a lot of questions. He is not lacking in people who want to advise him. The answer is in his relationship with God, not counselors. We mentioned they didn't even have the Law (five books of Moses) at this point. Look at verse 10 of chapter 32. "Therefore, I say, 'Listen to me, I also will declare my opinion."

I hope none of Job's counselors said, "I know how you feel." I have a hunch at least one did. No one knows what Job went through, unless you have been there. The best counselor we can seek of course, is God. You don't have to explain anything, God already knows where you are at.

I like something Dr. Charles Stanley said, "Because God is all-knowing He knows where you're at in the storm. Because He is all-present He is with you in the storm and because He is all-powerful He will help you through the Storm." Paraphrased of course.

"Behold, God works all these things, twice, in fact, three times with a man, to bring back his soul from the Pit, that he may be enlightened with the light of life." (Job 33:29-30)

Just a word about Elihu first. Elihu reminds me of me, as a young Christian. It seemed the more I learned the more I thought I knew. Now, after over thirty years I realize just how much I had yet to learn. I think sometimes we confuse Bible knowledge with a relationship with the Writer, not necessarily so. Elihu strikes me as one of those guys.

I do like the picture here, "to bring back his soul from the Pit." I've heard so many stories of man's quest for God in their life. They don't have to look that hard. God is always reaching out to His creation. God desires a personal relationship with His creation. I believe that is a big reason, as I've said before, why God came down in the person of His Son Jesus.

The "he" of course is us. Anybody know anything about biology? Look in Genesis chapter one. Notice the order of creation. On the third day God created the plant life. One the fourth day He created the sun, moon and stars. I was always taught that plants could not survive without sunlight. Have you heard the theory that these days represented thousands of years? So, there were thousands of years between creating plant life and the sun, seriously?

I have heard that the light prior to the sun, moon and stars was the Light of God. I can buy that. Of course, in John chapter one we read, "In Him was life, and the life was the light of men." (v. 4). The Light that brings us back from the Pit is of course Jesus Christ!

Of course, Elihu got it right at the beginning of this verse. "God works all these things." If we ever fully grasp that concept. God is in charge. God provides for our needs, leads us in the path of righteousness, and communes with us in prayer. It's really all about God, isn't it?

We are nearing the end of Job. When I think of Job I pretty much think of those first three chapters. God included those verses in this book for a reason. I think He wanted us to get a glimpse into the fact that Satan can do nothing to us, but what He allows, and that for a reason!

He seals the hand of every man, that all men may know His work.
(Job 37:7)

Think about it, just how important is this fact imparted to us here? "That all men may know His work." So how do we know the workings of God? As His children, by the prompting of the Holy Spirit we simply must look around through the eyes of God. As His children, we can do that.

Here comes the challenge. How does a lost and dying world see God? For one thing, they see God through you! When God works in your life the lost world notices, when you praise Him! When you glorify God for things He has done, that helps the lost world to see God.

Be honest, Christian. How many times as a co-worker, or neighbor, or friend come to you to pray for them? Why is that? Because they see God in you. Like it or not, provided you give them reason to seek your prayers.

I like that word seals. One of the neatest promises I learned as a young Christian is the fact that the Holy Spirit is our "seal" that we are God's children. Look at 2 Corinthians 1:21,22, "Now He who establishes us with you in Christ and has anointed us is God, who also has sealed us and given us the Spirit in our hearts as a guarantee." Isn't that awesome!

Now the verse in Job says, "He seals every man". Don't leave off that last part. "That all men may know His work." That is the key. Without a relationship with God there is no seal. No receiving of the Holy Spirit. The requirement is that you believe. If you don't believe there is a God, how can you be sealed with the Holy Spirit who only inhabits believers?

If you haven't figured it out by now that is my big message in this book. A personal, intimate relationship with God. I have been blessed to slowly progress to that point. It's only after you recognize the God of the Bible and grasp His plan for your life can you really begin that walk we talked about. "If thou shalt confess with your mouth the Lord Jesus and believe in your heart that God has raised Him from the dead, you will be saved". (Romans 10:9) It's really just as simple as that. Trust, ask, believe and let the Holy Spirit seal you!

And the Lord restored Job's losses when he prayed for his friends.
Indeed, the Lord gave Job twice as much as he had before. (Job 42:10)

This is one of my favorite verses in Job. I love this. I'm not big on philosophical arguments, especially pertaining to God. A good movie to watch is "God Is Not Dead" it kind of takes this approach. But all through the movie you see examples of how God really works. I think we have moved from the days of Jesus, where miracles were very visible, to God working in each individual life. Please, that doesn't mean God doesn't do those things. Like scene where the car that wouldn't start in the movie. Of course!

Of course, we overlook the power of prayer. Even God's children think that is the last resort, if all else fails try praying. It is even featured at the END of Job. And of course, look at what Job prays for. The restoration of his family? A better understanding of God's will in his life? A closer relationship with God? No! He prays for his friends who have for the most part accused Job of all kinds of things, and trying to "explain" God.

Job prays for his friends. It's stretching it to call them friends. But, that is the catalyst to God blessing him with double what he had before. I heard an interesting theory. God gave him double of everything except his children. Some preacher argued that when he went to heaven he would have all twenty-four. The point is God blessed him when he prayed!

I hope your keeping up with these daily readings. I know it's hard. I think you've come through the hard part. Today concludes the book of Job. Now we begin days of walking through the book of the Psalms. Take the time each day to pray and ask God to speak to you through His word. He will, but you must ask Him.

I used to get so mad that while I was reading I would lose my train of thought. I would be trying to pay attention to the text and these thoughts kept creeping into my mind. Then I realized that maybe God was trying to say something to me. My mind was on God's word why would He not try to say something to me. It's like setting in front of the TV and all of a sudden you get this idea to call a friend or relative. How many times have we dismissed that or put it off? Think about it!

O Lord, our Lord, how excellent is Your name in all the earth, who
have set Your glory above the heavens. (Psalm 8:1)

I probably shouldn't bring this up again but "Your name" just keeps bringing it
up. Let me give you a couple of verses: "Therefore God also has highly exalted
Him and given Him the name which is above every name, that at the name of Jesus
every knee should bow, of those in heaven, and of those on earth, and those under
the earth, and that every tongue should confess that Jesus Christ is Lord, to the
glory of God the Father." (Philippians 2:9-11).

Why are we afraid to use His name at the end of our prayers? I just don't
understand that. It just gets my blood pressure up. I won't quote the whole passage
but in Acts chapter three Peter, by using the name of Jesus Christ raised a cripple
to walk. Maybe our prayer loses some of its power by not invoking Jesus' name.
Think about it.

Just this once I want to remind you that most, not all, but most of the Psalms
were writing by king David. Not sure when he wrote them, it's not important.
Could have been as a shepherd out in the fields or as king. Psalm 51 is said to
be written after his confrontation with Nathan over Bathsheba. I just want you
to think about the man who wrote these. We talked about this in the book of
Kings. The relationship that David had with God, I would think, would give some
credence to what David says.

Jesus has so many names throughout the Bible. Alpha and Omega, the Lion of
Judah, the Lamb of God, etc. I think someone even made a poem or a song taking
a name for Jesus from each book of the Bible. That's great, it's interesting to think
about. But to me there is nothing more powerful, more endearing, or more heartfelt than the name of Jesus. When I was first saved it was hard for me to get used
to using the name God in a sentence. My upbringing of reverencing God. But I had
no problem talking about Jesus. A "personal" relationship. That, I believe, is what
God intended. To show mankind that God was not this all-powerful, vengeful,
tyrant. God loves us, John 3:16.

What is your relationship with God. Do you know Him? How much do you
know Him? If you follow these devotions clear to December 31 it's my prayer that
you will have a closer and more personal relationship with our heavenly Father.

And those who know Your name will put their trust in You; for You
Lord, have not forsaken those who seek You. (Psalm 9:10)

"And those who know Your name." Just think about that for a moment. Just knowing the name doesn't get you anything but another name. I'm sure that's not what the Psalmist is talking about. Probably another way of saying it might be: "And those who know YOU." I'm pretty sure that's what David was talking about.

There is a huge difference from knowing the name and knowing the person. For many years I kept the Sunday school rolls. I would see these names every week. Many times, I would later connect the names with the person. I'd meet them in the church service or in a fellowship of some kind. Then I could "connect" a name with a face. So, from then on when I saw the name I had a face to go with it.

It's sad that today so many people think that because they know the name, they know the person. Not true! God seeks a relationship not just an acquaintance. I wonder how many people have been moved one day in a worship service. Went forward and made a profession of "faith" but never really became acquainted with Jesus, the Son of God. To me a symptom of a relationship is the desire to be in God's house on the Lord's day. There is a desire to worship, and read His word, and pray that wasn't there before.

Notice, in the second half of that verse. God is always there for a relationship. That word seek reminds me of that verse in Jeremiah, "And you will seek Me and find Me, when you search for Me with all your heart." (Jeremiah 29:13). And of course, Luke 11:9, "So I say to you, ask, and it will be given you; seek, and you will find; knock and it will be opened to You." (Also, Matthew 7:7).

God is always there when we seek Him. That's a promise from God. David knew that. Even with his sin with Bathsheba, when Nathan confronted him David acknowledged his sin and repented. There were still consequences which David accepted. That is the evidence of David's relationship with God. We all make mistakes, with others and with God. It's what we do after that, that makes the difference. David trusted God, even with the loss of the child.

> Let the words of my mouth and the meditation of my heart be
> acceptable in Your sight, O Lord, my strength and my Redeemer.
> (Psalm 19:14)

What an awesome prayer. How many times have we said things we wished we could retrieve? We can apologize, ask forgiveness, etc. But the words are there. The best thing is to ask God to control your tongue. Oh, that reminds me of verse in James, remember? "Even so the tongue is a little member and boasts great things. See how great a forest a little fire kindles!" (3:5) And, "Out of the mouth proceed blessing and cursing. My brethren, these things ought not to be so." (3:10). This whole chapter (James 3) is worth meditating on.

So how can we control something so unruly? Of course, we can begin with the Holy Spirit. That assumes you're a Christian. There is no Holy Spirit unless you are a child of God. Second, we need to listen to that Spirit. He can convict us all day but if we don't listen, it's useless. Here's another thought, think before you speak. What a novel concept I know. Someone once said, "That is why God gave us two ears and one mouth."

How about we begin the day, in our devotions, with this prayer, "Let the words of my mouth and the meditations of my heart be acceptable in Your sight." What an awesome way to begin the day. Notice God also, as author of scripture, says, "the meditation of my heart." You see if we did that the chances of saying something we shouldn't are far less likely. Think about it.

And then there's the key at the end of this verse. David acknowledges where the ability to do comes from. "my strength and my Redeemer." The strength and ability to control the tongue comes from God. Like we said earlier, the Holy Spirit. How many times has God brought a verse or a story to your mind that you needed at the time to witness to someone? The same principle works for your mouth. As a former truck driver one of the first things God changed in my life was my language. I love what someone told me once. "Profanity, is ignorance made audible." I said that once on my CB and another driver wanted to dispute it at the next truck stop. The truth hurts sometimes. Think about those words!

The secret of the Lord is with those who fear Him, and He will show them His covenant. (Psalm 25:14)

I have long held this problem. As someone who was saved at the age of thirty-five I've wondered how to express this thought. It's almost like Alice and the Looking Glass. Now that I'm on this side of God's grace why those on the other side don't see it? Is that weird?

Because once you have accepted Christ as your Savior your whole world changes. Your priorities change, your attitude changes, your language changes, your thought patterns change. I just wish I had the way with words to explain what I'm trying to say.

Look at this verse. "The secret of the Lord is with those who fear Him." You see? You must be on this side to understand and fully grasp what this verse says. But to get here you must have enough faith to ask Jesus in your heart. It's like going to heaven then coming back and trying to explain it to someone who doesn't know God. You can't!

I explained earlier what the term "fear of the Lord" meant. It's not fear as we understand the word it really means a "reverence." Just like the last part of this verse, "And He will show then His covenant." We have come far enough through the Old Testament to understand what a covenant is. It's an agreement between two parties, a pledge if you will. God makes a pledge to us. If we ask Jesus to become our Savior God will come into our hearts in the person of the Holy Spirit and walk with us the rest of our lives.

What would it mean to you to have God walking with you forever? What do you think that means? To me I guess the first word that comes to mind is "peace." Peace to know where I'm going when I die. Peace to know that God is in control of my life. Peace to know that God has a plan for my life (Jeremiah 29:11). Peace to know that when bad things happen that God has a purpose for it and I need to learn what God is doing. Peace to know that I can talk to God at any time through prayer and that He hears my prayers and will answer according to His will.

There's that frustration again. I'm on this side, I love it! You are on that side. Have no idea what I'm talking about. Come on over! Just pray and ask Jesus to come into your life. He will, and change your life.

That I may proclaim with the voice of thanksgiving, and tell of all Your
wondrous works, Lord, I have loved the habitation of Your house, and
the place where Your glory dwells. (Psalm 26:7-8)

I have to jump on that last part. Since the day I was saved I have always believed in the work of the church. I used to tell others that I've held every job in the church, from janitor (that's a funny story) to pastor. I used to say there were two jobs I hadn't done. Lead the choir and lead the ladies group. In Freeman where I pastored I got lead the singing on Sunday nights. In another church, I had the opportunity to lead the Ladies Bible Study group in a study on the Holy Spirit. So now I can say I've done every job in the church. So, what? I have loved every minute of it.

Too many people want to find fault with the church. Be it spiritual or personal. So-in-so said this or so-in-so did that. Really? And what has God said? The purpose for worship is just that, worship the Almighty God, Creator of the Universe, Father of the Son who bought your salvation. I love the picture I read once that church is like a fireplace. You put one log in there and you can't maintain the heat. You put three logs in there and you got a FIRE! That's church.

Now take that first part, "That I may proclaim with voice of thanksgiving, and tell all your wondrous works." That is so important. Most of us think that is what church is for. That's where we get up and tell what God has done for us. That's nice but it needs to be more outside than in. We need to proclaim the wondrous works of God to those who don't know God. A personal testimony is the most powerful weapon God has. You need to use yours, outside the church, as well as in.

"Tell of all Your wondrous works." Can you? Do you even notice what God is doing all around you? I can look back and see so many instances where God has saved my life. The doctor caught colon cancer soon enough to cure it! I didn't feel good one Easter Sunday after church. I wanted to go home. My wife and kids talked me into going to hospital. Said I had blood clots in both my lungs. I should be dead. I had a bad accident on the highway driving for U.P.S. I should have been killed, instead just some bruises. Oh, I'm running out of room, that's just the highlights. Praise God!

> For the word of the Lord is right, and all His work is done in truth. He loves righteousness and justice; the earth is full of the goodness of the Lord. (Psalm 33:4-5)

Have you ever tried to convince someone of something that was in the Bible and their response was, "why should I believe the Bible?" Let me ask you this, "how long would you trust someone who lied to you?" Not long I suspect. The Bible has withstood the test of time and trial and still emerges as the most purchased book in history!

Just think, for a moment, what you hold in your hand. This is a letter from the Creator of the universe. Your Creator. After God, freed Israel from the bondage of slavery in Egypt He took them to Mt. Sinai for a time of fellowship and refreshing, NO! He took them there to give them the rules to live by, instructions for life.

One of my favorite books of late is "Total Money Makeover" by Dave Ramsey. Great book, changed my whole approach to managing money. Why, because the author consulted the word of God. The guidelines and principles are founded on the word of God. Every self-help book worth its salt should be based on scriptural principles. The foundation is there, we just need to incorporate it into our lives.

I love the numerous stories about professors, theologians, other "learned" people who set out to disprove the Bible and ended up becoming Christians. It's amazing, really!

I like this part of the verse above, "He loves righteousness and justice." Much of our jurisprudence is based on the principles of scripture. The Founding Fathers were men of faith and Bible readers (contrary to popular believe). They were raised on the truth of scripture and thus their mindset incorporated that thinking into their writings and thus the Declaration of Independence, the Constitution, and other government documents. Many of the original state constitutions contained biblical references. It's an amazing study if you're interested! Let me recommend writings by David Barton if you're interested!

"The earth is full of the goodness of the Lord." It's there if you open your eyes and look around. Do some research read about our American heritage and our Founding Fathers (one of my favorite subjects). You will be amazed at what you find!

> The steps of a good man are ordered by the Lord, and He delights in his way. Though he fall, he shall not be utterly cast down; for the Lord upholds him with His hand. (Psalm 37:23-24)

Psalm 37 is one of my favorite psalms. Twice it tells us to "wait" on the Lord (v. 9,34). Look at verses 3 thru 8 there are commands at the beginning of each verse. This is a good psalm to spend a little extra time on.

Look at the verse above, "The steps of a good man are ordered by the Lord." Did you notice the Lord gives us no more than the steps we take one by one? One of the most frustrating things about following the Lord is that He will NOT reveal what's next. He just says, "trust Me!" Back to Jeremiah 29:11. God has a plan, in fact He created us with a plan in mind. The great thing, depending on how you look at it, is that we have the option to follow that plan or not. Think about it. Which would you rather follow, the One who created you, or your own intuition?

Oh, I missed the good part, "And He delights in his way." In whose way? Yours of course. God wants only the best for His children. He wants to bless us, but He also requires obedience. Think about your own children, you want them to obey you, don't you? How do you feel when they do what you told them? That's how God feels!

Wait a minute, "Though he fall," but if God wants only the best for us why would we fall? Again, back to your own children. Do they not fall occasionally? Especially when they try something new. Of course, they do. Now, look at the end of that verse, "For the Lord upholds him with His hand." We are going fall, but isn't is reassuring to know that God is right there to pick you up and comfort you and encourage you to continue that walk with Him.

Now for me the hardest part of this psalm is the word "wait". I have never been a patient person! God has been working on me for thirty years to help me in this category. I was told a long time ago never to pray for patience. God won't "give" you, patience He will teach you, patience. He's been doing just that for a very long time, I am getting better. For more about patience look at the first chapter of the New Testament book of James!

Many, O Lord my God, are Your wonderful works which You have
done; and Your thoughts toward us cannot be recounted to You in
order; if I would declare and speak of them, they are more than can
be numbered. (Psalm 40:5)

I could fill this whole page with blessings God has done for me. But what would
that matter to you? The question is, what has God done for you? I challenge you
to begin keeping a daily journal of what God is doing in your life. Because, many
times, God works a step-by-step event to bring you to a certain place.

I remember when I first thought about getting a church. I was an associate
pastor at the time and my pastor kept urging me to create a resume and submit
it to the association. I kept putting it off. I hated the thought. One day I got my
daughter to help me create one and I turned it in. Not long after that a church in
Freeman, Missouri called me. The point I want to make and a lesson I learned then
was: There are things we need to do and then there are things God does. Until
we are obedient to God's prompting and do those things we need to do God will
not take a hand.

I'm kind of curious about this first part of this verse. Is David talking about
the things around, nature, etc. or is he talking about the things God is doing in our
everyday life? "Your wondrous works" can mean either or both. I think the thing
I have learned is that God is always at work around us. We just don't recognize it.
The worst word for a Christian to use is "luck". Luck has nothing to do with it. As
you can probably tell I believe fully in "providence" nothing happens by accident.

Again, to quote Henry Blackaby in "Experiencing God" "Find out where God
is at work and join Him there." That applies to the events around us. When we
begin to notice what God is doing around us and get in on those things then we
can know the full extent of God's activities in our life.

Just a note about this psalm. Notice how it starts, "I waited patiently for the
Lord," Do you know how hard that is? Part of that recognizing God working
around us is looking back over, maybe a long period of time, and remembering
how God brought you from point "A" to point "B". God is always at work, take a
minute and think back,

Oh, clap your hands, all you peoples! Shout to God with the voice of
triumph! For the Lord Most High is awesome; He is a great King over
all the earth. (Psalm 47:1-2)

Now why would Korah use the word "triumph" instead of joy? You would
think, if you were reading this that you would fill in the word "triumph" with
a different word. Why triumph?

That's exactly what God gives us. Triumph over sin, the grave, depression,
guilt, hurt, sadness, you name it. We have victory over these feelings when we
remember just what God has done for us.

I touched on this earlier. Being on this side of God's grace is hard to explain
the joy that exists to someone on the other side. You must join me to understand
that feeling.

I'm glad to see that Korah likes the word "awesome" too. It is probably the
best word to describe a relationship with God. Korah was a chief musician in the
temple. The "song leader" if you will. Music is such an important part of worship.

I remember watching our church progress from not clapping for someone
who sang a beautiful solo, to clapping in praise for their offering to God. I've even
seen our church applaud for the pianist piece that was played during the offering.
I'm glad to see us get past that. Applause is in appreciation for an extra effort to
glorify God. And we can honor that person for their offering.

I have heard countless stories of the Song Leader preparing his list of songs
for Sunday and then on Sunday finding out that the music fits perfectly with the
pastor's message, without either of them conferring.

It seems most of this psalm about singing. Have you ever had a hymn stick in
your memory after Sunday worship? I think sometimes that's the way the Holy
Spirit works. He keeps whispering over and over in our minds, either something
to do or something that needs to be addressed. Just that "still small voice" that
keeps speaking to us.

Look at verse 10 in Psalm 46, "Be still, and know that I am God." Sometimes
that's what it takes. Listening to God prompting in your heart. He wants your
attention, He wants to speak to you, He wants to encourage and guide your
footsteps toward His will for your life. Are you listening?

> Restore to me the joy of Your salvation, and uphold me by Your generous, Spirit. Then I will teach transgressors Your ways, and sinners shall be converted to You. (Psalm 51:12-13)

What an awesome psalm. If you've been in church any length of time you know that supposedly David wrote this psalm after his affair with Bathsheba and God's rebuke. I just wonder how many "old" Christians have ever prayed this prayer? "Restore to me the joy of my salvation." Think back. Remember how you felt when you asked Jesus to come into your heart. The realization that your sins were forgiven by God and that you have a relationship with the Almighty! Remember?

I love this word "teach". One of my dearest verses, especially as a teacher is, "If anyone speaks, let him speak as the oracles of God. If anyone ministers, let him do it as with the ability which God supplies, that in all things God may be glorified through Jesus Christ, to whom belong the glory and dominion forever and ever. Amen." (1 Peter 4:11) That verse has always been an encouragement to me as a teacher. The ability is all from God.

Take a look at David's heart here: "The sacrifices of God are a broken spirit, a broken and contrite heart—These O God, you will not despise." (v. 17). I believe that is what cemented David's relationship with God. His heart for God!

It wouldn't hurt to read this psalm over a couple of times. What a picture of repentance! We have talked about the many mistakes David had made. But David always came back to God. Always sincerely repented and sought God's forgiveness. Again, God knew his heart.

I don't know if I mentioned this, I probably have, but these are all songs the Hebrews would sing. Either in worship or in the quiet time. Imagine learning and singing this hymn. It just really speaks to my heart!

This is a good psalm to examine our own hearts. Is there anything between you and God that would hamper your relationship. If you're not sure, in your quiet time, ask God to reveal it to you. Mark this psalm in your memories (address). Check on it regularly. Remind yourself of two things, one, God loves you and desires an intimate relationship. Two, He is forever willing to restore a broken heart.

Hear my cry, O God; attend to my prayer. From the end of the earth
I will cry to You, when my heart is overwhelmed; lead me to the rock
that is higher than I. (Psalm 61:1-2)

"Attend to my prayer." Isn't that the prayer of each of us? Have you ever experienced a time when your prayers went no higher than the ceiling? It's not a pleasant feeling. I imagine David felt that way the night he lost the child born to Bathsheba.

What would it take to overwhelm your heart? Extremes of high and low, maybe. How about the nearness of God? You can just sense His presence, either in your quiet time or a worship service. It is an awesome feeling to sense God's presence. I suspect David felt that many times out in the field in the evening as the sun was setting, watching the sheep in the pasture. Just knowing the presence of God.

I wonder if you notice the familiar hymn in this verse? I'm hearing the Statler brothers in my mind right now (the last phrase in this verse). I can't remember the name of it right now. Then of course there is "Rock of Ages." What a great picture of our Lord.

Look at 2 Samuel 22:2, "And he (David) said, The Lord is my rock and my fortress and my deliverer; the God of my strength, in whom I will trust; my shield and the horn of my salvation, my stronghold and my refuge; my Savior, You, save me from violence." So, how was David's relationship with God?

Can you say that? First it requires complete trust in God's sovereignty, does it not? Remember the numerous opportunities David had to rid himself of Saul, who wanted to kill him? What was David's response? I will not raise my hand against God's anointed. David had respect for His servants, God's chosen. I'm sure that strengthened David's relationship with God.

A short psalm, only eight verses. A powerful psalm that speaks to God's desire for us to pray. He is there just waiting to hear from us, to open our hearts and share with Him our burdens.

We are coming up on the mid-way point in the Psalms. 150 Psalms, a 150 Hymns, to praise God. Just a trick. For the most part, it doesn't always work with a study Bible but generally if you split your Bible in half you will open to the Psalms.

God be merciful to us and bless us, and cause His face to shine upon
us, Selah that your way may be known on earth, Your salvation among
all nations. (Psalm 67:1-2)

Someone once told me that the word "Selah' meant "Amen." Not sure but sounds
good. Think about those words for a minute. "And cause His face to shine upon
us." What does that mean to you? We have been talking about walking with God.
This is part of that picture. For God's face to shine on us, what do you think must
happen. First, we've got to be on the same path, walking with God or we won't see
His face. Next, we must be, if we are on the path, walking in God's will. Doing
what He wants us to do. Of course, that would make Him happy.

Someone once asked, "Do you want justice or mercy?" Of course, we want
mercy. If it weren't for God's mercy we all deserve the cross. That's why Jesus took
our place. To pay what we could not. That's another point. ONLY the Son of God
would have the authority to pay for our sins, past, present and future. And He
did it willingly.

There is the challenge for of each of the children of God. "That Your way may
be known on earth." We are the one's God has chosen to bring that message. That
doesn't mean we are all to preach on the corner and try to win as many to Christ
as we can. That's the purpose but not the method. The method is in our daily walk
and how we treat those we come in contact on a daily basis. There are so many
opportunities just in the people we meet just to offer a kind word, encouragement,
compliment, etc. That's how we make "His way" known in the earth.

Have you ever watched these missionary programs on Sunday on TV? It is
amazing what is happening around the world. You say, "why haven't they made
a difference?" You know the story of a guy walking along the beach, throwing
starfish back into the ocean. Another person comes along and says, "you're wasting
your time, you're not making a difference. There are thousands on the shore. The
other guy says, "It makes a difference to that starfish." Let me remind you of the
shoe salesman named Kimball who witnessed to D.L. Moody, did that salesman
make a difference? Think about it.

We simply share with others what Jesus has done in our lives, sow the seed,
God takes care of the crop that springs from that seed!

> The humble shall seek this and be glad; and you who seek God, your hearts shall live. For the Lord hears the poor, and does not despise His prisoners. (Psalm 32-33)

Don't misunderstand this verse. It does not mean that God can't use the rich. Far from it. It's like Jesus taught. Too many times for the rich, the money becomes a god, and replaces the true God. That is the danger. That is why God seeks not just the poor but the "poor in spirit" as well.

It's funny that David uses the picture of us seeking God. "And you who seek God." We have this picture that at some point in our lives we decide to seek God. It doesn't work that way. God is always seeking us. His Spirit convicts us of our sin. Convicts us that there is something missing in our lives, starts us searching for that missing piece. His Spirit is what prompts us to search. God is looking for us. Look at John 4:23, "But the hour is coming, and now is, when the true worshippers will worship the Father in spirit and truth, for the Father is seeking such to worship Him."

Back up to verse 29. "But I am poor and sorrowful; let Your salvation, O God, set me up on high." Again, a reference to poor. But here it's a reference to poor in spirit. I have heard so many testimonies about those who have come to God, only, when they have reached the bottom. No hope, nowhere to go, etc. Then they look up, they seek God. God was there all the time they just needed to get to the point of looking up. Sometimes you must reach the bottom before you look up.

Do you remember what it was like when you met your first love? Just the ache in your heart when you weren't together. That's what David is talking about "your hearts shall live." You come alive when Jesus comes into your heart. It's a feeling you can't describe. It's not like the love of a boy and girl, it's the kind of love that brings peace, contentment, joy, excitement, etc. To me it was the anticipation every day to see what God was going to do in my life. The almost, daily miracles that He did all around me. Now I saw them for what they were, God making Himself known to His child. Showing me He was there, He cared, He would walk with me daily if I let Him. That's knowing God in your heart.

> But it is good for me to draw near to God; I have put my trust in the
> Lord God, that I may declare all Your works. (Psalm 73:28)

There is the picture I have been drawing throughout the psalms and other passages. "Draw near to God." I have always enjoyed walking. I can't run much anymore but I love walking. I was walking with my mother once and she told me to slow down, she couldn't keep up. That's an important part of walking with someone. Each has their own pace. That is not a problem walking with God. Of course, God always knows what's ahead, but our challenge is to trust God's leadership. Stay in step and stay close. If you get too far behind you miss where He's leading, Never, get too far ahead. That is dangerous! I know from experience.

The second part of this verse is exactly what I'm talking about. When you choose to follow someone or to walk with them you must have confidence that they know where they are going. Because God knows where we are going we can have the assurance the course is the right one. It's when we decide to go our own way, we get into trouble.

The other day we set the GPS in our car to take us to a place in Kansas. We thought we knew a better way. A faster way on the highway. When we took a strange exit, we hadn't thought of, my wife says, "I never would have thought to go this way." That's exactly how God works. Too many times we think we know better than God. God who knows the future way in advance, yet we want our way.

That last illustration is exactly what I'm talking about. When we get to the point when we can see God's principles all around us then we can know that we are walking with God. When we have the assurance of His presence and trust in His leadership the journey becomes so much easier and pleasant!

This verse reminds me of Moses. Notice how God drew Moses to Him to enlist him in God's work? The burning bush. How would you like to be a burning bush? God can use you much the same way. People will see God working in your life and be drawn to what God is doing in your life and want to know how they can know God. That is such a draw. Remember Moses and the burning bush when you are around strangers. Are you demonstrating God's power in your life? Are your words and actions pointing people to Jesus?

> We will not hide them from their children, telling, to the generation
> to come the praises of the Lord, and His strength and His wonderful
> works that He has done. (Psalm 78:4)

I have talked before about the importance of keeping a journal. The funny thing about keeping a journal is that you can't look back and say, "I wish I had written down my past." Unless of course you have an excellent memory. A few years ago, I had the opportunity to try that. Using the many places, we had lived growing up as a guide I wrote down memories from each location. After writing over 280 pages I still have reminders of things I forgot to include.

So why is that important? Look at this verse. "Telling, to the generation to come the praises of the Lord." The nice thing about writing those pages is I got to give my testimony of how God saved me and what God has done in my life since. I made three copies. One for me and one for each of our daughters. Hopefully they can pass them on to their children.

I can't stress how important it is to pass on what God has done in our lives. It's not too late. Stop right now. Find a notebook or buy one and start writing while the memories are still there. Use locations as a point of reference. Dates are hard but you can usually remember places you have lived. "The old home place," etc.

Another benefit of writing these things down is you can look back over the years and see where God has brought you from, to where you are now. See God's hand in the events that brought you here. It will really strengthen your faith, believe me.

This psalm, in a sense, is a prophecy. Look at verse 2, "I will open my mouth in a parable; I will utter dark sayings of old." One of Jesus most effective teaching methods was His teaching with parables. I can't tell you how many sermons I have heard on the "Prodigal Son."

Today is the first day of the second half of this year. A good time to buy a special notebook and begin recording your thoughts and events. The day you write them down they will seem so insignificant, almost boring. It's the accumulation and reflection that pays off years from now. Try it. Pray and ask God for guidance!

For the Lord God is a sun and shield; the Lord will give grace and
glory; No good thing will He withhold from those who walk uprightly.
O Lord of hosts, Blessed, is the man who trusts in You! (Psalm
84:11-12)

Did you notice toward the end of this verse the word "blessed?" I did an exercise
with a youth class I was teaching once. We were going through the Be-
Attitudes, I challenged the class that there are many more "Be-attitudes" in the
Bible. I brought a box of Snickers candy bars to the class and told them if anyone
could find another Be-attitude in the Bible they would get a Snickers. It worked
for a while until I started asking them what the blessing was that was used in the
verse. All they had to do was look in the concordance in the back of their Bibles
for "blessed". It was fun anyway.

One of the points I wanted to make was that most of the time, the blessing
came with conditions. Look at the verse above. Do you see the condition? "Who
trusts in You." Check it out! It's a good exercise.

This is a good verse for "literalists" those who take the Bible at face value.
Don't miss understand. I am a inerrancy believer myself. But some carry it way
too far. The point I want to make is, here it says, "God is a sun." It doesn't say God
is LIKE the sun. That's SUN not Son. This would make Egypt's worship of Ra
(the sun god) ok. It's not. Sorry to split hairs but I have known literalists like that
before.

Look at the promise in this verse. Oh, yes most of the promises in the Bible
come with conditions as well. "No good thing will He withhold from those who
walk uprightly." Now I'm reminded of an old gospel hymn sung by Red Foley and
Tennessee Ernie Ford, "Just A Closer Walk with Thee." Even the hymn writers
know what I'm talking about.

That might be a good Bible study. Look up the word "walk" and see how many
refer to walking with God.

I got to thinking, now that we are starting the second half of the year. I have
talked a lot about walking with God. Like God is some sort of buddy. Never forget
that God is the Sovereign of the Universe! God Almighty! Creator of all that is!
He desires a relationship with us!

> Give ear, O Lord, to my prayer; and attend to the voice of my
> supplication. In the day of my trouble I will call upon You, For You
> will answer me. (Psalm 86:6-7)

Isn't that the prayer of most Christians? We pray that God will hear us, yet we spend little or no time listening to God. We want God to respond to our requests but when God asks us to do something we refuse or ignore Him. Why is that? Even in the rest of the verse. When do we usually call on God? When we are in trouble, and then as a last resort. When we have messed things up so bad then we want God to fix them.

But look at the confidence of David, "For you will answer me." wouldn't you love to have the confidence of David? So how do you think David got that confidence? Look again at David's life. David saw God do miraculous things even as a shepherd. He had the confidence to trust God against Goliath because David saw what God did against a bear and a lion. That's why God works miracles in our lives every day, to prepare us for the time we will need a special miracle.

We have passed the halfway mark in the year. Soon we will pass the halfway mark in the Bible. How are you doing? I hope you are keeping up. I was thinking about this just this morning. If we focus on the New Testament we have a drawing in pencil. No color, no definition. Once we add the details of the Old Testament them we have filled in the lines with color. The picture becomes clearer, more defined. It makes a big difference.

I wonder why David would say, "Give ear, O Lord." Does he think that God may not be listening? I would love to know the chronology of these psalms. Just when David wrote them. What point was he in his walk with God? It would help in knowing his frame of mind. Curious.

I like verse 11 as well. "Teach me Your way, O Lord; I will walk in your truth; unite my heart to fear Your name." Isn't that awesome? When I began this project, I chose verses I had already selected from a previous trip through God's word. As usually happens when I read over them God points to a different verse. That is the miracle of scripture. You can read the same chapter 10 days in a row. Each day a different verse will catch your eye, get your attention, show you a different perspective of God's glory!

> He who dwells in the secret place of the Most High shall abide under
> the shadow of the Almighty. I will say to the Lord, "He is my refuge
> and my fortress; my God, in Him I will trust." (Psalm 91:1-2)

Years and years ago our youth group did a play using this scripture. I remember the verse from that play. I believe it was called something like, abiding under the shadow of God's wings. Notice the "peace" in the following words, "He is my refuge and my fortress, my God, in Him will I trust." chew on that phrase a minute.

I told myself I wasn't going to use that phrase (chew). It's just my way of saying meditate. It makes me think of a cow in the pasture. He gets a mouthful of grass and chews, and chews, and chews, until He has every last bit of nourishment from it. That's the idea when I say chew on that verse.

This is an interesting verse. Who is the He? Is it God who dwells in the secret place of the Almighty? That doesn't make sense, does it? Is it YOU who dwells in the secret place? That makes sense, but do we really feel like we are dwelling there? It seems we are dwelling in a world that is falling part. Look at this, "If you were of the world, the world would love its own. Yet because you are not of the world, but I chose you out of the world, therefore the world hates you." (John 15:19). When we become a child of God we are no longer members of this world. We are passing through. We are destined for the shadow of God's wings. The great thing about that. As children of God we can have the peace of that "secret place" here on earth. Just the knowledge that God has our back. He is watching over us.

Underline that first verse. That is such an awesome promise from God. I remember seeing this picture of an eagle's nest during a rainstorm. The mother eagle hovers over the nest with her wings spread wide to protect the eaglets from the rain. What a great picture of God's protection for us. But wait, bad things still happen. Of course, they do. What happens when those baby eagles try to fly too soon? They are not ready to leave the nest. Too many Christians think they get a few verses under their belt and they are ready to take on Satan. It doesn't work that way. We need to mature, get our wings, learn to trust God!

Inter into His gates with thanksgiving, and into His courts with praise. Be thankful to Him, and bless His name. For the Lord is good; His mercy is everlasting, and His truth endures to all generations. (Psalm 100:4-5)

I wonder what the first part of this verse means. I would think he's not talking about heaven. It sounds like it, doesn't it? "Enter into His Gates." Can you imagine coming into God's presence? I want you to try something next time you pray. Just in your mind's eye imagine you are walking down this long stretch of huge marble columns. You are approaching the throne of God. God is seated on His throne. How would you approach? Crawling on your hands and knees? Bowing to the ground, prostrated on the marble floor? Just bowing at the waist? Think about it.

You see here is the paradox. As His servants, which we certainly are, we would approach humbly, bowing, etc. As His children, we have the authority to approach the throne as heirs. Look at Romans 8:16-17, "The Spirit bears witness with our spirit that we are children of God, and if children, then heirs—heirs of God and joint heirs with Christ, if indeed we suffer with Him, that we may also be glorified together." What an awesome picture. Understand, even as joint heirs we are to approach our Heavenly Father with awe and respect. Look at the proceeding verse, 8:15, "For you did not receive the spirit of bondage again to fear, but you received the Spirit of adoption by whom we cry out, "Abba. Father." These two verses give us a glimpse of our relationship with God the Father.

I want to contrast these verses with the picture we get of God in the Old Testament. Judging, punishing, rejected by Israel, ignored and disobeyed. Power! I really believe that is Why God sent His Son to show us that human side of God. He so desires that personal, intimate relationship with us. To the point of saying, "Abba". (daddy).

Digest the two verses from Psalm 100 again. It just gives an invitation to inter into God's holy presence, not as servants but as His children seeking approval, and in return offering our praise of thanksgiving because of that special relationship with a holy God. A relationship made possible only by God's grace and the blood of Jesus!

> But the mercy of the Lord is from everlasting to everlasting on those
> who fear Him, and His righteousness to children's children, to, such as
> keep His covenant, and to those who remember His commandments
> to do them. (Psalm 103:17-18)

This could almost be a command to memorize the Ten Commandments. "Who remember His commandments to do them." What do you think? That has always been God's desire for us. Not just to know His word but to follow and obey it!

Look at Isaiah chapter one. The whole chapter is God's frustrations toward Israel. They offer up these sacrifices and they mean nothing. They obey God in all the "rules" and neglect the relationship. There it is again in this 18th verse. "to such as keep His covenant." I guess God is saying, "It's just empty words." Say what you mean, and mean what you say. I can see this bumper sticker in Israel, during the time of Moses.

Did you notice that God's mercy has a catch to it? "Those who fear Him." We talked about fear before. I think it is consistent throughout scripture. Remember John 14:15?

God has gone to great lengths to bring His message to us through His great prophets and servants and teachers throughout the Bible. It's not complicated and it's not hard. I have given you a set of instructions to follow. If you follow them you will prosper (do a word search on "prosper"). A certain amount of obedience is required for salvation and to become children of God. "IF you will confess with your mouth the Lord Jesus, and believe in your heart that God had raised Him from the dead, you will be saved." (Romans 10:9) There is something for us to do (believe) then God does the rest. Those are His instructions. There's no other way. That's the path that God has established.

God is willing to wait for us to learn the truth. "The mercy of the Lord is from everlasting to everlasting" The problem is, the longer you wait the less opportunity you must enjoy that blessing and that relationship with Almighty God. Don't put it off. If you have read this far in our schedule chances are you are saved. To the lost this will make no sense. Rejoice in your walk with God!

> Oh, that men would give thanks to the Lord for His goodness, and
> for His wonderful works to the children of men! For He satisfies the
> longing soul, and fills the hungry soul with goodness. (Psalm 107:8-9)

Ain't gonna happen! As long as we feel the need to take credit for the miracles of God we will never acknowledge the true source of our blessing. One of the greatest downfalls of the nation Israel was to turn their backs on God and begin trusting in "things". Remember Nehushtan? 2 Kings 18:4. God instructed the creation of this thing to heal Israel from snake bites, it later became an idol. If you notice the ark of the Covenant became the same thing until the Philistines captured it. The most dangerous thing we can do is attribute the blessings in our life to either self, or substance!

I love this phrase because He has definitely done this for me. "He satisfies the longing soul." I love the principle that says if we don't receive the answer that we want from God, God will change our "want to". God changes our priorities, our desires, to fall in line with His and thus gives us a special peace that the things of this world can't give!

To go along with that, look at these words, "and fills the hungry soul with goodness." This is so important! God changes what is important to us. Our fleshly desires are replaced with God's perfect will. That seems to be the biggest struggle today. Our will verses God's will. Can you look a year into the future and make plans accordingly? Of course not! God can. God can lead us down that path that leads to His perfect will and His perfect outcome. We just need to trust His vision for our lives.

The next two verses, 10 and 11 say the same thing I just said, only better. Thank, you Lord!

I'm encouraging you to follow this reading plan. I believe it's the best to get the most out of your Bible. Here is another option. There are 150 Psalms and thirty chapters in Proverbs. Some have suggested reading a chapter of Proverbs and five Psalms each day. The insight and wisdom you will receive is unbelievable. At the start of each Proverbs chapter write the five Psalms chapters. It doesn't really matter which plan you use, just have a plan. Commit to it and stick to it.

> The works of the Lord are great, studied by all who have pleasure in them. His work is honorable and glorious, and His righteousness endures forever. (Psalm 111:2-3)

It is so hard to come up with different approaches to basically the same principles. I hope you didn't look at these devotions as a commentary. I am simply sharing my thoughts on these verses. God's word has meant so much to me through the years I just wanted to share some of that passion with you.

That's an interesting start to this verse, "The works of the Lord are great, studied by all who have pleasure in them". The Old Testament and the gospels is a great place to study "the works of the Lord." As far as the Bible goes. But what about, in your life? Has God done anything great in your life? Do you think it was an accident that you met your wife? Surely you don't think your children just happened? How about your occupation, do you think that was all your doing? Where do you suppose you got that specific talent? So many things that we think were just accidents or genetics or whatever, all stem from God's hand in your life.

One of my favorite hymns is Amazing Grace and I really love the last verse that says, "When we've been there ten thousand years, bright shining as the star, we've no less days to sing God's praise than when we first begun." Apologies to the writer. THAT is what forever is. That verse describes "forever". The verse above says, "His righteousness endures forever." God has always been on the throne, and God will always be there, no matter what. Just chew on that for a minute. In a world that has so totally changed in the last twenty years God has never changed. His love for us, His desire to have a relationship with us has remained constant.

God tried one approach in the Old Testament. His creation would not accept His offer of leadership. So, God sent His Son to be born in Bethlehem, to grow up to preach and teach the grace of God. To demonstrate God's love so dramatically that He offered His life on a cruel cross to demonstrate how much God desired an intimate relationship with His creation. So, what more can He do? It's up to you now!

May the Lord give you increase more and more, you and your children. May you be blessed by the Lord, who made heaven and earth. (Psalm 115:14-15)

In this set of verses let me draw your attention to a passage that is so important. Look at 115:4-8. This is a great picture of what God hates. Idols! Anything that comes between you and God. The psalmist draws a drastic comparison between the God of the Bible and "objects" that people put their trust in. I wonder how many of us carry around "objects" in our pockets, four-lead clovers, rabbit's feet, a trinket of some kind because they think that gives them good luck. This passage exposes that myth. The God of the Bible has demonstrated His passion for our success.

Look at the first part of this verse. "May the Lord give you increase more and More." May I remind you of Joshua 1:8? Of course, there are conditions to this promise. Overall, I think the clearest condition is, get to know God through His word. Walk with God. Believe God, Trust God and obey God, it's really that simple.

Now it's interesting that God says, "You and your children" the point being that it's up to us to pass on this information to the next generation. Dave Ramsey has gone to great lengths to, not only give financial advice for us to get out of debt (scriptural advice) but has also provided tools for parents to teach their children. It is so important to pass this concept on to the next generation.

Our pastor was teaching on Psalm one this morning and guess what word popped out to me? Speaking of a Christian, "He shall be like a tree planted by the rivers of water, that brings forth it's fruit in its season, whose leaf also shall not wither; and whatever he does shall prosper." (1:3).

Check the concordance in the back of your Bible. Look up the word "prosper" then look at the verses it lists. Do a little Bible study. Then pray about what you have read. Idols can do nothing but occupy a space. God wants the best for His children. Again, the condition given in Joshua 1:8, you must read God's word and obey Gods commands to do things God's way brings God's blessings! "May you be blessed by the Lord."

You are my portion, O Lord; I have said that I would keep Your words. I
entreated Your favor with my whole heart; be merciful to me according
to Your word. (Psalm 119:57-58)

This is one awesome psalm! 176 verses of exhortation to read and heed the
word of God. Statutes, ordinances, commandments, laws, etc. All these words
throughout this psalm. Challenge us to think about who or what rules we are
living by. What guides the decisions we make? Proverbs will spend a lot of time
on knowledge and wisdom. Both are great, but if we don't "follow" them what is
the point. We have filled our heads with all kinds of facts that mean absolutely
nothing until they are put into action.

When I was little, I loved going into my dad's workshop. He had tools hanging
on the wall over his workbench. Tools I had no idea what they were for. Sometimes
I would catch him working on a piece of wood. He would use a certain tool to
accomplish a certain task. The point is, you can have all the tools in the world but
unless you use them the way they were intended to be used they just occupy a space
on a wall above your workbench.

Did you notice, in the verse above, how dedicated the psalmist was to doing
God's words? "With my whole heart." That's what God wants! That's God's desire,
that our commitment to obedience be complete, fully committed! Of course, to do
that you must know what God's word says, don't you! I hope you haven't given up
on reading through the Bible. Just make a commitment to do it at least one time.
When you see the way, it speaks to your heart. Verse after verse lifts, encourages,
challenges, inspires, chastises, moves you to a closer relationship with the Father
of heaven. You will want to do it year after year just to absorb God's message and
wisdom.

Is it any wonder that the "heart" of the Bible would be about His word? Here is
a little side study if you're interested. It was fascinating to me when I studied it. Get
a book about the creation of the Bible that we hold in our hands. The painstaking
methods used to determine which books would be included and why they were
chosen. The purpose for writing the King James Bible. All the history behind this
fantastic book. You will realize that God was in the process all along!

I was glad when they said to me, "Let us go into the house of the Lord." Our feet have been standing within your gates, O Jerusalem! (Psalm 122:1-2)

When my wife and I went on vacation I would always look for a church to visit away from home. I wanted to experience how others worshipped. Ever since the day I was saved I have always felt that the Lord's day was meant to be enjoyed in God's house. It's just right! When I have rarely been sick and missed a Sunday it just felt weird and depressing! My place, as a child of God, is in God's house on the Lord's day. I really enjoy Wednesday night prayer meetings. Even the business meetings. That's God's business with God's money (tithes and offerings). You just can't separate God's house from a relationship with God.

It might be different if Paul or Peter had suggested forming a church. Of course, the Old Testament equivalent would be the tabernacle. It was Jesus, the Son of God who instituted the concept of the New Testament church. Of course, it has been corrupted and mismanaged thru the years but that is because of man, not God.

I know it's kind of hard to walk through the story of Solomon and all the detail of constructing the temple. It can get boring. But you notice that the grand building that was erected didn't keep God from judging His people. A severe lesson Israel had to learn. God doesn't dwell in buildings made with hands. He dwells in the hearts of His children through the Holy Spirit.

I've mentioned that I have been saved over thirty years. Served as deacon, Sunday school teacher and director, even pastor for a time. This Sunday our pastor preached on Psalm one. I heard several things that I had to make a note of. Not new stuff but things I needed right then. I had to underline three words in verse one. "walk, stand, sit" walking with God, standing (that meant, taking a stand, to me) and then sitting in God's house on the Lord's day and taking in the nourishment of hearing God's word proclaimed. Either in a Sunday school class or from the pulpit. A real blessing comes from hearing testimony and insight from those in our class. Those who have experienced God working in their lives and how it impacted them. That is such a blessing! I always look forward to being in God's house every week!

How precious also are Your thoughts to me, O God! How great is the
sum of them! If I could count them, they would be more in number
than the sand. (Psalm 139:17-18)

We have been there before, but I want to remind you of the words of Jeremiah
29:11, "For I know the thoughts that I think toward, you, says the Lord,
thoughts of peace and not evil, to give you a future and a hope."

That word hope recalls a scene in "The Hunger Games." The head guy asks his
assistant, "why do we have a winner in the Hunger Games?" He replied he didn't
know (or something like that). Anyway, the head guy says, "to give the people hope.
If they have no hope they wouldn't survive." Hope is such an important part of our
makeup. Many times, it's what keeps us going, through enormous odds.

As a Christian the hope of heaven, many times, can encourage us, even to the
point of death, as in the lives of the martyrs. It's one of the great promises that God
has given His children to sustain us through hardships and trials.

This is a great couple of verses but how can we know God's thoughts toward
us? Well, we see just a portion in the verse in Jeremiah. The rest of scripture also
reveals how God feels and thinks of us. Another great example is to study the life
of Christ in the four gospels. Here we have four different perspectives of what Jesus
taught, said, and acted to show us the mind of God.

There is a story in the gospels of Jesus heading somewhere important. He was
determined to reach that point. On the way, a woman touches his garment. Jesus
senses some healing had taken place. Instead of just moving on to His destination
He stopped and spoke to the woman and marveled at her faith, and complimented
her faith. (Matthew 9:18-24). He didn't have to do that, He was on a mission. But,
He stopped to minister to her. That's the thoughts of God. God cares about each
and every one of us. He wants to minister to His children. We are the ones too
busy to stop and talk to God. To spend a few minutes learning the mind of God by
reading His word. Is it any wonder we have no idea what God wants to do in our
lives? The plans He has for us, to bless us, and to lead us to a closer walk with Him.

> Cause me to hear Your lovingkindness in the morning, for in You I do trust; Cause me to know the way in which I should walk, for I lift up my soul to You. (Psalm 143:8)

God, begin my day seeking your guidance and wisdom. Keep me on track, keep me walking in your will and purpose for my life. You demonstrated Your love on the cross at Calvary. Make your presence known to me throughout this day. Guide each and every step. Let me not put one foot out of place. Thank you for Your presence in my life, bless your servant today.

I know it's easy to tell someone when they should have their quiet time. When I was working it was easier to have it in the evening. But since I have retired I always begin my day with my quiet time, reading and praying. When I was working sometimes I had to force myself to shut the TV off and have my time with You. We get so busy, especially early in life. So many things to get done in so little time.

I like this saying, "He is so earthly minded he is no heavenly good, and he is so heavenly minded he is no earthly good. Neither are good. But there comes a time, preferably early in life when we establish what our priorities are. If God's not at the top of your list, why should we be at the top of His?

"Cause me to know the way in which I should walk." There's that word walk again. Because it's an ongoing thing. As we travel from one end of life to the other, there are so many detours, and forks in the road sometimes it's hard to know where to turn. What do you do who you reach a fork in the road? Do you stop, look up each road, maybe ask someone? Or do you toss a coin and off you go. Why not ask someone who knows what's at the other end. Is it a dead end, or does it lead to life more abundant?

Remember John 10:10b? "I have come that they may have life, and that they may have it more abundantly." Jesus said, that's why I came. To bless you. To prosper you, to guide you into the Father's perfect will. And when He left He promised to send the Holy Spirit to continue to guide us along this path. To help us know whether to go left, right or straight ahead. But if you don't listen to the guide the fault is yours, is it not?

He does not delight in the strength of the horse; He takes no pleasure
in the legs of a man. The LORD takes pleasure in those who fear Him,
in those who hope in His mercy. (Psalm 147:10-11)

I thought this verse was funny because I have a friend who raises horses. Also, I will not wear shorts, for obvious reasons!

But don't ignore the point of this verse. "The Lord takes pleasure in those who fear Him." I know it's a little late in this journey through God's word. I want you to know the difference in the word Lord. The editors of our current Bible make's a distinction between the two words, Lord and LORD. In Bible time's many kings and those in authority were referred to as "Lord." Jesus, and even God can be referred to as LORD. That's why I have capitalized it here. If you notice in the text that is how the publishers distinguished between the two. Take a close look next time. Even in this verse you can see LORD.

I think we talked earlier about knowing the mind of God. Here's another example. The scripture reveals what is important to God. Saul was a good example. Saul was a head taller than most Hebrews. (1 Samuel 9). He was handsome of course. He lacked the one quality that God needed to be His servant; A heart for God. David, on the other hand was the opposite of Saul. David's heart sought after God. That's what God wants from us.

Have you ever heard the hymn, "Sweet Hour of prayer?" I heard a pastor say one time, "Can you pray for an hour?" Not likely. He said that a good way to pray for an hour is to read the psalms to God. It's no accident that the heart of the Bible is the psalms. The psalms, full of praise and worship. If we meditate in this book. Read a portion every day. We will find our relationship growing deeper and deeper with our loving Lord.

Did you notice anything about these last five psalms? Look at the first word of each psalm. "Praise" you can put this word next to "fear" in your priority list of God's priorities. Fear (reverence) and praise will bring you into God's presence quicker than anything else we can do. Repentance comes in there too. Confession, seeking God's direction, etc. All this of course, in our daily prayers. If you praise God it means you recognize who He is and who you are!

> Trust in the Lord with all your heart, and lean not on your own understanding; in all your ways acknowledge Him, and He shall direct your path. (Proverbs 3:5-6)

This is one of those verses to commit to memory! Basic stuff here! There are four simply components. Let's break them down:

Trust in the Lord with all your heart.

It's a full, heartfelt, commitment to trust God. To walk daily by His side and trust God to make the right moves. Like I pointed out before. God knows the bends and turns up ahead, you don't. When I drove over the road, I had occasion to drive in dense fog. I could keep going while I kept my eye on the white road lines in the middle of the road, slowly for sure but that line kept me on the right track. That's the way walking with God is. Trust Him to lead you.

Lean not upon you own understanding.

This is critical! Sometimes God will take us to places and circumstances we just don't understand. Trust Him, there is a reason He has brought you here. Either a much better path or to avoid a danger up ahead. God always has a reason for the direction you are traveling. To bring you to a certain point that will bless you and glorify Him!

In all your ways acknowledge Him.

Simple isn't it. Not really. To acknowledge Him it must be His will and not yours. Giving God the reins, allow Him to lead. No arguments, no back talk, no grumbling. "Not my will but yours God!" That must be our attitude. Until you are willing to let God take the lead there will always be those sidetracks that only bring disappointment and discouragement. Trust that God knows what He's doing.

And He will direct your paths.

That's the point, isn't it? You see, when He created you in the womb, He has a purpose for you to fulfill. Your one of His children and He wants only the best for you. So, you must trust His guidance. Stop, turn left, go ahead, etc. Wait for His guidance, trust that He knows what's best. Would you lead your own child into harm's way? Of course not! Neither will God. God wants only the best for His children. The wonderful thing about it is that He has the knowledge and the desire to lead you to the very best only God can offer!

My son, give attention to my words; incline your ear to my sayings. Do not let them depart from your eyes; keep them in the midst of your heart; for they are life to those who find them. (Proverbs 4:20-22)

Now what do you suppose Solomon is talking about here? The word of God of course. That's the point of this devotion. If I can encourage one more person to spend a little more time in Bible study, I have accomplished my task. The time you spend in God's word is an investment in your future. An investment in your relationship with God the Father. And an investment in understanding the God of the universe that wants only the best for you.

There's that reference to a heart again. Now why didn't Solomon say keep them in your mind? Because "head-knowledge" will not bring a relationship with God. In the very beginning God deals with the heart. In my Bible I have underlined, in the early chapters of Exodus, how many times it say's "and God hardened Pharaoh's heart." God had a purpose for all those plagues. So, when Pharaoh didn't harden his heart, God did. God deals in the heart. Later when Samuel is looking to call a king to replace Saul he goes to Jesse's house. Looks at his sons. Samuel picked one out, but God said, "For the Lord does not see as man sees; for man looks at the outward appearance, but the Lord looks at the heart." (1 Samuel 16:7).

You notice he says, "keep them in the midst of your heart." It is a daily exercise to maintain that storehouse of scripture. If it is just reading it you will be surprised at how much you retain. I think I have read through the Bible over ten times and each time I find new and exciting verses and truths that bless me.

See that in the last part of this verse? "For they are life to those who find them." It's like panning for gold. You scoop and sift, scoop and sift, every day, day in and day out. Then one day you find a small nugget. That's what reading the Bible is about. Think about what the miner does with that small nugget. He saves it, puts it with other nuggets and soon he has enough to change his life. To live comfortably. To relax and enjoy life, etc. That's what reading the Bible is like. You daily add to your pouch of gold nuggets. The more you add to that pouch the more you begin to have a peace about the future, don't you?

The fear of the Lord is the beginning of wisdom, and the knowledge of
the Holy One is understanding, for by me your days will be multiplied,
and years of life will be added to you. (Proverbs 9:10-11)

The book of Proverbs is a hard book to follow. I thought of this analogy. Eating
a handful of mixed nuts. I love mixed nuts, they are different and their flavor
blends together in mouthful of blessing.

Each verse in Proverbs, is a study. You could meditate on a verse each day.
Each is rich with God's wisdom and instructions for living a godly life.

There are those two words that you will see throughout the Proverbs, wisdom
and knowledge. They are so different from each other yet we think they are alike.
Think about this definition when thinking of these words: "Wisdom is the right
application of knowledge." Some call it "common sense." I mentioned before that
I've known some people with all kinds of degrees, all kinds of "knowledge" but
not a lick of sense.

Now notice that both wisdom and knowledge are linked with the fear
(reverence) of the Lord. Without that connection to God both wisdom and
knowledge are simply a pile of facts. It's like a trivia contest. You know a whole lot
of "facts" but you can't find your way home.

Notice the last part of verse 10. "The knowledge of the Holy One is
understanding". You see it's that relationship with God that brings all these facts
into focus. You begin putting each in it's place and you begin to understand just
what God is trying to tell you.

It's a lot like the lesson I was trying to teach my high school Sunday school
class. I gave each one, every Sunday, a Lego cube. The more they attended the
bigger their Lego block became. The facts and information we gain from daily
reading God's word begins to accumulate in our minds, it's more than just wisdom
or knowledge, it's Godly facts that help bring us closer to God and His will for
our lives.

How's this for a promise from God. "And years of life will be added to you." It
would be an interesting study to see if there is a correlation in how much scripture
you know, how close your walk with God is, to how long you live. Of course, you
can't measure your walk with God in any numerical fashion. It would be hard to
measure. I've known some godly people who die way too early. Interesting thought.

The lips of the righteous feed many, but fools die for lack of wisdom.
The blessing of the Lord makes one rich, and He adds no sorrow with
it. (Proverbs 10:21-22)

There's that word wisdom again. Let's stop a minute and remember who the
author of Proverbs is. You're right, it's Solomon. The one history has proclaimed
the smartest man in the world at that time, maybe for all time. Notwithstanding
his mistakes later. It's clearly told us that God gave him the wisdom to lead God's
people. Solomon's wisdom came from God. Too bad he didn't always follow it.
Much like we are.

Solomon uses so many metaphors to teach the wisdom he is trying to impart.
What do you suppose he means by, "The lips of the righteous feed many, but fools
die for lack of wisdom!" I almost made a common mistake in reading the Proverbs.
I tried to separate A from B. If you notice most of the Proverbs have a plus and
a minus. Do this, don't do that, etc. You can't separate A from B. Sometimes B
can clarify A.

A: The lips of the righteous feed many. B: But fools die for lack of wisdom. See
what I mean. I know you've heard the story about two options for feeding the poor.
You can give him food to eat for the present but if you teach him to fish he has food
forever. That's the point of this Proverb. Do you know anyone who can talk a good
game, but never played it? That's what I get from the Proverb. What do you see?

O.k, lets, look at the second Proverb. Does this mean that riches come from
God? If we walk with God and follow His instructions we are guaranteed to be
rich? If you've been a Christian for any length of time you know that's not what it
says. When we receive the blessing of the Lord you can't measure it in monetary
numbers. Define rich! Someone once described blessings from God as an "Amen".
Amen simply means you agree with what was said. When God gives us a blessing
have you ever thought of saying "Amen"? Just to know that will bless us can give
us the feeling of being rich.

I think the second part can mean that though we suffer hard times and may
not understand why certain things happen in our walk. As Christian's we also
understand that God is right there with us, to comfort, and to continue that walk
with us and let us know we are not alone in our sorrow. Just His presence is a
comfort.

In the fear of the Lord there is strong confidence, and His children will have a place of refuge. The fear of the Lord is a fountain of life, to turn one away from the snares of death. (Proverbs 14:26-27)

It would be interesting to know just how many times the phrase "fear of the Lord" is used, just in Proverbs alone. Why? I think it is a critical phrase. To me it denotes a relationship with the Lord. A "close" relationship. Why didn't Solomon, in the verse above, just say in the fear of the Lord there is confidence. Instead he said, "Strong" confidence. The strength of a relationship is determined by the trust between the two parties. When you can trust God with confidence that He will do what He said He will do. That's STRONG confidence.

In the next sentence, it is likened to a fountain of life. That fear of the Lord is life. I want to remind you of the day you were saved. Think back to that feeling you had at that moment. If you are not saved now is the time to change that! Ask Jesus to come into your heart and change your life! Now, do you remember that day? Did you feel something different? More alive, more energized, more connected to God? That's the fountain of life Solomon is talking about! The sensation of being connected to God through His Son Jesus Christ. Like the New Testament says, "joint heirs with Christ." (Romans 8:17)

Solomon tries to make his point by offering contrasting points. Look at both verses. The good, then the bad. Do this, don't do this, etc. I've pointed out before that you almost must take these pills one at a time. In 1 Kings 4:32 it says Solomon wrote over 3,000 proverbs. We have pithy sayings today. It's cultural. Except these Proverbs are wisdom from God given to us by the pen of Solomon. Soon we will be looking at the book of Ecclesiastes. It's fascinating because Solomon had the wealth and wisdom to try everything, as he say's "under the sun" and he does, and he comes to one conclusion—fear God. He had the ability to check out the mysteries of his world. To test wisdom and knowledge and his conclusion: fear God!

When you accept the advice of someone you want to know by what "authority" they make their assertion? Based on their "experience" and testing you may choose to accept their findings. Check out Solomon's authority, his findings.

He who mocks the poor reproaches his Maker; He who is glad at
calamity will not go unpunished. (Proverbs 17:5)

It's tough to read this in the context of our world today. Is there calamity today?
It is unbelievable, and the sad part is that it is deliberate! Maybe we don't, as
such, mock the poor as much as we use the poor. Governments use the poor to
gain sympathy for their decisions. Did you notice the word maker is capitalized?
Solomon is referring to God. To mock the poor, you might say use also, is a
reproach to God. Interesting how God might deal with them.

One of my favorite verses is in 1 Corinthians 14:40, "Let all things be done
decently and in order." Now there's a proverb. The sad thing is most people thrive
on chaos. If there is disruption there is no leadership. I think the term today is
"drama". There is too much drama in our lives. The solution, walking with God
brings order and discipline and peace.

In an earlier reading I had also circled 17:15, "He who justifies the wicked,
and he who condemns the just, both alike are an abomination to the Lord." It is
scary how relevant these verses are today. If you have a reasonable excuse you can
do just about anything you think is right. Doesn't matter the results or who gets
hurt. Don't even get me started on lying. That is an abomination, in today's world
it is accepted.

That's the method Solomon is using. The contrast, the good vs the bad, etc.
The task is translating the truth to today's world. Today the lines are so blurred
it's hard to tell sometimes. I love to watch movies. I have noticed in some movies
that the censors will bleep out some profanity but it's ok for them say GD. Why is
that? Maybe they don't believe that there is a God who said, "Thou shalt not take
the name of the Lord in vain." (Deuteronomy 20:7) Maybe I'm misinterpreting it.

I want to remind you of a good alternative Bible reading schedule you might
try for a month (30 days). Read one chapter of the Proverbs then five chapters of
the Psalms. If it was me, I would write in my Bible beside Proverbs Chapter one
1-5. Then Proverbs Chapter two 6-10, etc. Then when I read the Proverb for that
day I can see what psalms to read.

Every way of a man is right in his own eyes, but the Lord weighs the
heart. To do righteousness and justice is more acceptable to the Lord
than sacrifice. (Proverbs 21:2-3)

Does this phrase sound familiar? "Every man is right in his own eyes". Remember
the theme of the book of Judges? (Judges 21:25) We saw how that worked
out. The more you read and learn from the Bible the more you realize that this
book could be written today. Of course, no one would, it would "offend" too many
people. What if the world were ruled by man's standards rather than God's. We
can see throughout the Old Testament the results of that fiasco!

Man looks on the outward appearance, God looks on the heart. A paraphrase
of God's response to Samuel looking for a new king for Israel. (1 Samuel 16:7)
What a scary truth. Scary because it says we cannot hide anything from God.
We can say the right words, even do the right things but God knows what's in our
hearts. We may fool others, but not God.

Isn't this interesting. How much of the Old Testament, especially Leviticus
talks about the process of offering a sacrifice to God? Yet, here God is saying,
through the pen of Solomon, that God would much rather that we live by His
commands that make these sacrifices. God wants obedience rather than sacrifice.
It's just that simple!

I have really been thinking about this idea of a deeper study of Proverbs. This
book is so rich in simple instructions for a better life and a closer walk with God.
With a notebook, make two columns. On the left-hand column, you write the
"Pro" aspects of a verse. What we are supposed to do. In the right-hand column,
you list the "Cons" the things we are to avoid. Under the "Pro" fact you can write
what that fact means to you, how does this apply to me personally. Likewise, the
same with the fact in the right-hand column. What a Bible study. It would take you
months to go through Proverbs. Just think what you might learn from God's word!

Let's look at a verse and see: "The plans of the diligent lead surely to plenty."
The positive side. "But those of everyone who is hasty, surely to poverty." (21:5)
This on the negative side. Now just think for a moment, what this simple verse
gives of wise counsel. I was so guilty of this as younger person.

Train up a child in the way he should go, and when he is old he will
not depart from it. The rich rules over the poor, and the borrower is
servant to the lender. (Proverbs 22:6-7)

Have you ever had someone argue against this proverb? They say, "I took my
kids to church all through their childhood and now they won't have anything
to do with church, or God." Have you heard that? Why is that? Maybe they saw
the hypocrisy all around them. People saying one thing and doing another. That's
tough to argue. But remember that those biblical principles are in their hearts.
They may rebel against those facts for now. But God is not through with them.
Those seeds were planted. One day God will get their attention and they will
return to those truths that were planted as youths.

Maybe I'm reading more into this than is there. But notice the gap between
"child" and "old". I believe that children and youths, who have been raised in the
church, once they graduate high school feel they must try the world. One of the
hardest Sunday school classes to start and maintain is the College and Career
class. The class for those just out of high school and beginning their careers. They
are so distracted. Their schedules and priorities are so overwhelming that they
can't seem to fit God in their schedule.

A lot of times it takes beginning a family that can get their attention and
slowly bring them back to their roots. Those things I learned as a youth are
true, and they start getting hungry to refresh those principles again with these
new responsibilities. Just keep praying for them. God has a way of getting their
attention.

Verse seven is one of the key verses in Dave Ramsey's "Total Money Makeover"
book. It is so true. I learned the hard way this biblical truth. Most people need
to learn the hard way. Right now, I can say I am almost debt free. I still have a
mortgage but I'm working on that. The thing that this verse doesn't relate is the
peace that comes from being free of bondage to a debtor. Think about it this way.
Who has control over your hard-earned income? You or a debt that must be paid.
When you get your check you start thinking, "who do I have to pay?" Why not
say, "Now, what can I accomplish with MY money?" That is the question to ask!

A word fitly spoken is like apples of gold in settings of silver. Like an earring of gold and an ornament of fine gold is a wise rebuke to an obedient ear. (Proverbs 25:11-12)

I have a book of poetry entitled, "Apples of Gold in Settings of Silver." Notice the prelude to these words, "A word fitly spoken" that is so important. I have a funny story that illustrates this.

As Sunday School Director, we were having teachers meeting on Wednesday night for our teachers to talk about the various lessons and other concerns for our Sunday school. The meetings were held an hour before the regular prayer meeting. This night, one of our teachers came in for the prayer meeting and didn't attend the teacher's meeting. When she walked in I said, "You're an hour late." Well, the teacher did an about-face and left. After the prayer meeting I went to her house and apologized. Too many times we make comments about things we know nothing about.

That's where this word "fitly" comes in. Do you remember the old saying, "If you can't say something nice, don't say anything at all!" They could have taken that from this proverb. Too many times we just say whatever comes to mind instead of thinking before we run our mouth.

How do you take criticism? For most people the first response is, "how dare you, who do you think you are." Right? Why is that? We tend to have a natural rebellious attitude don't we.

Of course, this goes all the back to the Garden of Eden, doesn't it? Think about it. The nerve of God to put that tree there and then tell Adam and Eve they can't eat from it. Who does He think He is? He is God that's who. Their attitude got them kicked out of the Garden. So many time's our attitude brings us grief instead of blessing. How do you respond when God lays on you to do something? Where, on your priority list, does God's request rank?

Did you notice this proverb is different? There is no plus and minus, good and bad side to this proverb. Just good advice. Pay attention! Flowery words of course but chew on the truth of this proverb. I guess it could be boiled down to attitude. How do you respond to criticism? Do you examine your words before they are thrown out there?

Every word of God is pure; He is a shield to those who put their trust in Him. Do not add to His words, lest He rebuke you, and you be found a liar. (Proverbs 30:5-6)

What is Solomon talking about? The word of God. One of my favorite chapters, besides John 14, is John 1. "In the beginning was the Word, and the Word was with God, and the Word was God. He was in the beginning with God." Who was with God? Look at verse 14, "And the Word became flesh and dwelt among us." Verse 1 says God was the Word. Verse 14 says God became flesh and dwelt among us. God in the person of Jesus Christ came to visit His creation. So how important is the Word of God? Jesus / God was referred to as The Word!

As a writer, I am very aware of copyright laws. So, I wondered one day where the copyright for the Bible was. Of course, if you have a study Bible the copyright is for the study notes. The copyright for the Word of God is found in Revelation 22:18, "For I testify to everyone who hears the words of the prophecy of this book: If anyone adds to these things, God will add to him the plagues that are written in this book." Now some have said this verse only applies to the book of Revelation. So, this word of God is more important than the rest of the word of God? I don't think so.

Today we have so many translations and variations of the original text it's hard to know what exactly is truth. Are you a "King James Only" person? Did you know there was a more popular Bible before the King James? The Geneva Bible. The point is that God's word, in the original text, was in Hebrew and Greek and Aramaic. I want to renew my challenge to consider the history of how our Bible was assembled, how they chose which books to include and which not to. Look at the history of the writing of the King James Bible. It's really interesting.

The other day I was trying to remember the name of a college student that was determined to disprove the Bible and discredit Jesus. His name was Josh McDowell. After much study Josh wrote several books. One of his books, "Evidence That Demands a Verdict" is about historical evidence that Jesus was who He said He was!

> He has made everything beautiful in its time. Also, He has put eternity
> in their hearts, except that no one can find out the work that God does
> from beginning to end. I know that nothing is better for them than to
> rejoice, and to do in their lives. (Ecclesiastes 3:11-12)

I hope you understand who the author of this book is. This is Solomon, the author of Proverbs. The king that succeeded David to the throne. The king that God appointed to construct the Temple in Jerusalem. The one that God granted his wish to receive wisdom to lead God's people. I can't stress enough the "authority" that Solomon had to write this book. Ecclesiastes is an interesting book. We talked about it before. Solomon had the wherewithal to do whatever came to his mind. To experiment, to research anything and everything he wanted. You will see that in this book.

These verses follow the famous "A time for" verses in chapter three. You know, the ones that the Turtles made into a hit song in the sixties. Just look at those verses and you see the depth of his wisdom. You also see the "fatalist" mentality we see throughout this book. Solomon, to me, gives the impression there is no hope. How many times does the author say, "Vanity, vanity all is vanity."? The problem is that Solomon was looking at things from a human perspective. From that perspective, even today there seems to be little or no hope. But from God's perspective it's totally different.

To some extent, Solomon recognizes that in the verses above. He acknowledges the hand that God has in the world around him. The problem is Solomon, of all people, doesn't see the part where God works in the individual's heart. Granted he said, "He has put eternity in their hearts." It seems detached from the God who seeks a relationship with us.

Look at the last part, "Except that no one can find out the work that God does from beginning to end." That's not true. Our problem is, and Solomon's, is that we are not looking for God's handiwork. We either take the credit ourselves, give it to "luck", or happenstance. Really? We are missing what is right in front of us. God is trying to get our attention, to get us to look up. Imagine if Solomon had realized that early in his reign. It might be different!

Do not hasten in your spirit to be angry, for anger rests in the bosom
of fools. Do not say, "Why were the former days better than these?"
For you do not inquire wisely concerning this. (Ecclesiastes 7:9-10)

"Ah, the good old days". Have you heard that? I once told my youth class, "I
have lived, what you have to look forward to. You have lived, what I have
left." We are looking at things from two different perspectives. My past, their
future. We can look back and see, lower prices, simple living, etc. But we forget
we were only making $1.25 an hour (high-end). Sure, things were cheaper but we
made less money. Things were slower but it took a week or more for a letter to
travel across state. (no jokes). Each generation has its benefits and its deficiencies.

Thank God for the time you live in and the country you are a part of. Notice
the end of this verse, "For you do not inquire wisely concerning this." If we spend
too much time looking back, or always looking to the future we are missing what
is right in front of us. God's mighty works!

I learned very early that anger never accomplishes anything. Oh, I get mad
sometimes but for some reason God has given me the ability, the madder I get the
quieter I get. I will not argue, I hate confrontation. In a sense that is how God
operates. Look at Jesus! The only place it is said that Jesus got upset was in the
temple cleansing. He never got violent with the scribes and Pharisees. He told
them off once or twice. God is the same way. Most of the time God just sits back
and let each of us hang ourselves. We do enough damage on our own. When we
reach the end of the rope, and cry to God, then He may take a hand, if we are
sincere.

Anger and profanity never accomplishes anything! Mark my words. Step
back, take a breath, and talk. Before I became a Christian, I had this famous motto,
"I don't get mad, I get even." After Jesus came into my life I realized, according
to the Bible, that God will handle my battles a lot better than I could. He knows
their weaknesses far better than I do.

The wisdom of Solomon. Ask Solomon how his dad dealt with anger. After
Saul throws a few spears at him, how did he respond. God took care of the
situation and David knew that God would handle it. What a blessed peace to
know God is in charge.

Let us hear the conclusion of the whole matter: Fear God and keep
His commandments, for this is man's all. For God will bring every
work into judgment, including every secret thing, whether good or
evil. (Ecclesiastes 12:13-14)

In the late fifties, there was a weekly drama entitled, "The Millionaire". It was
about this multi-millionaire who would give away a million dollars (in those days
a lot of money) to someone out of the blue. The catch was they couldn't tell anyone
how much or where it came from. I wish I could get my hands on a DVD of that
series. I think it ran for three seasons. In those three seasons only two people gave
the money back.

Solomon had more money that anyone in history to that point. He could buy
anything and do anything (he was the king) he wanted. Day after day whatever he
thought of, he could bring it to pass. Remember what his attitude was? "Vanity of
vanity, all was vanity." (1:2) I'm sure you've never thought what you would do with
a million dollars, right? Ever buy a lottery ticket?

After all his research, we see the conclusion of the matter as Solomon would
put it. The verse above is so profound. Contrast this conclusion with the conclusion
of the book of Judges, "In those days there was no king in Israel; everyone did what
was right in his own eyes." (21:25) What is your attitude today?

Ecclesiastes can be a depressing book. It seems hopeless. Then you read the
conclusion that Solomon came to. Our hope is in Christ! Just think how hopeless
things would be without the gospels and the New Testament. Read the back of
the book, we win!

"Fear God and keep His commandments." I want to use reverence instead of
fear. It's a more accurate meaning. We think of fear as afraid. That's not what the
writer meant.

I think it's interesting how the council arranged the books in the Bible. After
the depressing book of Judges God inserts Ruth and after this depressing book
God inserts Song of Solomon. A love story about our relationship with God.
Solomon destroyed his relationship with God when he started drifting into idol
worship because of his many wives. He drifted away. How is your relationship?

I am the rose of Sharon, and the lily of the valleys. (Song of
Solomon 2:1)

Iam one of those who question why this book is in the Bible. I get the picture it
is trying to portray and all that but there are other ways of telling us that God
loves us. The cross for instance. How would you describe God's love?

O.k, a commentary uses the concept of marriage as the message of this book.
I can understand. The gospels, in the words of Jesus, portrays the church as the
bride of Christ. Look at Revelation 21:9, "Then one of the seven angels who had
the seven bowls, filled with the seven last plagues came to me and talked with me,
saying, "Come, I will show you the bride, the Lamb's wife." and then in Matthew
9:15 Jesus says, "Can the friends of the bridegroom (Jesus) mourn as long as the
bridegroom is with them? But the days will come when the bridegroom will be
taken away from them, and then they will fast." It accepted that in the gospels the
bride of Christ is His church.

If we use that analogy and then read this book maybe we can get a perspective
on God's relationship to His church, His Son's bride. Think about it. That would
be a favorable standing with the Father.

The "Rose of Sharon" is one of the names for Jesus that many quotes. They
try to find a "name" for every book of the Bible. This is for Song of Solomon. Some
believe the Shulamite woman in this story was the maid brought in to comfort
David as he was dying. I don't know. Commentaries can be interesting. They can
clear up a lot of things. Take them for what they are. One person's learned opinion.
You decide.

I heard a radio preacher once use this book to do a study on marriage. It wasn't
bad but it took liberties with the text. Read this book for what it says. The people
who included it had their reasons. I stated earlier I believe they were divinely
inspired. So, I must accept they had their reasons.

One thing is sure. If these words convince you of how much God loves you
then they have achieved their goal. I think that is the point.

O my love, you are as beautiful as Tirzah, lovely as Jerusalem,
awesome as an army with banners! (Song of Solomon 6:4)

Did you catch the contrast? Beautiful, lovely, then like an army. That really is a good picture of God. In the Old Testament, we see the "army" side of God. Sorry, but that's just what I see. God, stern, forceful, demanding, leading, pushing, trying to bring Israel to both a personal and spiritual point in the nation's history. Dealing with Israel as a "nation".

In the New Testament, you see God dealing with both Israel and mankind in a more personal, one-on-one relationship. So much so that He rejects Israel's lack of understanding when the Messiah is in their midst and don't recognize Him. When we get to the New Testament in October I want you to notice how many times Jesus commends Gentiles for their faith and chastises His own disciples for their lack of faith. It's amazing.

Song of Solomon is about love. My favorite New Testament book about love is First John. Look, "In this the love of God was manifested toward us, that God has sent His only begotten Son into the world, that we might live through Him. In this is love, not that we loved God, but that He loved us and sent His Son to be the propitiation (payment) for our sins." (1 John 4:9-10)

That word love can be over used to the point that it has lost its meaning and effectiveness. Anyone can say, "I love you" but how have they demonstrated it? Do you love someone enough to make a lifetime commitment to each other? To swear before God and witnesses that you will love, and honor each other the rest of your life. That is love. Love that is demonstrated in a commitment.

God also demonstrated that love in the Old Testament with covenant between Him and the nation Israel. Of course, we just said that Jesus rejected Israel and turned to the Gentiles. He hasn't forgotten that covenant with Israel. Read the book of Revelation. God still uses Israel and eventually restores Israel and that relationship.

I use the word relationship a lot, I know. That word best describes what God wants with us. It's not a religion, it's a relationship. I don't think that when you get to heaven God is going to ask if you're a Baptist, Catholic or Methodist, He is going to ask if you know Jesus!

> "Come now, and let us reason together", says the Lord, "Though your
> sins are like scarlet, they shall be white as snow; though they are red
> like crimson, they shall be as wool." (Isaiah 1:18)

There is so little of this today. Have you heard that on college campuses they riot to prevent a conservative from speaking? What are they afraid of? Maybe they are afraid of "reason". Reason can be a powerful force. God gave us a mind and common sense to guide our thoughts. When you begin to appeal to common sense, many are afraid of that.

The following verses explain what the reasoning is about. God laid down some basic rules in the Old Testament. Isaiah is telling Israel that it is not unreasonable to expect obedience in return for His blessing. All through God's conflicts with Israel that was the basic argument. The thing that Israel did that turned God from them was idol worship. Idols infuriate God more than anything. An idol is a false god that comes between His people and Him. There is no relationship if you worship idols.

Now look at the picture the verse above draws. Have you ever marveled in the fall at the first snowfall? Especially if it is two or three inches deep. Everything is so "white", so clean. Exactly what Isaiah is talking about. There is absolutely nothing that we can do to bring this about. We can live perfect lives, never do anything wrong (like that's possible) and we would still be "red like crimson". It's not the outward deeds it's what's in our hearts. It's not our hands that need cleaning it's our black hearts. Look at Jeremiah 17:9, "The heart is deceitful above all things, and desperately wicked; Who can know it?"

One day I asked myself, "Why did Jesus have to die on a cross?" I knew He did, I accepted that to become a Christian. I just never questioned why. Then I read, and understood, Exodus 13. The Passover. Why God spent the whole Old Testament to teach us the cost of sin. That there is a payment to be made to God for that sin. That payment is blood. That is the cost that God established from the very beginning. (Genesis 3:21). The only one worthy, with the authority, to pay for our sins, past, present and future was the Son of God. And God was willing to make that sacrifice to establish a relationship between us and Almighty God.

I love Isaiah. His writing style is different from the other prophets in my view. I just like his style!

> Therefore, as the fire devours the stubble, and the flames consumes the chaff, so their root will be as rottenness, and their blossoms will ascend like dust; because they have rejected the law of the Lord of hosts, and despised the word of the Holy One of Israel. (Isaiah 5:24)

Do you know who the four major prophets are in the Old Testament? Major in the sense of volume not substance. Let me give you a hint: J-E-D-I. Jeremiah, Ezekiel, Daniel, Isaiah. What a neat way to remember those significant prophets. JEDI.

Isaiah was a prophet prior to the southern kingdom going into captivity in Babylon. The tribes of Judah and Benjamin. Judah is significant, that this the tribe the Messiah would come from. I'd like you to take note of the warning in this verse.

The consequences of rejecting God's word, God's principles, God direction can be catastrophic, basically reduced to nothing. Notice the prophet uses different references to God's word. He uses "law" and "the word". To us today that means the Bible. Now in Isaiah's day of course, The Law referred to the five books of Moses. The amount of instruction in those five books would govern Israel for centuries. The consequences of disobeying those instructions affect us today!

Simple instructions, the Ten Commandments, for example. Four commandments pertaining to our relationship with God, and six to our relationship with our fellow man. Simple. Why are they so hard to obey? Because of our enmity with God. Our rebellion against any authority be it God or anyone else. "You're not going to tell ME what to do!"

Always note in writing the word "therefore", ask yourself what is that "therefore" there for? It refers to the previous comments. Because of what was said previous, this is our response.

Back up to verse 18 in this chapter. Five times the prophet uses the "woe" to warn Judah that they are headed for doom. They are headed for destruction. They are going the wrong way. Just as in the verse above Isaiah gives a description of the consequences of their rebellion. That's why God has given us the Bible, the word of God, to warn us both by words and by the example of Israel's history. There are dire consequences for not obeying God's written word! As we look at these four major prophets think about what God is telling you!

For unto us a Child is born, unto us a Son is given; and the
government will be upon His shoulder. And His name will be called
Wonderful, Counselor, Mighty God, Everlasting Father, Prince of
Peace. (Isaiah 9:6)

Recognize this verse? You, no doubt, have some old Christmas cards with this
verse. This verse is prominent in many Christmas Cantatas. A very familiar
verse. So, familiar that, I think, just like John 3:16 it may have lost its meaning.
The familiar becomes invisible. I hope not!

I've tried to remember if I've read any reference to a Messiah after Genesis
3. I don't recall any. If so, Isaiah in this verse is drawing a significant picture for
Judah prior to their being taken captive by Babylon. There is hope. There will be
a ruler, there will be a King above all kings. Did Jesus fulfill that in His earthly
ministry? No. This can be seen as thousands of years between, "A Son is given,"
and "the government will be upon His shoulder." The last part of that verse is yet
to be fulfilled.

Let me give you another example of this concept, look in Luke chapter 4
beginning in verse 16. Jesus goes into the synagogue and opens the book of Isaiah
and reads from Isaiah 61:1-2. Now look at the passage in Isaiah. Jesus quotes this
passage but stops midway through verse 2. Jesus does not say, "And the day of
vengeance of our God." Why is that? Because He did not come to fulfill THAT
part of the prophecy, not yet!

The same way the verse above is split from past (Christ's birth) to Christ's
reign on earth. The next time you see this verse at Christmas time think about
that split prophecy!

Look at the contrast in these descriptions: Counselor vs Mighty God, or
Mighty God vs Prince of peace. That's our God. He is mighty in His power and
judgment but also wants to walk with us in our daily walk following His guidance
and trusting Him for each step we take. What a fantastic relationship to have.

Many years ago, I got the privilege to have a popular Disc Jockey as a friend.
I got to stand in the studio with him while he did his show. I was in awe that I
knew someone like that. Above all, he invited us to his house. Take that feeling
and magnify it a thousand times and that's how we should feel walking with God
on our pilgrimage.

AUGUST 2

ISAIAH 14-18

> The Lord of Hosts has sworn, saying, "Surely, as I have thought, so it
> shall come to pass, as I have purposed, so it shall stand. (Isaiah 14:24)

Who can make a statement like this except God? Isaiah is now talking about God's judgment on the nations around Israel. Those whom God has chosen to punish and remove the various tribes from the country. To judge Israel for her disobedience and rebellion. In this passage, he is talking about Assyria. The previous verses are about Babylon. Notice He uses these nations to punish Israel then He brings judgment on these same nations.

God may choose to do the same thing in our lives. He can use circumstances we don't understand to bring us the where God wants us to be. We fight, we rebel, we refuse to obey His guidance and we end up either suffering much more than we need to, or we are completely out of His will which is not where you want to be.

I remember, as a child, when my brothers and I were ignoring the instructions of our parents they would sit us in a corner facing the wall. After a while we started going to sleep in the corner so our parents needed to find another way of "getting our attention." God has been doing this with Israel for years.

This half of the Old Testament is full of prophets who tried to warn Israel of their rebellion. They were not treated well. All were ignored and scoffed at. Much like Jesus was when He tried to warn Israel they were missing His message from God. Jesus was the long-awaited Messiah, yet Israel totally missed Him. Why? They were looking for a king (again) and missed the Messiah.

What are you looking for from God? A miracle worker? Someone to give you peace and comfort, maybe riches, and blessing? Ok, so are you doing what God asked you to do? Do you have enough faith to obey and trust God every day? Or are you disputing with God about who makes the decisions in your life. I learned the hard way about knocking down doors that God hasn't opened. If you wait and let God open the door He wants you to go through, it is so much better! That's part of walking with God, trusting Him to decide which path to take, which move to make, even what to say. Trust Him!

> And it will be for a sign and for a witness to the Lord of hosts in the land of Egypt; for they will cry to the Lord because of their oppressors, and He will send them a Savior and a Mighty One, and He will deliver them. (Isaiah 19:20)

Here He is dealing with Egypt. Notice that God has a way of revealing His will in certain situations. Here again, God is using neighboring nations to punish those who refuse to honor Him. It's funny sometimes how God's word can be timeless. Notice this phrase, "He will send a Savior and a Mighty One, and He will deliver them" applies both to Egypt then and us today.

Have you ever thought of Jesus as "Mighty One"? Remember the verse 9:6 earlier? What was one of the names of Jesus? Was it not "Mighty God?" Do you ever picture Jesus as Mighty God? Yet His mastery over nature pretty much goes ignored. My favorite is finding a coin in the fish's mouth to pay their taxes. Think about that. Another one, how about Peter walking on water. Jesus, we can accept but a common human like Peter, how did he do it? The power of Jesus. Oh, I forgot about Lazarus.

I would say "Mighty God." That's great, but greater still is Savior. If Jesus hadn't gone to the cross we would still be sacrificing sheep to pay for our sins. Which of course meant nothing to most of God's people. Just a ritual to go through having no "spiritual" effect. Much like our going to church today. Do you go to meet God or your friends?

Notice why God is using these various nations to bring about His judgment. They are a sign to Israel at this point that His judgment is about to fall. He is trying everything He can to get Israel's attention to get them to turn from the idols and return to Him. Let me remind you of a critical passage in the psalms. Psalm 135:15-18. Concerning idols, I like verse 18, "Those who make them are like them; so is everyone who trust in them." Read these verses, that is what Israel was worshipping.

Is God dealing with you about something in your life? Maybe you have allowed an idol to creep into your life. Money is a good example. Has it come between you and following God? Maybe it's friends, prestige, things, anything that is more important to you than God is an idol. Think about it, do some meditating, ask God to reveal it.

You will keep him in perfect peace, whose mind is stayed on You, because he trusts in You. Trust in the Lord forever, For in YAH, the Lord is everlasting strength. (Isaiah 26:3-4)

Do we really know what peace is? We have seen earlier that Jesus is the Prince of Peace. Just what does that mean. What will it take to bring you peace? Think about it. When you go to bed at night what is keeping you awake? What is it that you can do right now that will give you "perfect peace"? The answer is in this verse. Trust in God.

When we were in Proverbs we looked at Proverbs 3:5-6. Let's review: "Trust in the Lord with all your heart. Lean not upon your own understanding. In all your ways acknowledge Him. He will direct your path". When I can't sleep at night I don't count sheep. I recite this verse over and over.

Look at the middle of the verse above, "Because he trusts in You." That's the key. You see, you can't MAKE things work out. You can't change circumstances. Oh, you can to some degree, and you might effect some changes. Some things are just out of your control. Those are the things that keep you up at night, isn't it? Why fret about things you can't control? Leave them with God.

One lesson I have learned is that God will not work on something if your hands are on them. When you let go, God will take over. You must "turn" them over to God. Trust Him to bring to pass what is best for His children. Remember that Father-child relationship with God. He wants only the best for His children.

Have you ever prayed and got a busy signal? Of course not! God is always there. The neat thing about that is that God knows what's going to happen, tomorrow, next week, next year, etc. God has it all worked out. The key, and the hardest part, is to trust Him. Just take one day at a time and trust God for the next step.

Here is a verse you need to write in the front of your Bible on one of the blank pages. Matthew 6:34, "Therefore do not worry about tomorrow, for tomorrow will worry about its own things, sufficient for the day is its own trouble." Those are the words of Jesus! He should know.

Can we have perfect peace? I think so. It takes practice and continually trusting God for His direction!

> Therefore, the Lord will wait, that He may be gracious to you; and
> therefore, He will be exalted, that He may have mercy on you. For the
> Lord is a God of justice; blessed are those who wait on Him. (Isaiah
> 30:18)

I don't like verses with the word "wait" in them. That is the hardest thing that I deal with God about. We will see it again the fortieth chapter but It's all through the Bible. Psalm 37 also talks about it. Remember what we talked about yesterday? Trusting in God. The biggest part of that peace is "waiting" on God to DO SOMETHING isn't it.

The hardest thing in life is waiting, isn't it. We are so impatient. I was told early on as a new Christian never to pray for patience. God never grants patience He teaches it through trials!

Look at James 1:2-4, "My brethren, count it all joy when you fall into various trials, knowing that the testing of your faith produces patience. But let patience have its perfect work, that you may be perfect and complete, lacking nothing." So how do you have patience? Through trials, trusting God.

Notice in this verse, "The Lord will wait." I am so glad that God has patience. He waited on me for thirty-five years to finally come to Him for salvation. I can look back on those years and see times when I could very well have died. I served a year in Vietnam before I was saved. I was so thankful that God allowed me to return home, find my bride and live till I accepted His Son as my Savior. God waited on me. He's waiting for you, if you haven't made that decision yet!

Isaiah is still trying to get Judah's attention here. Judah doesn't trust God's provision. They are looking to Egypt for help against Assyria. Of course, we know Assyria is not the nation that will conquer Judah. But Judah's faith is not in God. Isaiah is trying to get them to trust God not Egypt.

That's the battle we face today. Everybody wants us to trust this system, this game plan, this program, even this church doctrine. The only thing you can trust is the blood of Jesus Christ and the power of God to work in your life if you trust Him. If you can't wait on God you will turn to any other quick fix you can get your hands on. It won't work, trust me. Wait on God!

> And the ransomed of the Lord shall return, and come to Zion with singing, with everlasting joy on their heads. They shall obtain joy and gladness, and sorrow and sighing shall flee away. (Isaiah 35:10)

I believe it was 1948. Before then there was no nation of Israel. I believe it was called Palestine. In 1948 the nation was restored. Prophecy? You decide. Isaiah, in this verse, is prophesying the eventual return to Israel. Wait a minute, didn't Israel return under Nehemiah and Ezra? A remnant returned to rebuild the temple and the wall around Jerusalem. After Jesus time the nation was overrun by various nations. The temple was destroyed in 70 A.D. Not until 1948 was the nation recognized as Israel again.

To me Isaiah could be called the "Jesus Prophet" so many key verses in Isaiah refer to the coming Messiah. Wait till we get to chapter 53. Fantastic chapter.

Again, Isaiah was written as a warning to Judah prior to them going into captivity in Babylon. Written to Judah and Benjamin, the southern kingdom. Isn't it interesting that God not only warns Judah of the coming captivity (judgment) but at the same time gives them hope by talking about the coming Messiah (deliverer).

I think sometimes we can't join the two. Some see God as this great judge sitting behind His bench and proclaiming His sentence on mankind, judgment! Judgement! Judgement!

At the same time this same judge is offering up His Son to pay our penalty for our sin to the point of dying on a cruel cross at Calvary. This same judge who seeks to reconcile Himself to us and to have an intimate relationship with us. What a contrast. But make no mistake it is the same God.

He wants to bring us into His family. He also wants our obedience to His laws and instructions. He wants us to trust Him and follow Him in faith. In today's speech "there are strings attached to the blessings." As there should be.

All the way from the Garden of Eden it has always been our choice to make. Accept the blessings of God by obedience to His wishes or go our own way and accept the consequences. It's our choice, and always has been. The same goes for Israel.

> But those who wait on the Lord shall renew their strength; they shall mount up with wings like eagles, they shall run and not be weary, they shall walk and not faint. (Isaiah 40:31)

For a long time this was my "life verse". I found it by accident of course. Our music director found this little chorus for the congregation to sing prior to opening our worship. It really grabbed me! There is just a slight addition to the verse, in the chorus we sing: "Teach me Lord to wait." At that time, I needed that so much. God was doing great things in my life and I just wanted it to go fast. I had a hard lesson to learn. There is much more to this chorus. In the movie, "Rise Up and Walk: Dennis Byrd Story" his wife sings the whole chorus to him as he lays paralyzed in a hospital bed. I love the chorus!

One thing I noticed in this verse. It talks about running and walking and does not say anything about sitting. There are things, plans, that God has for our lives. That's why the gift of the Holy Spirit comes with a "spiritual gift" that is to be used to serve and glorify God. There are way too many Christians that are not using that special gift that God has given them. That's sitting! That's occupying a space. Not serving!

When you are exercising that God given gift and serving the Lord it's just like the verse says, "Mount up with wings like eagles." That is such an awesome feeling. My wife and I, before we even knew about this gift, started working in the church. We started by cleaning the church on Saturdays, before Sunday service, then I started teaching.

Sometimes, I would get annoyed that my wife would hang around after the service and visit with people. We're talking 30 minutes or more. Then I realized that that was her gift. The gift of compassion, helps, etc. So, I wait patiently till she is ready to go. I let her exercise her gift.

There are surveys and ways to find out your spiritual gift. I encourage you to find out your gift, then use it. Like the verse says when you are serving the Lord with the gift He has given you it's like soaring with eagles. Take it from someone who knows. This devotional is a product of the gift that God has given me. To teach the unsearchable riches of God's word!

> Fear not, for I am with you; be not dismayed, for I am your God. I
> will strengthen you, yes, I will help you, I will uphold you with My
> righteous right hand! (Isaiah 41:10)

Sorry, I just must use that word again, awesome. What an awesome verse. Have you ever felt alone, neglected, no future, no hope? Of course, you have. I can look back at different times and remember having that feeling. The thing is those were all days prior to accepting Christ in my heart. Then there was no hope. I was in control of the foreseeable future and it was bleak. I could see no way out.

After Jesus came into my life God began doing things in my life I never thought I could do. When I was in high school if I had to make an oral book report, stand in front of the class, I would stay home. I was so shy it was terrible. After Jesus came into my heart the courage was there because I knew God was with me and would give me the words to speak. I did things I NEVER thought I could do.

You have battles that seem impossible, don't you? Of course, you do. Let me ask you first, are you a Christian? That is the key. You see if you are a child of God you have a heavenly Father that loves you and wants only the best for you. He loves you so much He is ready to push you out of that comfortable nest and force you to learn to fly. Many time's it takes something like that for us to trust God enough to take a step of faith.

One of my favorite stories is in Joshua 3:15-16, "And as those who bore the ark came to the Jordan, and the priests bearing the ark of the covenant before the people, and as those who bore the ark came to the Jordan, and the feet of the priests who bore the ark dipped in the edge of the water (for the Jordan overflows all its banks during the whole time of harvest), that the waters which came down from upstream stood still".

Now think about what they did. They are looking at a raging river overflowing its banks. God did NOTHING until they stepped into the water. Until they took that step of faith, trusting God to get them across, God did nothing. Until we have enough faith to trust God to take that step out of our comfort zone, God's waiting for us to trust Him. It's just that simple!

Tell and bring forth your case; yes, let them take counsel together. Who has declared this from ancient time? Who has told it from that time? Have not I, the Lord? And there is no other God besides Me, a just God and a Savior; there is none besides Me. (Isaiah 45:21)

I hope you are keeping up with the daily reading. It's important that you see the background to these verses. Maybe each day as you read you may want to bracket your own verses that speak to you. Everyone is different and God uses different verses at different times to speak to our heart.

So how do we know there are no other gods? It's just like the people that argue there are several ways to get to heaven. Why is Jesus the only way? First, Jesus said so, in John 14 Jesus said, "I am the way, the truth, and the life. No one comes to the Father except through Me." So why should I believe Jesus? It's the same question, "Why should I trust the Bible?" Do you have several friends? Do you trust some more than others? Why? Maybe someone has let you down, or even lied to you, do you trust them now?

No one has been able, over thousands of years, to discredit the Bible. I told you earlier about Josh McDowell. There are countless stories of atheists who set out to disprove the Bible and end up being Christians. It's the same with God's word. If you doubt it, fine. Do you accept the consequences if it is right?

I forget where I heard this, are you willing to bet eternity in hell that the Bible is not accurate? Think about it. O.k, some is true, some isn't. Ok, are you qualified enough to determine which is true and which isn't? It's the same story with working your way to heaven. How much is enough, what counts and what doesn't? If you just count the King James Bible which was assembled in 1611. The Geneva Bible goes back much further than that. We won't even consider the original text. Just the King James that is over 400 years. There have been scholars, skeptics, professors, all kinds of "learned" people who have tried to discredit the Bible. It is still the largest selling book in history. Why is that?

"I am the Lord and there is no other." Let those words sink in. If this is true, are you trusting in Him for eternity?

Thus, says the Lord, your Redeemer, the Holy One of Israel; I am the
Lord your God, who teaches you to profit, who leads you by the way
you should go. (Isaiah 48:17)

That is one of my favorite words in the Bible! In Matthew 28, Jesus says, "Go
therefore and make disciples of all nations, baptizing them in the name of the
Father and the Son and of the Holy Spirit, **teaching** them to observe all things
that I have commanded you; and lo, I am with you always, even to the end of the
earth." (Matthew 28:19-20).

"But I'm not a teacher!" Look at 1 Peter 4:11, "If anyone speaks, let him speak
as the oracles of God. If anyone ministers (teach), let him do it as with the ability
which God supplies, that in all things God may be glorified through Jesus Christ,
to whom belong the glory and the dominion forever and ever. Amen."

Don't let me get started on that word "profit". Do you see what Isaiah is
conveying? It's not you! It's being obedient to the Spirit of God. Just trusting God
to give you the words to speak. I have known so many Sunday school teachers
through the years. Not a one believes they are anything special. They will be the
first to admit, it's God doing the teaching, they simply give voice to God's Spirit!

I was looking once for a teacher for 3rd and 4th grade children's class. I asked
this one lady if she would try it. She was very hesitant, she just knew she wasn't
a teacher. Six months later when the year ended and we usually filled vacancies.
When I went to her she begged me not to take her class away. She loved it and
teaching. She just needed to trust God and try! Of course, she didn't know in a
Baptist church once you take a class it's yours for life.

Don't overlook the last part of that verse. "Who leads you by the way you
should go." That's the key. If God's not walking beside you, you're on your own.
But God promises to be there all the way. I skipped a key verse in Matthew 28.
And Jesus came and spoke to them, saying, "All authority has been given to Me
in heaven and on earth." You see if God calls you to teach, that's important, you
have His authority. You have His power through the Holy Spirit. I can't tell you
how many teachers have told me that the best way to learn the Bible is to teach. I
know that don't make sense, but it's true!

But He was wounded for our transgressions, He was bruised for our iniquities; the chastisement for our peace was upon Him, and by His stripes we are healed. All we like sheep have gone astray; we have turned, everyone, to his own way; and the Lord has laid on Him the iniquity of us all. (Isaiah 53:5-6)

Here's another set of verses that you need to note in the front of your Bible. What an awesome picture of the purpose of Christ's coming and our relationship to His coming. You really ought to note the whole chapter. Take a minute and read this chapter over.

Look at the beginning of verse 6. "All we like sheep have gone astray; we have turned everyone to his own way." Sound familiar? Try the end of the book of Judges. It's theme throughout the Bible. Man's will vs God's will. This passage gives us the reason God had to send His Son to die on the cross. As ignorant sheep, we are lost without a shepherd.

This must be the most beautiful passage in the Bible. A movie that came out a few years ago was called, "The Passion of Christ" I heard enough about the movie that I was sure I didn't want to see it. It was so vivid in the depiction of Christs' death on the cross, it was just not to my liking. If I want a picture, this 53rd chapter of Isaiah is enough for me. I don't need to see it. I know what Jesus did for me at Calvary. He paid my sin-debt in full. I've accepted that by faith and now I'm a child of God.

Just for a minute I'd like you to put yourself in Isaiah's shoes. He's sitting at his desk writing. Suddenly, the Holy Spirit gives him these words to write. What do you think went through his mind? Remember this is hundreds of years before the actual event. They didn't have crucifixion in Isaiah's day. At that time, it was stoning. Just a note when you get the chance, we've already went through the psalms, but read psalm 22. That too will sound familiar, if your familiar with the crucifixion story.

I mentioned before that the psalms were the heart of the Bible. I think this passage can be the heart of the message of the Bible. This is what it is all about. God restoring His relationship with mankind and opening up a relationship with His fallen creation.

> The Lord will guide you continually, and satisfy your soul in drought, and strengthen your bones; you shall be like a watered garden, and like a spring of water, whose waters do not fail. (Isaiah 58:11)

What a great picture of what I've been talking about. Notice the word, "continually"? That's why I love the picture of walking with God. Your both on the same path (hopefully). You share as you walk, things on your mind, concerns you have, then God encourages you, strengthens your walk. You walk at His pace not yours. You take the turns He takes not yours. It's really a great picture.

When I was in my early teens I had this experience I'll never forget. I was laying on a hammock outside about midday. I had almost drifted off to sleep. It had started to sprinkle. Someone, somehow had laid newspapers over me. I heard the rain hit the newspaper but had no thought of getting up and going inside. It was the most peaceful moment I can ever remember. I still cherish it today.

Walking in a garden after a spring rain, it smells so fresh and alive. That's what it feels like to walk with God. I know I sound like an expert. No, I do have brief memories of doing just that. The problem is too many times we part ways. God wants to go one way and for some weird reason we want to take off on another path. It takes so much longer to backtrack and find God waiting at the fork where you left Him.

Do you remember the first thing Israel complained about when God freed them from Egypt? They had crossed the Red Sea and they were headed to Mt. Sinai. Three days and they ran out of water. Instead of asking God, they started complaining. What do we do when the road gets bumpy? We start complaining don't we. God your right there, why won't you do something? Instead you might want to ask, "O.k, God what is the lesson you want me to learn in this trial?" Instead of complaining start paying attention. Is there some reason God has decided you needed this detour? Some lesson you need to add to your growth as a Christian?

I think an interesting principle is that God has a plan for you. That plan may take you places you've never been before, do things you've never done before. Before that, He needs to teach you some things, listen!

For since the beginning of the world men have not heard nor perceived
by the ear, nor has the eye seen any God besides You, who acts for
the one who waits for Him. (Isaiah 64:4)

Wow. We are at the end of Isaiah already. Does this verse sound familiar? If you've read the New Testament this might sound like, 1 Corinthians 2:9, But it is written, "Eye has not seen, nor ear heard, nor have entered into the heart of man the things which God has prepared for those who love Him." You might know it would be from the pen of Isaiah.

Chew on this verse a minute. Think of all the movies you have seen that try to depict heaven. They pale in comparison to what it is really like. Stories of people with "out-of-body" experiences, etc. They try to paint a picture of heaven. They can't do it justice.

Just like those who try to tell us what we will be doing in heaven, etc. No one knows. Look at that verse again, either one. God is telling us, through Paul and the prophet Isaiah, you can't imagine in your wildest imagination what it will be like.

This is interesting. Did you pick up on these words, "since the beginning of the world" is God saying it will be like the Garden of Eden or is He saying it will be better. There is a vague picture of heaven in the book of Revelation. But again, it's not that clear. When we read passages like those in Revelation we wonder why God didn't do a better job of describing it. I told our Sunday school class one Sunday, "If God told us everything we wanted to know we would not be able to carry the books." Let's just say that God told us enough to get us there!

I hope you've enjoyed reading Isaiah. I said before he is my favorite major prophet. His writing is so different. That's the miracle of the Bible. God allowed the author to keep his personality and style while at the same time conveying God's perfect truth to the writer. Maybe I'm off, but I can also tell the difference between the gospel of John and the gospel of Luke. We'll touch on that when we get there.

One thing about this description of heaven. As a Christian we can say, "soon and very soon." but if your lost. You haven't asked Jesus into your heart, what do you have to look forward to?

> At that time Jerusalem shall be called The Throne of the Lord, and all the nations shall be gathered to it, to the name of the Lord, to Jerusalem. No more shall they follow the dictates of their evil hearts. (Jeremiah 3:17)

That's interesting isn't it. Just recently our president said that the United States embassy would be moved to Jerusalem. Quite an uproar too. Just fulfilling prophecy. Of course, it's not because it is known as The Throne of the Lord. I mentioned before the middle three letters in Jerusalem.

Of course, Jeremiah was talking of the end times. For such a small country, it sure does draw a lot of world-wide attention.

In Isaiah, I called him the "Jesus Prophet" Jeremiah already has a name, "The Weeping Prophet." It is unbelievable how much this prophet goes through trying to warn Judah of their pending captivity. Why were they going into captivity? Rebellion, disobedience, refusing to obey the commands God gave them through Moses.

Is God dealing with you about some rebellion in your own heart? Notice the last part of the verse above, "They follow the dictates of their evil hearts." It's the heart that God judges not their actions. We can "do" all the rights move's but if our motives are amiss God knows.

How are you doing in your daily devotions? In your Bible reading? What kind of information are putting into your mind and heart and journal? Godly information and reading I hope.

Jeremiah, just like Isaiah, is trying to warn Judah that God is at the end of His patience. They have disobeyed God's law about letting the land rest one in seven years. Now the payment is due. Do they repent? Do they turn from disobedience? I'm afraid not. Is God trying to get your attention about something? Has He sent a prophet into your life to warn you of your disobedience? You might want to do some praying and ask God to reveal anything that hinders your walk with God. He will tell you if you ask.

In your reading, does your mind wander? Do you think of things other than what you are reading? Think about it. Is God trying to get through your thoughts and concentration to tell you something. Pay attention to where your mind wanders while reading God's word!

Thus, says the Lord, "Stand in the ways and see, and ask for the old paths, where the good way is, and walk in it; then you will find rest for your souls." But they said, "We will not walk in it." (Jeremiah 6:16)

Y ou didn't know my "walking with God" was biblical did you. Look what Jeremiah says! Walking with God is the good way, He commands us to walk in it. I've already talked a lot about this. Why? It's important that you get this concept. When Israel "walked with God" godly leadership, godly direction, God blessed their efforts. God gave them victory after victory over their enemies.

When God brought them into the Promised Land think about it. They didn't have to plant vineyards, already planted and producing. They didn't have to build cities, or homes to live in. They were already built. On and on what they needed was already there! God provided all of it. They were walking with God. Then comes Ai. One man disobeyed God's instructions, the nation was routed! When they got right with God they destroyed Ai. When God is walking with us we can achieve fantastic things. When we walk our own path it's nothing but frustration, hardship, and heartache.

Notice he says, "the old paths" we are constantly looking for some new way to do things. That's good in some things. They still haven't replaced the Bible. We want some new "self-help" book. Some guru to tell us how to achieve what God has already achieved, peace! God is the one who created us. He knows what makes us tick. Why not go to the Maker to find what is lacking?

But then, alas, the end of the verse. "Rebellion"! What is the one thing that frustrates a parent more than anything, rebellion! Your kids know more than you do. They are bound to walk their own path. What happens? More times than not the parent ends up bailing them out of trouble. Rebellion never accomplishes a good result. Look at the Bible.

"Then you will find rest for your souls." Is that what we are looking for? The answer is right here. Walking with God brings that rest. Worshiping with God on the Lord's day. Being in God's house on the Lord's day. Reading God's holy word. Praying, talking with our heavenly Father. Listening to the leading of His Holy Spirit as it leads us along this path called life. The destination, the presence of God!

"But let him who glories glory in this, that he understands and knows Me, that I am the Lord, exercising lovingkindness, judgment, and righteousness in the earth. For in these I delight," says the Lord. (Jeremiah 9:24)

I love movies. Movies with a message, a story line, etc. Here are three movies I like, "The Love Letter", "The Longest Ride," "The Christmas Wish," These three have something in common. The first two revolve around letters, the third around some diaries. The point is that in all of these a relationship is born from reading these articles. There is one more, "The Notebook" revolves around a notebook a man uses to restore his wife's memory of their long marriage together. The point being we can learn a lot from the writings of another.

The line in the verse above, "That he understands and knows Me." is so important. I've talked a lot about walking with God. You get to know someone by walking with them. You get to know them by reading the letters that they wrote. God has blessed us with a huge storehouse of letters to get to know Him. To learn what pleases Him and what doesn't. How to get on His good side, and how not to! God shares with us, as we walk, His will for our lives.

God is not stuck in the ancient days, God is relevant today. The greatest thing about knowing God is that He knows the future. Of course, He's not going to tell us what's going to happen next week. That's not the point. He does tell us when we are headed down the wrong road. He won't tell us why sometimes, but He knows why! He just wants us to trust Him. Sometimes that turn will not seem logical, but God knows and that's all that counts!

He wants us to trust Him. To follow His leading. The first line of Proverbs 3:5-6, "Trust in Lord with all your heart!" That's His desire. It comes from reading His word and learning about God and why He desires a relationship with us.

I just mention four movies but there are so many others that have the same story line. Letters from someone in the past that change our lives and the direction we take. I hope you are staying in the Word through these devotions. Reading and getting to know God in a deeper way. Ask Him to reveal His will for your life!

This is your lot, the portion of your measures from Me, "says the Lord, because you have forgotten Me and trusted in falsehood." (Jeremiah 13:25)

We talked yesterday about God's love letter to us. The method of getting to know God and having a relationship with Him. There is another component to those letters, truth. Spiritual truth and relational truth. That is our relationship with Him, is demonstrated in these letters God has written to us. When we get to know God through His letters we get to know what is important to Him and how He feels toward us.

Most Christians understand, I hope, that God loves them. We got that. But there is so much more in His word. There is truth. Basic facts that we need to do daily to, not only have a closer walk with Him but to have a better life here.

Take the book of Proverbs. There is so much truth there that if someone practice all the precepts that are written there it would greatly change their life! You notice the word Jeremiah uses in the verse above? "Trusted". It's one thing to hear lies and false hoods but it's quite another to live by them to trust them for your life decisions.

I told you about the description of idols in Psalm 135. They don't speak, hear, talk, etc. Then how in the world can a person listen to an idol? Obey an idol? Yet we do. If they don't speak who are we listening to? Our own desires, our own wants, our own wisdom, not God's.

Don't forget the lesson of Solomon. He had all the wisdom God could provide, yet his wives led him into idols and thus led him away from God. You might say he knew the truth but denied it anyway. We can do the same thing. Who are our counselors? Where do we seek the wisdom to make our daily decisions? If it isn't God and His word we are fooled!

It may have been a blessing that I was not saved until I was thirty-five. I can look back on the uneasiness, the fear, the uncertainty, of a lost world. And compare it with the amazing peace and direction I feel today. Oh, I have my moments, we all do, but I can keep coming back to God to reassure me of His love for me, His direction in my life, and renew that walk with Him for however many days we have left. That is a peace that passes all understanding!

I, the Lord, search the heart, I test the mind, even to give every man according to his ways, according to the fruit of his doings. (Jeremiah 17:10)

Do you see the contrast? First God searches the heart, then He rewards according to his doings. The point is, God looks at both sides of our relationship with Him. He doesn't look at just our heart. Our heart may be in the right place but our deeds don't reflect that. Conversely, we may do all the right things but if our hearts aren't right it will make no difference.

Also notice that He test the mind. Let's think about this word "test" a moment. First, in one of my favorite chapters, 1 Corinthians 3 we read, "Each one's work will become clear; for the Day will declare it, because it will be revealed by fire; and the fire will test each one's work, of what sort it is." Interesting thing about this chapter, it doesn't say which works are gold, silver and precious stones and which works are wood, hay and stubble. It does say our works will be tested. Look at 2 Corinthians 13:5, "Examine yourself as to whether you are in the faith. Test yourselves. Do you not know yourselves, that Jesus Christ is in you? - unless indeed you are disqualified." Interesting verses, are they not? You are to test yourselves to see if the Holy Spirit is within you.

I believe God is always testing us. Not to see if we are worthy, no! He tests our faith. To what degree He can trust us and use us. How many times in the gospels does Jesus say, "Oh ye of little faith." Look at Matthew 25. Jesus is giving His parable of the talents. I encourage you to read the whole thing. Right now, look at verse 21, "His Lord said to him, 'Well done, good and faithful servant; you were faithful over a dew things, I will make you ruler over many things. Enter into the joy of the Lord.'" God tests our faithfulness, commitment to serve Him, our obedience. If we are faithful in the simple tasks He continues to use us in greater and greater ways.

As a long time, Sunday School Director, I've often wondered at what point do you "graduate" from Sunday school? The only graduation will be when you stand before the Lord and He say, "Well done thou good and faithful servant." Inter into My joy!

"The instant I speak concerning a nation and concerning a kingdom, to pluck up, to pull down, and to destroy it, if that nation against whom I have spoken turns from its evil, I will relent of the disaster that I thought to bring upon it. (Jeremiah 18:7-8)

If God's people had only listened. Remember, Jeremiah is talking to Judah prior to their Babylonia captivity. They had a chance to repent and to turn back to God. Can you picture Jeremiah standing before the leaders and telling them that God has this message for them? If you've read Jeremiah you know they treated him shamefully. Totally disregarded his message and thus God's message.

Has God spoken to you through the Bible? Has His word convicted you of some misdeed? What are you doing about it? God doesn't "wink" at disobedience.

When you read through Leviticus were there some "laws" you thought were, maybe meaningless? Not important. Those that can be disregarded? Ever thought that about our current laws? I see people not stopping at stop signs, running through yellow lights, etc. As long as they are not caught they will keep doing it, right? The problem is that one time they run into a van with children in it. Then it's too late!

I love this. They talk about "petty thieves." Sure, they don't steal much here and there. Of course, the lowest is those who steal from homes during a natural disaster. Anyway, have you ever heard of a thief that said, "O.k, I have enough I will quit now?" I don't think so. The only way they will quit is when they are caught. One last thing. Did you notice in Exodus that anyone taking from someone else, must pay restitution? Why did we get away from that?

This chapter has the story of the potter and the clay. What a great analogy. We are the clay of course. God wants to make a masterpiece but if the clay isn't pure it will crack, then it is worthless. One of my favorite country songs is "The Old Violin" it was either Johnny Paycheck or Merle Haggard, not sure. The violin was to be auctioned, it was battered and torn. No one bid on the violin. Then a master picked it up and played beautiful music. Then the price kept going up and up. God wants to play some beautiful music in your life. Are you willing to let Him clean you up and tighten the strings?

"I will set up shepherds over them who will feed them; and they shall fear no more, nor be dismayed, nor shall they be lacking," says the Lord. (Jeremiah 23:4)

A great verse. Let me share three stories from my experience as a pastor. There is a lot more to being a shepherd that preaching from the pulpit.

The very first call to my office, as a pastor, was to tell me that a young couple in our church had just lost their baby to S.I.D.S. (Sudden Infant Death Syndrome). I rushed to the hospital. Praying all the way there, "what do you tell a family at a time like this?" There were no words. I was just there. Later I made several visits with them. Prayed with them. Answered what questions I could. Prayed for and with them. When I later left the church, the mother had just gotten news that she was expecting again. I was so happy for them!

Once I got a call from a family who was having life-support turned off from their father. They asked if I would be in the room when it happened. Shortly after I got there the family was in turmoil. Angry comments, accusations, etc. Then they turn the machines off and removed the tubes. Everyone was watching the monitor. You could feel the tension. Waiting, waiting. It just seemed like he wasn't ready to go. Forty-five minutes and still no sign of his departure. Soon the family began talking about the memories of when they were children. The mood changed, friendlier. Then he left. The line went flat. I believe he was waiting for them to get along before he left.

I had just resigned from the church. I felt a calling elsewhere. I got a call from a family who wanted me to come to the nursing home where hospice was ministering to the father. I told them I was no longer pastor but they wanted me there anyway. I sat and talked with the family members, prayed with them. They had questions, comments, we talked till 4:00 in the morning. It was an awesome experience. The opportunity to comfort and encourage in a time of grief.

These are the stories of being a pastor. Many joke about a pastor only works a few hours a week. A pastor's calling is 24-7. His message? Hope! His mentor is the word of God. His strength comes from the power of the Holy Spirit. Thank you, Jesus!

For I know the thoughts that I think toward you, says the Lord, thoughts of peace and not of evil, to give you a future and a hope. Then you will call upon Me and go and pray to Me, and I will listen to you. And you will seek Me and find Me, when you search for Me with all your heart. (Jeremiah 29:11-13)

The more I have gotten to know this verse the more it is part of my life. There is so much here about God's relationship with us. You just must meditate on it more and more. Not sure what I could say that hasn't been said but we'll see.

I like the NIV choice of words in the first verse, "I know the plans I have for you." That's the point. God had a plan for our lives when He formed us in the womb. Look at chapter 1 verse 5 (speaking of Jeremiah) "Before I formed you in the womb I knew you; before you were born I sanctified you; I ordained you a prophet to the nations." God had a plan for Jeremiah before he was formed.

Notice in the verse in Jeremiah, the word isn't used but the thought is there, Prosper! God wants the best for us. He always wanted the best for Israel but they rejected God's plan. How about you? Are you seeking God's purpose in your life?

Look at 12 and 13, "call, pray, seek search, find." that is what God expects from us. To seek His will and purpose for our lives. I found out yesterday that our pastor turned down a six-figure job to become a minister. That is seeking God's purpose for your life. That is putting God's priority first in your life. Are you arguing with God about a direction? Don't!

Notice the condition for this guidance, "with all your heart!" Have you ever heard the term "half-hearted"? Of course, you have. I wonder how many "half-hearted" Christians today that are missing God's best because there is only a half-hearted commitment to God's direction and guidance.

Notice God's promise? "and I will listen to you." God is always there, always willing to listen. God will never let a prayer go unanswered. The problem is if we don't hear the answer we want, or expect, we think He didn't answer. I like what someone said once, If, you pray a couple of times then you move on, it must not have been important!

> The Lord has appeared of old to me, saying: "Yes, I have loved you
> with an everlasting love; Therefore, with lovingkindness I have drawn
> you. (Jeremiah 31:3)

Jeremiah is talking about the final restoration of the nation of Israel. After Jesus' return in the book of Revelation, God will restore His people to their rightful place. So, what does that mean to me.

Do you remember, as a youth, the day in the revival service when you went forward and accepted Jesus as your Savior? Do you remember how excited you were? So, what happened? Why did you drift away? Day by day slowly the things of God meant less and less. You gave up going to church, it was too convicting. You slowly tuned out the prompting of the Holy Spirit. You think you drifted farther and farther from God. You did but God is still right there.

It's like the story of the couple in the front seat of their car. The wife says, "I remember when we were first married we used to sit close to each other holding hands, etc. Now we sit on opposite sides of the seat. What happened?" Then the husband says, "I didn't move." That is what God is saying to you right now.

God will always love you, with an everlasting love. He loves you so much He was willing to allow His Son to take your place on the cross to pay for your sins. That kind of love never fades. You are the one who has drifted away. Slowly allowed other things to come between you and your heavenly Father.

Now is a good time to take a minute and pray and ask God to forgive your turning your back on Him and ask that He would renew a "right Spirit" within you. Draw you back into that relationship you once enjoyed.

Someone in our prayer meeting last night talked about what happens when, as Christians, we sin. What does that do to our relationship with God? I said, "The fellowship may be broken but NOT the relationship." You are still a child of God if you have asked Jesus into your heart. But that fellowship, that walk with God, has been broken. It just takes a simple prayer and turning back to God to restore that fellowship with the Father. That's the promise from this verse. God's wants that relationship to flourish and grow!

> Call to Me, and I will answer you, and show you great and mighty
> things, which you do not know. (Jeremiah 33:3)

W hat is required? You must first call on Him. To expect God to work
miracles in your life just because He can, isn't going to work. You must
have enough faith to ask!

Have you ever asked God to give you an Amen? A fella once told me that when
your faith begins to dim, pray and ask God for an "Amen" something that day that
will renew your faith. Let you know that God is there and wants to be an active
part of your life. So, I tried it. Yes, He did something that day that only God could
have pulled off. So, being the human that I am, I asked for another the next day.
Of course, it didn't take God long to catch on. But I will never forget that blessing!

What is God doing in your life? Do you feel His presence, is He doing things
in your life you can't explain? Try this little experiment. But remember it's only
good once. The point is to strengthen your faith, to let you know that He is there
and is part of your life!

Did you notice where Jeremiah is at, when he received this encouragement
from God. Look at verse 1 in this chapter, "Moreover the word of the Lord came
to Jeremiah a second time, *while he was still shut up in the court of the prison, saying.*"
(emphasis added) This is where Jeremiah spent most of his ministry. The king
didn't like his prophecy so he throws him in prison. Yet God encouraged him
with the words above.

Speaking of prison. Paul spend many years at the tail end of his ministry
in prison. Instead of saying woe is me, Paul began witnessing to his jailors. So
much so, I'm told, that the king had to keep rotating them so they didn't become
believers. Paul took advantage of his "hopeless" situation. In another jail, he was
singing. (Acts 16:23)

What about you? Where are you and your relationship (walk) with God? I
remember sitting on a dock waiting for help to arrive, as a UPS driver. Thinking,
"is this all there is?" Will, I ever get out of this rut? Not long after that I signed up
for over-the-road training. I would have never thought I could drive those big rigs.
In a couple of years, I was pulling a "train" (two 40-foot trailers) to Wichita. We
never know what is just around the bend. Oh, this was before I was saved. Even
then God was watching out for me, waiting for my heart to turn to Him!

"For I will surely deliver you, and you shall not fall by the sword; but your life shall be as a prize to you, because you have put your trust in Me," says the Lord. (Jeremiah 39:18)

How far are you willing to go? How much trust do you have in God's plan and direction for your life? Let me remind you of this verse, Then He touched their eyes, saying, "According to your faith be it unto you." (Matthew 9:29). That verse intrigues me. All through the gospels Jesus comments on the degree of someone's faith. Let's look at a couple, (Matthew 6:30) "Now if God so clothes the grass of the field, which today is, and tomorrow is thrown into the oven, will He not much more clothe you, O you of little faith?" Jesus teaching about worry. Look at this one (Matthew 8:10) When Jesus heard it, He marveled, and said to those who followed, "Assuredly, I say to you, I have not found such great faith, not even in Israel." This Jesus said to a Roman Centurion.

How would you "measure" your faith? How far are you willing to trust God? God uses the faith of His children to be a testimony to a lost world, to demonstrate His power to the faithful. When God works through a child of God the world sees what God has done and forces them to decide.

Many a Christian, in the work force, is amazed at how many co-workers come to them for prayer. The testimony of your faith in God draws the lost world to come to you to reach God. When all they must do is ask Jesus into their heart and they have the same access to the throne of God. This is something I will never understand.

Just a note, take a look at 39:15. I mentioned this before. The whereabouts of Jeremiah.

This promise wasn't even to Jeremiah but to someone who came to Jeremiah for counsel. Think about Jeremiah's faith. Here he is in prison and he can encourage someone who comes to him for encouragement. I wonder if, when we are in a storm, can we trust God enough, in our own storm, to encourage someone going through their storm?

Notice the condition to God's deliverance? "because you have put your trust in Me." Until we are willing to turn the trial over to God, He will withhold His deliverance until we trust Him!

"Whether it is pleasing or displeasing, we will obey the voice of the
Lord our God to whom we send you, that it may be well with us when
we obey the voice of the Lord our God." (Jeremiah 42:6)

There is that nasty word again, obey. Just a reminder that Jeremiah was a
prophet to the southern kingdom (Judah) prior to the Babylonians taking
them into captivity. The people have come to Jeremiah to ask God not to remove
them from their land. They have asked Jeremiah to intercede for them. The verse
above is Jeremiah's response. Again, they promise obedience. Have you ever tried
to bargain with God?

Then when it seems God did not fulfill His end of the bargain, what was your
response? Blame God? How many times has Israel or Judah said, "We will obey
the word of God." Only to turn right around and do their own thing? Too many
times I'm afraid.

I hope you are keeping up with the daily reading schedule. Did you see what
happened in the following verses? God promised the Remnant that if they "trusted"
Him enough to remain in the land God would protect them from Babylon. If they
went to Egypt all bets were off. Guess what they did?

Do you know what one of the duties of the Holy Spirit is? Some will give
credit to the conscience, but if you are a Christian it's the Holy Spirit speaking. He
warns us not to go down that road, not to do something that is contrary to God's
will. That's one of the benefits of this walk we are taking with God.

We are about to take this fork in the road. God is going right, we want to go
left. The road looks smoother, wider, more pleasant to the eye. God's way looks
bumpy, barren, not headed anywhere. So, we leave God and take the road that is
pleasing. Just around the corner we wish we had never left God's direction. So, we
double back and hope that God is still there. He is, waiting patiently. But we have
lost valuable time to a foolish mistake.

Lip service is so easy. Israel was good at it. Whether in the desert after leaving
Egypt, or the many other challenges God delivered Israel from, yet as soon as the
road gets bumpy they bail.

How about you. Can you look back at some choices you made that you wish
you hadn't? Some wrong turns? Listen for God's still voice!

> For because you have trusted in your works and your treasures, you also shall be taken. And Chemosh shall go forth into captivity, his priests and his princes together. (Jeremiah 48:7)

Tell me what you really think! That's clear. The sad part is that this is where we are today. We talked yesterday about the degree of faith we have in God. O.k, let's take a measure of how much faith we have in the two things listed in this verse. Works and treasure.

If your trusting in works (good deeds) to get you to heaven, how much is enough? Where is the passage in "God's word" that lists what we can do to earn our spot in heaven? How many points do we get for giving to charity? How many points do we get for helping a neighbor and not asking payment? Where is that list? Even in Corinthians three it talks about works, but no list. Look in James, he's good about comparing works and faith. Look at this verse, But, someone will say, "You have faith and I have works." Show me your faith without your works, and I will show you my faith by my works." (James 2:18). You see? That is an argument going back to biblical days. Even this argument doesn't talk about getting into heaven.

I once posed the question, "Suppose you could buy your ticket to heaven for $1,000. They would be lined up around the block to buy a ticket." It's just like faith it can't be measured in dollars and cents. It is so rare that Jesus marveled at any display. He was even more surprised that, for the most part, the faith was demonstrated by the Gentiles.

Here's another question, "Where is the verse in the Bible that gives a monetary amount to get into heaven? Try this verse, "For by grace you have been saved through faith, and that not of yourselves; it is a gift of God, not of works, lest anyone should boast." (Ephesians 2:8-9).

Besides Jeremiah there will be other prophets that chastise Israel for trusting in treasures and works to get God's blessing. God wants faith not fortune. He wants trust not works. God's grace is not for sale. That "price" was already paid at Calvary. The greatest cost you can imagine, the death of the very Son of God. He paid your sin-debt for all eternity!

I hate to be so crass but, "Do you have your ticket?" if not, why not? It just requires faith, not riches or good deeds.

> They shall ask the way to Zion, with their faces toward it, saying,
> "Come and let us join ourselves to the Lord in a perpetual covenant
> that will not be broken. (Jeremiah 50:5)

This always fascinated me. Here God uses Assyria and Babylon to punish Israel and Judah for their disobedience. Then He turns around and punishes both nations. God can use anyone or anything to bring us where He wants us to be. Assyria removes the Jews from the northern kingdom (ten tribes). Then Assyria sends in their people to occupy the northern part of Israel. Have you noticed what this land is referred to as? Samaria. Does that sound familiar in Jesus day? The Samaritans were a mixed race of Jews and Assyrians. That's why they were shunned by the Jews in Jesus day.

We talked about the Babylonians removing the southern tribes (Judah and Benjamin) from the land. The difference is that God allowed them to return because of the covenant God made with David that there would always be a remnant in Israel. Much as there is today. God's word is always true! God kept His covenant with David.

Just a note. When we get to the prophet Danial you will note that when Daniel prayed he would always face east. Facing Jerusalem.

I have a two-pronged approach to teaching. Number one: The Historical Perspective. The history behind a passage, you can't fully understand a passage unless you get the context of what is happening. That's why it's important to read these chapters each day. Number two: Personal Application. How does this passage apply to me personally? There is always a spiritual truth in God's word that can help us better understand God's will for our lives.

We have looked at the historical part now the personal application. Look at the end of this verse. "In a perpetual covenant that will not be broken." This makes me think of the covenant God made with me when I got saved. God promises in His word that when we ask Jesus into our hearts we are saved. (Romans 10:9). That is a perpetual covenant. That is a promise God makes to us, because His Son died on the cross to make this covenant sure. Some have said that if we could lose our salvation through some sin, that Jesus would have to die over and over. Jesus died once for ALL!

AUGUST 28   JEREMIAH 51-52

The Lord has revealed our righteousness. Come and let us declare in
Zion the work of the Lord our God. (Jeremiah 51:10)

We are nearing the end of Jeremiah's prophecy. Think about this, two dynamic prophets, Jeremiah and Isaiah, preaching to the southern kingdom (Judah and Benjamin) that God's judgement is coming and what do they do? They refuse to listen. God sends in Babylon to remove them from their land.

God sends His only, Son, Jesus, to preach essentially the same message but in a different way. What do the people do? We see it through Paul's writings up to the book of Revelation. We refuse to listen. Now after the judgments in the book of Revelation Satan is taken out for a thousand years. Look at chapter 20 in Revelation verses 7-8a, "Now when the thousand years have expired, Satan will be released from his prison and will go out to deceive the nations which are in the four corners of the earth." Even after a thousand years of God reigning on the earth the nations still fall for Satan's lies.

So, what's the point? It all comes down to a personal decision, doesn't it? The nations are deceived, what about you? Are you falling for Satan's lies or do you want a personal relationship with the God of the universe? Just ask Jesus to come into your heart!

Do you see the message of Jeremiah? "let us declare in Zion the work of the Lord our God." That is what Isaiah and Jeremiah and the rest of the prophets in the Old Testament have done. Declared God's judgment and challenged the people to come to God in repentance. I hope, as we work through these daily Bible readings your heart has turned to God. If you're already a Christian I pray that you are checking your walk with God. Are you tuned to God's prompting, God's leadership in your life?

God put the writings of these prophets in His word for a reason. Israel is our example of disobedience and the consequences of "doing it our way".

It's my prayer, as we finish up the Old Testament in the coming weeks, that the scriptures have given you a new perspective and a new and fresher relationship with God the Father. Listen to the prophets as they try to turn Israel back to God. Are you listening to the prompting of God's Spirit in your own life?

"Through the Lord's mercies we are not consumed, because His compassions fail not. They are new every morning; great is Your faithfulness. The Lord is my portion," says my soul. "Therefore, I hope in Him!" (Lamentations 3:22-24)

This book may be the reason Jeremiah was called, "The Weeping Prophet". His burden for Jerusalem was tremendous. This book focuses on the destruction of Jerusalem. Think back to the time of David and how important it was to David that the ark be brought to Jerusalem.

Even today there is a lot of controversy over the city. The Palestinians claim it as their capitol, the Jews of course claim it. The United States has announced it will move it's, embassy to Jerusalem and the uproar that caused. Jesus always made it a point to go to Jerusalem on Passover and the last time He was crucified in Jerusalem. The importance of that one little city in world history is amazing!

When Ezra and Nehemiah return to rebuild the nation, they returned to Jerusalem and rebuilt the wall, and the temple within it. The focus of the return from Babylonian captivity.

In this verse, we can see God's comfort for Jeremiah. He relies on the mercy of God, the comfort that only God can provide. That recalls my favorite verses on this subject. 2 Corinthians 1:3-4, "Blessed be the God and Father of our Lord Jesus Christ, the Father of mercies and the God of all comfort, who comforts us in all our tribulation, that we may be able to comfort those who are in trouble, with the comfort with which we ourselves are comforted by God.

What awesome verses. Our comfort is in the mercies of God. The verses above are as comforting. If anyone needed comforting Jeremiah did. Jeremiah knew where to go, do you?

Where do you turn in trials? Where do you go for encouragement, support, peace, direction, compassion? I hope it begins with God, first through His Spirit, then turning to His word. One of our deacons, when he prays for those in need he says, "May You wrap Your ever-loving arms around them" what a wonderful way to put it.

For Jeremiah's preaching, all he ever received was punishment. But Jeremiah had the comfort of knowing God's presence in his life!

Turn us back to You, O Lord, and we will be restored; Renew our days
of old. (Lamentations 5:21)

W hat is the most precious commodity today? Gold, silver, 401K's, stocks,
investments, pension funds, your current wage? It's all based on a monetary
amount, isn't it? No, the most precious commodity today is time. I was shocked
a few years ago when I learned that high school students needed to carry a "day-
planner." Today it's all kept on their phones. To have a schedule so tight that you
needed to track it is just amazing.

Let's look at a couple of verses. First, Psalm 31:15, **"My times are in Your
hand;** deliver me from the hand of my enemies, and from those who persecute
me." Do you see who is in control of our time? You can have all the, day-planners
and smart phones but God can throw you a curve at any time! Here's another one
from the New Testament, "But when the **fullness of time** had come, God sent
forth His Son, born of a woman, born under the law. (Galatians 4:4) Everything
happens in "God's time". But we continue to plan, scheme, and prepare.

I like what someone once told me, "Want to know how to make God laugh?
Tell Him your plans." There is a point to this line. How much "time" do you give
God? Simple question. Reading His word, praying, church, etc. God allows us 168
hours in each week. Can you "sacrifice" 3 hours on Sunday? Think about it. Does
it give an insight into your priorities?

Look at this verse again. "Renew our days as of old." If you can find one hour
in the morning (preferably) to have a "quiet time" with God. You will not believe
the benefits it will bring you. Is there a challenge coming up in the day ahead?
Give it to God. Maybe Jeremiah, at the end of his prophecy is reminding Israel to
remember what God has done in the past. If Israel would only remember. But we
know they have VERY short memories. Remember what they did right after God
freed them from Egyptian bondage, they complained about no water.

Take that time in the morning. Forget about the day ahead. Put it in God's
hands. Praise Him for the blessing of having a job, of getting out of bed, of each
breath you take. Be thankful!

> Then the Spirit entered me when He spoke to me, and set me on my feet; and I heard Him who spoke to me. (Ezekiel 2:2)

There is an interesting lesson in Ezekiel's comment here. You see the Holy Spirit worked differently in the Old Testament compared to the New Testament, thank heaven. In the Old Testament, the Holy Spirit would come and go as God saw fit. To inspire, to empower, to teach, etc. But, in the New Testament once a person has given their life to Christ. Asked Jesus to come into their heart, at that time they receive the Holy Spirit as a "permanent" resident! As an example, look at 3:24. Ezekiel says the same thing, "then the Spirit entered me."

A couple of things. First, in Ezekiel the scene has changed. In Isaiah and Jeremiah, the prophets were speaking to Judah prior to the Babylonians taking them into captivity. Ezekiel is preaching to a nation in captivity in Babylon. Second, you're going read some weird things in Ezekiel. Visions that Ezekiel has. This same principle can apply to some of the visions that John had in the book of Revelation.

Suppose your only frame of reference was what you knew in Bible times. How would you describe a car? How would you explain an airplane? That's the problem these prophets had at the time. They would describe them in terms they could relate to. Imagine you were taken 2,000 years in the future and you saw some things you couldn't explain. How would you describe them? In terms of what you know now wouldn't you?

I heard a message on this passage and in the course of that message it was pointed out how many times Ezekiel referred to Israel. Seven times in chapters 2 and in 3 was Israel called "a rebellious house". O.k, Ezekiel, what's your point? We have seen it all through the Old Testament. As long as Israel wants to do things "my way" they continue to rebel against God's direction. The thing that is so funny to me is that they are basically saying, "I know better than God."

I pray that is not your attitude. Start by turning the day over to God. "O.k, God whatever You want for me today it's in Your hands. My time, my direction, my thoughts are Yours to do with as You please." I know that is risky, isn't it? That night, reflect on what God did today.

"Yet I will leave a remnant, so that you may have some who escape the sword among the nations, when you are scattered through the countries." (Ezekiel 6:8)

Remember Ezekiel is written to the Jews who are in captivity. The king of Babylon has conquered Israel (Judah) and brought the people to Babylon to assimilate them into their country. The book of Daniel gives us that picture of how it was done. Do you remember why God would not destroy them all together? Yes, a promise made to David and a covenant with Abraham. God's promise!

This sixth chapter of Ezekiel deals with idolaters. To me I think the greatest sin Israel ever committed was idolatry. Remember the golden calf at the foot of Mt. Sinai? At that time God wanted to destroy the whole lot and start over, Moses talked Him out of it. God hates anything that comes between us and Him, ANYTHING! (Exodus 32)

It also recalls the few who followed Ezra back to Jerusalem to rebuild the temple and the wall. There were a few there, a remnant, to return and rebuild. God provided and protected the nation during this time. In chapter seven we see God, again warning Israel that the time is near to pay for your disobedience. Ezekiel was one of those taken captive. Daniel and his friends will join him.

The point of all these prophets was to warn Israel (Judah) to listen to the warnings, pay attention to what God is trying to tell them. Have you heard the saying, "Don't shoot the messenger."? We want to blame the messenger for the message. Look at the life of Jeremiah especially.

Today we have preachers on TV we can turn them off. We have the Bible but you don't have to open it. We have friends and relatives who want to tell us about Jesus, just ignore them. How is that any different than Israel's response to these prophets. How are the consequences any different? Is God trying to get your attention about something? I think it's interesting how He can work on someone who is lost. There is a piece missing in the lost person that only God can fill. They search and search for that missing piece but until they turn to God and ask Jesus to change them their search is futile!

"Then I will give them one heart, and I will put a new spirit within them, and take the stony heart out of their flesh, and give them a heart of flesh." (Ezekiel 11:19)

Beautiful picture of what I was talking about yesterday. God changes the heart not the mind. It is amazing the changes that take place when we've asked Jesus to come into our heart and change us. This verse is a great illustration.

We were talking in Sunday school the other day about how God changes us. I hope you haven't gotten the idea that the change is instant. It's not. When the Holy Spirit moves in He begins cleaning house. Kind of like "Spring cleaning." He takes one room at a time and begins systematically removing the things that don't belong there. It may be language (that's a hard one to clean up) God will give you a new vocabulary. Then He might move to habits we have that aren't pleasing. You fill in the blank. Habits are SO easy to start and SO hard to break.

When I was working nights, I would stop at the lunch room and get a Snickers before starting my shift. I did this a few times then I realized I couldn't pass the lunch room without getting a Snickers. I made sure I had the change, etc. It is so easy to fall into a habit. So, hard to break it. The hardest part is recognizing you have one.

How many times have you heard the term "comfort zone"? All that is, is a set of habits, routines, that you do all the time. It scares you to omit or break that routine. When Jesus becomes your comfort zone you find you can do so much more and better too! You learn new things. You exchange your heart of stone for a heart of flesh.

What does the picture of a "stony heart" bring to mind? Someone who doesn't care, right? Exactly. Jesus gives us a heart for people a heart that cares about the things around us. A new awareness of people who are hurting and suffering. As Christian's we now can pray for that person or that need. We recruit God's power into the situation. We have compassion for that person and that need, why? Because God has given us a heart for Him.

"Nevertheless, I will remember My covenant with you in the days of your youth, and I will establish an everlasting covenant with you." (Ezekiel 16:60)

Ever feel like God has forgotten you? I'm sure most of us have at one point or another. I mentioned I was saved at age thirty-five. Once, when I was ten years old I had made a profession of faith in a Salvation Army church. Sometimes I wonder what might have happened if the church had followed up. Of course, being ten they might have and my parents didn't say anything. I don't know. When I look back I can see times when God was watching over me. I think this verse is very true. Don't disregard those decisions made as a youth or younger.

That "everlasting covenant" was established on the cross of Calvary. Notice this verse in Hebrews, Let, your conduct be without covetousness; be content with such things as you have. For He Himself has said, "I will never leave you nor forsake you." (Hebrews 13:5) That is a promise from God. So, what does the term "everlasting" mean to you? Forever, permanent, consistent, that's just a few. What does it mean to you? When do you usually seek God's presence? When you're at the end of your rope, isn't it? Why is that? Why not begin each day, just reminding yourself that God is in your heart in the person of the Holy Spirit? It will make the day much easier.

I hope you are having that quiet time with God and reading through the Bible with me. Here's an exercise you might try. Once when I read through I would find one verse that spoke to me that day. One verse will attract your attention. Mark, it somehow. A dot beside the verse, a bracket, something to note the verse. It will help you find key verses.

One word to keep an eye out for is the word "blessed" It's a promise from God. It doesn't just appear in the Be-attitudes. It's all through the Bible. Next, when you see the word ask yourself, "What is the promise here?" Second, look for the condition to that promise. God will bless us in so many ways but He also requires a response on our part. Something we are to do for that blessing. Rarely does He bless us without a response on our part.

Keep with the schedule. It's so hard to catch up when you get behind. If you fall behind just start where you're at and continue!

"Cast away from you all the transgressions which you have committed,
and get yourselves a new heart and a new spirit. For why should you
die, O house of Israel?" (Ezekiel 18:31)

Have you ever heard someone say, "When I get my life straightened out, I will ask Jesus in my heart?" That is so sad. Because you will never get to that point on your own. God is in the "fixer-upper". If you call on Jesus to come into your heart, He will. Then He will begin the process of rebuilding your life from the ground up. A closer relationship with God will do wonders for cleaning up your life.

Now it seems that this verse is saying the opposite. But Ezekiel is talking to Israel about turning away from idols. We do need to reject the false gods. That happens when you receive Christ. You have rejected the false gods and turn to Christ. Then when God gives you the new heart and the new spirit then He begins to work on your life. Notice He changes your heart. That is the first step in changing your whole outlook on the things around you.

God can change your "wants", your language, your habits, your desires, etc. I shared before that the night I was saved at 35, I found an enormous hunger for God's word. I think the reason of course was that I understood it better. Not completely of course, but, through His Holy Spirit, it just made more sense. Without the light of the Holy Spirit it is almost impossible to fully grasp the word of God.

Just a reminder. Isaiah and Jeremiah were written prior to Judah going into captivity in Babylon. Ezekiel and Daniel were written during their captivity. While the Jews were making a life in a foreign country. Ezekiel continues to encourage them to come back to God. To remember the God who brought them out of Egypt. The same God they turned their back on and refused to obey His commands.

Were you saved at an early age? Have you remained faithful through the years? It's hard to maintain that close relationship during your "college" years (early twenties). Then when you begin to think about getting married, having a family, your heart turns back to God. Why is that? Maybe during those early years, we think we know more than God. That's sad. Maintaining a relationship with God takes a commitment! That is the key. Work on that!

> I am the Lord your God: Walk in My statutes, keep My judgments, and do them; hallow My Sabbaths, and they will be a sign between Me and you, that you may know that I am the Lord your God. (Ezekiel 20:19-20)

There is an interesting take on this verse. You might read it as these statutes and judgments are God's sign that He is with us. They are, in a sense, signs of His authority. I want to take a different look or tack.

I want to look at these statutes and judgments as a sign that we will walk with God. By our obedience we acknowledge who God is, what kind of relationship He desires to have with us. By our obedience to these commands we demonstrate our faith in His sovereignty! There is no greater demonstration of faith in someone than when you do as they ask.

God explains this further earlier in this chapter. Look at verses 11-12. And I gave them My statutes and showed them My judgments, which if a man does, he shall live by them. Moreover, I also gave them My Sabbaths, to be a sign between them and Me, that they might know that I am the Lord who sanctifies them. What is the promise here from God? Listen to Me, obey Me and you will live.

In both cases, notice the reference to the Sabbaths? God, in the very beginning (Genesis) set aside one day in seven to rest. To reflect on what God has done. In the New Testament that has become Sunday, when Jesus rose from His tomb to everlasting life. Sunday was established as that one day in seven when we acknowledge the authority of God in our lives, or is it.

What has Sunday become today? I remember as a boy how everything was closed. No one worked. I had a paper route and I threw papers on Sunday morning till around nine in the morning. The rest of the day was rest. We could have gone to church if we were so inclined, but we didn't. Still it was a day of rest. I want to get past that thought. Sunday is a day set aside to worship God. We might have our Wednesday night prayer meetings, etc. Sunday is a day of worship. To me, it's not just three hours on Sunday morning (Sunday school and worship). My favorite worship service is Sunday night. I enjoy the less formal atmosphere. The Bible study, the singing. Since I have become a Christian I make a special effort not to do any work on Sunday.

"So, I sought for a man among you who would make a wall, and stand in the gap before Me on behalf of the land, that I should not destroy it; but I found no one." (Ezekiel 22:30)

I think it's significant that it says, "I sought for a man." Not a nation, not a church, not a city, but one man. One man to do what? Stand in the gap, to make a difference. Does that term sound familiar today? That seems to be a clarion call for some to say, "I want to make a difference."

One of my favorite stories is about a Sunday school teacher named Kimball. In Chicago, he became determined to witness to every boy in his class. One boy was a shoe salesman. Mr. Kimball led the boy to the Lord. End of the story? Not so, that shoe salesman was Dwight L. Moody. Maybe you've heard of the Moody Bible Institute? Dwight L. Moody is responsible for leading thousands to a saving knowledge of Jesus Christ. If you follow his spiritual genealogy D.L. Moody, in a chain of events and evangelists leads directly to Rev. Billy Graham. How many countless individuals would Bro. Graham be responsible for leading to salvation in Jesus? One man named Kimball started it all.

God isn't looking for someone to just stand there. Look at the verse again. "A man who would make a wall." You see God has a task for each of us. It may be like Mr. Kimball, a simple Sunday school teacher whom God laid the students in his class on his heart. Mr. Kimball obeyed the prompting of God's Holy Spirit and did the best he could. It doesn't say whether all his boys came to Christ. One did! That one boy changed the Christian world forever and enlarged God's kingdom.

Let me take you back to Mt. Sinai. Moses had returned from the mountain and Israel had built the golden calf. God wanted to destroy the whole bunch of them and start over. But Moses interceded, Then Moses returned to the Lord and said, "Oh, these people have committed a great sin, and have made for themselves a god of gold! Yet now, if you will forgive their sin—but if not, I pray blot me out of Your book which You have written." (Exodus 32:31-32) God's anger was abated by a man who stood in the gap for his people and stayed God's judgment. Remember Abraham, and Sodom and Gomorrah?

I, the Lord, have spoken it; it shall come to pass, and I will do it; I
will not hold back, nor will I spare, nor will I relent; According to your
ways and according to your deeds they will judge you," Says the Lord
God. (Ezekiel 24:14)

Testimony! Did you know that Moses saved God's testimony? Look at Exodus
32:11-12, Then Moses pleaded with the Lord his God, and said: "Lord, why
does Your wrath burn hot against Your people whom you have brought out of
the land of Egypt with great power and with a mighty hand? Why should the
Egyptians speak, and say, 'He brought them out to harm them, to kill them in the
mountains, and to consume them from the face of the earth'? Turn from your fierce
wrath, and relent from this harm to Your people." Moses used God's testimony
to the nations to stay His hand against a rebellious Israel. Does the threat of your
testimony being tarnished motivate your actions?

As a young Christian, I had to deal with this in my workplace. Many had come
to know that I was a new Christian. Funny how that word gets around. Anyway,
several wanted me to know that one of our mechanics, a Christian, was fired for
stealing. It was tough for a while. Believe me when I tell you that the "world" is
watching you as a Christian. Does your testimony live up to your calling?

Remember that when you discredit your testimony your discrediting the God
you serve. I know that's harsh, but true. The world will be oh, so quick to point out
when you fall. Even though we are not perfect, just redeemed, the world is looking
for an excuse to bring you down to their level. Think about chances you might
take that are against your beliefs. Know that someone, including God, is watching

If you finished this chapter you notice that God took Ezekiel's wife as a
testimony of His judgment against Israel. God can, and will use whatever is
necessary to get our attention. It seemed hard for Ezekiel but he also knew
the mission he was on. To warn Israel of the disobedience and the judgment
that accompanies that disobedience. Is God trying to get your attention about
something? What is your response?

"They will judge you." The people were watching Ezekiel. They knew he was
a prophet of God. Ezekiel was God's messenger and Ezekiel obeyed God and
carried His message.

"And they will dwell safely there, build houses, and plant vineyards; yes, they will dwell securely, when I execute judgments on all those around them who despise them. Then they shall know that I am the Lord their God." (Ezekiel 28:26)

If you want a picture of this prophecy (the verse above) read the book of Ezra. When you read these prophets, you need the context of when it was written to understand it better. I've talked earlier, the difference between Isaiah and Jeremiah, then Ezekiel and Daniel. You can get a good idea from the first chapters of Daniel. Ezekiel is kind of between Jeremiah and Daniel chronologically. That is one of the reasons that Bible study is not something you do here and there. I have read through my Bible at least ten times and am still amazed at what I learn each time.

Then, the preaching from our pastor each Sunday and the Sunday school classes all add to the knowledge of God and His word. It can, and usually does take a lifetime in God's word to come close to an understanding of God's desire for a relationship with us.

I love the story of the building of the wall. Those around them tried to discourage them, then threatened them through Cyrus the king. Then at one point they were building with a shovel in one hand and a sword in the other. Satan tried everything he could to deter the building of the wall around Jerusalem. God was watching over both the construction of the temple and then the wall.

Has God laid on your heart to do something? Maybe teach a class or take on a certain ministry? Let me tell you a certainty, the devil will begin quickly to put doubt in your mind. "Who do you think you are?" "You're not educated enough to tackle this." "You will never succeed!" Don't listen to those lies. God is about to do something fantastic through you, and you know who will get the glory? God!

You get the blessing of seeing God do something in your life that you know was impossible. That will strengthen your faith and lead you to bigger and more challenging efforts, all to the glory of God. Because you trusted Him enough to get out of your "comfort zone" and trust God. The blessing is yours, the glory is God's and God accomplishes His will in your life!

> Then whoever hears the sound of the trumpet and does not take
> warning, if the sword comes and takes him away his blood shall be
> on his own head. (Ezekiel 33:4)

In my early years as a Christian I got involved with the youth group in our church. They called themselves the "Certain Sound Singers". I can't find the scripture right now. In several places, the Bible talks about a trumpet making a certain sound. In the beginning Moses had several trumpets each sound would signify something. It was a great idea.

In this passage Ezekiel is talking about giving attention to the warning of the trumpet. It usually meant a "call to arms". A warning that danger is about.

I was thinking this morning what these prophets must have felt. Here they have a clear message and warning from God to the nation Israel and no one will listen. It had to be so frustrating! I guess no less frustrating than trying to lead a friend to Jesus. You give your testimony, you show them the Bible verses, you pray for them and still they reject the message. Now you know how these prophets must have felt.

Notice who is responsible. Not the trumpet blower, not the message, not the warning, the one who refuses to listen and obey. Too many Christians who tell others about Jesus and share the gospel message feel inadequate because there was no response. That's not what God tells us to do. It's not us that turns someone to God but the Work of the Holy Spirit in that person's heart.

In the gospels Jesus exhorts us to "sow the seed," or the word of God. We are not responsible for the crop, just to sow the seed. Of course, there would be no crop if the seed was left in the bag, would there?

The prophets were called by God to warn the nation. Through persecution, torture, death, they gave the message, they sounded the trumpet. It was up to Israel to respond.

It may be cruel but I've thought about being here when the Rapture takes place. And as I'm ascending into heaven looking down and saying, "See, I told you so." maybe that's wrong but it's frustrating, sometimes isn't it?

"I will put My Spirit within you and cause you to walk in My statutes,
and you will keep My judgments and do them. Then you shall dwell
in the land that I gave your fathers; you shall be My people, and I will
be your God. (Ezekiel 36:27-28)

What must Israel think of this passage today? This follows what we talked about yesterday. Notice, "I will put My Spirit within you." It's the work of the Holy Spirit that brings people to God. Jesus, talking about the work of the Holy Spirit when He is come, after Jesus ascends to heaven, here in John's gospel 16:8-10 "And when He has come, He will convict the world of sin, and of righteousness, and of judgment: of sin, because they do not believe Me; of righteousness, because I go to My Father and you see Me no more; of judgment, because the ruler of this world is judged." That's the work of God's Holy Spirit who is at work today.

This must have been a comforting verse for Ezekiel. Knowing one day God will bring all things to pass. "You shall be My people, and I will be your God."

So, how are we to do God's work? We need more classes, more teaching, more memorizing Scripture, etc. Look at this verse again. "I will put My Spirit within you and cause you to walk in my. . . "did you catch that? It's only by the power of God's Spirit that we accomplish anything. Think about what's going on here. The Holy Spirit is empowering you to tell others, and the same Spirit is at work in that lost person to bring them to God. You can't lose! Why we feel so defeated is beyond me.

Of course, it all takes place on God's timetable. So many stories of relatives praying and sharing with a family member then one day it happens. It's not the messenger it's the recipient. Keep praying, keep sharing and in God's perfect timing He will win their hearts.

There's that word "walk" again. We walk this path only by the grace of God. It could be us someone is trying to reach. Remember those days? As we are walking this path with God we will encounter all kinds of people. Some will laugh, some will scoff, some will listen, even some will give their lives to God. Just remember as you are sharing with that person that God is walking right beside you!

"So, I will make My holy name known in the midst of My people Israel, and I will not let them profane My holy name anymore. Then the nations shall know that I am the Lord, the Holy One of Israel." (Ezekiel 39:7)

Where were you? Anyone who remembers that day remembers what they were doing and where they were. It shook our world. It got our attention, didn't it! Something else I remember about that time. How everyone that could walk or crawl was in church that next Sunday. They even remarked about how full the churches were. Why is that?

We are no different that Old Testament Israel, are we? Oh, there were some at the time who preached this was the hand of God. Maybe you can make a case, maybe not. It doesn't matter. What matters is how this affected you. Did it bring you back to God? For how long? Yes, it didn't take long until the churches were back to "normal". What about you?

We've been looking at these Old Testament prophets and their message to the nation. Suppose we had a prophet before 9-11 that told of the judgment. What do you suppose our response would have been? You guessed it. The same response that Isaiah, Jeremiah, Ezekiel and all the other prophets got.

Have you noticed how prevalent the words "GD" are in the movies today? God makes a statement in this verse, "and I will not let them profane My holy name anymore." If there is anything that gets under my skin it's the use of these two words. But now, it seems, unless a movie has used it at least once they can't get an audience. That's sad.

Besides being the third commandment God condemns the practice over and over. Don't pass over the end of this verse, "Then the nations shall know that I am the Lord, the Holy One of Israel." Don't forget the New Testament words of the Apostle Paul, For, it is written, "As I live, says the Lord, every knee shall bow to Me, and every tongue shall confess to God." One more. Philippians 2:9-11, Therefore God also highly exalted Him and given Him the name which is above every name, that at the name of Jesus every knee should bow, of those in heaven, and of those on earth, and those under the earth, and that every tongue should confess that Jesus Christ is Lord.

> And the glory of the Lord came into the temple by way of the gate which faces toward the east. The Spirit lifted me up and brought me into the inner court; and behold, the glory of the Lord filled the temple. (Ezekiel 43:4-5)

I'm sure, as a Christian, you have experienced this. If you have attended church any length of time, you have felt the presence of God. There is no denying the presence of God in His house. Of course, your heart must be listening. Not your ears, your heart. If you haven't figured it out by now I believe in God's institution, the church. Jesus made a point of instituting its function in the gospels, in Matthew 16:18 we read, "And also I say to you that you are Peter, and on this rock, I will build My church, and the gates of hell shall not prevail against it." I heard a preacher say once that this verse is so powerful that despite all the bad preaching it has prevailed!

I'm not going to debate about Peter. Anyone who has the Bible knows that Jesus is talking about the gospel of salvation through faith in Christ is the "rock" Jesus is referring to. Notice that Jesus says, "and the gates of hell shall not prevail against it." He is warning us ahead of time that Satan will do everything in his power to destroy or at least water-down the power of the church. It keeps preaching the message of salvation through Jesus Christ. If your church is not preaching the word of God, you need to leave!

Think back. How many times have you read from Exodus to here, about the "glory of the Lord filled the temple?" From the first completion of the tabernacle, to the completion of Solomon's temple, God blessed the work. Let me impart one more picture if you will.

Here's a verse to underline, I Corinthians 6:19, Or do you not know that your body is the temple of the Holy Spirit who is in you, whom you have from God, and you are not your own?" Paul, by inspiration of the this very same Spirit tells us that God dwells within us Christians. Just as God filled the temples in the Old Testament He wants to fill us today. He wants His presence known and felt in every believer. That's a promise from God. We simply need to ask. There is a difference between being filled and the Spirit simply residing in us. Anyone who has experienced the difference knows!

> Also, He brought me by way of the north gate to the front of the temple; so, I looked and behold, the glory of the Lord filled the house of the Lord; and I fell on my face. (Ezekiel 44:4)

I remember, as a fledgling preacher, trying to preach a message on the tabernacle. Would that I knew then what I know now. I guess we can all say that about one thing or another. There are so many messages about the furniture, the meaning of each piece, etc. The construction, who carried what, etc. One wish I have always had, as I read through Exodus and the building of the tabernacle, would be to see a life-sized replica. With all the gold, the bronze and silver and the various colored fabrics, it would be awesome.

I was thinking this morning as I was reading the description again, after the construction of the temple by Solomon what happened to the items listed in Exodus? Some, I'm sure, were incorporated into the temple. It's like they moved on from a temporary house to a grand temple. The problem is that it did nothing for the people's relationship with God. They still rebelled!

We talked yesterday about the church, and our bodies as the temple of the Holy Spirit. I'd like to ask you a question. Have you blamed "the church" for your relationship with God? Oh, I can worship in my own way at home. Is that biblical? O.k, we have the Holy Spirit living within us, does that negate our commitment to the institution God set up through His Son?

One nice thing about the church today. If you get upset there is always another church, right? You're just exchanging one set of problems for another. Is that what God wants us to do? God wants us to make a difference not be nomads!

One of the greatest New Testament writers was the apostle Paul. His writings make up a majority of the New Testament. What was Paul's calling? To establish churches throughout Asia. Three "missionary" journeys in the book of Acts. All to set up churches in pagan cities. Many of the New Testament books are letters written to churches. Oh, don't forget the first three chapters of Revelation, addressed to churches. God's word is the lifeblood of the church. Anemic churches are ones who ignore the word of God!

"And it shall be that every living thing that moves, wherever the rivers go, will live. There will be a very great multitude of fish, because these waters go there; for they will be healed, and everything will live wherever the river goes." (Ezekiel 47:9)

The prophet Ezekiel is speaking of the millennial kingdom. It's interesting that one characteristic is water. Even in Revelation it talks about the fountains flowing from the throne. (Revelation 22:1). Of course, you know how to find water in a desert, look for an oasis where the trees are growing. You might want to read the last part of Psalm 1, He shall be like a tree planted by the rivers of water, that brings forth it's fruit in its season, whose leaf also shall not wither; and whatever he does shall prosper. Who is the Psalmist talking about? The beginning of the Psalm, "Blessed is the man."

A humorous thought to this fish. I used to tell people that it's great that we will get to eat in heaven. The Bible says, "Beloved, now we are children of God; and it has not yet been revealed what we shall be, but we know that when He is revealed, we shall be like Him, for we shall see Him as He is. (1 John 3:2) O.k, we will be like Jesus. Now look at this verse, Jesus then came and took the bread and gave it to them, and likewise the fish. This is now the third time Jesus showed Himself to His disciples after He was raised from the dead. So, when they had eaten breakfast. (John 21:13-15a). The point being that Jesus ate after His resurrection as we will eat in heaven. I'm clinging to that picture!

One point from the verse above, there will be no want. No hunger, no need. Ezekiel, as he finishes up his prophecy takes his listeners to that day when God will reign and the nation Israel will be one again. Not divided, not scattered, but one nation again in the Holy Jerusalem.

What do you think of, when you think of the book of Revelation? Vengeance of God, terrible judgments, final reckoning? What comes to your mind. It's a hard book to read granted. The picture God wants His children to see is the gathering of His children in a heaven that has no tears, no want, no thirst, no hunger, where His children will live in peace and contentment for eternity. In this world, we can't imagine that utopia. Of course, most of the book is spent on judgment but the last couple of chapters gives us a glimpse of heave. Ezekiel got a glimpse of it here as he concludes his prophecy.

> "Look!" he answered, "I see four men loose, walking in the midst of the fire; and they are not hurt, and the form of the fourth is like the Son of God." (Daniel 3:25)

I like the New King James version. I think the King James has it "son of the gods." I just have one question how does Nebuchadnezzar know what the Son of God looks like?

We have skipped a great introduction to Daniel. When him and his three companions are taken to Babylon from Jerusalem. Remember Daniel was written during the seventy years of captivity. Daniel makes the best of his situation, much like Joseph.

Speaking of which, there are only two individuals in all the Bible, besides Jesus, who, it is said, there is nothing negative said about them. You guessed it, Daniel and Joseph. There are a lot of parallels between the two.

What's interesting is that Daniel is not in this episode. Here his three companions defy the king's edict to bow before a golden image. At least someone got the message about idols. There is another verse I want to talk about.

Look at verse 17-18 of this chapter, "if that is the case, our God whom we serve is able to deliver us from the burning fiery furnace, and He will deliver us from your hand, O king. But if not, let it be known to you, O king, that we do not serve your gods, nor will we worship the gold image which you have set up." Do you see their response? Underline that word "But". They have confidence that God will deliver them, one way or another, but it doesn't matter to them, they are going to do the right thing. You see they didn't know for sure what God's plan was. They had no assurance of God's deliverance but were still willing to be obedient. I love that.

When God leads us down a certain path we don't know the outcome. God does! He wants us to trust Him and the outcome will be to God's glory! Faith, trusting God each day alone this path to lead us where His will is. It's when we start wanting things our way we get in trouble. We think we know better than God what is best for us.

Daniel is a book of trusting God. Doing what is right. Whether it's what he eats or whether he prays, the kings will, or God's will!

> I thought it good to declare the signs and wonders that the Most High God has worked for me. How great are the signs, and how mighty His wonders! His kingdom is an everlasting kingdom, and His dominion is from generation to generation. (Daniel 4:2-3)

Is that not an awesome job description? That is our job description as well. I have said this before. The greatest witnessing tool is to tell others what God has done in your life. That is assuming He is working in your life. Is God using you in some fashion? Has He blessed you in a way that you can share it with others? Or, has He blessed you and you haven't even noticed? You might want to take a minute and write down your testimony. I've heard that's the best way. For now, just run through your mind what God has done in your life.

If you're a child of God, you have a testimony. God doesn't just leave us the way He finds us. The moment we ask Jesus into our heats He begins doing a work in our lives. First, if we are listening, he might ask us to do something that is totally out of our comfort zone. Here is a crucial moment. If we trust Him and do it we have demonstrated that God can work through us. If we refuse and don't trust Him we are put aside until out faith can grow to be of use to Him.

I know this is true because I've seen it so many times. Not only in my own life, but in so many others. Ask people serving in your church if they thought they would ever be doing what they are doing. I know of one fellow, wanted nothing to do with the church. His wife came regular, then one day, during a Progressive Dinner fellowship he gave his life to Jesus. Soon he began leading the music in our church. God opened up a whole new world to him because he was willing to walk by faith and trust God one day at a time.

The sad part is that when God works a miracle in our lives we are generally the only ones who know about it. Those who know us might see the difference. But that is the kind of miracle that God means for us to share with others. Those who don't know what it's like to have an intimate walk with God. To know the joy of seeing God do things in your life that you never thought He would. First, you must take that step of faith. If God lays something on your heart, don't question Him just take a step of faith and do it! You will see a miracle!

> Then to Him was given dominion and glory and a kingdom, that all peoples, nations, and languages should serve Him. His dominion is an everlasting dominion, which shall not pass away, and His kingdom the one which shall not be destroyed. (Daniel 7:14)

I'm not big on prophecy. When, specifically this event happened or is going to happen. It's not important to our everyday lives. What it does for me is give me a peace that God IS in charge, WAS in charge and will be forever. There is a peace in knowing that. O.k, so what does that mean to me now? I'm sure you've noticed the chaos in the world today. North Korea, Iran, etc. God has it all under control!

One of my pet peeves is this idea that mankind could destroy something that God had created. The audacity is unbelievable to me. I'm not saying we should not be good stewards of all that God has given us. We are to take care of our world. But, to think we could destroy it, if there is any destroying it will be by God if we get out of control.

There is a flavor of the book of Revelation in this book. I see some of the Tower of Babel, even pre-incarnate Christ. The book of Daniel was written to the exiles in Babylon. The book was to give them hope that God had not forgotten them, He has not abandoned them. God still has a plan for His people. They just need to trust Him.

That is the same message for us today. God knows where we are at. Hopefully He's walking right beside you today. If not, you need to change that. Are you making the decisions today or is God? That is what you need to be concerned about, not the chaos in the world around us. Now, understand I don't think we should be some cocoon or something. We should be informed and make appropriate decisions. But don't get down!

Twice in this verse Daniel uses the word "dominion". What does that mean to you? It simply means that God is in total control. There is nothing that happens that catches God by surprise, nothing! If God is walking with you, He knows which forks in the road to take. What decisions to make because He knows what's up ahead, far better than you do. You just need to trust His leadership and guidance and make the choices that will glorify Him and be consistent with His plan for your life (Jeremiah 29:11). Trust Him!

"At that time Michael shall stand up, the great prince who stands watch over the sons of your people; and there shall be a time of trouble, such as never was since there was a nation, even to that time. And at that time your people shall be delivered, everyone who is found written in the book. (Daniel 12:1)

One of my favorite books is called, "The Miracle of the Bells". In it a press agent comes to put his faith in the Archangel Michael. It is said that Michael is the archangel of the army of God. Michael does the fighting for God. This press agent came to God through his faith in Michael. It has a Catholic theme to it. There is no surprise that Daniel talks about Michael and the end times. Michael and Gabriel are featured in the book of Revelation.

There is another phrase that is mentioned in Revelation, "one who is written in the Lambs book of life." The book of Revelation and Daniel are so closely entwined that you need both books for a serious study of the end times. Look at this verse, "But there shall by no means enter it anything that defiles, or causes an abomination or a lie, but only those who are written in the Lamb's Book of Life. (Revelation 21:27). Of course, John is referring to those who have accepted Christ as their Savior.

Just a note, those names are written in ink, they can't be erased!

Daniel only has twelve chapters, but like I said it goes hand in hand with the book of Revelation. Daniel helps to clarify some timelines mentioned later.

I read this story that a Jewish professor did some calculations, and using the date of the completion of the wall, using the Jewish calendar of 360 days to a year, and counting the days, it concluded at the time Jesus made His triumphal entry into Jerusalem. The point being that Daniel, led by the Holy Spirt, gave calculations that even he didn't understand. This being in the prophecy of the 70 weeks, etc.

I think another thing we might overlook. God has a plan. From creation to a whole new world in Revelation. From beginning to end it is all in God's plan. Let me use that to remind you again about walking with God. I think this has turned out to be the theme of this devotional book. Just to remind everyone who reads the Bible that God has it under control, He has a plan to bring it all to a great climax!

> Let us know, let us pursue the knowledge of the Lord. His going forth
> is established as the morning; He will come to us like the rain, like
> the latter and former rain to the earth. (Hosea 6:3)

Hosea, like Isaiah and Jeremiah was written to the Jews prior to their going into captivity. Warning! Warning, you are about to witness God's judgment. You have disobeyed Me long enough, now it's time to pay up. This is an interesting concept. Because as Christians we want to know if God is keeping a ledger on us. Will there ever come a time when God will even our score? I hope, as a Christian, you understand that that debt was paid at Calvary on the cross.

Of course, that doesn't give us a license to do whatever we please now. God will chastise us if we get too far afield from His permissive will. Make no mistake, just like a parent with an unruly child. We still love that child but there must be boundaries!

"Let's us pursue the knowledge of the Lord!" This is an interesting statement. What do you suppose the prophet meant? Did he mean that we should pursue the knowledge that He has? Or should we get better acquainted with God? I think the latter. It's part of that walking with God that we have been talking about.

I love the picture in New Testament of the disciples walking with Jesus. We don't really get the picture because we can read through the gospels in an hour or so. Jesus walked, talked, and taught His disciples over a three-year period. Nights by the fire, or visiting with friends in their home, etc. Intimate times with His disciples must have been fantastic learning experiences.

My favorite is the two disciples on the road to Emmaus in Luke chapter 24. This takes place after His resurrection. Look at verse 32, And they said to one another, "Did not our heart burn within us while He talked with us on the road, and while He opened the Scriptures to us?" I just love that picture! At the time, they didn't know who He was. Then when He sat with them and ate they recognized who He was. What an awesome picture!

How would you "measure" your knowledge of the Lord? You can't measure it in any specific way. My guess would be to measure it by how close your walking with Him on your journey.

> Who is wise? Let him understand these things. Who is prudent? Let
> him know them. For the ways of the Lord are right; the righteous walk
> in them, but transgressors stumble in them. (Hosea 14:9)

Another reference to walking. Wow! Have you noticed that the more you walk with someone the more you get to know them? I had the opportunity once to go on a walk with my mother. I learned quickly not to walk so fast. I had to slow down to walk "with" her. God is the same way. Too many times we want to walk ahead. Sometimes we can get so far ahead we lose sight of His direction. That happened to me.

I've always wanted to pastor my home church. A small church in Independence, Missouri. At the time, I was pastoring in a small town in mid-state. An opening appeared and I preached as a candidate. They didn't call me. I just knew that was where I was supposed to be. So, instead of waiting for God to open the door, I resigned the church I was at, and my wife and I started attending the church in Independence. When God closes a door, He does a thorough job. Let's just say it didn't work out. I learned a valuable lesson that day. God opens the doors not us! But transgressors stumble in them. When the Bible says, wait on the Lord that is exactly what it means!

For the ways of the Lord are right. So, how do we know what is the right "way"? Like I just said, how many times in the Bible are we admonished to "wait" on the Lord? Besides Isaiah 40:31 and Psalm 37, too many to count. Yet, we still think we know better than God.

It reminds me of Israel in the wilderness. They couldn't wait for God to supply food and water, they had to complain to Moses. Do you think God wasn't aware of their need? Of course, He was. He knew what they needed but they couldn't wait. Saul is another example. I believe it was God's plan to make David king but Israel couldn't wait they wanted a king NOW!

The Bible says that God knows the desires of our heart. The catch is we must wait for God's timing and God's plan to be fulfilled. When we get ahead of God we risk losing it all together or at the least settling for second best. God wants to strengthen our faith by providing our desires in the most amazing ways so we know that it comes from Him and not our own making. Wait on God!

> And it shall come to pass that whoever calls on the name of the Lord
> shall be saved. For in Mount Zion and in Jerusalem there shall be
> deliverance, as the Lord has said, among the remnant whom the Lord
> calls. (Joel 2:32)

Joel, again one of the pre-exiled prophets. God sent so many prophets to warn the Jews of their disobedience. I wonder if we really pay any attention to those around us that might try to warn us? Sometimes God will try to get our attention as well, through circumstances. But are we really listening? Do we really care? Would we rather continue our present course or really want to listen to God?

I think it's interesting that an Old Testament prophet would give a New Testament challenge. "That whoever calls on the name of the Lord shall be saved." Now look at Romans 10:13, For whoever calls on the name of the Lord shall be saved. That tells me that God's plan was the same from the very beginning. Now wait, the Savior wasn't born till Bethlehem. How can this be? The Lord and God are one and the same. You could just as easily say, "whoever calls on God will be saved." same difference.

By calling on God, we acknowledge His existence and our faith in His saving power. Saved from what? Eternity in hell. That was God's plan since the Garden of Eden. Adam and Eve had a choice, their will, verses God's will. They chose their own. That is the same choice we have today. Our will verses God's. It is, and forever will be, our choice!

Have you ever heard anyone express the idea that God is a loving God and won't send anyone to hell? Then why did He bother putting the tree in the garden? Better still, why did He send His Only Son to the cross if He was going to save everyone? Doesn't make sense.

There is an interesting thought at the end of this verse. Among the remnant whom the Lord calls." God will always have a remnant. That is a promise to those about to go into bondage in Babylon. Remember how many Jews went to Egypt because of the famine? Seventy. How many left Egypt after God delivered them? I think the number was 600,000 + adults. If anything, this is confirmation of His promise to David that there would always be descendants of David. Even Jesus, had to come from the line of Judah and thereby David.

Seek good and not evil, that you may live; so, the Lord God of hosts
will be with you. As you have spoken. (Amos 5:14)

Would God have fellowship with evil? We have talked often of walking with
God. Do you think God would be walking with someone in disobedience
(sin)? Amos is another pre-exile prophet. Warning Israel they are headed down
the wrong road.

You could almost make a plaque of those first words, "Seek good and not evil,
that you may live." How many choices do we have each day to do one or the other?
My guess is more than we care to think about. Someone once said we make over
three-thousand choices a day. Most we don't even realize we're making. Too many
come naturally according to our heart. So, where is our heart in those decisions?

I wonder, once Babylon took the Jews to Babylon, their new home, how
many sought the Lord? How many just gave up, maybe turned to idols? At what
point, during the storm are you ready to give up, maybe blame God for your
circumstances? Just a refresher let me remind you of Psalm 135, The idols of the
nations are silver and gold, the work of men's hands. They have mouths, but they
do not speak; eyes they have, but do not see; they have ears, but do not hear; nor
is there any breath in their mouths. Those who make them are like them; so is
everyone who trusts in them. (15-18).

It doesn't matter what the idols are, today or in Bible times they all amount
to the same. I like what the Psalmist said, "Those who make them are like them"
what an awesome truth.

I think the point of this verse is "choice". Amos is reminding the Jews that
they always have a choice. The same with idols, you have a choice who you worship.
Where you seek counsel, who you listen to, and follow. Sometimes those choices
don't cause much harm. Sometimes those choices are with you the rest of your life.
That's why Amos pleads with Israel to make the right choices. They have a second
chance. They will only be in captivity seventy years (a generation). I wonder if they
bothered to teach their children the folly of the choice they made to disobey God's
command. I wonder.

Sometimes we don't have a lot of time to make the right choice. That's when
we need to have our hearts right with God!

> "Behold, the days are coming," says the Lord God, that I will send a famine on the land, not a famine of bread, nor a thirst for water, but of hearing the words of the Lord. (Amos 8:11)

Over my thirty years as a Christian I accumulated several Bibles. All of them I marked and made notes in, more about that later. Recently I made it a point to give each of my grandchildren one of the Bibles I had used through the years. No instructions just as a gift. What they do with them is between them and the Lord. I pray it will be a special blessing to them.

Many have their own thoughts on the subject but myself, I mark in my Bible. The words therein are, of course, holy. The book, to me is a textbook. If you've ever been to college and bought your own books you mark passages and items of importance that you want to remember. The same is true with my Bible. I have verses bracketed, underlined, stars, etc. My textbook teaches me what is important in life. It teaches me about, finances, companionship, relationship with God, living with my neighbor, how to treat others, what God expects of me, important things that enhance my relationship with God. These things I must make note of!

"Hearing the words of the Lord." I wonder if the prophet was talking about preaching? I don't suppose there is a household in this country that doesn't have a Bible of some sort. Of course, it may never get opened but it's there, right. I mentioned this before and it is a strong belief of mine. If your church doesn't preach from, and teach from the Bible you need to find another church. I'm afraid Amos' prophecy is all too clearly coming true.

For hundreds of years all Israel had was the first five books, The Law of Moses. That was there guide to life and a relationship with God. They couldn't even follow that. As we are working through these last books of the Old Testament they are all prophets to the nation. Preaching God's judgment, some even God's deliverance. Did they listen? Take a minute and read Ezra and Nehemiah.

Where is your Bible? How much time do you spend in it? I hope this devotional will motivate you to spend a little more time. Take the challenge to read through it this year. You will be surprised!

"When my soul fainted within me, I remembered the Lord; and my prayer went up to You, into your holy temple. (Jonah 2:7)

Say the word Jonah and what comes to mind? The big fish, or whale, right? That's sad because there are many great lessons from this prophet. We might think of it as a great Vacation Bible School story but it is an illustration for the nation Israel. They ran from God, now God is trying to get their attention by sending them into captivity. Will they learn as Jonah did?

An old, old story. When you get to the end of the rope THEN you ask God for help. Jonah had all he wanted, he finally gave up and prayed. I like the way it is rendered, "I remembered the Lord." Isn't that always the case. He heard God clear enough, when God told him to go to Nineveh, didn't he? Yet in the storm on the boat Jonah knew why the storm was raging.

I heard this message from Dr. Charles Stanley that was so true. He said, "because God is all-present, He is with us in the storm. Because God is all-knowing, God knows where we are at in the storm. Because God is all-powerful, God will bring us through the storm." That is so awesome. Are you going through a storm? Do you think God has forgotten you? Not a chance if you're a child of God. I saw a plaque in Branson that read, "If God brought you to the storm, He will bring you through the storm."

Jonah had his own issues concerning Nineveh. He didn't want them spared. He knew that if he preached repentance to Nineveh they would turn to God. What a sad story, God was not only reaching out to Nineveh but was trying to reach Jonah's heart. The story ends abruptly. I wonder if Jonah ever realized what God's purpose for him was?

How about you? Has God asked you to do something you just know is not what you want to do? Are you going through a storm? What will it take for you to remember that God wants only the best for you. He wants to get you out of that comfort zone, to trust Him, to take that step of faith that will bless your socks off! Try it.

Next time you hear the name Jonah, don't think about a fish think rebellion!

Many nations shall come and say, "Come, and let us go up to the mountain of the Lord, to the house of the God of Jacob; He will teach us His ways, and we shall walk in His paths." For out of Zion the law shall go forth, and the word of the Lord from Jerusalem. (Micah 4:2)

What beautiful words, "He will teach us His ways, and we shall walk in His paths." The prophet Micah, looking past the book of Revelation to a world where the God of Jacob is worshiped! Micah is one of those pre-exile prophets. They haven't even faced captivity yet. A picture that God will rule in the end.

There is that word walk again. Have you ever walked on a path in the woods? My brothers and I walked along this path along a creek. There is no room to wander. It winds and turns and is real narrow. You either walk in front or behind someone. You can't see very far ahead either in front or back or on either side for that matter, the weeds are so high. There are only two ways to go, forward or back. In this case the path leads in God's direction and His will.

You're on a path right now whether you know it or not. Your future is being determined by. . . That is the question right now. Is someone leading on this path? Are you all alone? Do you know what is ahead? If you had God leading on this path you can have the assurance of knowing that the "guide" is taking you the right way. He knows what is up ahead. You can trust Him.

Maybe you have left school behind. You have graduated, dropped out, finished in one way or another. Do you think your learning has stopped? Surely not! You are learning every day whether you know it or not. The problem is what are you learning, what habits are you picking up and adding to your lifestyle? It's time to do an inventory. Think this trough for a moment.

Are you actively learning the ways of God? Do you attend church? Do you read your Bible? Do you have a relationship with God that you can go to Him in prayer and talk about the path you are on, and the decisions you need to make?

One more thing. This path your walking on, do you have a blindfold on? That's crazy, of course not. If your walking alone you do. You have no idea what's ahead. I wish you the best!

> He has shown you, O man, what is good; and what does the Lord require of you but to do justly, to love mercy, and to walk humbly with your God? (Micah 6:8)

The first part of this verse is important. "He has shown you, O man" That's the problem. Both, with us now, and with the Jews in those days. That is the point of the Old Testament. God has shown His people what He is capable of, and still they turn to idols, to their own wisdom. Micah is giving a summary of the simple requests God has made of His people. Three things, do justly, love mercy, walk humbly.

Are any of these contrary to what Jesus taught and did? Of course not. If anyone had the right to boast it was the Son of God. Look at the temptation in the wilderness in Matthew 4. Satan did everything he could to get Jesus to "show Himself" He did not. He quoted Scripture.

Just look at the Ten Commandments in Exodus 20. Is there anything in the last six Commandments that are contrary to these three? The first four Commandments, of course pertain to our relationship with God, as the last of these ten pertain to our relationship with our neighbors. Simple commands. I started to say requests but these are not requests, they are commands. None are that difficult but we, and Israel seem to go out of our way to break them. No wonder God is so frustrated with His people and His children.

I hope you are still with me in this journey through God's word. There are some dry places, places we really don't quite understand but overall this journey will profit you enormously in your daily walk with God. Be patient, be diligent, be consistent and this journey will end before you know it. You will look back at what you have accomplished, and learned, and be so excited you will want to go again next year.

Listen to the prophets. There warnings to Israel can be warnings to us today. The prophets simply tried to get Israel back on track, to get them to look up. To remember who brought them out of bondage and gave them their Promised Land and yet they refused to obey His simple rules but instead turned to idols.

Keep pressing on. Maintain that daily walk with God through His word. Trusting God for each direction, in each fork in the path seek God's direction. If things seem strange, trust in God, make sure you are in His will then follow His direction.

> God is jealous, and the Lord avenges; the Lord avenges and is furious.
> The Lord will take vengeance on His adversaries, and He reserves
> wrath for His enemies. (Nahum 1:2)

Now see, this is the God of the Old Testament, isn't it? Nahum, again is a prophet prior to the captivity. Trying to tell Judah what was about to take place. Nahum is a sequel to Jonah. After, through the preaching of Jonah, Nineveh repented and God spared them. Later they turned back to their old ways and God is judging them. Kind of like we do. Especially when we are first saved.

How easily we slip back into our old ways. That "spirit-filled experience may last a day, maybe even a week. But soon we get back with our peers and that "profession of faith" is a distant memory. It doesn't take long before we have totally left that experience in the dust. That's where the word of God and church attendance comes in. Those first few months are essential to staying on track with God.

Daily getting into the word and reading about God's relationship with us, and our walk with Him. Learning from fellow Christians, etc. I think the second or third week my wife and I were saved a couple in our church invited us to their home for Sunday dinner. I'll never forget that.

It is also our responsibility, to encourage and disciple new Christians to help keep them on the right path. That's where Sunday school is so important. That "small group" setting to learn and share with others the trials you face each day, their encouragement and prayers. By listening to other Christians pray you learn that God is there whenever you want to talk.

God is a jealous God. What is He jealous of? Our faith and trust in anyone or anything other than Him. He wants our total commitment, faith, and an intimate relationship with Him. Just seeing us trusting in anything but His direction and counsel makes Him furious. That's how strongly He desires our devotion. Does that verse above seem "wishy-washy" to you? I don't think so. It's pretty clear about how God feels about our relationship with Him.

The neat thing about the verse above. Your enemies become His enemies and God will fight your battles with those who would mistreat you.

> "Look among the nations and watch—be utterly astounded! For I will work a work in your days which you would not believe, though it were told you. (Habakkuk 1:5)

Another pre-exile prophet. How many times has God warned Judah about God's judgment? How many times has God tried to get your attention about your walk with Him? Don't criticize Judah for ignoring God's warnings, we do the same. We may not go into captivity in Babylon but we sure can't expect God's blessing or guidance if we rebel against His direction.

Awesome verse. Exactly what can happen when we walk with God. We will be amazed at what God does in our lives. The problem is, most of which we may never even know.

Do you get upset when you are stuck in traffic? Do you think God had anything to do with that? Have you ever, after sitting for a long time in traffic, come upon a bad accident? Where would you have been had it not been for the traffic? Think about it. The same is true in so many other instances. We may never know what God has prevented by a simple delay in our lives. Time belongs to God. We can't change it or alter it. We must trust that God is in control and what has happened is God watching over us!

That is the main reason I encourage you to keep a journal. God may take several days, or months to work His plan. If you write down each day's events you can look back and see God's hand in the process. Too many times we forget what happened yesterday and fail to see where God was at work through the whole process to bring us to this blessing.

Unless you can take the time to write these daily notes to yourself you will be as the end of this verse. "Which you will not believe, though it were told you." We you can connect the dots and see God's hand that brought you to exactly where God wants you to be, you will not believe that God was amid this miracle. Start today. Write down the events of the day. Maybe your prayers. How will you know if God answers a prayer unless you write it down somewhere? Because God will not answer it in your time, but in His!

God wants to show Himself to you and what He can do which in turn will strengthen your faith in Him!

> "The Lord your God in your midst, the Mighty One, will save; He will rejoice over you with gladness, He will quiet you with His love, He will rejoice over you with singing." (Zephaniah 3:17)

Do you realize how blessed we are to live in this time? In the Old Testament, it was rare for God's presence to work in the life of a believer. There were exceptions, Moses, Abraham, Judah, Joseph, etc. Today God's presence is in every believer! Look at the verse above. Zephaniah had that same experience that every believer has today. If they are open to it.

God is with us in sorrow, trials, rejoicing, heartache, you name the emotion and God is with us. We are the ones who turn away, ignore His presence, and just plain forget that He is there. In the trials is where God is most evident and where we are the last to recognize that.

In over thirty years as a Christian I have learned to recognize God's presence. It wasn't easy. I made some bad mistakes, but guess what, after the pity-party, God was there to pick me up and get me back on the path. The problem is that a lot of us turn our backs on God at those times and ignore His arms around us and shrug off His comfort and encouragement and think that one, we don't need God, we can handle it, or two, that God is to blame for the mistakes we make.

I am so blessed that our family has not had to go through some of the trials some families have had to endure. A family in our church lost four little children in a fire, then a few days later the mother died from injuries. As a father, I often think what must be going through his mind. Is he walking with God during this time, or is he blaming God. I pray the former. I pray there are Christians friends and relatives around him to comfort and grieve with him.

We all have those times we don't understand what God is doing. If we hold on to Him, rest in Him, trust Him, we may one day understand. If we blame God and lean to our own understanding, we may never know. Much of life makes no sense because we are looking at it from our "limited" perspective. Trust God who knows the future and loves us that His will is perfect, and God never does anything without a purpose in mind. God is there to comfort if we will open our hearts to Him and trust Him!

> Now therefore, thus says the Lord of Hosts: "Consider your ways! You have sown much, and bring in little; you eat, but do not have enough; You drink, but you are not filled with drink; you clothe yourselves, but no is warm; and he who earns wages, earns wages to put into a bag with holes." (Haggai 1:5)

I heard a powerful sermon on this passage once. How appropriate for today. God is speaking through this prophet reminding us to think about our relationship with Him. How much is God a part of our everyday living? How often do we consult with His Spirit about a direction or a decision we are about to make?

Notice the prophet tells Israel, since they returned from captivity to remember where they were and the lesson they should have learned. Did they learn that material things are nothing without God? That is such a major lesson for today's generation.

I wonder if Haggai was yelling, "Wake up! Listen to me!"

I am a "people watcher" I love to sit at a Wal-Mart or outside a store, or in a mall and watch people. It is fascinating! You can learn so much about people. What's important, how they respond to the actions of others. Of course, none of them know I'm watching. That's the way God is. He's watching.

Try something. Do you have a movie camera on a tripod? If you carry it around the people know your there and will act accordingly. If you put it on a tripod in a corner soon no one will remember that it's there and will begin to act normal. I did it once at a birthday party. It was quite interesting. How we act when we think no one is watching, and how we act when we think someone is watching.

Twice in this first chapter Haggai says, "Consider your ways." Here, Israel has spent seventy years in Babylonia Captivity. They were conquered and taken to a foreign land. After God's judgment, and they begin returning, God had to admonish them to "consider your ways" as usual it didn't take them long to return to their old ways.

How about you. Do you remember your commitment and pledge to God when you were saved, that you were going to live for God? How long did that last? God always has His arms open to welcome us back. Just like the father of the Prodigal Son. Turn back now!

> So, he answered and said to me: "This is the word of the Lord to
> Zerubbabel: "Not by might nor by power but by My Spirit," says the
> Lord of hosts. (Zechariah 4:6)

Wait a minute. I thought the Holy Spirit didn't come until Pentecost in the book of Acts. We've talked about this before. In the Old Testament, the Holy Spirit came and went as God had need of someone. Look at Genesis chapter 1, The earth was without form, and void, and darkness was on the face of the deep. And the Spirit of God was hovering over the face of the waters. (v.2) Just a sample of His power. That's what Zechariah was talking about.

That same power lives within us. We, our bodies are the temple of the Holy Spirit (1 Corinthians 6:15). You should underline this verse, this biblical principle. The power of God resides within us as children of God.

My daughter asked me one time how God could be everywhere in the world. It's simple through the person of His Holy Spirit. If God's children ever fully grasped that fact there is no telling what God could accomplish through us.

Besides this verse, I have a few other words underlined in my bible. Look at verse 10 of this chapter, "For who has despised the day of small things." One of my biggest pet peeves is the idea that we tend to put God in a box. That is, we can't conceive of God doing anything that we can't imagine. If we can't see how it could be we think God can't accomplish it. That's sad!

God wants to work miracles in your life. He wants to accomplish great things with you. But, you must take the first step. You must trust Him, to leave your comfort zone and trust God to do what He has asked you to do. One principle, I've noticed in over these thirty years of ministry. God will start with a simple task. S-t-r-e-t-c-h your faith a bit. When you accomplish that step of faith, then He will put another task in front of you. The more you trust Him the greater He will use you.

It's not in our own strength or wisdom but it MUST be in God's power. The power of the Holy Spirit. When we can learn to trust God, there is no limit to what God can do in our lives. Trust is a learning trait, it grows the more you practice it!

"Yes, they made their hearts like flint, refusing to hear the law and the words of the Lord of hosts had sent by His Spirit through the former prophets. Thus, great wrath came from the Lord of hosts. (Zechariah 7:12)

I don't think anything frustrates God more than when His children refuse to listen and obey. The same with parents and their children. How much time do we spend trying to teach our children to obey us? I've had my backside tanned a few times trying to learn that lesson. Just as God has done with His children, the nation Israel.

Ever tried to talk to someone who just won't listen? It's the most frustrating thing there is. "Just listen!" I can hear God shouting from heaven through all the Old Testament prophets. Even His Own Son had the same problem. Even with all the miracles Jesus did in front of His disciples He was still amazed at their lack of faith. Zechariah mentions that in this verse.

You see, there is a limit to God's patience! One of my favorite verses is Numbers 14:22, "Because all these men who have seen My glory and the signs which I did in Egypt and in the wilderness, and have put me to the test now **these ten times**, and have not heeded My voice." I'm not sure God keeps score but you get the idea, God's patience was at an end. This takes place when Israel refuses to enter the Promised Land.

How many times has God laid something on your heart but you're were too scared to try it? Too many times I dare say. Been there! Done that! When I think of the blessings I missed out on because I wouldn't trust God and take a step of faith, it's sad!

We have one more prophet after Zechariah. One more man filled with God's Spirit that tried to speak to God's people. These two prophets, Zechariah and Malachi were prophets to Israel after their captivity. You would think they would have learned, they didn't. We are the same way. God could work a miracle or chastise us, we know without a doubt who and why but we still would ignore the message.

The disciples didn't take notice until they saw Jesus after His resurrection. I don't have room here but look at John's gospel 20:24-29. Read all of it, it will make sense then!

"So, I will strengthen them in the Lord, and they shall walk up and down in His name," Says the Lord. (Zechariah 10:12)

Just what does that mean? "I will strengthen them in the Lord." We have talked a lot about our walk with God. We kind of get that I hope. But there is a lot more to walking with God than a relationship. God is not only with us, daily, walking with us but God gives us the strength to make it through each day.

There were days I came home from work just exhausted. For years I used to drive over-the-road. For a long time, I drove to St. Louis and back to Kansas City every day. My wife wouldn't understand, I spent the day setting, why should I be tired? Many don't understand that stress can be just as draining as physical labor. God helps us to deal with that stress. There are a lot of ways God strengthens us in our daily walk.

You've had those days when noting seems to go right, right? Try something, when you have those days, take a moment and read a chapter or two in the psalms. See if the word of God doesn't change your outlook on the past day. We need to be reminded sometimes who's in charge!

There's that word "walk" again. The question is, are you walking "In His name." Are you trusting God for every step? We had an interesting lesson in Acts this morning. In chapter 20:23 it says, "except that the Holy Spirit testifies in every city, saying that chains and tribulations await me." Paul was told in advance what awaited him in Jerusalem. What would we do if God told us that next Tuesday we would be in chains and maybe beaten? Yet Paul continued to his destination. Would we? That's the kind of commitment Paul had. Isn't it a blessing that we don't know what lies ahead each day?

God gives us, each day, the strength to get through this day. He doesn't tell us what's up ahead. Why? He wants us to trust Him for every step, every day, every hour that we walk in His presence. That's called faith. Faith to know that God knows the end from the beginning and we simply trust that God wants only the best for us and we walk every day trusting Him to bring His will to pass.

Any trials coming up? Just remember who is in charge!

> "Bring all the tithes into the storehouse, that there may be food in My house, and try Me now in this," Says the Lord of hosts, "If I will not open the windows of heaven and pour out for you such a blessing that there will not be room enough to receive it." (Malachi 3:10)

This was one of my biggest struggles as a Christian. We can talk about faith, teach faith, encourage faith but when it comes to money that's a whole other story. Let me share my story.

It started with Dave Ramsey's book, "Total Money Makeover." My daughter encouraged me to read it. I got it and read it. I made a commitment on January 1, 2009 that we were going to get out of debt. It's funny that Dave spends little or no time talking about tithing. It's, a given.

Well, I was so in debt. I would send a hundred dollars to Home Depot, then five days later max it out again and charge eighty. Once I sent a hundred dollars to a credit card. I was a little late. The statement said I owed more after sending the hundred dollars than I did before. That was it! I'm getting out. Every penny I made each week was taken up in creditors. So where to start?

I prayed! I said, "God I want out of debt. If you will tell me who NOT TO PAY, I will start tithing." At the time, we were living in a trailer in a trailer park. I can't go into all the details. But by the end of one month we paid off the trailer and moved into another house we owned. The cost we saved by getting rid of the trailer and leaving the trailer park rent—was exactly the amount of our tithe. God kept His word. Now, each month we had enough to tithe. But again, we were back to a commitment for every dime I made. I made a promise to God and I kept my end.

Six months later I was running the numbers in my head on the way home from work. Guess what? The "extra" money we had that month, that didn't have a home in some creditors envelope was EXACTLY the amount of the tithe. So, in a sense, he doubled the amount of the tithe. I have heard countless stories like this. But nothing seeped in until it happened to me. I'm glad to say I am a faithful tither now.

Just take a minute and look at the challenge God gives us in this verse. IF, you will trust Me, look what I promise!

"And she will bring forth a Son, and you shall call His name Jesus, for He will save His people from their sins." So, all this was done that it might be fulfilled which was spoken by the Lord through the prophet. (Matthew 1:21-22)

Take note of these words, "which was spoken by the prophet." Matthew will use a variation of the phrase throughout his gospel. Sometimes he will say, "according to the Scriptures" or a variation of those words. The gospel of Matthew was written primarily to the Jews, the nation of Israel. He continually refers to the Old Testament writings to point his people to Jesus.

This prophecy was from Isaiah 7:14, a familiar Christmas verse. Now realize that Isaiah wrote this 800 years before Christ's birth. Led by God's Holy Spirit to write something he would know nothing about. Imagine what went through his mind when the Holy Spirit told him that a child would be born of a virgin.

The name Jesus is the Greek form of the Hebrew name Jehoshua or Joshua, meaning Jehovah is salvation. I like the way John the Baptist made the Old Testament connection when John said, "Behold! The Lamb of God who takes away the sin of the world! (John 1:29) You can't escape his reference to the Lamb. The Old Testament sacrifice for sin. The blood that was shed to pay for sin in the Old Testament. John knew "exactly" who Jesus was.

The genealogy of Jesus in the beginning of Matthews gospel can be interesting since you have read through the Old Testament. Look at these names, Judah, Jacob had twelve sons, here the line passes through his fourth son, Judah (v. 3). Remind yourself of Genesis 38? Why was this story inserted in the narrative of Joseph, now you know? Notice Boaz in verse 5. Boaz was born of Rahab, who was Rahab? Rahab was the woman in Joshua chapters 2 and 6. The harlot that was spared at the destruction of Jericho. Ruth the mother of Obed, another Gentile who followed Naomi to Bethlehem to marry Boaz. You see these names become familiar when you've read the Old Testament.

Let me make this point here. God can use anybody to complete His will in His time and place. He can use even YOU!

"But seek first the kingdom of God and His righteousness, and all
these things shall be added to you. Therefore, do not worry about
tomorrow, for tomorrow will worry about its own things. Sufficient
for the day is its own trouble." (Matthew 6:33-34)

Do you want three chapters to know the mind of Christ? These three chapters
(5-7) will change your life. Want a short passage to "chew" on for weeks, check
out these three chapters! They are so full of meat it will be hard to digest in one
day for sure!

Here God gives a simple priority list. Seek FIRST the kingdom of God. There
are all kinds of commentaries written on the difference between "kingdom of God"
and "kingdom of heaven" that's not important to us right now. Let's focus on the
word "kingdom" which is where we want to be. We want to be where God is. As
a Christian that is right here, right now. The Holy Spirit lives within us so what
are we going to do. Seek FIRST the kingdom of God. What is God's will for our
lives? God didn't save you to sit. God has a specific plan for your life. He is leading
you in that plan right now.

Your priority is to find what God wants you to do. So, how do I do that? First
you pray! Ask God! When you were saved, along with the Holy Spirit you received
a "spiritual gift." This is a very special gift for you alone. It is your road map to
service. God gave you that gift to serve Him! First you need to find out what it,
then you need to start using it!

Do you see what else is in this verse? Don't worry. I heard a song the other day
that works for me. "Don't worry, be happy" easy for you to say. No, it's easier to do
than you think. Because when you realize that God is in control, and that you can
do NOTHING about tomorrow, your worries tend to decrease!

Another way to say that last part is, "Let today's troubles be sufficient for
today." Let me ask you this. Can you change anything about tomorrow by worrying
about it? Will that change anything. I will tell you who CAN change tomorrow,
God! Have you taken your "worries" to God? Now He can change things.

Just keep in mind the most important thing, the kingdom of God, and His
righteousness!

"Ask, and it will be given to you; seek and you will find; knock and it will be opened to you. For everyone who asks receives, and he who seeks finds, and to him who knocks it will be opened." (Matthew 7:7-8)

What a promise from God! More about that in a minute. Have you noticed anything interesting about ask, seek and knock? The three words spell A.S.K. To me that is the most important aspect of our relationship with God. There is no relationship without ASKing Jesus into your heart. Our prayers are about asking God for direction, needs, help, wisdom, etc.

It is important that we ask the question, or request. Look at James 4:3, You ask and do not receive, because you ask amiss, that you may spend it on your pleasures. What we ask for must be within God's plan for our lives. Must glorify God. I could do the whole concordance reference on the word ask. Have you ever heard the phrase, "be careful what you wish for"? Be careful what you ask for.

Remember the verse we looked at yesterday? Seek first the kingdom of God. Look at this promise, what you seek you will find. But first, we must seek it with our whole heart. These three must be done with a heart for God. What do you think Jesus is saying here? We are toward the end of His sermon on the mount. What do you think He is getting at?

Heaven is for our asking. A relationship with God is for our asking. A prayer must be prayed before it can be answered. God's will can only be found by seeking it from God. It falls on us to want these things, these answers.

One of my favorite verses gives this very picture. Revelation 3:20, "Behold, I stand at the door and knock. If anyone hears My voice and opens the door, I will come in to him and dine with him, and he with Me." God is simply a prayer away. Just outside the door of our heart. We must open the door. God will not force Himself on us or our will. It must be relinquished voluntarily. We must ask, we must seek, and we will find that special relationship with God by our initiative!

Anyone who has done any of these three will testify that God keeps His word. It's up to us to accept it!

"Come to Me, all you who labor and are heavy laden, and I will give you rest. Take My yoke upon you and learn from Me, for I am gentle and lowly in heart, and you will find rest for your souls. For My yoke is easy and My burden light." (Matthew 11:28-30)

Just what we were talking about yesterday. The action is on us. We must come to Him. God is there willing to work miracles in our lives, but we must seek Him, seek His hand His will in our lives.

You want to give up? You want to quit? There is no hope! Really? That's not what Jesus says here. He says bring it to me. One thing I've noticed since my early days as a Christian. Altar calls are for joining the church. Rarely do you see someone come forward for salvation. Another thing that is missing is "rededication." That is even more rare.

For several years I used to go with a youth group to a Christian youth camp. Each year several of the youth would "rededicate" their lives. I guess that is old fashioned anymore. Maybe it's not acceptable anymore. Rarely did those rededications prove effective. I guess we can do that now in our quiet time at home. So how many is enough? Maybe we might want to think about doing it every morning in our devotions. In our quiet time with the Bible and prayer. Reflect on our walk to that point and see if we may need to rededicate our walk.

"Find rest for your souls" Are we looking for that today. So many of us have become accustomed to a fast-paced lifestyle we wouldn't know how to wind down. I think I mentioned this before. Here's a challenge, some evening, turn EVERYTHING off. The TV, the phone, everything, and just sit still for fifteen minutes. Don't laugh until you try it. What starts going through your mind? Things you need to do, right? Your "to-do" list. Try and focus on your relationship with God through Jesus Christ. See if that doesn't bring a peace you haven't felt in a long time?

The cares of this world are exactly that! Look what Jesus said in John 16:33, "These things I have spoken to you, that in Me (Jesus) you may have peace. In the world, you will have tribulation; but be of good cheer, I have overcome the world." That is exactly what Jesus is talking about in the verse above. No one can give you that peace except Jesus because He has the authority to do so!

"Now he who received seed among the thorns is he who hears the word, and the cares of this world and the deceitfulness of riches choke the word, and he becomes unfruitful." (Matthew 13:22)

This is such an impactful verse. Read it again! First, they received the seed. In verse 19 Jesus explains what the seed is, "When anyone hears the word of the kingdom." The word is the gospel, the word of God. They have heard the word of God. Either someone has shared it with them. They read this devotional, or the Bible, they attended a church service, any number of ways they "heard" the word of God.

What is one of the preparations for sowing seed? You need to break up the soil, don't you? You need to ready the soil to receive the seed. It could be a person, after person witnesses to them. Then one day the seed takes root. Who knows how many times they have been cultivated until the seed takes root. This whole parable is so important to sharing our faith.

I like the principle in the book of Galatians 6:7, "Do not be deceived, God is not mocked, for whatever a man sows, that he will also reap." Too many today have forgotten that basic biblical principle. I like what Dr. Charles Stanley says, "We reap what we sow, more than we sow, and later than we sow," He calls it the principle of Sowing and Reaping.

I used to drive a truck between Kansas City and Topeka, Kansas. Many times, along the turnpike near Lawrence there is this large flat field. Many times, I've seen this farmer on a tracker pulling this thing that distributed the seed in rows. About twenty feet behind him was a huge flock of birds. Eating the seed, he planted. Funny thing though he still had a crop each year.

This is such a key principle to all those Christians who think they are wasting their time telling others about Jesus. Think of it as planting a seed. You never know when that seed will produce a crop. Sometimes it may be like the verse above. It may not take root. What do you do? You keep sowing. It just takes one seed to produce a plant. God is also fertilizing each of those seeds we plant with the power of His Holy Spirit. If you notice we are not responsible for the crop only the sowing of the seed! Remember that!

> But when he saw that the wind was boisterous, he was afraid; and beginning to sink, he cried out, saying, "Lord, save me!" And immediately Jesus stretched out His hand and caught him, and said to him, "O you of little faith, why did you doubt?" (Matthew 14:30-31)

I love this story. Just think how much faith it took for Peter to step out of that boat. Sure, he got distracted, so do we. But to have that much faith is amazing to me. Yet we cringe if God asks us to teach a Sunday school class, or sing in the choir, or lead a Bible study, or even to become a deacon. I truly believe the hardest thing to do in a church is to recruit volunteers.

Peter is so much like we are. How many times did Peter step out of line, make a rash statement, question the words of Jesus? He even denied Jesus three times, after he said he would die with Jesus. We're the same way. God must drag us kicking and screaming to do some deed for Jesus. But when we take that step of faith we are amazed at what God can do through us.

I'm curious just how far out of the boat Peter got. A few feet, more? I wonder. He was doing fine if he kept his eyes on Jesus. We are the same way. God can do miracles through us, but as soon as we get puffed up, scared, lacking in faith, we begin to sink, don't we? Why do we do that?

There is another fact to keep in mind. Where was Jesus when Peter began to sink? Right there, close enough to grab him before he went down. That's where Jesus is to us when we take that step of faith. I can tell you from experience that when we put our trust in God and get out of our comfort zone we will see God do things through us we never thought possible!

I have always wanted to do a little Bible study in the gospels. How many times, and to whom did Jesus say, "O ye of little faith", or "I have not seen such great faith". Faith is my favorite word in the Bible. When I get a new Bible the first thing I do is go through the New Testament and underline the word faith. It only appears twice in the Old Testament, in the King James version. It is a fascinating word to me. And of course, I told you about Matthew 9:29.

What do you suppose God could do through you if you trust Him?

He said to them, "But who do you say that I am?" Simon Peter
answered and said, "You are the Christ, the Son of the living God."
(Matthew 16:15)

It's always been a curious question for me. At what point were the disciples "saved?" This statement by Peter raises that question. Pete announces, "Thou are the Christ, the Son of the living God." Does this mean Peter has asked Jesus into his heart? We can look at his actions from here but is that evidence? How about you? Do you recognize Jesus as the Messiah, the Son of God?

You see, many have said that we are only eighteen inches from heaven or hell. Eighteen inches from the head to the heart. It's one thing to acknowledge who Jesus is. Even to admit, historically, that He might have been raised from the head. But, the question is, have you asked Him into your heart? That is the difference. Too many people think that by acknowledging who Jesus is that will get them to heaven

Look at these verses, "Not everyone who says to Me, 'Lord, Lord,' shall enter the kingdom of heaven, but he who will do the will of My Father in heave. Many will say to Me in that day, 'Lord, Lord,' have we not prophesied in Your name, cast out demons in Your name, and done many wonders in Your name?' "And then I will declare to them, 'I never knew you; depart from Me, you who practice lawlessness!" (Matthew 7:21-23).

See Jesus can see through our "works" and see our heart. We can talk a good conversion but God sees the heart. That's what I meant about eighteen inches from heaven or hell. It begins with the heart. There are a lot of people who can talk the talk, how many have walked the walk? That is one of the saddest things about being a Christian because those who are not saved but talk the talk give those who have made that commitment a bad name.

I don't think there is any doubt Peter became a Christian. Think about this. When Peter got out of the boat and walked on water was he "saved" he had faith? Was it saving faith? Peter makes this statement here, was it fact or faith? When Peter denied the Lord three times, was he saved? When Jesus asked him three time, "do you love Me?" was he saved? Interesting questions, have you asked yourself the question?

Jesus said to them, "Have you never read in the Scriptures: 'The stone which the builders rejected has become the chief cornerstone. This was the Lord's doing, and it is marvelous in our eyes?'" (Matthew 21:42)

What an indictment of the Pharisees! They had all the Old Testament scriptures, they studied and taught from. They missed Him. Much like we talked about yesterday. They had the facts but missed God's Son.

If you have ever done any "wall-building" you know the importance of a corner stone. You set the two corners then you run a plumb-line between the two corners that helps to make the rest of the wall straight. The rest of the wall is aligned with the corners. Who or what keeps your life aligned?

What gauge do you use to determine what course you will choose? The Lord gave me this last night and I guess this is a good place to use it. "Are you living by book-learning, or are you learning the book?" What is your plumb-line based on? Is it based on truth or conjecture? Is it fact-based or experience based? Where do you go to help make a critical decision in your life? Tough questions. The earlier you lay that foundation of scripture to make your decisions the easier and more fruitful your life!

Jesus here is quoting from the psalms, 118:22. Remember how He defeated Satan in the wilderness? Jesus knows His scriptures. How about you? How much of God's word have you put into your heart? It took me a while to find this verse in the Psalms. I truly believe the concordance is inspired. Many times, a verse or passage will come to mind but I'm not sure where it's at. I will keep at it till I find it. You just need some key words and that's where knowing the word of God comes in handy.

Think about Jesus' question here. Who is He asking this question of? Look at verse 23 of this chapter. "chief priests and elders" you would think they knew the Psalms. I don't think it did them much good for their egos to have this itinerate preacher quoting the Torah.

I heard a gospel song the other day. Its title was "Dust on the Bible" of course there was a country song entitled, "Dust on the Bottle." Sad! Which in your house has the most dust?

Jesus said to him, "'You shall love the Lord your God with all your heart, with all your soul, and with all your mind.' "This is the first and great commandment. And the second is like it: 'you shall love your neighbor as yourself.' "On these two commandments hang all the Law and the Prophets." (Matthew 22:37-40)

Do you see what Jesus did? In the Sermon on the Mount Jesus said, "Do not think that I came to destroy the Law of the Prophets. I did not come to destroy but to fulfill." (Matthew 5:17). Here the Scribes and Pharisees are trying to trap Jesus by getting Him to admit that He was above the Law. You see His response.

Jesus simply broke down the Law into two key components. Laws one through four pertain to our relationship with God. (Exodus 20). The last six Laws pertain to our relationship with our fellow man. That's why He said, "On these two commandments hang all the Law and the Prophets." You might want to reread the Sermon. How many times does Jesus say, "But I say to you."? If you look at the Laws He's talking about He takes them one step further.

I don't know how many times I've heard this quoted and the speaker says, "with all you're MIGHT." Look what it says. With all your MIND. It's not all based on faith. "Heart, soul, and mind" it must be complete. You can't walk with God halfway.

Why do you suppose this lawyer was asking this question? We've already said it was to trick or trap Jesus into making a statement that would discredit Him before the people. Of course, it was not successful. As you read through these four gospels note how many times the religious leaders try to trap Jesus. He is confronting their hypocrisy. If you've read the verses for today did you notice that right after this exchange Jesus chastises the very same leaders by saying, "Woe to you, scribes and Pharisees, hypocrites." Jesus spends the 23rd chapter calling out these leaders for their hypocrisy.

Two, very simple commands that encapsulate the Ten Commandments Moses received from God on Mt. Sinai. Love God, love your neighbor. Yet Jesus had come and corrected the leaders of the Jews on their own law. God's Law was given to encourage a relationship with God and with our fellow man!

"Then the sign of the Son of Man will appear in heaven, and then all the tribes of the earth will mourn, and they will see the Son of Man coming on the clouds of heaven with power and great glory." (Matthew 24:30)

Son of Man is one of Jesus terms for Himself. Do you remember anyone else using that description for himself? The prophet Jeremiah referred to himself as "the son of man." What a great picture.

As a young Christian, I remarked to a youth leader once that it would be exciting to return with the Lord and fight beside Him. He told me, "We won't be doing any fighting. Jesus will simply speak and the armies will be defeated!" What an awesome thought.

Now why do you suppose the tribes of the earth will mourn? Every person at this point will be given the opportunity to accept or reject Jesus as Savior. There will be no, "I didn't know" excuse. Those mourning will be those confronted with the truth and realizing they were wrong and that their fate is sealed!

I wonder how many people think that they can get away with denying God here, in this life and when they stand before God say, "Oh, it is real, o.k, I accept Christ as who He says He is." Well then, it's too late. When you're confronted with the truth it's too late!

Just like Adam and Eve in the Garden. God gave them specific instructions. But they had to try and test God. They suffered the consequences. As we do today. When we think we know more than God, we go our own way, then when confronted with the results of our actions we say, "I didn't know" it won't work.

This is a great chapter, Jesus talking about the signs of the end times. So many have used this passage to look for signs of His return. Look at verse 36, "But of that day and hour no one knows, not even the angels of heaven, but My Father only." It will be when we least expect it. It's like the person that thinks he can wait until he is on his death bed to get saved. You don't know when or the circumstances of your death. It may be instant. Then when you stand before God what will you say? "I didn't have time!" Really? You can't fool God. Once you've heard the truth you will be accountable for the truth, and how you responded to it!

He went a little further and fell on His face, and prayed, saying, "O My Father, if it be possible, let this cup pass from Me; nevertheless, not as I will, but as You will." (Matthew 26:39)

I can't tell you how important prayer is. Even our Lord put a priority on prayer. When He faced the most difficult time in His life He went to prayer. Jesus knew what was coming. When we look at what He endured it's unimaginable to think of.

So, what place does prayer play in your life? How often do you pray? Once a week, Sunday, only when you're in trouble or facing a challenge? How about when you need a miracle or a blessing? What motivates you to pray? Is God your Santa Claus? Or is God your confidant that you go to every day and bring your concerns, needs, petitions, etc.?

In my Bible, I have a list of maybe thirty names. I've never met them I have no idea who they are. The list was made during a revival in our church. I took a portion and I pray for them every day by name. I may never see them. I hope when I get to heaven maybe one of them will come up to me and thank me for praying for them, who knows. It's not important, God knows them and their need.

I always pray for my family! We can all use some prayer. I also pray for my pastor and our church. God is working in our church, and I want to seek His power and input in our ministry.

How about taking your concerns, your decisions, your plans to God for guidance? You are recruiting the wisdom of God in your decision-making process. You might ask Him to open some doors or to close them to give you direction.

How about thinking of prayer and your relationship with God just as His Son Jesus thought of it. Remember, Jesus was God in the flesh. If He thought it was necessary to go to the Father for strength, and assurance of the Father's perfect will, why not us?

Prayer must be an integral part of our Christian life. Our relationship with God will not exist without that daily communication with the Father. One thing we must never neglect to do is ask a blessing on our food. Wherever we are at. It reminds us of where our sustenance comes from

But the angel answered and said to the woman, "do not be afraid,
for I know that you seek Jesus who was crucified. He is not here; for
He is risen, as He said. Come, see the place where the Lord lay."
(Matthew 28:5-6)

W here do you look for God? Here is another opportunity to pray. Mary was
looking for Jesus. She went where she thought He would be. He wasn't
there. She continued to seek Him. God used Mary to tell the disciples of His
resurrection. Why? Because she sought Jesus. The same principle will work with
us. Are you seeking Jesus?

She "expected" to find Him in the tomb. God is never where we "expect" to
find Him. Therefore, we must seek Him. Remember that verse, "But seek first
the kingdom of God and His righteousness, and all these things will be added to
you" (Matthew 6:33). Seek first God, then He will use you to accomplish miracles!

Of course, Mary wasn't going there, thinking He had risen. She went to anoint
His body for burial. Many of us seek God for various reasons. The question is
what do you do when you have found Him? Do you allow Him to change your
life, or do you forget the experience and go on with your life as you planned it?
It's your choice.

Why would the angel take Mary to see the empty tomb? We are creatures of
"seeing is believing" aren't we? Remember Thomas? One of my favorite passages,
"The other disciples said to him, "We have seen the Lord." (after His resurrection)
So he (Thomas) said to them, "Unless I see in His hands the print of the nails, and
put my hand into His side, I will not believe." And after eight days His disciples
were again inside, and Thomas was with them. Jesus came, the doors being shut,
and stood in the midst, and said, "Peace to you!" Then He said to Thomas, reach
your finger here, and look at My hands; and reach your hand here, and put it into
My side. Do not be unbelieving but believing." And Thomas answered and said to
Him, "My Lord and my God!" Jesus said to him, "Thomas, because you have seen
Me, you have believed. Blessed are those who have not seen and yet have believed."
(John 20:25-29)

That is a challenge to us. Are you seeking an empty tomb and do you believe
Jesus is all He said He is and can give you eternity in heaven?

> And He said to them, "The Sabbath was made for man, and not man for the Sabbath. Therefore, the Son of Man is also Lord of the Sabbath." (Mark 2:27-28)

Do you remember what God told Moses about this commandment? Remember the Sabbath day, to keep it holy. Six days you shall labor and do all your work, but the seventh day is the Sabbath of the Lord your God. In it you shall do no work: you, nor your son, nor your daughter, nor your male servant, nor your female servant, nor your cattle, nor your stranger who is within your gates. For in six days the Lord made the heavens and the earth, the sea, and all this is in them, and rested the seventh day. Therefore, the Lord blessed the Sabbath day and hallowed it. (Exodus 20:8-11)

Now of course we know that God was telling Moses to rest one day in seven. The Sabbath to the Jews is on a Saturday. It begins at 6:00 P.M. on Friday and ends at 6:00 P.M. on Saturday. When the Lord instituted the church, Jesus was raised on a Sunday. That became the Lord's day. So, the church celebrates the Lord's day on Sunday. The concept is the same. One day in seven to rest. As Christian's we recognize that day to be Sunday.

Maybe your old enough to remember when it was a priority in our country. Stores and businesses were closed. There are a few, Hobby Lobby, Chic-fil-a, others recognize that tradition. The Lord will bless their faithfulness. What about you. Since we are empty-nesters my wife and I eat out after church on Sunday. That makes us hypocrites. If the restaurants had no waitresses and servers they would not be open. Our not going will not deter them from being open.

The point I guess I want to make is that we do attend church every Sunday. The Lord is the Lord of the Lord's Day. We worship Him and praise Him on the Lord's day.

What we are missing in this passage above, is that the Pharisees were using that day to trap Jesus. They made it much more than God intended. He challenged them on it. Watch in the gospels how much Jesus challenged them on the Sabbath. He would deliberately heal someone on the Sabbath to challenge the religious leaders in their strict rules which were not of God but their own making. Jesus point exactly!

However, Jesus did not permit him, but said to him, "Go home to your friends, and tell them what great things the Lord has done for you, and How He has compassion on you." (Mark 5:19)

One year, as pastor, I determined to preach Jesus from Christmas to Easter. Trying to connect the two events. Of course, there were over three years in Jesus public ministry. It was a blessing. This is one of the stories I used. There is a good lesson at the end. After Jesus had cast out the demons into the swine and healed the guy. The one healed wanted to follow Jesus. What did Jesus tell him to do? That's the verse above.

He was to go and tell others what Jesus had done for Him. The woman at the well, after learning who Jesus was went and told others. Look at John 4:28-30, The woman left her water-pot, went her way into the city, and said to the men, "Come, see a Man who told me all things that I ever did. Could He be the Christ?" Then they went out of the city and came to Him. That's how people come to Christ.

We simply tell others what Jesus has done in our life. We invite people to Sunday school. Because we hear the teachings of Christ. The Bible, etc.

Jesus could have added many more followers. Remember when Jesus began His Sermon on the Mount there were thousands following Him. They all gathered to hear Him speak. He fed them then taught them. Later, He explained to them what it meant to follow Him. Many left Him so much so that He asked His disciples if they would leave also.

What would be your response if Jesus asked you to take up His cross and tell others what Jesus had done to change your life? This also happened to Jesus. I believe there were three examples of followers that wanted to follow Him but had other things to do first.

An interesting thing about this episode. When Jesus cured this guy by casting the demons into the swine and the swine ran off a cliff. The towns people begged Him to leave. They were afraid of the power that Jesus exhibited. They didn't care that this guy who had been afflicted with demons, for who knows how long, was cured they wanted Him to leave. They feared His power. Interesting story.

Have you told anyone lately what God has done in your life?

> He answered and said to them, "Well did Isaiah prophesy of you hypocrites, as it is written: This people honor Me with their lips, but their heart is far from Me." (Mark 7:6)

Isaiah 29:13. Even in the days of Isaiah, then in Jesus day, and even today the same is true. People talk the walk but there is no personal relationship, intimate walking with God. Of course, we don't see what goes on in their personal life. They may have their quiet time. Their time of prayer but there is no outward sign of this commitment. Should that make a difference? Notice in the verse above, "But their heart is far from Me." That is the difference Jesus is talking about.

Israel, in many instances said, "Yes we will obey God, we will follow Him." The turn around and rebel or turn to idols. How frustrating it must have been for God. Isaiah, a prophet prior to their going into captivity tried to warn Israel. Isaiah saw first-hand the inconsistent behavior of the nation.

Jesus saw it in His day. In Jesus' day, it was the religious leaders that frustrated Him. The people followed but as soon as it got serious they turned away. Even His disciples fled when confronted by the leadership. After Jesus ascended to heaven then Peter and John and later Paul had to deal with the hypocrites. Even today!

Here's something that frustrates me. I think the last poll was 80% of Americans claim to be Christians. The divorce rate is skyrocketing, the abortion rate is still way too high. The pornography business is flourishing, alcohol and drugs are still profitable, etc. Who is buying this stuff if not Christians. We are not making a difference. They say one thing on Sunday but it's a different story the rest of the week.

So, what to do. I think it comes down to that intimate relationship with God AND His word. I think the more time you spend in prayer, reading God's word and walking with the Lord. The more God will begin to work in and on your heart. The more time you spend with a person the more you become like they are. God can have a real effect on your life if you let Him.

I hope these devotions have spurred some thought, maybe encouraged a reflection on the time you spend in God's word. Maybe added a different perspective to what you have read.

"For whoever is ashamed of Me and My words in this adulterous and sinful generation, of him the Son of Man also will be ashamed when He comes in the glory of His Father with the holy angels." (Mark 8:38)

Tough verse! What would it mean to be ashamed of Jesus and His words? Do you ever show, in a public setting, your devotion to God? Do you ask a blessing on your meals when you are in public? Do you do it at home? What's the difference? Do you talk of Jesus or the Bible in a public setting? Not forcefully but in course of the conversation. Have you ever shared, in a public setting, what God has done in your life recently? Do you share with family?

Are you ashamed of your faith? It was very hard for me as a young Christian to use the word God. My parents had always taught me a "reverence" for God but not a relationship with the Father. As I grew closer to God and my relationship grew, things changed. It was no longer God but Father. That's when I began to be more comfortable talking about God in a public setting. When my relationship changed my openness changed.

I think it's interesting that Jesus included the word "words" in this context. Have you ever said to someone, "The Bible says."? Why not? Maybe you weren't sure of exactly what it said so you didn't say anything. Why do you not know, for sure, what it says. How many sayings do you think in the Bible are simply "wives' tales." Ever heard, "Cleanliness is next to godliness?" Of course, you have. That is not in the Bible. How about "God helps those who help themselves" that also, is not in the Bible. You need to know the difference.

The Holy Spirit will help if your listening to Him. Spending time in the Bible helps. When you finish this one year trip through God's word go back and do it again. Make it a daily commitment. The more you can read the more is stored in your warehouse of thought. It will be there when a friend needs to hear what "the Bible says."

It's interesting that Jesus calls His generation an "adulterous and sinful generation. That could be said of every generation from then till now. We realize we can't change our environment, but we can change the next generation. Talking and teaching the word of God to our relations can make a difference in OUR next generation!

> But when Jesus saw it, He was greatly displeased and said to them, "Let the little children come to Me, and do not forbid them; for of such is the kingdom of God." (Mark 10:14)

Jesus was upset that His disciples were restraining the children who were following Jesus from coming near Him. It's an interesting dilemma in the church. I've been in both situations. Do you allow, say, and eight-year-old, who believes he has asked Jesus into his heart to come forward in church? We won't even get into baptism. The point I think is whether we encourage a child in the faith.

What's Jesus' response? Of course, you encourage them. There we go again trying to judge the heart. God is the only one qualified to do that. We all know that children mature at different stages in life. Some may be thirty before they mature spiritually. The point is, God never set an age limit on a relationship with Him. I mentioned before I wasn't saved until I was thirty-five. Yet, I had a "spiritual experience" when I was ten. So, which was real. Both were real. At what point was I saved? Does it matter?

I do want to make a point. When I had that experience at ten I was not encouraged or disciple beyond that Easter morning. Either by the church or by my parents. Maybe that's the point Jesus was making. When a child (whatever the age) seeks a relationship with God through Jesus we should encourage and disciple at every opportunity. The Holy Spirit is dealing with that child. They may not understand all that is going on but they should always be encouraged and taught about a relationship with God.

I think it's interesting how displeased Jesus was at this event. How often do you see where Jesus is "greatly" displeased? Have you heard the phrase "faith of a child"? What do you think that means? Their hearts are open, not cluttered with the politics of religion. Anyone who has been around the church very long knows about the politics of church life. It is inevitable. Anytime you have human nature involved you will have politics. Thankfully God can overcome it and still uses a church and individuals to reach a neighborhood for His glory!

We should always encourage a deeper relationship with God no matter the age!

"And you shall love the Lord your God with all your heart, with all
your soul, with all your mind, and with all your strength. This is the
first commandment." (Mark 12:30)

Does this look familiar? Of course, it does. How many times do we need
reminding of our fundamental duty? Love God, love our neighbor. But my
neighbor is impossible! Where is the commandment that says they must return
the honor? It's the same with the principle of giving. Do you expect a response
when you give? Then you have given for the wrong reason. The best way to give is
anonymously! I like to do that. I get a kick at how much it drives the receiver crazy.
Why? Because that MUST thank someone. They must give a return for the gift.
It frustrates them to no end, watch!

You know that God expects a response to His love? Look at John 14:15, "If
you love Me, keep My commandments." There are strings attached to loving God.
Understand me. The best way we can demonstrate to God how much we love Him
is in our obedience. Not our giving!

This has always been an interesting problem for me. How can we be obedient if
we don't know the rules? Have you memorized the Ten Commandments? Probably
not. Do you know where the are at in the Bible? How many DO you know? That's
a start. How about the gospels, Matthew, Mark, Luke and John? How much of
them do you know? How are you going to be obedient if you don't know the rules?

One of my favorite games, as a child, was Monopoly. We had the basic concept
down and we played it that way for a long time. Until I took a close look at the
rules. You should do that some time. Any game you play you need to understand
ALL the rules. It makes a better game.

The same is true when walking with God. You can follow Him blindly but
it will never make any sense. Until you read this book, that God put out, that
explains all the rules in depth. Then you can better understand why God chooses
a certain path. Why He says no to certain things, you don't understand. When
you know the rules, it is so much easier to be obedient!

Don't pass on this familiar verse! Read it over again!

Jesus said, "I am. And you will see the Son of Man sitting at the right
hand of the Power, and coming with the clouds of heaven." (Mark
14:62)

There is an interesting verse in the longest chapter in the book of Acts. It's
after the stoning of Stephen. Stephen was a deacon elected in the 6th chapter
of Acts. Stephen preached Jesus. I encourage you to read his brief career. In the
verse above we see Jesus "sitting" at the right hand of the Father. Now look at this
verse in Acts, But, he (Stephen), being full of the Holy Spirit, gazed into heaven
and saw the glory of God, and Jesus **standing** at the right hand of God, and he
said, "Look! I see the heavens opened and the Son of Man **standing** at the right
hand of God!" (Acts 7:55-56).

What an awesome honor for a martyr for the gospel of Jesus Christ! Jesus, of
course in this verse in Mark is referring to His return at the end of the tribulation.
Basically, encouraging His followers that, in the end, the victory is ours!

Did you notice the context of this statement? Jesus is being tried before His
crucifixion. This was His response before the chief priest. The most amazing
thing about this whole final story before His death on the cross is that Jesus knew
what was coming. He may not have understood the extent of pain but He knew
this was not going to be easy. YET, He was willing to endure what He endured to
accomplish the will of the Father.

There is one argument, to me, that dispels any idea that this whole "movement"
could be a hoax. Think of all the martyrs from Stephen till today that died for this
mission. If it were not true, by some weird circumstance it was a lie. You're telling
me that all those throughout history, including Stephen died for what they knew
was a lie? I don't think so.

When you believe in something so much that you are willing to die rather
than deny what you believe, to me, that's unwavering faith in the word of God the
Father. What He has told us in His word. What history tells us. To me that is
the miracle of the word of God. It has endured through the centuries and remains
the truth though Satan has tried his very best to water it down, distort, and deny
it, it still stands!

But he said to them, "Do not be alarmed. You seek Jesus of Nazareth, who was crucified. He is risen! He is not here. See the place where they laid Him." (Mark 16:6)

Why do I keep highlighting the same verses in each gospel? You tell me how many times you need to hear something until it becomes true. There is a story about a famous old-time, preacher who preached every Sunday over and over, "Look unto Me, and be ye saved." Over and over he preached the same message. One day, of course, someone asked him why he preached the same message. I will preach the message until all are saved. I wish I could remember the exact quote. But you get the message.

How many times have you read or heard John 3:16? So many times, it becomes invisible. If you've been a Christian for a while try reading it right now. Your eyes skim over the words. It's in your head so it almost becomes invisible. It's really sad when the things of God become invisible because of familiarity!

That's why I encourage you, when you've finished this trip through the Bible, that on January 1st you turn back to Genesis one and do it again. New verses will catch your attention each time through the Scriptures. New verses will touch your heart, make an impact and they become your new favorite verses.

When I was first saved I found Galatians 2:20. Pretty soon I came across Isaiah 40:31. That lasted a long time until I discovered Jeremiah 29:11-13. Each one touching me in a different way at a different time. The more time you spend in God's word the more you will grow fond of it!

Sure, we've read this similar passage before, and will again but don't let that take away from the point of the passage. The tomb is empty. How many messiah's can say that? Look at these verses, "Now if Christ is preached that He has been raised from the dead, how do some among you say that there is no resurrection of the dead? But if there is no resurrection of the dead, then Christ is not risen. And if Christ is not risen, then our preaching is empty and your faith is also empty." (1 Corinthians 15:12-14).

You see it all centers on the empty tomb!

> And the angel answered and said to her, "The Holy Spirit will come upon you, and the power of the Highest will overshadow you; therefore, also that Holy One who is to be born will be called the Son of God." (Luke 1:35)

What must have been going through Mary's mind? Maybe we can get a glimpse in verses 47-55. It's called "Mary's Magnificat." How humbling that must have been.

There has been a lot of discussion about Mary's questioning the angel in verse 34. Zacharias question the angel in verse 18. Zacharias said, "How can I know this?" And Mary said, "How can this be, since I do not know a man?" Do you see the difference?

In the Old Testament book of Isaiah "and shall call His name Emmanuel" (Isaiah 7:14). In Matthew we read, "And called His name Jesus" (Matthew 1:25). Look at Matthew 1:23, "Behold, the virgin shall be with child, and bear a Son, and they shall call His name Immanuel," which is translated "God with us." If you check, those last three words are not in the Isaiah passage. Matthew is giving us the translation of Immanuel. Remember another version of Jesus is Joshua which means Jehovah-Savior.

One of my favorite Baptist hymns is "Jesus, Jesus, Jesus" There is something about that name. To me the name Jesus just says, "friend, comforter, confidant" I think that's what God was trying to get across to us when He decided to come to earth and bring His word in Person. He desired that intimate contact, the personal relationship, not demonstrated in the Old Testament.

Maybe that is the hardest part about accepting Jesus as your Savior. When you finally realize that this same Jesus, the comforter, companion, is also God Almighty, the Creator of the universe, my Creator! One in the same. We might try to separate the two but it's not possible. They are one in the same God!

Oh, don't forget that same God, Jesus, God Almighty, and the One that overshadowed Mary, One in the same God! The One who overshadowed Mary now dwells in every believer today. If God's people could ever get their minds around these facts and this relationship with God it would change a lot of heavenly relationships!

> Then the shepherds returned, glorifying and praising God for all the things that they had heard and seen, as it was told them. (Luke 2:20)

It began with a simple, lowly servant girl named Mary. Then we move to the shepherds tending the flocks in the hills. Simple people no one payed much attention to. Then, as we will see later, then we move to the three kings from the East. From servants to kings. God can use anyone at any time to accomplish His perfect will. Zacharias was a priest, Elizabeth his wife. Two of my favorites in this same second chapter, are Simeon and Anna these God chose to verify the credentials of the Messiah. God spoke to them long before Jesus' birth. Told them to get ready for a blessing.

Here's our commission. Look at that verse again, "Praising God for all the things they had heard and seen." What things have you heard or seen. I can't tell you how many times I've come home from a worship service or prayer service and been blessed by someone in the service. Sometimes yes, the pastor, but usually it might be someone I see before or after that says something to me that reminds me of God's love.

I'm not a people person. I know that sounds funny, but I'm not. I used to get mildly upset when the service was over I'm ready for lunch. But Mary, she will stand and talk, and talk, while I wanted to go. Then one day I realized that that is her gift. The gift of compassion. When I understood I just started looking for a place to sit. I have no problem. Mary is exercising her gift. Oh, it's a blessing to watch her!

In this verse, the shepherds had returned from visiting the manger scene. They saw the baby Jesus. They return to their task, praising God for what they had seen. Have you seen God work in someone else's life? Maybe God blessed them in some way. Can you praise God for His blessing someone else? I sure hope so! If not, you and God need to have a serious conversation.

Let's finish with a trivia question: Who is the most prolific (wrote the most) writer in the New Testament? Most would say Paul. The truth is, in volume Luke has written more in the two books he wrote, Luke and Acts, than Paul. That's not counting Hebrews. Not sure who the author of Hebrews is. But combined Luke wrote more words.

"But that you may know that the Son of Man has power on earth to forgive sins"—He said to the man who was paralyzed, "I say to you, arise, take up your bed, and go to your house." (Luke 5:24)

I love this passage. I think that was the point of all His miracles. To demonstrate exactly who He is. Did you see who motivated this statement? Look at verse 21. The scribes and Pharisees. The religious leaders of the day. Those who studied the Scriptures. They denied who Jesus was.

Notice also Jesus' method of demonstrating who He was. "Power on earth to forgive sins." He didn't say power on earth to heal the sick. He said to forgive sins. That was the "authority" of the priests. That was the tradition of the sacrifice, the temple ceremonies. Jesus said that power now resides in Me.

Again, this demonstrates the necessity of Christ going to the cross. God established the payment for sin in the book of Genesis 3:21. God's law never changes. That was the price to be paid. The extraordinary thing about the power of Christ's sacrifice was that it was sufficient to cover our sins, past, present and future. The key is the application. Until we accept Christ as our Savior the blood sacrifice is not applied to our lives.

Wait a minute! Don't get carried away. This, by no means, gives a license to sin. There will "always" be consequences for sin. But those consequences will not keep us out of heaven. Some may be, while here on earth, some may be in removing of rewards but God will be just in His judgment.

Here, in a sense, Jesus is fulfilling His statement, "Do not think that I came to destroy the Law or the Prophets. I did not come to destroy but to fulfill." To fulfill the Law of blood being the payment for sin in the form of a sacrifice Jesus fulfilled that on the cross of Calvary.

What does that mean to you. It's simple. Either you have applied the blood of Christ to your sins, have been forgiven and seeking a relationship with God. Or you have denied the truth of Scripture and rejected God's sacrifice and thus rejected God, and will spend eternity in hell. Really a simple choice. And how to receive the power of Jesus' sacrifice? Just ask Jesus into your heart, sincerely trust in Him!

"But he who heard and did nothing is like a man who built a house on the earth without a foundation, against which the stream beat vehemently and immediately it fell. And the ruin of that house was great." (Luke 6:49)

Wow. This verse goes along with the truth of yesterday's devotion. We talked about making that choice. Here Jesus tells of someone who rejected the truth. It is sad just how many people think they can get along without God. They may be prosperous, healthy, famous, but at some point, they will meet the Judge. What will be there defense?

One of my favorite passages, speaking of foundations is in 1 Corinthians 3. Mark this passage down! 1 Corinthians 3:11," For no other foundation can anyone lay than that which is laid, which is Jesus Christ." This whole chapter is worth a day's mediation. The point being about the verse above, look at the contrast between the two foundations. Who or what is the foundation of your life built on?

Looking here reminds me of another principle. We have talked about sharing our faith. You might want to note verse 6. "I (Paul) planted, Apollos watered, but God gave the increase." We talked earlier about planting seed. Maybe in your Bible, beside that parable Jesus used, you might put 1 Corinthians 3:6. Here is the principle. Paul traveled through Europe planting seed. On subsequent missionary journey's he returned to see how the seed was doing.

We are called to sow seed. The cultivating, watering, weeding, etc. may be done by others. And of it, is God who gives the increase. It's God, through His Holy Spirit that causes that seed to bloom!

Of course, if you don't sow there is no crop. It's that simple. But you don't make it happen God does.

Did you notice something in our verse for today? "But he who heard and did nothing." We've talked about those who did nothing. How about the responsibility when you have heard? It doesn't matter when or where or by whom. It could be Billy Graham on a rerun of his sermon. The source doesn't matter. Once you have heard of Jesus and His sacrifice on the cross then you are responsible for what you've heard. Once you know the truth it is up to YOU to respond. You no longer have the excuse, "I didn't know."

"Those by the wayside are the ones who hear; then the devil comes
and takes away the word out of their hearts, lest they should believe
and be saved." (Luke 8:12)

I hope you have read this teaching moment from the Lord. Let me give you a
couple of scenarios. Do you remember hearing, as a child, the story of Johnny
Appleseed? Here is a guy who was supposed to go throughout the countryside and
just throw apple seeds hither and yawn. Some have said there are apple orchards
today because of his sowing.

Next, we have the picture of a farmer who plows, cultivates, fertilizes, and
does everything he can to prepare the soil for planting. I told you the story of this
farmer in Kansas where the birds follow behind him and eat the seeds, but he still
has a crop.

Now, let's look at this teaching moment by the Lord considering these two
examples. I see the "Johnny Appleseed" approach in this lesson. The seed is cast
out and it takes root where it can. I understand what the Lord is trying to teach
here. We MUST sow the seed. The seed, of course, being the word of God. (v.
11). It challenges the hearer to evaluate how they have received the word and what
impact it has made in their lives.

I want to use the scenario of the farmer to offer maybe another approach. Do
you "cultivate" your sowing of the Word of God? That is, to talk with them, share
your testimony, encourage them to read the Bible? Different ways to prepare the
soil. In Jesus picture preparation of the soil would have eliminated some of the
pitfalls for the seed to take root.

Understand, as a former Sunday school teacher I love this illustration. Jesus
is forcefully extolling the need to sow the word of God. I'm simply saying, do some
ground preparation first. There is, of course, a place for the "Johnny Appleseed
approach" but there is also plenty of need for the farmer who works to prepare
the soil.

Don't miss the point is this discussion. The point being to sow the word of
God. That is one of the main goals of this book of devotions. If I can get you to
spend a little more time in God's word I have succeeded in sowing a few seeds.

> "Nevertheless, do not rejoice in this, that the spirits are subject to
> you, but rather rejoice because your names are written in heaven."
> (Luke 10:20)

I hope you've read the verses leading up to this verse. The disciples have gone out, sent by Jesus, and have seen God do some miracles through them. They come back, in a sense, bragging about what they had accomplished. Jesus points them back to God. It's not what they did but it is their relationship with God that matters!

The following verse is the correct response. (10:21) Praise God!

Has God used you in some way to lead someone to faith in Jesus? I hope so. Did you put a notch in your Bible? That's not the correct response. I met a guy in youth camp once who had to tell me that he had led over 3,000 youths to Christ. That's great. I would have loved to ask him, where are now? Again, as a teacher my concern is not notches on my Bible but discipleship. How much have they grown in their relationship with the God who created them.?

Well, you say, if Jesus sent me out with the power that these seventy had I would see miracles too. Well, friend HE HAS! When you become a child of God you have received the same power these seventy disciples received. Notice it was seventy not twelve. Not the inner circle but "followers" who trusted Christ enough to do what He sent them out to do, be witnesses of what Jesus did for them. Or, you might say, "sow some seed". Sorry, couldn't resist it.

Notice the power that Jesus gave these disciples. The power over the demons, over Satan's minions. We have spiritual power that we have never tapped. Satan has no power over us except what we allow. I'm sure you remember Flip Wilson's excuse, "The devil made me do it." Friends the devil can't "make" you do anything you don't allow him to do. You're in control, unless you give it away.

Something I forgot to mention about the book of Luke. We said that the gospel of Matthew was written to Jews that's why Matthew keeps referring to the Old Testament. Luke was written to the Greeks. The Greeks love stories, philosophy. You will find this gospel full of parables, stories to illustrate the message Jesus was preaching. Think about this as you read this great gospel.

"Therefore, you also be ready, for the Son of Man is coming at an hour you do not expect." (Luke 12:40)

What do you suspect Jesus is talking about when He says, "Be ready"? Does He mean are your bags packed? Does He mean, do you have your ticket? What does this question mean to you? Maybe He's asking, have you done enough good works? Have you led enough people to Jesus? You fill in the blank.

To me He means, are you a child of God? If you are, you have nothing to worry about. Your one of the family.

One of my favorite verses is in 1 Thessalonians 4. For the Lord Himself will descend from heaven with a shout, with the voice of an archangel, and with the trumpet of God. And the dead in Christ will rise first. Then we who are alive and remain shall be caught up together with them in the clouds to meet the Lord in the air. And thus, we shall always be with the Lord. (4:16-18).

Do you know why the dead in Christ will rise first? Because they have further to go. Sorry, I had to get that in.

Is this a fantastic picture? Isn't it funny that the word "rapture" is not found in the Bible but here it is? That time when Jesus comes for His children. Here's another little saying: "If you are born once you will die twice. If you are born twice, you will die once, maybe." Have you heard that before?

If you have been "born again" (John 3) then you will only die once, maybe. The maybe is that if Jesus comes back while you're still alive you will not even die once. But If you haven't received Christ as your Savior, you will die twice. A physical death then a "spiritual" death, and spend eternity in hell.

Cute little saying but it all pertains to this time when Christ returns for His church, the bride of Christ. Some question as to when this event occurs. Is it before the seven years tribulation or does this event occur at the end of the tribulation in the final battle when Jesus defeats Satan and casts him into the lake of fire. Don't get caught up in the time tables, the point of this verse in Luke is, be ready for whenever Jesus returns.

I hope you've made a commitment to finish this tour with me!

"Salt is good; but if the salt has lost its flavor, how shall it be seasoned?
It is neither fit for the land nor for the dunghill, but men throw it out.
He who has ears to hear, let him hear!" (Luke 14:34-35)

I think the phrase today is, "making a difference". The problem is most of us won't be around when that criteria is measured. The lives we may influence may be in the subsequent generations. I'm in my seventies right now. I'm thinking more and more about what I am leaving behind. What kind of "testimony" I'm leaving my grandkids and children.

It's simple what Jesus is talking about here. Do you influence those around you by your words and actions? Are you pointing people to Jesus or away from Jesus? Are you involved in the lives of those who can make a difference.

Let me offer a suggestion. Get involved in your local church. I went to prayer meeting last night. I looked around and at least 90% of those attending, were over 60. Then I realized that the young people in our church were working in our AWANA program. Teaching children about Jesus. Working with children. Because they weren't in the prayer service didn't mean they weren't making a difference. We need to stop and think about the various ministries in our church! How we can support those ministries.

Sometimes the only way we might "make a difference" can be in our giving. We are not able to teach or do physical things later in life but we can always find a way to give. Giving is a critical way of making a difference. If you feel that you have no spiritual gift to contribute think about what you are doing with the resources God has blessed you with.

It's interesting that Jesus uses the metaphor of salt. I don't use salt, never could tell the difference. But in Jesus day it was the thing used to preserve meat, and many other functions besides flavor. Here Jesus uses the aspect of flavoring. A sour disposition can sour those around you. Sometimes just a kind word or encouragement can turn a person's day around. There are plenty of opportunities to be "salt" in our daily lives. It's our option. Jesus exhorts us to think about how we affect the world around us. Are we making a difference?

But Jesus called them to Him and said, "Let the little children come
to Me, and do not forbid them; for of such is the kingdom of God.
Assuredly, I say to you, whoever does not receive the kingdom of God
as a little child will by no means enter it." (Luke 18:16-17)

O.k, we've seen this verse before. I knew this verse was coming up and I got to
thinking this morning. Jesus public ministry lasted three and a half years. A
little less than 1,300 days. We can probably read these four gospels in a morning
setting. Just a few hours. We can't begin to grasp the brevity of all that is in these
four books. Look what the apostle John wrote, "And there are so many other things
that Jesus did, which if they were written one by one, I suppose that even the world
itself could not contain the books that would be written." (21:25).

The point I want to make is, if the Holy Spirit, who was directing the writer of
this gospel thought it was important to include this picture, this episode more than
once then I think we should give it some attention. Someone once said that when
Jesus uses, "verily, verily" that means pay attention! When God thinks something
is important enough to repeat it, then it's worth noting.

I wonder what He means by, "receiving the kingdom of God as a little child?"
Children have not been exposed to "adult think" maybe. Their minds have not
been cluttered by "facts" to dissect every little event in our lives. They don't "over-
think" something. They accept it as truth until proven otherwise. God wants us
to come to Him with that mindset. You've heard this before, "God said it, I believe
it, that settles it." That's great, except others have added, "God said it, that settles
it." It doesn't matter if you believe it or not. It matters if you want to get to heaven!

It doesn't matter if you believe it as far as fact goes, of course! The miracle of
the Bible to me is proof enough that it is God's word. God gave us the Bible to make
that connection between His mind and our heart. To tell us just how much He
loves us and wants the best for us. And finally, to let us know that the relationship
between us and the Almighty are predicated on our choice. It's our option to
believe and accept or to deny and reject. We are responsible for our choice!

And He said to them, "Render therefore unto Caesar the things that
are Caesars, and to God the things that are God's." (Luke 20:25)

Again, the religious leaders trying to trap Jesus. Trying to get Him to say
something that will trip Him up. Do you have some friends like that? They
ask you questions like, "Can a fish really swallow a human being?" "Is the Bible
really true?" "Did Jesus really exist?" Those are the only ones I can think of right
now. The point is those around us are looking for us to trip up. Just as they did
in Jesus' day.

There is an interesting challenge in this verse. What are the things of Caesar?
Jesus is looking at a coin with Caesar's likeness on it. Is that what He's referring
to? Not likely. Then what? The "things" in our life can be put into two categories.
The things of God and the things of this world. Basically, everything belongs to
God. But Jesus is trying to get us to set some priorities.

To distinguish the things that glorify God and the things that don't. They
were using taxes as an example. Nobody likes or wants to pay taxes. It's the law.
We are commanded to obey the civil government (Hebrews 13:17). The spiritual
leaders were trying to trap Jesus in denying this law. It didn't work (look at verse
26). Later Jesus will pay their taxes with a coin from the mouth of a fish. God
provided!

Our priorities get so mixed up. Sometimes we can't separate the things of
God and the things of man. What was Israel's biggest complaint after they were
freed from Egyptian bondage? The flesh. Water, food, nothing of spiritual needs.
They had God walking with them and they still focused on their physical needs.
That's the message Jesus was trying to get across. Where is your focus? The things
of God or the needs of the flesh.

Look at Matthew 6:33, "But seek first the kingdom of God and His
righteousness, and all these things shall be added to you." That is the priority.
God will supply the daily needs if we seek His direction, His provision, His will in
or lives. This lesson was not for the religious leaders but for those watching Him.
Where was His faith? Again, Jesus points to God for provision. When we start
trusting plastic instead of God's provision we are trusting Caesar instead of God.

"Then they will see the Son of Man coming in a cloud with power and great glory. Now when these things begin to happen, look up and lift up your heads, because your redemption draws near." (Luke 21:27-28)

Look at the previous verses again. If you've read these two chapters you've seen this. Jesus is telling us that when the people get to the point of "no hope" look to the heavens. We are not there yet. Does it seem we are getting closer? It is meant to be. In our generation or the next, or the next. Only God knows. Why does God tarry?

That is a simple question to answer. God wants to give every single person on this earth the opportunity to accept Jesus as their Savior. He will wait as long as necessary to bring as many as possible into His kingdom.

There is an interesting question in these verses. Who will see Jesus coming in the clouds? Will it just be Christians as the Rapture takes place? Will the lost see His coming and regret their denial? I'm thinking this is His first return, meaning the Rapture of the church. So, the lost will not see Him. They will only see the Christians disappear. Which will signal the Tribulation period.

"Now when these things begin to happen" What things? The things in the previous verses. Also in Matthew 24. I could get political but this isn't the place. For the lack of a better description let's say, "All chaos will break loose." Which is a good description! The normal things of this earth will be turned upside-down.

I just read a commentary that says this isn't the Rapture. You decide. There are two occasions when Jesus returns. One, at the Rapture of the church. The other at the end of the Tribulation period. Either time will be a time of judgment. The first, Jesus will remove His children prior to His judgment of the earth. The second to conclude God's judgment on those who, after seven years of hell, refuse to acknowledge Jesus as Savior. Which will you be a part of?

Here is another verse that is repeated. Repeated for a reason. When you stand before God. Either after your death on at Jesus second coming it's too late. You must make that decision prior to facing God!

> And they said to one another, "Did not our heart burn within us while He talked with us on the road, and while He opened the Scriptures to us?" (Luke 24:32)

This verse has a special meaning in my life. At our old church, I was asked to bring the message at a "Hobo Convention" fellowship our church held each year. It was one of my first attempts at preaching. I used this verse for my text. It describes, I think, how I felt reading God's word after I was saved. This verse just spoke right to my heart!

Notice here again, it wasn't head knowledge it was the heart. That is where God deals with us. We can memorize the whole Bible and miss heaven. We can have John 3:16 in our heart and be welcomed into God's presence! I mentioned before about missing heaven by 18 inches. The distance from our head to our heart.

Even before Jesus revealed Himself as they ate, they felt something as He spoke the truth. That is what should happen to us when we hear the truth, the word of God. It should stir our hearts as no other words should. One of the reasons the word of God has survived these hundreds of years.

I remember reading that one of the criteria to determine whether a book should be included in the Canon was whether the book had an impact on the people. Did the people recognize its heavenly quality! That is so important!

I hope you have stayed with me through this devotion. Reading day by day the words of this marvelous book, the Bible. I truly think that once you have finished this first year you will want to go back year after year and continue feeding your spirit with the truth of God's word!

Notice Jesus reference in verse 23, Then He said to them, "O foolish ones, and slow of heart to believe in all that the prophets have spoken!" Some are harder than others. Their heart screams "believe" but their head wants to dissect the facts. The heart says, "believe" the head says I can't. Remember Thomas at the end of the Gospel of John. (John 20). Read that last chapter as well. Jesus also had to deal with Peter.

What will it take for you to put your faith in the word of God? I'm not talking about salvation. I'm talking about the truth of scripture. The standards we are to live by. Trusting the word of God!

"He who believes in Him is not condemned; but he who does not
believe is condemned already, because he has not believed in the
name of the only begotten Son of God." (John 3:18)

There it is again. Faith not fact. Understand that I'm not discounting fact. There is plenty of historical evidence but that's not what God wants. He wants us to trust Him. "By grace you have been saved through faith, and not of yourselves; it is the gift of God, not of works lest anyone should boast." (Ephesians 2:8-9) Look at this one, If, you confess with your mouth the Lord Jesus and believe in your heart that God raised Him from the dead, you will be saved. (Romans 10:9) I don't see anything there that says you must KNOW! It says with your heart! Look at the next verse, For, with the heart one believes unto righteousness, and with the mouth confession is made unto salvation. (Romans 10:10).

You see it is very simple. That's what makes it hard. Huh! For something so life-changing we want to make it difficult. We must jump through fifteen hoops, and memorize fifteen verses, etc. God just says "believe". Until you can acknowledge that Jesus is who He said He was you can't be saved. This is God's plan and you can't change it. Maybe you have a better idea, doesn't matter you're not the one offering salvation, God is.

Man must make things complicated! Just look at the church through the centuries. Do this, do that, be baptized, walk this way, that way, etc. No!

Have you ever seen this sign at a football game, "John 3:16"? What does that mean to you? If you're a Christian you probably know what it says. If you're not what does it mean? If your lost you might not even know who John is, let alone 3:16. Besides that, unless the Holy Spirit is working on you, you might still not know.

This is probably one of the most significant chapters in all the Bible. It's all here. Jesus talking with Nicodemus, explaining what it means to be born again. That has always been a challenge to me. We (Christians) are on this side of the mirror. The lost are on the other side. How do you convince them that they MUST step through the mirror to the other side to know what a difference it can make!

> "But the hour is coming, and now is, when the true worshippers will worship the Father in spirit and truth; for the Father is seeking such to worship Him. God is Spirit, and those who worship Him must worship in spirit and truth." (John 4:23-24)

If you have done your reading you know this is the story of the woman at the well. Here's where the Old Testament knowledge comes in. This woman is in Samaria. Jesus, as a Jew, was not supposed to be there. The Jews shun the Samaritans.

When Assyria conquered the northern ten tribes of Israel they send Assyrians in to replace the Jews who were removed from the land. In so doing they had become a mixed race. In the Jewish eyes "unclean". Besides this, the Jewish men rarely if ever talked to women in public. What Jesus was doing, again, was contrary to the Law. It seems Jesus was frequently pushing against the restrictions the religious leaders had enforced.

"In Spirit and truth." What an awesome truth. Today, as children of God we worship God in the Holy Spirit and the truth of the word of God. Too many believe they don't have to go to church to worship God. That's true. So, when Jesus instituted the church, and Paul spent his whole life establishing churches at Jesus command, that wasn't necessary?

God desires His people, His children to regularly gather, not just for worship, but fellowship, encouragement and discipleship. Look at the first chapters of Acts. They gather daily in fellowship and prayer. Oh, but we don't need that today, right? We need it more than ever!

Here's another person, that when Jesus spoke to her need, she ran to tell others. She recognized that He was sent from God. He got her attention by telling her things that she thought were hidden. He saw her heart. That's how God operates. His word will penetrate the heart and open it to the truth of God's love.

You can't hide anything from God. God knows the heart and God deals with the heart. You may be able to fool those around you, but not God! I don't think you would have gotten this far in your reading without asking Jesus in your heart, but if you have what a time to open your heart and begin a personal relationship with a God who loves you!

"And this is the will of Him who sent Me, that everyone who sees the
Son and believes in Him may have everlasting life; and I will raise Him
up at the last day." (John 6:40)

Even here, Jesus recognizes the will of the His Father. He may debate it in the
garden before His crucifixion but He will accomplish what God has asked
Him to do.

You notice that it isn't enough to see Jesus. So many of His followers SAW
Him but how many believed in His message. I reflect to John 20:28-29. The story
of Thomas. Of course, that is at the end of this gospel but the illustration is so
dramatic! "Blessed are those who have not seen yet believe". I love that because
that's where we are today! Is it not?

Have you ever heard this old country song? I don't know if it's the title or the
chorus, it goes, "I just can't eat without bread." The older ones might remember
it. I loved that song as a kid. In this chapter four times Jesus refers to Himself as
"the bread of life." Bread is such a vital part of our diet. Even more so in Jesus' day.
Remember the feeding of the five thousand? (Matthew 14). Bread and fish. It was
a staple for the Jews. I dare say it is today, although in variations. ·

I love the gospel of John, it's my favorite. I'm not sure exactly where but it
seems at least half of the book takes place in the upper room just before going to
the cross. So, this was Jesus' final time to teach His disciples.

I heard a story once about when Jesus ascended to heaven. One of the angels
asked Him if He had a plan "B"? If the disciples fail to spread the message was
there another plan? Jesus replied, "No, this is God's plan to reach a world, dying
and going to hell." Interesting story but God doesn't make mistakes.

God had a plan from the very beginning. If you think God didn't know what
Adam and Eve would do, you don't know God. God has had this plan from the
very first creation. He could have created us like the angels, no free will, just
servants. God took a huge risk. He created mankind with the ability to "choose"
whom they would serve. He gave them the ability to choose to follow Him or
follow their own desires. It's our choice. Therefore, it's our consequences!

> Then Jesus spoke to them again saying, "I am the light of the world. He who follows Me shall not walk in darkness, but have the light of life." (John 8:12)

This comment follows Jesus' encounter with the woman caught in adultery. I've heard preachers tear these accusers apart. That is where we are today. I am so frustrated with all the lying and deceitfulness in the world today. It's unbelievable! People don't even want to know the truth, they simply swallow whatever is told them and refuse to search for the truth, hence the woman accused of adultery!

That, I think, is what Jesus is talking about. The darkness of ignorance. "Just accept, don't question" just continue walking in darkness that way you don't have to take a stand. You don't "make waves" you just go with the flow. "What you don't know won't hurt you!"

I think one of the problems about knowing the truth is that then you are accountable for that truth. No more excuses! You can't claim ignorance anymore. Jesus sheds light on lies. He exposes the lies to the light of His truth.

One nice thing about walking in the darkness is that no one sees you. You can do whatever you want. Ever see a brightly lit bar? You think you get away with things in the dark you don't get away with in the light. It doesn't work that way. Jesus knows what's going on and has His way of shinning a light on sin!

There's that word "walk" again. Ever walk around in the dark? It's scary you don't know what you will encounter. Danger lurks there. You turn on a light and it's an amazing feeling when you can see!

The youth camp I used to go to had this large hill with a cross at the top. The first time I went they had this exercise where the youth would form a very large circle at night in front of the cross. Each would have a candle. One or two at the foot of the cross would light their candle. Each would light the others. In less than two minutes the hill was lit with candlelight. It was the most awesome sight! When the candles were lit, the whole hillside was lit. You might say the light chased the darkness.

When we ask Jesus into our heart He brings His light with Him. To light the hidden places in our heart that needs to be cleansed. Ask Him!

"My sheep hear My voice, and I know them, and they follow Me. And I give them eternal life, and they shall never perish; neither shall anyone snatch them out of My hand." (John 10:27-28)

Get a hold on the last part of this verse, "neither shall anyone snatch them out of My hand." That includes you. You cannot lose your salvation! Once you have asked Jesus into your heart you become a child of God. Nothing and no one can change that.

Don't misunderstand. As Paul says, this is not a license to sin. Those children who get out of God's will can expect correction from the Father! Let's ask one question. Who determines what it takes to lose your salvation? Who determines what it takes to get it back? How many times can you lose it? There are just too many unanswered questions to that scenario. The Bible says it's permanent.

Hearing Jesus' voice, picture this, we are walking with Him close enough to hear it. We are not way ahead of Him nor are we lagging. We must be within His will to hear it clearly. You might want to check your hearing. Can You hear His voice clearly? If not you might want to check your walking distance.

What does the word "eternal" mean to you? Jesus uses it in John 3:16 as well. That would be an interesting search. How many times does Jesus use "eternal" referring to our salvation? I guess you could substitute eternal with forever. Would it make any difference in your concept of eternity? Once you become a child of God it is permanent, eternal, everlasting, etc.

This chapter is entitled "Jesus the Good Shepherd." The verse above is talking about sheep and the Shepherd. I don't know how many preachers have used the analogy of the ignorance of sheep. They will go anywhere, and do anything not knowing where or why. It's like yesterday's verse about light and darkness. Without direction, we are lost sheep. (Isaiah 53) We try so hard to "make it on our own" don't we. We are the masters of our fate. Seriously.

I think that's the first time I used that word seriously. Not one of my favorites but appropriate! We access "self-help" books, tapes, videos, conferences looking for guidance. When all the time all we need is right here in the word of God! Check it out!

"I have come as a light into the world, that whoever believes in Me should not abide in darkness. And if anyone hears My words and does not believe, I do not judge him; for I did not come to judge the world but to save the world." (John 12:46-47)

Did you catch that phrase? "If anyone hears My words and does not believe." The option is yours. So how do we hear of the words of Jesus? The word of God. I love my Bible. It's God's written communication with me. His verbal communication is through His Holy Spirit. If we could get our minds around that fact. The pathway we are traveling would be so much easier!

This is important. Look at John 3:17, "For God did not send His Son into the world to condemn the world, but that the world might be saved." Look at that! He says pretty much the same thing in the verse above. Basically saying, "It's your choice," God puts it squarely in your hands. God isn't forcing anyone to accept Jesus. It is totally up to you. The thing is by doing salvation that way YOU are responsible for that choice.

Here again Jesus is using light to describe His ministry. Darkness is ignorance, not accepting truth when it is presented. The world is always seeking what is true. I know there's not much evidence of that right now. That's sadly funny in a way. Men would rather believe a lie that seek the truth.

Did you notice what Jesus said about the unbeliever? They "abide in darkness." They live there. They are content there. It's those who feel there is something better, nothing in truth that they are lacking in their lives.

I mentioned before that I like to write in my Bible. It's God's textbook of His holy word. In John 3:16, whenever I get a new Bible I go there and cross out "the world" and fill in my name. For God, so loved Lonny that He gave His son... It's personal! When Jesus gave His life on that cross at Calvary He paid my sin-debt in full. I can come before God knowing I have accepted the truth and God's promise to me. That because of Jesus I have access to the throne of God as a "born-again" child of God. That is an awesome feeling. I seek His guidance and comfort through the trials of this world. He is my heavenly Father!

"Peace I leave with you, My, peace I give to you; not as the world gives do I give to you. Let not your heart be troubled, neither let it be afraid." (John 14:27)

Where do you seek peace? Better yet, how do you find peace. Do you play these audio tapes of quiet music? Do you find a quiet place to meditate? Do you just sit quietly in the dark and meditate? Where and how do you seek peace? You know where I'm going with this. The only true peace is a relationship with Jesus. Not just accepting who He is but a true relationship with the Son of God.

Here's a clue. Take another look at chapter 15. Now, if you don't mind underlining, find the word "abide" and underline it. I found eight references in verses 4-10. Read those again. What is the key? Abiding in Christ. How do you "abide" in someone? You listen when they speak, you do what they ask, you trust their counsel.

Notice the illustration He uses. A limb attached to a vine. The strength, the blood, the life itself comes from our "attachment" to the branch. Look out. In verse 10 Jesus says, "if you keep My commandments." There it is again. Being attached to the vine means we obey His principles.

Don't miss these metaphors. Earlier Jesus is the Light that leads us out of darkness. Here He is the lifeblood of the branch that sustains the vine. It all goes to what I have preached through-out this book. That intimate relationship with the Father through His Son Jesus Christ!

"Let not your heart be troubled, neither let it be afraid." Can you really say that? With the everyday worries, concerns, trials, and decisions that are mandatory daily can you truly say you are at peace? Of course, you can. Jesus said, "Because of your unbelief; for assuredly, I say to you, if you have faith as a mustard seed, you will say to this mountain…" (Matthew 17:20a). It doesn't take much, just enough.

I wonder, if you we're able to measure faith. How much faith did Peter must have to get out of that boat and walk on water to Jesus? How would you measure that? Let me give you some advice from experience. The more you trust God the greater your faith will grow, believe me, I learned the hard way.

> "I do not pray that You should take them out of the world, but that you should keep them from the evil one. They are not of the world, just as I am not of the world. Sanctify them by Your truth. Your word is truth." (John 17:15-17)

I have noticed something about the various books in the Bible. They can be broken down into two basic categories: Narrative or story, and instruction or teaching books. Of course, the easier to read are the story books. After this next book (Acts) we will get into the teaching books. Books like Proverbs, and Psalms, and Romans are "teaching" books. Fundamentals that God wants us to apply to our daily lives.

Of course, the gospels are story or narrative books.

Jesus, talking to God has asked God's blessing on those disciples He has left behind to carry on the work of spreading His message, thereby the message of God, throughout the world. Just think about that a minute. Twelve disciples, twelve men whom God chose to be the messengers of God's grace and salvation to the whole world. Were they successful? I should hope so! Aided by the word of God.

Speaking of the word of God. Something we need, also, to keep in mind as we read these last remaining books. There was no Bible in the early church days. Beside the Old Testament books of Moses and a few of the prophets, maybe some letters that Luke, Matthew, John and Mark wrote to the churches there was no Bible as we know it. The book of Revelation wasn't written until ninety years after Jesus.

It's always good to keep in mind the culture of the day as you read. Maybe even put yourself in their place. You can better understand where they are coming from. Throughout the Bible God uses simple men just like you and I to accomplish extraordinary things, how, by being available and willing to be used of God.

A tax collector, shepherds, fishermen, a tent maker, a Pharisee, simple professions throughout the Bible that were willing to heed God's call to take His message, no matter the cost, to a lost world.

Has God tapped you on the shoulder? Remember the excuses that Moses tried to use? It's easy to make excuses but if God moves on to someone else you're the one who missed His blessing and seeing His power work a miracle in your life!

And Thomas answered and said to Him, "My Lord and my God!" Jesus said to him, "Thomas, because you have seen Me, you have believed. Blessed are those who have not seen and yet have believed." (John 20:28-29)

This is such a key passage. We are ending our visit to the gospels. Here Jesus makes a final appearance to His disciples. The first time, Thomas, one of the disciples, missed the meeting. When the disciples saw him, they told him they had seen the Lord. Look at his response, the other disciples therefore said to Him, "We have seen the Lord." So, Thomas said to them, "Unless I see His hands, the print of the nails, and put my finger into the print of the nails, and put my hand into His side, I will not believe." (v.25) Now this isn't some stranger who just showed up after the crucifixion, Thomas was one of the original disciples called by Jesus. What does it take for some to believe?

Later, Jesus returns to the upper room, this time Thomas is there. I have to repeat what Jesus said, "Thomas, because you have seen Me, you have believed. Blessed are those who have not seen and yet believed." (v. 29). What a fantastic message for us today. Unless you have seen Jesus recently this message is for you!

Thomas professed his faith AFTER he saw Jesus. Today that is the work of the Holy Spirit in the life of an unbeliever. The Holy Spirit convicts them of their unbelief. Assures them of God's love and His desire for them to accept the message of Jesus through faith and become a child of God.

Isn't it interesting that once you have made that decision, in faith, there is a peace that we can't explain. The assurance of the truth of the love of God. We can't explain it unless you experience it. If you haven't there is an emptiness in your soul you can't explain. Jesus will fill that emptiness.

As far as I can tell, I think Jesus is in the upper room for the last time beginning in chapter 13. To me this is very important. This was Jesus' last opportunity to teach His disciples the truths He wanted them to remember as they faced the world. Take these chapters and Matthew 5-7, the Sermon on the Mount and mark them to read several times. Teachings that will change your life!

"But you shall receive power when the Holy Spirit has come upon you; and you shall be witnesses to Me in Jerusalem, and in all Judea and Samaria, and to the end of the world." (Acts 1:8)

We talked before how God could use simple men to accomplish such an amazing task. Here is your answer. "You shall receive power from the Holy Spirit." As a Christian of over thirty years I can fully testify to this fact. I've seen God do some amazing things through me, that I could write a book about. Including this devotional. When I started this task, I had some doubts. What would I write, what would I say? When I set down the words just start flowing. I am in awe!

We talked about these men reaching a world with the gospel. Notice the game plan. They started in their hometown, Jerusalem, then their state, Judea and Samaria and finally the whole world. We are a part of that last challenge. If you support your local church you can support missions which, in turn, reach the whole world. Too many think they must go out into the mission field to fulfill this challenge and Matthew 28:19-20. You can be an important part just by giving!

"You shall be witnesses." Wait a minute. I never saw Jesus OR His disciples. How can I be a witness? Simple! What has Jesus done in your life to change your life, if you're saved of course! That's the witness Jesus is talking about. Witness to the life changing effect of the salvation gospel. You are the best tool God could use to lead others to salvation in His Son.

But I can't speak, I don't know what to say, I'm shy, unlearned. Sounds like Moses to me. Remember something very important! It's not you, but the power of God through His Holy Spirit that speaks. Believe me you will be amazed at what God will bring to your mind, if your listening and willing to say what God lays on your heart! As a pastor, I made several visits to people I had never met before. What do I say? What is my approach? It's simple, God chose you, and created you, to be you. I used to wish I could preach like Chuck Swindoll or Charles Stanley! Then one day I realized the world already had a Chuck Swindoll and a Charles Stanley what it didn't have was someone like me, with my personality that God could use to reach those in my sphere. God can use ANYONE!

"This is the stone which was rejected by you builders, which has become the chief cornerstone. Nor is there salvation in any other, for there is no other name under heaven given among men by which we must be saved." (Acts 4:11-12)

We have seen this passage before. I believe Jesus quoted a variation of it. Here Peter is quoting from the Old Testament Psalms 118:22. Here referring to Jesus of course. This must be the favorite verse to stick it to the religious leaders of the day. This always fascinated me, although it shouldn't have. These religious leaders were supposed, to know the Old Testament prophecies of the Messiah. Yet Jesus wasn't what they "expected" so they missed God's visit!

Of course, we can do the same thing. People who come up to you and ask them to pray for someone or something don't realize that they have the same access to God as you do, if they were saved!

It was interesting. Something I have noticed for years. The way Hollywood shies away from the name Jesus. They can use God's name in vain in a movie but let's not mention Jesus. Our president mentioned Jesus in the yearly Capitol Prayer Breakfast. You should have heard the news stories. He used the name "Jesus" they couldn't get over it. Sadly, that is our culture today. You can say anything, but don't bring up the name Jesus!

As a Christian, we know there is power in that name. Next time your thumbing through the hymnal in church notice how many hymns use the name Jesus. Of course, they tried to get the word Christmas out of our culture. God's people would have none of it. It took a couple of years but I think they've given up on that idea. There will be other attempts to silently remove it from our language. Won't happen!

Look at verse 13, Now when they saw the boldness of Peter and John, and perceived that they were uneducated and untrained men, they marveled. And they realized they had been with Jesus. How could they do that? Remember where the power comes from. "They had been with Jesus." You can say the same thing when you ask Jesus in your heart. He will give you the ability to testify about what He has done in your life and complete the Great Commission in Matthew 28:19-20 and in Acts 1:8. God can use even you!

So, the eunuch answered Phillip and said, "I ask you, of whom does the prophet say this, of himself or of some other man?" Then Phillip opened his mouth, and beginning at this Scripture, preached Jesus to him. (Acts 8:34-35)

I want you to notice who initiated the conversation here. How many people around you have asked you questions about your faith? What was your response? Were you able to do as Phillip did? Start in Isaiah 53 and lead them to the Lord. Do you know enough about the Lord and the Bible to do this? Why not?

I gave a challenge to my youth class once, "I can take anything subject you bring up and take it to the Lord." Could you do that? Do you know the Bible enough to take any subject to Jesus? You can, if you know God's word. You must spend time in it. Reading and praying.

The events leading up to this exchange have God written all over it. Phillip was in a revival in another city, God sent Phillip to witness to this representative of Ethiopia.

I'm sure you've heard stories, if you've been in church any length of time, of a pastor being told by God to change his message at the last minute. He doesn't know why, but God instructed him to change it by the Holy Spirit. Why, there was a visitor or a member that needed to hear a different message. God works that way.

God will send someone into your life that will help point you in the right direction if you let him. There was one such person in my life that God used to help me get my first church as a pastor. God bless you Henry!

You can be that person in someone else's life. If you are open to the leadership of the Holy Spirit. Just like that person we mentioned who comes to you about questions in the Bible. But it's up to you to be prepared in the word. I'm not talking about college courses or anything like that. I'm talking about reading the Bible through. Implant those precious words into your soul. God will bring them to your mind when the need arises. If you're like me, He will bring the verse or parts of it and you need the concordance to find it. I've always said the concordance was divinely inspired. It has helped me so many times. Of course, you need to know some key words in that verse!

Then Peter opened his mouth and said: "In truth I perceive that God shows no partiality. But in every nation whoever fears Him and works righteousness is accepted by Him." (Acts 10:34-35)

Here's a lesson Peter had to learn. This is following his vision on the rooftop about a blanket full of food. God said eat, etc. You have already read the story in this chapter. Peter is a Jew. They have strict eating rules. Again, go back to Old Testament books of Moses. Then God had to convince him that everything was lawful to eat.

I don't know if you notice, in your reading, how God changed the diet of mankind through the centuries. In the Garden of Eden, they were vegetarians. Later God gave Israel a whole list of what meat they could eat and not eat. Later in this passage the diet was changed to anything God created.

It's the same progression in our salvation. First, God had to teach us the penalty for disobedience (sin) to His instructions. In Exodus 12 God gives us the "Passover" picture of applying the blood of a sacrifice to the door to ward off the death angel. Then Isaiah 53 description of the suffering Savior. This picture in the Old Testament was to help us understand the purpose of Christ in the New Testament. We see that in John the Baptist words when he sees Jesus, the next day John saw Jesus coming toward him, and said, "Behold the Lamb of God who takes away the sin of the world!" (John 1:29) So the picture is complete with Christ's death on the cross the sacrifice was made as required in the Old Testament in Genesis 3:21.

Peter learned from God's lesson on the rooftop, that God's message of salvation is open to all, throughout the world. A lesson he would be reminded of by the apostle Paul. There was a great dissension in the early church about allowing Gentiles (Greeks) in the church. A lesson the early church had to resolve.

It's amazing to me to look back through the process of reading through the Scriptures how God slowly brings His children to the lesson and point He wants to make. It's the same way the Holy Spirit works on a new convert. God doesn't "clean" him up all at once, He can, but most of the times it's changes here and there a little at time. "He's still working on me!"

"And when He had removed him, He raised up for them David as king,
to whom also He gave testimony and said, 'I have found David the son
of Jesse, a man after My own heart, who will do My will.'" (Acts 13:22)

Saul or Paul's first missionary journey. To establish churches, his mission, that
God called Paul to reach the Gentiles. Interesting that in each city that Paul
visited for a long time. He began by going into the synagogues. The more the Jews
refused to hear his message the more he reached out to the Gentiles. Finally, Paul
gave up and focused entirely on the Gentiles (Acts 18:6). By the end of Acts Paul
had reached Rome.

I've mentioned before the unique relationship God had with David. Here,
quoted in the New Testament a phrase that should be the goal of every child of
God today, "a man after My (God) own heart, who will do My will." There are
so many challenges in life. If we could say, at the end of the day, I have done what
God asked me to do. That is a good day!

Look at verse 23, "From this man's seed (David), according to the promise,
God raised up for Israel a Savior—Jesus-." The promise? That was made to
Abraham in Genesis 12. God has always had a plan and a purpose for His people.
Just as He has a plan and a purpose for His children, born-again of the Spirit of
God through Jesus Christ!

One of my greatest joys was being able to trace God's genealogy through
Adam, Seth, Abraham, Isaac, Jacob, David, Solomon to Jesus! When you make
those connections, you can see God's plan working to bring about His will and
purpose. That has always been interesting to me to look back and see the steps that
God had a hand in to bring me to a certain place "His perfect will". Until you are
able to do that you can't fully appreciate God's working in your life.

From that day that God saved me at our kitchen table that night, to thirty-five
years later being able to sit and write these devotionals God has blessed, taught,
encouraged and chastised me into His perfect will. It's hard sometimes, we think
we know better than God but that is never the case. When we can fully surrender
to His will, the blessings are amazing. The neat part about it is, now you can see
God's hand in this path we are walking called life. That is the greatest blessing.
Just to watch and see what God is doing in your life!

"So, God, who knows the heart, acknowledged them by giving them the Holy Spirit, just as He did to us, and made no distinction between us and them, purifying their hearts by faith." (Acts 15:8)

otice how God works? Twice in this verse Paul mentions the relationship between the heart and God's working in a person's life. We have become so proficient at fooling people, with our facial expressions, knowing just the right words to say. But God knows the heart. Thankfully, through the working of the Holy Spirit most of the time we don't fool our Christian friends. There Spirit bears witness that something isn't right.

Notice where this Holy Spirit comes from. Yes! When you have prayed and asked Jesus to come into your life, that same moment you receive the third person of the Trinity, the Holy Spirit. I've used this analogy several times. Once the Holy Spirit comes to dwell in you we tend to put Him in a closet and lock the door. We only let Him out on Sunday, maybe, but the rest of the time we lock Him up. Why? Because when He comes to dwell in our hearts He begins to clean house. He begins to try to make changes in our lifestyle to bring us closer to the Father.

But, we don't like change! So, instead of listening and trying to be obedient to His promptings we lock Him in a closet. The thing about the Holy Spirit is that He will not FORCE Himself into any life. The same with our conversion. God doesn't force anyone to decide to follow Him. It is all voluntary. When you decide that you need God in your life He will come in. The amount of control God has in your daily walk is up to you. Let me caution you though. The less you allow His working the more of God's blessings you are missing. The more you allow God to work in your life, the closer your walk with God, the more you will see God work amazing blessings in your life.

When God's Holy Spirit prompts you to do something out of your "comfort zone" it is strictly voluntary. He won't force you to do anything. BUT, if you refuse to take that step of faith you will miss a blessing and the opportunity to see God do something with your life you never thought possible. Which, hopefully, will encourage you to take more steps, greater steps, and thus receive a greater blessing and it will grow your faith like you never thought possible!

These were more fair-minded than those in Thessalonica, in that they received the word with all readiness, and searched the Scriptures daily to find out whether these things were so. (Acts 17:11)

I love this verse. I mentioned before the testimony of Josh McDowell. He was in college and many of his friends would try to witness to him. He would have nothing to do with Christianity! He got so tired of them that he decided to research and prove them wrong. After much studying and research Josh, accepted Christ, it changed his life. He then, wrote a book entitled, *Evidence That Demands a Verdict*. His research led him to discover Jesus. He has written several books since.

I love the history of our country. It's founding and the early men who wrote our historical documents. There is a story of one, Blackstone I think. His judicial writings became the foundation of our legal system. There was another, I can't remember his name. This judge, by reading Blackstone's commentaries, which were loaded with Scripture, turned to Jesus as his Savior. Just by the Scripture that was included in his writings. I love it!

Godly men, versed in the word of God, becoming leaders of our country. God continues to bless those who live in God's word! Who feast on the Scriptures and have an intimate relationship with God through His word.

The biggest reason I undertook this endeavor is my love for the Bible. From the day, I was saved I have feasted on God's word. I've tried all kinds of study courses, etc. The best way to learn God's word is to spend time in it. I've heard stories of professors that will spend their lives studying God's word and still they haven't scratched the surface.

How much time do you spend in the Bible? If you read these two or three chapters, then this devotion, then pray, for those who are sick, those in leadership in your church, and of course your family members who need the Lord, I've found it can take thirty to forty-five minutes a day. Is that too much time to fellowship with your Creator? To commune with the Father of heaven and earth. With the Jesus who died for you on the cross of Calvary. Open your heart to the promptings of the Holy Spirit who lives within you to guide you and encourage you and direct your path as you walk with God.

"But none of these things move me; nor do I count my life dear to myself, so that I may finish my race with joy, and the ministry which I received from the Lord Jesus, to testify to the gospel of the grace of God. (Acts 20:24)

I have been talking about walking with God on this path of life. Paul likes to use the analogy of a race. I can't run anymore so I like to walk. Either way there is a destination we are headed for. Let me give you a couple more verses, "I have fought the good fight, I have finished my race, I have kept the faith." (2 Timothy 4:7). Then there is this picture in Hebrews, "Therefore we also, since we are surrounded by so great a cloud of witnesses, let us lay aside every weight, and the sin which so easily ensnares us and let us run with endurance the race that is set before us." (Hebrews 12:1).

I'm sure you've heard life referred to as the "rat race". It depends on your perspective. If you're in it with God at your side it can be fascinating and exciting. If not, it can be discouraging, disheartening, and seeming to take forever.

To the apostle Paul the daily events and sufferings, and trials meant nothing to him except how he ran his race. Look at 2 Corinthians 11:24-28. Paul gives a detailed list of the sufferings he endured for the gospel of grace. You could include this list in his comment above, "" But none of these things move me." At what point would you have given up? We talked yesterday about obeying the Holy Spirit. Jesus told Paul, in the very beginning, that he would suffer for the cause. Look at Acts 9:16, (Jesus speaking to Paul) "For I will show him how many things he must suffer for My name's sake." Ask yourself, what will it take for me to give up on God?

People have turned their backs on Jesus for far less than what Paul had endured. Paul was a person, no more special than any of us. Paul made a commitment on that Damascus road that he would followed Jesus to the very end. When you accept Christ as your Savior the only commitment was that Jesus would be with you the rest of your life. He asked nothing of you. You simply surrendered your life to His grace. There are no strings attached. Yet, if you decide to walk a closer walk with God you will be surprised what God will do with a willing soul!

Now as he reasoned about righteousness, self-control, and the judgment to come, Felix was afraid and answered, "Go away for now; when I have a convenient time, I will call for you." (Acts 24:25)

There is so much here. How many people think they can hear the truth and then decide in their own time. Like they are in control of when God will call them home, and how. We all have this "death-bed" scenario that when the time comes we'll just simply ask Jesus to forgive us and off to heaven we go. Can you truly say how you will die?

I heard an illustration of the difference between someone who gets saved at twenty versus someone who gets saved at sixty. The sixty yea-old missed forty years of God working, teaching, blessing, and walking in his life, he missed it! Where the twenty-year-old had who knows how many years of God's blessing, comfort, encouragement, God walking with him daily in his life. Which would you choose?

Everyone, at some point in their life will have the same opportunity as Felix did here. A chance to make a choice. I can't guarantee there will be other opportunities. There may be that one, or there may be others. We don't know. God will see that we have one!

Paul had the opportunity to witness to two kings before going to Rome. Agrippa and Felix. We may never get such an opportunity. It matters not the status of the one we tell about Jesus. It matters not whether they accept the message you share. That is the soul, responsibility of the Holy Spirit and the willingness of the hearer. Your full responsibility is to tell them. What they do with that is between them and God. Just like Felix here.

We are about to conclude our journey through the book of Acts. Have you noticed the reception Paul receives in most cities? In one he is stoned to near dead. Some think he did die. At what point would you be ready to quit? To say it's not worth this. Even if you had a calling such as Paul's. A person of note would be Mark. Follow his story in Acts. He gave up, but later he would go back to the program.

Did you notice Paul's approach to Felix? Paul spoke of the sin in Felix's life. Paul confronted him with the gospel of salvation through Jesus Christ. The work of the Holy Spirit is to "convict" that conviction leads to repentance, which leads to salvation!

> To open their eyes, in order to turn them from darkness to light, and
> from the power of Satan to God, that they may receive forgiveness
> of sins and an inheritance among those who are sanctified by faith in
> Me. (Acts 26:18)

The word that jumps out to me in this verse is "inheritance". Are you expecting an inheritance when you die? Chances are for most of us we are not. If anything, we will need to deal with funeral arrangements, and maybe debts left behind, of our kinfolk. Very rarely can we foresee any inheritance. But look what Paul says here. Paul says we, the children of God, will receive an inheritance.

Look at this verse, "In Him (Jesus) also we have obtained an inheritance, being predestined according to the purpose of Him who works all things according to the counsel of His will." (Ephesians 1:11) Here's another, "To an inheritance incorruptible and undefiled and that does not fade away, reserved in heaven for you." (1 Peter 1:4). One more if you will, "The Spirit Himself bears witness with our spirit that we are children of God, and if children, then heirs—heirs of God and joint heirs with Christ, if indeed we suffer with Him, that we may also be glorified together." (Romans 8:16-17) Chew on that verse a minute.

If God's people ever truly grasped that verse. We are joint heirs with our Savior Jesus Christ. That's why many times through these pages I refer to those who have accepted Christ as their Savior as "children of God." For such we are. As Jesus is the Son of God so we also are "adopted" into God's family through our profession of faith in Jesus. Let's look at these two verses, "For as many as are led by the Spirit of God, these are sons of God. For you did not receive the spirit of bondage again to fear, but you received the Spirit of adoption by whom we cry out. 'Abba, Father.'" Then we pick up verses 16 and 17 of Romans 8, above.

When you have yielded to the Spirit of God and have asked Jesus into your heart, you become a child of God. And as a child you are entitled to the full inheritance of the kingdom of God. "Joint heirs with Jesus!" Let that sink in a minute. You are adopted by God into His family. Do you think there is any force that could change that?

> For I am not ashamed of the gospel of Christ, for it is the power of
> God to salvation for everyone who believes, for the Jew first and also
> the Greek. (Romans 1:16)

Now, we see here what Jesus was talking about when He told Peter, "Upon this rock I will build My church." That rock is the Gospel of Jesus Christ, and/ or Jesus Himself. That is the gospel of Jesus Christ. "That whosoever believes on the name of Jesus will be saved!" (Acts 2:21) The truth of the gospel is that "Jesus saves!"

Are you afraid of being embarrassed? I told my daughters one time that they couldn't embarrass me. I'm am so confident in myself that I can't be embarrassed. And I'm confident enough in the power of God that I can't be embarrassed in sharing it with others. I will admit I'm more comfortable in a public setting, than one on one. Either way I'm willing to tell others.

Let me ask you this, why would you be embarrassed? What is there to be embarrassed about telling someone the truth? Maybe that's it. You are not confident enough that it is the truth. I hope that's not the case. You can be assured that the word of God has been proven over and over. The world, and Satan want you to doubt. That weakens your resolve and your message.

Notice in the verse above, "It is the power of God to salvation." Always remember that you are sharing with the power of God's Holy Spirit within you. The same Holy Spirit that will call to your mind, events (testimony) and Scripture that will connect with the one you are trying to reach.

Maybe a better word would be "win". When you win someone to Christ that means the devil loses! God wins! That's one less person that Satan won't be taking to hell with him. You win every time you lead someone to faith in Jesus Christ.

If anyone wasn't afraid, it was the Apostle Paul. He would walk boldly into a synagogue full of Jews and preach Jesus. Even after being stoned he got up and went right back into the town that just stoned him. (Acts 14:19-20)

I guess it's a simple question. Do you believe in the power of God or your own strength?

Now hope does not disappoint, because the love of God has been poured out in our hearts by the Holy Spirit who was given to us. For when we were still without strength, in due time Christ died for the ungodly. (Romans 5:5-6)

I remember this scene in "The Hunger Games" that has just stuck in my mind. The President asks his assistant "why do they have a winner in the Hunger Games"? Twenty-four people are sent to battle each other and the winner gets to live. Why do we have a winner? The President responded, "To give the people hope. Without hope they will die." I'm paraphrasing. The point is hope!

That's what the Apostle Paul is talking about here. The hope of one day being with Jesus in heaven. My greatest hope, of course, is to hear Jesus say, "Well done good and faithful servant; you were faithful over a few things, I will make you ruler over many things. Enter into the joy of your Lord." (Matthew 25:21)

Is this not awesome? Look what Paul says, "Because the love of God has been poured out in our hearts by the Holy Spirit." We have talked often about walking with God. Having that intimate relationship with the Father. Here is how that happens. We "listen" to that Holy Spirit within us. That Spirit of God that seals us, to be forever a child of God.

I remember the first time I left home. It was a scary feeling. I was on my own now. I had to make decisions on my own. I was responsible for the decisions I made. Our heavenly Father will never leave. We can't leave Him either. He will always be there, whether we listen or not. We can never have that feeling of being "on our own". God will always be walking beside us. So, we always have counsel in making those decisions. So, we can know we make the right ones as long as they are based on God's word.

That is something we can't grasp. It says, "For when we were still without strength, in due time Christ died for the ungodly." Here's another way to put it, "But God demonstrates His own love toward us, in that while we still sinners, Christ died for us. (Romans 5:8). Part of the Romans Road. Make a note of these verses: Romans, 3:23, 5:8, 6:23, 10:9-10, and a good close is Revelation 3:20.

"That if you confess with your mouth the Lord Jesus and believe in
your heart that God has raised Him from the dead, you will be saved.
(Romans 10:9)

The final step on our Roman's Road. Only two conditions! Confess with your
mouth, believe in your heart. What to believe? That Jesus Christ was raised
from the dead. Do you remember what Thomas refused to believe in John 20? The
disciples said they had seen Jesus after His crucifixion. Thomas wanted proof.

Did you notice the progression in the Roman's Road? In 3:23 we acknowledge
we are all sinners. Until you acknowledge your sick you will never be cured! Until
you acknowledge you're a sinner, born a sinner, born separated from God, you
will never seek a cure. Notice the word Paul uses "ALL" have fallen short of God!

In 5:8 it talks about how much God loves us. John 3:16. It was nothing we
earned! Notice he doesn't say we need to clean up our act before coming to God.
"While we were yet sinners" God came to us as a doctor to a patient seeking
healing. That is the picture. God acknowledges our sinful condition and wants
to rectify it.

In Romans 6:23, here God explains the consequences of our sin. Separation
from God. Wages are compensation for work done. The compensation for our sin
condition is eternity in hell. Notice also the cost of this redemption, "gift" there is
nothing we can do or give to buy our way before God. The gift is free to us but it
cost God the life of His Son Jesus.

And finally, the verse above. You might want to include verse 10 as well, "For
with the heart one believes unto righteousness, and with the mouth confession is
made unto salvation." That's interesting. Do you see any mention of the head or
mind? Knowledge is nowhere to be seen. We can know the Bible front and back,
memorize all sorts of Scripture but if God isn't in our "heart" it matters not!

I was thinking this morning. Baptism is supposed to be our outward
demonstration of the commitment we made to God for our salvation. We
have accepted God's gift of salvation through His Son. And we are making
that commitment public. How is going to church different? It is an outward
demonstration of what is in our heart.

> I beseech you therefore brethren, by the mercies of God, that you present your bodies a living sacrifice, holy, acceptable to God, which is your reasonable service. And be not conformed to this world, but be transformed by the renewing of your mind, that you may prove what is that good and acceptable and perfect will of God. (Romans 12:1-2)

These verses are very important and personal to me. As a young Christian, our pastor asked me to lead an opening ceremony prior to the Sunday school hour and I was to encourage attenders to memorize Romans 12. These two verses have stuck with me ever-sense. More important, that helped me become comfortable and confident speaking from the pulpit. I'm not sure, if it wasn't for this weekly presentation, that I would have ever had the opportunity to pastor a church.

There is so much in these verses. Of course, one that a lot of preachers like to use, "have you ever seen a *living sacrifice?*" Remember back in Leviticus? Do you ever remember reading that the sacrifice that was brought to the altar was still alive? That's Paul's point. You are alive and therefore God wants to use you for something special. He has a purpose, but you must be willing to sacrifice self!

Think about this. If God created you to be saved. That was your whole purpose for being here. Why doesn't He take you home after you've been saved? Because, of course, there is more for you to do, a lot more. He didn't save you to sit but to serve.

Let me finish my thought from yesterday. Baptism is our outward demonstration that we have accepted Christ as our Savior. That is the only purpose for baptism. Not our salvation but a display of the decision we have made. Isn't attending church the same thing? Meeting with God once a week to praise and worship Him. To demonstrate our commitment to His work here on earth. A public display of what is in our heart!

Don't overlook verse 2. What do you suppose Paul means by being conformed to this world? It could go back to the point preceding this. The world likes to tell us we don't need church. That's like telling a car it doesn't need gas, really?

Please chew on these two verses a while! They are awesome!

For whatever things were written before were written for our learning,
that we through the patience and comfort of the Scriptures might have
hope. (Romans 15:4)

What do you think Paul was referring to? Remember there was no "Bible" at
that time. Paul was talking about the Old Testament as it existed at the
time. The Psalms the Prophets, the books of Moses the words that God passed
down to these men that God chose to reveal His plan for mankind. No wonder
Jesus talked so much about them. Remember Matthew? Matthew quotes and
refers to the Scriptures numerous times in his gospel.

If we really understood the fact that what we hold in our hand very the Word
from God, I wonder if it would really make a difference.

I asked once in my newsletter, The Ekklesia, if anyone knew of any gold or
silver in their house. I don't know if you noticed or not, but if you've bought a new
Bible recently the outside of the pages is covered with either gold or silver. For
some of us the pages are still stuck together, that's sad. I hope this devotional will
cure that. Anyway, does the gold or silver still exist on the pages of your Bible? I
am hoping that those colors have been worn off from use. Are they?

Why did Paul say these writings were preserved for us today? "for our
learning." I don't think I'm very far off when I refer to the Bible as a textbook.
God passed these teachings down to us, through various authors for one reason.
For our learning! To translate these teachings into our everyday life. To apply them
to our lives in a way that makes a difference.

There's that word "hope" again. Hope in what? Hope in our eternal fellowship
with the God of creation. The Father who loves us so much that He desires a daily
walk in His presence through the person of the Holy Spirit, walking with us all
day, every day, bringing peace, comfort, encouragement, strength and wisdom to
face our daily challenges in life.

I hope you have stayed with me through this journey. We are almost through.
One more month to go. Still several books and verses to explore. I hope you are
keeping a journal of the verses that have spoken to you and maybe made some notes
on these verses. What has God revealed to you through this journey?

But as it is written: "Eye has not seen, nor ear heard, nor have entered into the heart of man the things which God has prepared for those who love Him." (1 Corinthians 2:9)

Have you seen the movies? Different movies about "out-of-body" experiences, about people visiting heaven? Do you think Hollywood could begin to capture what heaven is really like? Don't miss the condition of this experience! "prepared for those who love Him." A relationship with God begins there.

We are at the end of November. I don't want to let this month go by without saying something about Thanksgiving. Isn't this a curious holiday? First, for some, it begins the Christmas shopping season. We almost ignore the holiday by focusing on Christmas. It is a national holiday. That means our government thinks it's important enough to pause and give thanks to the God who created us. Not only created us but by a miracle, lead certain Christians to venture to America and establish a country built on the precepts of Scripture!

Notice what Paul says, "as it is written" referring of course to the Old Testament. No New Testament now, our Bible, here Paul was quoting Isaiah 64:4, "For since the beginning of the world men have not heard nor perceived by the ear, nor has the eye seen any God besides You, who acts for the one who waits for Him." Paul taking some liberties with the original text. It's kind of how we memorize verses. Be careful we don't get TOO far off the text!

You get the point Paul was making?

It's a shame we skip over the third chapter of this book. That chapter was the inspiration for a Sunday school attendance program I had developed. Let me encourage you to spend some time in that chapter (3). Let me quote one verse if I may, "For no other foundation can anyone lay than that which was laid which is Jesus Christ." With this verse let me refer you to the first chapter of John. Remember how John described Jesus? Later he would call Him the Lamb of God, but here, look at verse 14, "And the Word became flesh and dwelt among us, and we beheld His glory as the only begotten of the Father, full of grace and truth." And the Word became flesh, Jesus was called the Word of God, God's message to us!

> Yet for us there is one God, the Father, of whom are all things, and we for Him; and one Lord Jesus Christ, through whom are all things, and through whom we live. (1 Corinthians 8:6)

What a tough verse. That's not true of the world today. There are hundreds of gods today. Social media is creating gods every day. The political world, Hollywood, the sports scene. You want a god, take your pick? But, look what this verse says! There is one God. The same God that created the heavens and the earth. Can any of these other gods claim that? How about this, can any of these other gods claim that they were willing to die for your sins? Have they?

You might be able to have a personal relationship with some of these other gods, but do they know your heart? Do they know what is going to happen next week? Can they change what is going to happen next week? The gods we created are so limited by our own limitations as humans. Yet there is a God who knows our heart. Who cares about our life, so much so that He will move heaven and earth to provide for your needs. The problem today is we don't know what we need, only what we want!

Catch that last part? "through whom we live." Do we? What do you think it means to "live" through Jesus? There is a constant battle going on for the supremacy of our heart. Who will reign? Who has control of our lives? Really, it's our choice, isn't it? God won't force Himself into our lives or against our will. We must "allow" Him to control our lives. That is so hard to do! Yet, if we are to have God's best He must be in control. You know what that takes? It takes faith!

Who is in control of your life? O.k, you're a Christian, how much control does God have in your daily walk? Who is leading in the walk on the path of life? The path is narrow, there is only room for one at a time. Single-file. Again, who is leading? If your leading how far back on the trail is God? Can you hear His instructions, or do you even care?

Paul is writing to a pagan city in Corinth. Every street corner has a god, or idol. Here comes Paul with another God. Why should they listen to him? Why should they listen to you? Is there any proof in your life that God is in control? Do you have a testimony that will draw people to your message? Think about it.

No temptation has overtaken you except such as is common to man; but God is faithful, who will not allow you to be tempted beyond what you are able, but with the temptation will also make the way to escape, that you may be able to bear it. (1 Corinthians 10:13)

Right now, I'm reading a book by Charles Stanley on temptation. He makes a good point. It's not a sin to be tempted. Jesus was tempted. The sin is in giving in to that temptation. The sin, is losing the battle of wills between you and the devil. The devil's goal is for you to trip up. To ruin your testimony, so others will not listen to you. If he can do that he's won a battle. The thing is he hasn't won the war. God will pick us up, put us back on track and restore our relationship with Him if we confess and repent!

Have you ever said to God, "You don't understand"? That's the point Paul is making here. We have no right to say that because Jesus endured all the temptations we have faced, and yet did not sin! That can give us courage. It's interesting to see the method Jesus used to conquer these temptations—the word of God. Matthew chapter 4. Three times Satan tempted Jesus, all the temptations wrapped up in three, the lust of the flesh (hunger), the lust of the eye (all the kingdoms), and the pride of life (He will rule). Each was answered with a passage from Exodus.

We, as Christians, will never fully grasp the power in the word of God. We are too lazy to spend an hour a day in God's word. It only takes maybe twenty minutes to read the chapters listed above. The rest of the hour can be spent in prayer and mediating on what God said. Read Joshua 1:8.

Did you notice where the power to overcome these temptations comes from, beside the word of God. God will give us a way out! His Spirit will give us the strength, through God's word, to find the exit. To find the solution, the way out, of this temptation. It must be done in God's strength! We are no match for the wiles of the devil. He has had so much practice, since the Garden of Eden. Remember how he tricked Eve? He got her to question God's spoken word.

What are you battling right now? Are you ready to give up? I hope not. Have you asked God for wisdom and strength? Try it!

Yet in the church I would rather speak five words with my understanding, that I may teach others also, then ten thousand words in a tongue.
(1 Corinthians 14:19)

I'm not going to get into the "tongues" thing. That's not the point of this devotion. Notice how important it was for Paul that the message be loud and clear in the church. You start talking about teaching and you're in my territory!

As a Sunday school leader and teacher for thirty years I have my thoughts and stories about the Sunday School Ministry. One illustration I used was that of a miner panning for gold. The Sunday school class is like the miner's pan. In each year, I discovered that a class will have double its average attendance pass through that class. Visitors, looking for a class that fits their need. As different ones pass through your class it's just like the miner's pan. The trick for that teacher, and the church, is to find those "nuggets" that God can use in His kingdom. Those who will one day mature into servants that want to serve God.

That's just an illustration. I've already told you about 1 Corinthians 3. One year it was the Olympics. Using that as a seed thought I came up with seven attendance awards, Diamond, Pearl, Gold, Silver, Bronze, Oak and Cedar. As awards for attendance. I think those who received them, liked them. Many were surprised that anyone recognized their faithfulness, which was the point.

I think what I'm trying to achieve here is an awareness of the importance of the Sunday School Ministry. It is really the "outreach" arm of the church. The "small group" opportunity that gives members and visitors the opportunity to share and be a part of a small group that encourages, prays, and supports members in ways the "congregation" can't.

Jesus in Matthew 28 exhorted His disciples to go into all the world and teach. To teach God must give you that gift. If you have tried it, and don't like it fine. There are so many with that gift who are afraid to try. Too shy? If you ever trust God and take that step you will find a ministry that will bless you to no end! I once taught a youth class in two different churches. It is so exciting to see those who used to be in my class serving the Lord.

> But thanks be to God, who gives us the victory through our Lord Jesus Christ. Therefore, my beloved brethren, be steadfast, immovable, always abounding in the work of the Lord, knowing that your labor is not in vain in the Lord. (1 Corinthians 15:57-58)

You talk about encouragement! Why would Paul so encourage his followers this way? When you look at the early church life. They needed encouragement. Pagan statutes, pagan rituals, eat this meat, not that meat, etc. So much confusion in the early church. Remember they didn't have the Bible as we know it then. Paul was writing letters to the various churches, some he started himself. Churches dealing with so many false teachers. I can see them devouring Paul's letters when they came.

If anybody was, steadfast, immovable always abounding in the work of the Lord, it was Paul. I think we need to take a minute and think about this "work of the Lord" thing. Just what does that mean? Most might think it means pastor or deacon. No, No! It can mean so much more!

Our church, the last few years, has started a basketball program on Saturdays for children. It gets bigger and bigger every year. An opportunity to reach families through their youngsters. My wife and I came to salvation from our daughters riding a church bus to church. I'm in the ministry because a pastor would not let me sit and occupy a space. There are so many opportunities and needs in the local church it's amazing. Our pastor's passion is getting new members "connected" in a ministry of some kind in our church. That's what serving is all about. Serving the Lord in His church.

If I thought a while I could fill a book about those who I've met who are willing to give a few minutes, a week, of their time to help in the church. That's a ministry. Whether it's cleaning the church on Saturday, handing out bulletins on Sunday, teaching a class, you name it—it's ministry! I knew a lady once, I took her class when she retired, who taught Sunday school for over fifty years. Faithful on the Lord's day to be at her post expounding the precious word of Truth! I think she is 103 now. Jesus said, be faithful in a few things I will make you ruler over many things. (Matthew 25:23) That's awesome!

> You are our epistle written in our hearts, known and read by all men;
> clearly you are an epistle of Christ, ministered by us, written not with
> ink but by the Spirit of the living God, not on tablets of stone but on
> tablets of flesh, that is of the heart. (2 Corinthians 3:2-3)

As Christian's we have the word of God to grow better in our understanding of God and how to have a closer relationship with God. But you see God isn't through writing yet. The apostle Paul realized something that most of us never come to know. God is active today writing more and more of His gospel in our hearts. Every time God does something in our lives He writes it down in our hearts. To reflect and enjoy until we meet Him in heaven.

How much of an epistle (letter) has God written in your heart? A couple of paragraphs, a chapter, how about a whole book, maybe even volumes. The neat thing about that is that you can read it anytime night or day. Just reflect on your life and notice the times that God was there in a special way. Boy, how quickly we forget that special day we asked Jesus into our heart. God began that day writing love notes in our heart to reflect on, when we have a down day, a discouraging day, maybe even a great day we get to praise God for His presence!

Paul is reminding those whom he had opportunity to minister to that he has left an impact on their lives. He has touched their hearts, just as he would expect them to minister to those they meet. Each sharing the blessings God did through their willingness to serve God.

God is always trying to make a greater impact on our heart. We begin as little children, no matter what age we are saved. Then He teaches, encourages, strengthen and stretches us till He has shown us His power through His Holy Spirit. It is truly amazing what God can do with someone who trusts Him enough to put their whole life in God's hands.

Every New Year's I praise God and thank Him for what He has done this past year and so look forward to what He is going to do in the year to come. I look with anticipation at the miracles He is going to perform, and be privileged enough to see His handy work. Why, because I've seen it before and will see it all through the years ahead!

Do you look at things according to the outward appearance? If anyone is convinced in himself that he is Christ's, let him again consider this in himself, that just as he is Christ's, even so we are Christ's. (2 Corinthians 10:7)

That "outward appearance" can be so deceiving. I wonder what the scribes and Pharisees thought when they heard this disciple of Jesus walking around and teaching the things of God.

I think I mentioned that I'm a "people watcher" you don't have to go to a mall or a super market. Just watching family and friends react to comments and things, especially "spiritual" things. Just watch their reaction. I've learned that you can learn so much just by watching. Now be careful, like Paul says, you don't get caught up in "outward appearances" many times we want to judge a person's heart by outward appearances.

The Bible says you can tell someone's heart by what comes out of their mouth (Matthew 15:11). Ever wonder why God gave two ears and one mouth? Now you know. It never hurts to just listen sometimes. Have you ever talked to someone who isn't listening to you but planning what they will say next? Have no idea what you just said, but they are ready to come back with a comment. They aren't listening, they are planning.

Like Paul says, the important thing is if Christ is in their heart. A Christian, through God's Spirit, can tell when someone is not in the family. They can say all the right things but the Spirit isn't there! There is lacking a relationship that is evident in the speech. If we listen!

Have you noticed what Paul "boasts" about in his letters? The things he has suffered in his ministry. How many times he went through hard times. Now understand Paul is not "boasting" these are Paul's credentials! These are testimonies to his authority, maybe his badge of honor. We might call it bragging but Paul always gives the glory to God. Glory to God for suffering? Paul has a right to use his suffering to glorify God.

What has God done in your life that you could tell others what God has done? How much has He changed your life, or has He? Has He given you any new habits? Taken away some bad habits? Changed your "want-to" I hope His Spirit is speaking to you right now!

> For though He was crucified in weakness, yet He lives by the power
> of God. For we also are weak in Him, but we shall live with Him by
> the power of God toward you. (2 Corinthians 13:4)

This was a thought I had once, until I thought it over. If you remember when the centurion came to the three crosses to remove the prisoners. The two on either side of Jesus had to have their legs broken so they would die quicker. Jesus was already dead. I thought He was weak. But remember prior to His crucifixion He was beaten near to death before He was hung on the cross. Besides, if His legs were broken He would not have been a suitable sacrifice (Leviticus).

But notice that His resurrection and life after His death on the cross was through the power of God. That same power that we have access to as children of God. So many Christians today feel they are hopeless and helpless. They have never really trusted God to get out of their "comfort zone." That's why they call it a "comfort" zone.

Until we can trust in the same power that raised Jesus from the dead we will never fully understand what it means to be a Christian. Think about how much faith it takes to give ten percent of your income to God. Now we are talking real faith here. Time, we can give. Encouragement, etc. But money, that's just going too far. Where is your faith in God's promise in Malachi 3:10?

Do you remember what Jesus told Pilate? "You could have no power at all against Me unless it had been given you from above. Therefore, the one who delivered Me to you has the greater sin." (John 19:11) The true power comes from God. Do you think God would allow anything to come upon His children that God is not in control of? You need to read the first couple of chapters of Job. God is in control, concerning His children, whether we believe it or not.

Remember that Jesus went to the Garden and prayed that this would pass? Imagine the hurt that God felt when He had to tell His Son that this was necessary. And then to watch what man would do to His Son. It's just amazing the love that God had, not only for His Son but also for us, in order to allow that to happen that we might have a relationship with our heavenly Father. What love!

Are you trusting God today for whatever happens?

> I have been crucified with Christ; it is no longer I who live, but Christ lives in me; and the life which I now live in the flesh I live by faith in the Son of God, who loved me and gave Himself for me. (Galatians 2:20)

This verse brings back so many memories. I hadn't been saved very long. Someone mentioned a "life verse". I came across this verse that spoke to me so strongly as a baby Christian. I claimed the verse. My daughter then told me, "Oh dad, that is a chorus we sing." It didn't deter me. I was drawn to this verse. Do you know the chorus?

The part, as a young Christian, that I loved was, "Christ lives in me, and the life which I now live in the flash I live by faith in the Son of God," If a Christian ever realizes that significant fact "God lives within us" through the Holy Spirit. It will change their life! Absorb these verses in the New Testament. They will change your life.

I have three life verses. Each touching me at different times in my Christian walk. This one of course, Galatians 2:20. As I struggled with learning to wait on God and trust Him daily I found Isaiah 40:31. That also was a chorus we sang. It's interesting that music plays such a vital part in our Christian walk! Then finally today it is Jeremiah 29:11-13. Even at seventy to realize that God has a specific plan for me is just exciting!

What does this portion mean to you? "I have been crucified with Christ, nevertheless I live." Remember we talked about Romans 12:1. "A living sacrifice"? Christ was our sacrifice for our sin on the cross. He paid for our sin as if we were crucified instead. So, what are we to do as "living" sacrifices? We are to serve not sit! There is work, to be done. God has created us to accomplish certain things in our life. If we refuse we are the ones missing out on the blessing. As God created us with a free will to obey or rebel we have that option. It's our choice. But don't forget the consequences are ours also!

Do you have a life verse? Why not? You haven't spent much time in God's word if you haven't. As you read there will be verses that just jump out at you. Don't hurry it. Just read. The power of God's word is amazing. I don't know how many times I had read Jeremiah 29. Then one day it just grabbed me and shook me! Find your verse!

> But when the fullness of time had come, God sent forth His Son, born of a woman, born under the law, to redeem those who were under the law, that we might receive the adoption as sons. (Galatians 4:4-5)

I love this! If you study history, I've heard it taught that Roman culture and their road system and all that goes into that. This was the "perfect" time for the Messiah to arrive. Just as the verse says. God's timing is perfect! God worked for hundreds of years to the right place at the right time. Remember that Israel (southern kingdom) was taken into captivity. God had to bring them back and develop a Jewish state for the birth of His Son. Herod had to proclaim a census to bring the Messiah's mother to Bethlehem. All in God's perfect plan.

My Bible says the psalms were written 1,000 years before Christ. Look at psalm 22. Do you see anything that might make you think of Jesus? Of course, you do. Look at verses 14-18. This was hundreds of years before the Romans devised crucifixion. Don't forget the words that Jesus quoted from the cross in verse one.

Don't miss the end of this verse. "that we might receive the adoption as sons." What better way to describe the relationship we have with our heavenly Father. It's great!

That's one of the reasons it's important to read the Old Testament. It builds a foundation so that when you get to the New Testament you understand a whole lot more. It removes some of the fog surrounding the New Testament passages. Paul even refers to the Old Testament in this verse. "born of a woman, born under the law, to redeem those who were under the law." If you remember your reading in Acts about Paul's argument against forcing Christians to obey the Jewish laws. It was very vehement to Peter and James and the Jerusalem Council. (Acts 15)

Just as God's timing was perfect to introduce His Son into the world. Remember Jesus' public ministry was only three and a half years. Less than our presidential term. Look what God accomplished in that short of time. It's important that we keep "time" in perspective. I have even started underlining, in the book of Acts, words that tell the length of time for certain events. We can read over them and not understand the time span that took place. It's important. Sometimes Paul spent "years" in certain locals. We need to note that!

For by grace you have been saved through faith, and that not of
yourselves; it is the gift of God, not of works, lest anyone should
boast. (Ephesians 2:8-9)

These verses are so important. Key Christian doctrine is wrapped up in these
two verses. If you were to have two sets of verses to base your Christian walk
these are so key. Try these, Proverbs 3:5-6 and These two here, Ephesians 2:8-9.
What do these two here tell us. There is NOTHING we can do to earn, buy,
inherit, grow our salvation. It is a "gift of God". Did you see why? Because it is
nothing we did, it is all Jesus. We can't boast of our good works (deeds) or our
standing in the world, it is all Jesus!

How would you define grace? There is an acronym "God's riches at Christ
expense." that's all well and good but does it explain grace? Grace is exactly what I
said in the previous paragraph. If there was one thing, you name it, that we needed
to do to "earn" our salvation it wouldn't be grace. Grace is the free will of God that
grants us a relationship with the Almighty simply because God desires it.

Have you ever had someone say, "When I get my act together then I'll come to
Jesus!" That's not grace. God will take us just as we are, in our worst condition and
transform us through the power of His Holy Spirit and make us a new creation.
Look at this verse, "Therefore, if anyone is in Christ, he is a new creation; old things
have passed away; behold all things have become new." (2 Corinthians 5:17) Now,
can you tell me where it says that we are to "clean up" before coming to Christ?
God does the cleaning up!

That is where grace comes in. Our society is based on merit. You work your
way up to a certain level, either in education, physically, talent, etc. Then you
have "achieved" that pinnacle, then you have "earned" that status. The Bible says,
"Whoever calls on the name of the Lord shall be saved." (Romans 10:13).

Don't skip over these two verses. Paul gives a clear picture of our salvation.
It's ours for the asking. It is so hard for us to accept that today. We MUST pay for
what we receive. Excuse me, but the price has already been paid. All the money or
deeds in the world could not accomplish what Jesus did on the cross!

And He gave some to be apostles, some prophets, some evangelists, and some pastors and teachers, for the equipping of the saints for the work of ministry, for the edifying of the body of Christ. (Ephesians 4:11-12)

Would you like a "job description" for a pastor, deacon, Sunday school worker, someone who serves in the church? Here it is! Paul even lists some positions. We might think this is for leadership positions, it's not. Notice the goal? "Equipping the saints for the work of ministry" Did you notice, I'm not splitting hairs here, but notice what Paul said, "for the work of ministry" not for the work of a ministry. There is a difference. "Ministry" is any job in the church or outside the church that teaches the love of God through a relationship with Jesus.

You could be working in a food pantry, serving food. You could be helping in a youth project to minister to the homeless. Any opportunity to help someone in need is "ministry". Look at this from Jesus, "For I was hungry and you gave Me food; I was thirsty and you gave Me drink; I was a stranger and you took Me in; I was naked and you clothed Me; I was sick and you visited Me; I was in prison and you came to Me. Then the righteous will answer Him, saying, 'Lord, when did we see You hungry and feed You, etc. And the King will answer and say to them, 'Assuredly, I say to you, inasmuch as you did it to one of the least of these My brethren, you did it to Me." (Matthew 25:35-40.) That is ministry!

My favorite part of the verse at the top is, "for the equipping of the saints" You see? That's our calling. To pass on to others what God has blessed us with and teach others that God can bless them as well. Don't you like that Paul calls us "saints" isn't that cool. Two purposes listed here: "equipping saints, edifying the body." That's part of that teaching thing.

We can "edify" in so many ways. In your Sunday school class have you ever had someone give a testimony of what God did in their life last week? Of course, you have, or you will. That's edifying! Anytime we can give testimony of God working in our life, good or bad, we are edifying the saints! God is working all around us and we need to share that with fellow believers, and unbelievers too for that matter!

Be anxious for nothing, but in everything by prayer and supplication with thanksgiving, let your requests be made known to God; and the peace of God, which surpasses all understanding, will guard your hearts and minds through Christ Jesus. (Philippians 4:6-7)

Do you know what "anxious for nothing" means? Stop worrying! Can you do that? Whenever I must go somewhere that I've never been I love to have someone who knows the way, lead the way. Then I can follow without worrying whether I'll get lost or not. There is a peace in that confidence. The same is true with following Jesus. He knows where WE are going. If we just relax and allow Him to lead the traveling is so much easier!

Did you notice something in this verse? It doesn't guarantee that God will GRANT our prayer. It just says that God will give us a peace about the matter. Too many times we not only want to pray about something but we want to tell God how to answer it. The point is we don't "let go". If it remains in our hands God will not touch it. Until we can learn to let go we will not see an answer!

Did you notice what kind of peace God will give us? "Surpasses all understanding!" Here we go! Getting out of that box, out of our comfort zone. I think the closest time we may have experienced that kind of peace was when we asked Jesus into our heart. Remember that feeling? Just a calm assurance that God was now in control of our life and not us. Truly a peace that passes all understanding!

Don't overlook that big word at the beginning, "everything" that means everything. God wants to be so involved in our life that we talk to Him about every little detail. He wants that intimate relationship that He can have with us because He knows our heart. He knows our needs as well but He would love for us to share them with Him. Trust Him, trust His direction and the leadership of His Holy Spirit!

Digest this verse a minute. Read it two or three times. Meditate on what God is trying to tell us.

Then ask yourself, "what am I worried about"? Can I give it to God and trust Him to take care of it? Remember Matthew 9:29b, "according to your faith be it unto you." How would you measure your assurance that God knows where He is going?

Let the word of Christ dwell in you richly in all wisdom, teaching and admonishing one another in psalms and hymns and spiritual songs, singing with grace in your hearts to the Lord. And whatever you do in word or deed, do all in the name of the Lord Jesus, giving thanks to God the Father through Him. (Colossians 3:16-17)

Wow! There is so much here! What do you think Paul meant when he said, "Let the word of Christ dwell in you richly"? The word of Christ I'm sure meant the Scriptures, but how would that dwell in you "richly"? Do you look forward to your quiet time each morning? I hope God has blessed this time we have had together. I know God's word has blessed you. I'm not big on memorizing. I'm seventy-one and my days of memorizing are past. Although as I type these devotions certain words or phrases will come to my mind and with the help of my concordance I look them up and share them.

God's word has been such an important part of my ministry. Within six months of being saved at thirty-five I was teaching a Sunday school class of high-school boys. I've been teaching ever sense. I love God's word! The riches of God's wisdom are right there! You must work at digging it out and applying it to your life.

My voice is almost gone from medicine I've been taking. When I go to worship service I still open my hymnal and mouth the words. I love the hymns. There is so much theology in those hymns. Remember my first two "life verses" were chorus our church sang. "Singing with grace in your hearts to the Lord." That's what is important, singing to the Lord!

I'm sure you noticed that word "whatever" in this verse. Everything we do at home, at work, at church, or "whatever" we do in word or deed do all to the glory of God. What a motto to live by. If we would filter our words and deeds through God's will for us, it would change a lot of things. Remember WWJD? "What Would Jesus Do"? Used to be a popular thing with the youth. I guess people realized they would have to study their Bible's to find out what Jesus would do, so it kind of faded away.

Here's another couple of verses to add to the MUST KNOW book we are keeping, maybe even a journal of God's truth!

> For the Lord Himself will descend from heaven with a shout, with the
> voice of an archangel, and with the trumpet of God. And the dead in
> Christ will rise first. Then we who are alive and remain shall be caught
> up together with them in the clouds to meet the Lord in the air. And
> thus, we shall always be with the Lord. (1 Thessalonians 4:16-17)

I wasn't sure about using these verses, it's a long passage. But you can't really pass on Thessalonians without embracing these verses. It's like every Christian's dream. I can't resist an old joke: "You know why the dead in Christ rise first? They have further to go. Ok, that's done.

These verses, by Paul were meant to encourage the early church. Remember, at the time they were expecting Jesus any day. Each generation asks, "Is this the generation". I teased my daughter once about this might be the time. She said, "Oh, no daddy, not till after I graduate!" Well there's a far more important reason why God is putting it off because He can. God wants every possible soul that can be saved to be saved!

Later in chapter five Paul tells the believers, "For you yourselves know perfectly that the day of the Lord so comes as a thief in the night." (5:2). I hope you have seen the "Left Behind" movie with Kirk Cameron. It's just a glimpse of the panic that will occur when suddenly millions of people just disappear. Imagine the panic. The timing is totally up to God, even Jesus doesn't know the time appointed!

That's perfect! Because we can't keep putting it off. Even though many do. It's still a case that when you stand before God IT'S TOO LATE! You have already made your choice. It's only by God's grace that Jesus hasn't come by now. Can you remember how many men in history, in recent years, were thought to be the Anti-Christ? From Hitler to Ronald Reagan to Kennedy, etc. Always looking for a sign.

Jesus gave us a lot of signs in Matthew 25, and other passages. When we think this world couldn't get any worse God seems to send a revival of some kind, to buy us a little more time. But it's running out!

"Therefore comfort one another with these words." The only ones these words will comfort are those who are adopted into the family of God through salvation in Jesus Christ. Those have their destiny sealed by the promise of God in Romans 10:9-10.

> And the grace of our Lord was exceedingly abundant, with faith and love which are in Christ Jesus. This is a faithful saying and worthy of all acceptance, that Christ Jesus came into the world to save sinners, of whom I am chief. (1 Timothy 1:14-15)

Do you remember our talking about measuring faith? Can you say the same about grace? I think not. Grace is all or none. There are no "degrees" of grace.

I was driving home from work one afternoon. Nearing retirement and just wanted work over with. I was speeding, cutting in and out, not signaling, no seat belt, etc. This Highway Patrolman had been following me for several miles. He finally had to use his siren to get my attention. When he came up to the truck HE WAS HOT! He took my license and insurance and went back to his vehicle.

All kinds of scenarios went through my mind. He was going to take my license right there. I would get fired for not being able to get to work. Trying to work out the inevitable punishment. I was thinking, "Why did you let this happen?" Finally, the officer comes back with my ticket.

The officer says, "I'm not going to give you a ticket. If you get pulled over in the next year I will add these 5 violations to your sentence." He gave my license and insurance card back and I left. From that day forward I was a changed driver. Seat belt, speed limit, turn signals, the works! God's grace was the lesson of the day!

God's grace is not receiving what we deserve! That lesson that day totally transformed my driving. I asked a question once at a men's breakfast using this illustration. The Question was, "How has grace changed your life?" God's grace, the realization of it, should change your life and your relationship with God.

Did you catch that last line? "Of whom I am chief." This is the apostle Paul! The one God used to bring the gospel message throughout Europe. "A chief sinner?" This is the same apostle Paul who threaten prison, and sought Christians, lead in the stoning of Stephen. Basically, persecuted the church of Jesus without mercy. The same apostle Paul who experienced God's grace to the fullest! Have you experienced God's grace? How has it changed your life?

> Let no one despise your youth, but be an example to the believers in word, in conduct, in love, in spirit, in faith, in purity. Till I come, give attention to reading, to exhortation, to doctrine. (1 Timothy 4:12-13)

"Woulda, coulda, shoulda" Ever use that phrase? Ever think back to your youth and thought, "If I knew then, what I know now." That thought often crosses my mind. I made a profession of faith at ten years old, in a Salvation Army church. What if the church or my parents had encouraged me at that point? Instead I wasted 25 years until God got a hold of me and changed my life. We all have those forks in our past and, maybe wonder, what if I had chosen, a different path?

So, how much good does that do? Does it change anything in the past? Does it change anything today? Maybe a lesson learned. How about your walk with God? Is, there things you wish you had done different? Can you change it now? I think the point of this verse is, we can't change the past we need to focus on the NOW and think about moving forward in God's grace!

I think every generation looks at the next generation and says, "There is no hope!" That's sad. You might ask yourself what are you doing to change that? Just because we might be retired doesn't mean we can't make a difference.

Many times, when I teach the older adults in our church, I think, why am I teaching them? They know as much if not more than I. Then I think about encouraging them to be a testimony to their grand-children, etc. We can always make an impact on those around us, no matter the age. That's part of what Paul is getting at.

Don't despise those youthful years, build on them. Use the lessons you've learned to teach the next generation. Share your "lessons learned" with those who might learn from your mistakes. Those examples can be great teaching tools that might touch some youth and put on the right track!

Our pastor shared some things he did as a young adult that he wasn't proud of, then he shared about his conversion. We can't sink so low that God's hand can't reach down and lift us to an intimate relationship with our heavenly Father. Forget the past, it's past. Trust God!

All Scripture is given by inspiration of God, and is profitable for doctrine, for reproof, for correction, for instruction in righteousness, that the man of God might be complete, thoroughly equipped for every good work. (2 Timothy 3:16-17)

Here is a verse to underline and make a note of in your memory! I usually have a hard time finding it because I can't ever remember if it's 1 Timothy or 2 Timothy but I know close enough to find it. This is such a key verse. The authority this gives to the inspiration of Scripture. Whether it's Isaiah, Jonah, Psalms, Proverbs, Malachi, Matthew, Luke, or James it's ALL God breathed. In other word's it all comes from God! It is so important to keep that in mind as you read!

Profitable? Joshua 1:8, Jeremiah 29:11-13, Genesis 39:3, Proverbs 22:7 God wants His children to have good success! Why, it is all to God's glory! It's not just the word that is prosperous, it's obedience to it. You have all the counsel in the world, by the greatest experts of our day. Unless you apply and obey their counsel it doesn't matter!

"That the man (or woman) of God may be equipped!" How many degrees do you have hanging on your wall? What do they accomplish unless you apply the knowledge gained for these degrees. The same is true with God's word. I said it before, you can memorize the whole Bible but until you act on that knowledge it simply takes up space in your mind.

Doctrine, reproof, correction, instruction, action words. They are the pathway to the abundant life that Jesus promises! Look at this, Jesus said, "The thief does not come except to steal, and to kill, and to destroy. I have come that they may have life, and that they may have it more abundantly." (John 10:10). God wants the best for His children! Who is the thief in this verse? Satan of course. Satan doesn't want us to prosper, he wants us miserable, to turn our back on God. If we do, he wins!

This is one of those key verses to remember the authority behind what we have been doing all this year. Reading the word of God and, hopefully, ingesting some of these truths into our lives, into our daily thinking and actions. Like I said, "But ye doers of the word, and not hearers only, deceiving yourselves!" (James 1:22).

> For the word of God is living and powerful, and sharper than any
> two-edged sword, piercing even to the division of soul and spirit, and
> of joints and marrow, and is a discerner of the thoughts and intents
> of the heart. (Hebrews 4:12)

Kool! Another verse on the word of God. You might want to take a minute and reread the Gospel of John 1:14. I don't think there is a book with the power of the Bible. Look what this verse says, "piercing even to the division of the soul and spirit!" I truly believe that is why so many people really spend so little time in the Bible. It convicts them. It tells them that there IS a God and who loves them and wants a relationship with them. They would rather keep God at arm's length. Only talk or worship on Sunday, if that.

Look what else we don't like about the Bible, "and is a discerner of the thoughts and intents of the heart." There's that word heart again. You see God bypasses the brain, the knowledge and goes straight to the heart, the seat of our emotions. God knows what's going on there. He can pierce through the mask and reach into our inner thoughts. Another reason to stay away, too convicting!

Oh, I don't want to dwell on the negatives of reading the Bible. If you have made it this far this year I'm proud of you! It's been a long journey through some tough passages but you have stayed true. I hope you will see this journey to the end.

I wanted to give a word of caution about here. Christmas is a week away. I'm sure you're caught up in the stress and excitement of the schedule for the Christmas celebration. Take this time, right here, take a breath. Open your heart to God. Ask Him for a special measure of peace through this season. Ask Him to help keep you focused on Him, not all the distractions. Keep your focus on Him and finish this journey. Walking with God in the lead, along this path, this journey that I know God has blessed already!

I hope our journey has given you a new appreciation for God's word, and I want to encourage you now, when the year is finished, that you go back to Genesis 1:1 and begin again. God will show you amazing things every year you make this journey. Verses you have read over and over will suddenly come to life!

This hope we have as an anchor of the soul, both sure and steadfast, and which enters the Presence behind the veil, where the forerunner has entered for us, even Jesus, having become High Priest forever according to the order of Melchizedek. (Hebrews 6:19-20)

Unless you have read the Old Testament, you would not know what the author (unknown) means about the veil. What would Jesus have to do with a veil? Look at Matthew 27:51, Then behold, the veil of the temple was torn in two from top to bottom; and the earth quaked, and the rocks were split. This occurred at the time of Christ's crucifixion. Now look at the Old Testament creation of that veil, You, shall make a veil woven of blue, purple, and scarlet thread, and fine woven linen. It shall be woven with an artistic design of cherubim. You shall hang it upon the four pillars of acacia wood overlaid with gold. Their hooks shall be gold, upon four sockets of silver; and you shall hang the veil from the clasps. Then you shall bring the ark of the Testimony in there, behind the veil. The veil shall be a divider for you between the holy place and the Most Holy. (Exodus 26:31-33)

You see, the veil separated the presence of God from the rest of the tabernacle. Only the High Priest could enter the Most Holy place. What Jesus did on the cross was to tear down that veil and allow us, every one of us, access to the presence of God. Jesus became our High Priest. He represents us to God which was the function of a priest in the Old Testament. Like it says in verse twenty above.

This is what I have been talking about. Because of what Jesus, the Son of God, did on the cross we have a very special relationship with God. An intimate fellowship with the Creator of the Universe. God desires that we walk with Him, talk with Him and trust Him to guide our lives in a way that will accomplish His plan for our lives and glorify Him!

From that day when Jesus tore that veil with His death on the cross we no longer need a priest. We have direct contact with God. We no longer need to take our questions, sins, wants, prayers to a priest we can go directly to God because of our new relationship, as children of God.

Personally, I love the picture of God as our heavenly father. Granted there are some who may not have had a favorable picture of their father. It might be hard for them to understand. But God is a loving Father that wants only the best for His children!

> But without faith it is impossible to please Him, for he who comes to
> God must believe that He is, and that He is a rewarder of those who
> diligently seek Him. (Hebrews 11:6)

I think I told you once, when I get a new Bible I go through the New Testament and underline the word faith. It is a fascinating word to me, a fascinating concept, if we ever fully grasped it would turn our world upside down. I mentioned the New Testament. The word faith only appears twice in the Old Testament.

Do you understand what the writer of Hebrews is saying? If we have no faith we don't have a relationship with God. He becomes this tyrant we see in the Old Testament and will never understand the potential relationship that is available by trusting in God.

Trust! That's the definition of faith. The word faith may only be in the Old Testament twice but the word trust is all through the Old Testament. The story of Abraham taking his son Isaac up on a mountain, as God instructed, to sacrifice him. That is faith. For Noah to begin building an ark, that took faith. In this very chapter, the author gives us a list of "The Hall of Faith."

The in chapter 12 the author talks about being surrounded by "so great a cloud of witnesses" I've often wondered if he wasn't referring to those listed in chapter 11.

It was tough trying to decide which verses to use here. I also have 10:24-25 circled, And let us consider one another in order to stir up love and good works, not forsaking the assembling of ourselves together, as is the manner of some, but exhorting one another, and so much more as you see the Day approaching. Both verses are very important to me.

Sometimes, on Wednesday nights, as I look around at those coming in the middle of a work-week to pray. It just strengthens my faith to see those who believe in God enough to make that special effort to meet for prayer and Bible study. I heard this once: the attendance on Sunday morning is a testament to the popularity of the church, those meeting on Sunday night is the testament of the popularity of the pastor, those who meet on Wednesday night are a testament to the popularity of God. Interesting, think about it.

Now may the God of peace who brought up our Lord Jesus from
the dead, the great Shepherd of the sheep, through the blood of the
everlasting covenant, make you complete in every good work to do
His will, working in you what is well pleasing in His sight, through
Jesus Christ, to whom be glory forever and ever. Amen. (Hebrews
13:20-21)

What do you suppose the author of Hebrews means by the phrase, "through the blood of the everlasting covenant"? If you have payed attention in the Old Testament it's all about the blood. In Leviticus, over and over God told Moses, after the animal is slain this is what you do with the blood. Don't forget Genesis 3:21. Adam and Eve were not allowed to leave the garden without tunics of animal skin.

Oh, my favorite is Exodus 13, the Passover Lamb, whose blood was applied to the door posts and lintel to ward off the death angel. Until you grasp the idea of the blood atoning for our sins you will never fully grasp the reason Jesus had to die on the cross. Jesus was the ultimate "perfect" sacrifice. A spotless, unblemished atoning sacrifice that paid for our sins, yesterday, today and forever! Only the blood of the Son of God had the "authority" to accomplish such a feat!

Notice, through that blood which makes us "complete" in Christ, God is then able to use us to accomplish His perfect will in our lives. If we were still in our sins God could not and would not touch us. It's only through the blood of His Son that we have an intimate relationship with God the Father.

God so wants to accomplish great things through His children. Sorry to say most of us miss out on that special blessing by ignoring or disobeying the Holy Spirit that lives within us. We miss out on so much by refusing to trust God and get out of our comfort zone and watch God work in our lives.

What is your challenge today? Something at work that you're afraid to try? Something at home that tests your faith? Have you prayed about it? Do you have His o.k.? Are you willing to trust God's working in your life? Has He blessed you in the past? Trust Him now! Take that step of faith! Then, this evening or tomorrow write down what God has done in your life, to encourage you later on.

> Pure and undefiled religion before God and the Father is this: to visit orphans and widows in their trouble, and to keep oneself unspotted from the world. (James 1:27)

Just another reminder. We are nearing the Christmas holiday. You've had nothing else on your mind for almost a month. Don't let the stress of the holiday cloud your attention from the real meaning of Christmas. Meditate on God's word. Take comfort in His presence. Let the world take care of the world. You focus on Jesus!

What is religion? Notice the verse above. The apostle James tries to describe it simply. It's loving others as God loves us. I love what someone told me once. "It's not a religion it's a relationship." If you're walking with God you will know what to do when the time comes to minister.

The scribes and Pharisees represented religion in their day. Religion is not a ritual. We can easily get caught up in the "sameness" of ritual. It's a great "comfort zone" to know what you're going to do and when to do it. That's not a relationship that is a ritual. If you want a relationship you need to spend a great deal of time in God's word! See how others, especially Jesus reacts to the situations He encounters. Jesus "notices" the people around Him. The needs of those following Him. Who was it that asked Andrew about feeding the thousands around Him?

As Jesus is walking along He notices the people and the needs around Him. We need to learn to open our eyes. Many people will hint at their needs if we are listening. Too many times we are so wrapped up in our own troubles and needs we fail to notice those around us.

That's what James is talking about here, "and to keep oneself unspotted from the world" the world has its priorities which usually include "self." Jesus says look around you, pay attention to those in need, stop focusing on you and think of others. The two great Commandments, love God and love others as yourself.

Don't mistake church for religion. Let me give you a heads up, people in church are hurting too. Church is a hospital. Some minister better than others, so the same with hospitals. The neat thing about church is that people are more apt to share their hurts in church!

> If anyone speaks, let him speak as the oracles of God. If anyone
> ministers, let him do it as with the ability which God supplies, that in
> all things God may be glorified through Christ Jesus, to whom belong
> the glory and the dominion forever and ever. Amen. (1 Peter 4:11)

This verse and Ephesians 4:11-12 are my "Sunday school teacher's verses! Anyone who has worked in ministry for any length of time knows this fact, anything we do is through the power of God. Can you figure out what the "oracles of God" are? I wonder how someone would be looked on if they spoke the word of God all the time? Not favorably I suspect. They would be laughed at.

So, what does it mean to speak the oracles of God? How about biblical "principles" in today's vocabulary? To do that, of course, you would need to know what the Bible says on any given subject. I guess the biggest change would be our language, no profanity. That's hard for some. Profanity is just an "easy" way to express yourself without giving it much thought.

When I preached in my early years I used to wish I could speak like Charles Swindoll, or Charles Stanley, etc. Then one day I realized God already had a Charles Stanley and a Charles Swindoll but there was only one of me. I realized that God created me just the way I am to do what God had planned for me. Just like verse above, "If anyone ministers, let him do it as with the ability which God supplies." The exciting thing is that it is usually above what we think we can do. It stretches us out of our comfort zone. We, if we trust God, can do things that we never thought we could. Why does God do that? Look, "That in all things God may be glorified." Maybe others may not know it but you do! You recognize that God has taken you somewhere you never thought you could go. It's an amazing feeling!

Teaching is a great example. Most of us never look at ourselves as teachers. But truly we are all teachers in one way or another. As a Christian, the lost world is always watching you, observing you, looking for mistakes usually, but at the same time trying to understand why you are different from them. Children watch their parents to learn. We watch those in leadership. If you want to be a teacher you must have a relationship with God first then let God work through you!

> For all that is in the world—the lust of the flesh, the lust of the eyes, and the pride of life—is not of the Father but is of the world. And the world is passing away, and the lust of it; but he who does the will of God abides forever. (1 John 2:16-17)

If you look at Jesus' temptation in the wilderness in Matthew 4 you will notice that Satan used these very same three temptations on Jesus. His response was the word of God. This verse says those temptations are of the world. That is the world trying to destroy us as children of God. There will always be a battle for the Christian, between the Spirit and the world. Look what Jesus says in John 16:33, "These things I have spoken to you, that in Me you may have peace. In the world, you will have tribulation; but be of good cheer, I have overcome the world."

What does Jesus tell us is waiting for us in the world? "Tribulation" have you heard of this word before in the Bible? The book of Revelation. Tribulation is that period of chaos before the great judgment. This world is in tribulation. Just watch 30 minutes of the news. All over the world, there is conflict, lying, deceit, greed, chaos! Remember that we are only passing through. God just doesn't want us to take up residence!

Did you notice the antidote? "but he who does the will of God abides forever." So, the question is how do we know the will of God? By reading and walking in God's word. Staying on the path that has prepared for us. Always moving toward His plan and will for our lives. Not settling for the world's best but God's best. Notice John says, "abides forever" you see, that is where we take up residence. Not in this world.

An interesting thing in this book by John. He references his followers, those who read this epistle as "little children". I think there are two reasons, one, he looks at them, in their Christian maturity. They have yet to commit to following the teachings of Jesus completely. And two, they are God's children, born of the Spirit of God. They must continue to grow in the grace and knowledge of Jesus!

Notice that Satan's weapons can be broke down into three categories, the flesh, the eyes, and pride. Which do you suppose he uses the most? Whichever will work on you! He knows your weaknesses. He also knows that once you trust in God he hasn't a chance!

In this the love of God was manifested toward us, that God has sent
His only begotten Son into the world, that we might live through Him.
In this is love, not that we loved God, but that He loved us and sent
His Son to be the propitiation for our sins. (1 John 4:9-10)

What an appropriate verse for Christmas Day!
One of my least favorite passages to teach on is the Christmas story. I
have struggled with this many times. My problem is that I think everybody knows
the story and has heard it as many times as I have and therefore, we can't add any
new things to the story. Then I realized, one, that not everybody knows it like I
know it. And, two, it is worth repeating!

You could almost put this verse right after John 3:16. I think the New
Testament, more than any other scripture, tries to convey to us the extent of
God's love. Even in the "Christmas Story" it's about love. Who doesn't love a story
about a baby. So, we get sidetracked by the "baby story" and miss the point. God
went to such lengths just to communicate His love for us in that He was willing
to put aside His omnipotence and become a mere man to bring Hs message to us!

That's what the Christmas story and this verse and John 3:16 all have in
common. God, so wants to demonstrate His love that He will go to any length,
even dying on a cruel cross to get that message across.

Let me do some house cleaning here. The word "propitiation" simply means
"payment" Jesus paid our sin debt that we may have the option of a relationship
with God. Underline "option" it's our choice. Always has been.

Did you ever want to get into the "manger scene"? Just to be there when the
Son of God was born? Such a cute, and loving scene? Don't forget that if Herod
had found this baby he would have had Him killed. Which he tried by killing all
the new born babies two years old and under. (Matthew 2:16). Be careful what
you wish for.

I hope you have not let the world rob you of this special holiday. Your focus is
on the reason God decided to put on humanity and come with His own personal
message for us. Look at the verse above again. It's all about God's love!

Behold, I stand at the door and knock. If anyone hears My voice and opens the door, I will come in to him and dine with him. And he with Me. (Revelation 3:20)

This is one of my favorite verses! I even have a copy of the portrait of Jesus in the garden knocking on the door. We all know the fact that there is no door handle on the outside. It must be opened from within. Just as our heart must be opened that God's Holy Spirit may enter and begin the process of developing that intimate relationship with our heavenly Father.

Did you notice, John writes, "If anyone hears My voice." God not only knocks but He calls our name. Yes, He knows our name. He knows where we are and He knows our spiritual condition. I think, as Jesus was such a teacher that God wants to start teaching us His desires and plans for our life. What do you think Jesus does after the supper? Remember in the gospels? What did Jesus do after the Last Supper? They adjourned to the garden.

After we have opened the door. Jesus comes in a has a meal with us. Then we get up and begin this journey. We begin our journey on the path that God has planned for us. We may stop here and there and Jesus will teach us a lesson through adversity or a mistake we might make. But in all the trials there are lessons to learn. Lessons that will draw us closer, a more intimate relationship with God.

There is comfort in that relationship. There is peace in that relationship. There are always lessons to be learned in this relationship. Maybe lessons on giving. Lessons on compassion. Lessons on teaching others about Jesus. Just so many lessons. We must look at them as lessons, not punishment or tests or trials but lessons to be learned to make us better servants to God's glory.

Opening the door is just the first step. YOU must take that first step. God doesn't have a key. He will not force the door. You must open the door to your heart and invite Him in. The rest is up to God. Take a minute and read Jeremiah 29:11-13. It is all there. Maybe you could note in your Bible, in the margin, Jeremiah 29:11-13. Don't stop at verse 11. Go on and read all three verses. It talks about seeking God. That's the open-door thing!

And they sang a new song, saying: "You are worthy to take the scroll,
and to open its seals; for You were slain, and have redeemed us to God
by Your blood out of every tribe and tongue and people and nation.
(Revelation 5:9)

This is such a neat verse. Don't miss this fact: nothing or nobody could have accomplished what Jesus did. I don't know if you noticed in your reading of the Old Testament how many millions of bulls, goats, sheep, etc. were offered at the altar. The mercy seat in the tabernacle of the congregation.

Look at this passage in Isaiah: "To what purpose is the multitude of your sacrifices to Me?" says the Lord. "I have had enough of burnt offerings of rams and the fat of fed cattle. I do not delight in the blood of bulls, or of lambs or goats." (Isaiah 1:11). Why do you suppose God would say this? It was God who instituted the practice.

Let me tell you why I think He said this. Because it meant nothing! Israel simply went through the motions and never actually felt anything. Look at the verse above. How did they greet the Lamb of God? With singing. When you sing there is feeling in your heart. You cannot just say the words, you can't sing and not mean it. God wants our devotion, our commitment, and our faithfulness.

There is so little commitment today to a relationship with God. We say the words, we go forward in church, we might even be baptized, why? To go through the motions. Just like Israel did at the tabernacle of meeting. God knows our heart. God knows when we are just going through the motions. God is dealing with them here in Revelation.

Being a Christian is so much more than going through the motions. Just like what we saw in 3:20. It is one thing to open the door. It is quite another to dine with the Lord and to follow Him through life with a new commitment to obey and following His leading.

Do you remember in the "Left Behind" story about the youth leader that said and did all the right things, maybe offered some lambs and bulls, yet when the trumpet sounded he was left behind? God knows the heart. That is what we are judged by, not how many "sacrifices" we have made. Not how many promises we make but our relationship with God that begins in our heart not in our deeds!

Then the seventh angel sounded: and there were loud voices in heaven, saying "The kingdoms of this world have become the kingdoms of our Lord and His Christ, and He shall reign forever and ever!" (Revelation 10:15)

We talked yesterday about that final judgment. This is the trumpet judgment. There are three sets of seven judgments. The scroll judgments, the trumpet judgments and the bowl judgments. Twenty-one times God tries to get their attention, tries to get them to turn to Him. It amazes me how deceived so many were, But, then again, look around you today. How many know the truth but think they can live their lives ignoring the truth and nothing will happen.

Have you noticed all that is going on in Israel today? A tiny little country surrounded by massive countries that want to destroy Israel. It would be no problem at all to wipe them off the map. For Egypt to invade and destroy them. Egypt tried that a while back, they lost. God is still watching over Israel! Even though the leadership has pretty much abandoned the God of this universe!

What do you think of the book of Revelation? I think it is interesting that whenever a pastor announces that he is going to do a study on Revelation the attendance doubles. Why is that? Do you think the pastor will give a date? Maybe he will uncover something that hasn't been known yet. Just the chronology of Revelation is hard to follow. It's just a fascinating book. We all love stories and/or predictions about the future. The question is, are you in it?

We like the story but don't want to be confronted with the facts. You must make a decision before that day. You must decide whose side you're on. I don't have to do that right now, do I? So, do you know when the Lord Jesus is coming back? You know more than Jesus does. I mentioned this before, God didn't save you to sit. If that's all He wanted from you He would have taken you home as soon as you were saved. He saved you to serve! To be a testimony of His grace and love. To tell others how He has changed your life. So, others might join you in the air when Jesus comes back.

Christmas is over. New Years is just around the corner. What are you looking forward to in the New Year? I hope a closer walk with God!

Then I heard a voice from heaven saying to me, "Write: 'Blessed are
the dead who die in the Lord from now on.' "Yes," says the Spirit,
"that they may rest from their labors, and their works follow them."
(Revelation 14:13)

In the world, today there is so little rest. Even if we sit quietly with noting on, our
minds won't let us rest, unless! Our minds are at peace with God. If we have that
relationship, that surpasses all understanding. That confidence in our soul that we
are a child of God. That we belong to God the Father. Let's look at a verse I found
last night at our weekly prayer meeting.

So, we are always confident, knowing that while we are at home in the body
we are absent from the Lord. For we walk by faith, not by sight. We are confident,
yes, well pleased rather to be absent from the body and to be present with the Lord.
Therefore, we make it our aim, whether present or absent, to be well pleasing to
Him. (2 Corinthians 5:6-9). I want to encourage you to read this whole chapter,
it is awesome!

I've talked much about our walking with God. The same path that God is
leading in. There is such a peace when we know that God is in the lead and we can
trust Him and His knowledge of the future. There is a certain peace as well, in
that we also know where we are going. After we leave this world there is a world
that we can't even imagine. In heaven with the God of our faith!

To have that assurance relieves so much stress of this world. Of course, God
knows our journey in this world. He wants us to be a testimony and help to point
others to salvation in Him. We trust that God will use us to His glory. Notice the
last part of verse 13: "and their works do follow the". The works that God puts in
our path that glorify Him!

When we get a job, we want to know what the benefits are. What do we receive
besides our hourly wages. Here is one of the benefits of accepting Christ as your
Savior. That peace that comes from knowing that when we depart this world we
will be in the presence of the Lord. (2 Corinthians 5:8). As Christians, when we
attend a funeral of a fellow Christian we understand and rejoice in this fact!

After these things, I heard a loud voice of a great multitude in heaven, saying, "Alleluia! Salvation and glory and honor and power belong to the Lord our God! (Revelation 19:1)

Tomorrow will be our last visit in our journey through the Bible. Every year we come to this point in the story of God's plan for mankind. Of course, you notice, that we win. I do want to remind you, as we have said throughout this saga, it is our choice which path we take. In the verse above we see clearly that God wins out in the end. His plan from the very beginning. We see that in the first couple of chapters of Job. Satan has no power but what God grants him. The same is true in your life.

All the way back to the Garden of Eden. God in His infinite wisdom created man with a CHOICE. Obey God and live in this perfect garden or disobey and travel your road on your own. So many people think they know better than God what is good for them. Many of them prosper and do pretty good by the world's standards. That may be fine for now, eternity has other rewards, anguish, torment, pain, sorrow, etc. What is this life compared with eternity?

We can scoff at Israel's disobedient, at Saul's rebellion, maybe even point out David's fall. Peter's denial, Paul's persecution of Christians until God got a hold of him. In every case there is always the opportunity for redemption. Again, it's our choice. The parable of the Prodigal Son, Jesus, in His own words tells us of the Father's heart. That will always be God's response to repentance.

This last week of the year, the week between Christmas and New Year's is, to me, a time of cleaning up loose ends. Things I have put off all year, some things that can be finished so I can begin the New Year with a clean slate. I try to take a vacation each year for this purpose. I want to begin the New Year looking forward to what God is going to do. Looking forward with anticipation, and excitement. I also want to take this time to reflect on what God has done this past year. That is what makes me excited about the year ahead!

I hope you have grown in your Christian walk, as we traveled this journey together. I hope you have grown closer to God and are open to His leadership and trust His guidance!

Then He who sat on the throne said, "Behold, I make all things new." And He said to me, "Write, for these words are true and faithful." And He said to me, "It is done!" I am the Alpha and Omega, the Beginning and the End. I will give of the fountain of the water of life freely to him who thirsts. (Revelation 21:5-6)

Here's a verse you may not have noticed in Genesis, Then the Lord God said, "Behold the man has become like one of Us, to know good and evil. And now, lest he put out his hand and take also of the tree of life, and eat and live forever"- So He drove out the man; and He placed cherubim, at the east of the garden of Eden, and a flaming sword which turned every way, to guard the way to the tree of life. (Genesis 3:22,24) It is ok for man to live forever now. Sin has been removed from his environment.

I talked some yesterday about our journey ending here. I pray that you will continue each year to go through this journey. Each time you will pick up new stones to add to your knowledge of God. Stones that will help you each day draw closer to God, enjoy His guidance to learn, each day, how to trust Him more.

In this devotional, I have shared my favorite verses as we travel through each book. Verses that helped me in my journey. I encourage you to do the same. My verses may not mean as much to you. Circle, underline, mark somehow those verses that speak to you as you make this journey again next year!

Remember that God gave us His word to instruct, to guide, and to encourage us to find a closer relationship with Him. His greatest desire, I have no doubt, is an intimate relationship with His children as He seeks to encourage us to glorify Him in the deeds we do to serve Him.

It's my prayer, one, if for some reason you have read this book and have not asked Jesus in your heart, do so right now. Stop and pray and acknowledge that you are a sinner and need a Savior, someone who has paid your sin-debt on the cross. Ask Jesus to come into your heart and change your life. Just like Revelation 3:20 open your heart and ask Jesus to come in. He will change your life. Thank you for joining me in this journey. May God bless the rest of your journey!

LONNY E. YOUNG

I was born in 1946 in Kansas City, Missouri and have lived here all my life.

I dropped out of high school at the age of sixteen and enlisted in the United Air Force and left for Lackland Air Force Base the day after my seventeenth birthday. I spend four years in the Air Force, with one year in Vietnam at Bein Hoa Air Base. I got my G.E.D. while in the Air Force.

My wife Mary, and I were married in June of 1967. I was discharged in August of 1967 and in September began my career with United Parcel Service. I was with U.P.S. for twenty-six years. During that time, we were blessed with two wonderful daughters. We moved from Kansas City to Levasy, Missouri and started attending Anchor Point Baptist Church in Independence. I was ordained to the Gospel Ministry at Anchor Point and later was called to pastor a church in Freeman, Missouri.

I was with Freeman Baptist Church for over two years. When I left there, I got a job with the National Archives and Records Administration. (N.A.R.A.) I spent nine years with the Archives.

I am retired now. We have 6 grand-children and two great-grandchildren.

The Word of God has always been my passion. For over thirty years I have worked in the Sunday School ministry. Today we live in Grain Valley, Missouri and I am still active in my local church, First Baptist Church of Grain Valley.

Printed in the United States
By Bookmasters